Gateway
2nd Edition

G000075054

Anna Cole
Ursula Mallows

macmillan
education

B1

Welcome
Introduction by David Spencer

Before I tell you about *Gateway 2ⁿᵈ Edition*, let me tell you a bit about myself.

After studying Modern Languages, I trained to be a secondary school teacher. And I'm still teaching in a secondary school now, over 25 years later. Being in the classroom every day is a great help when writing a course like *Gateway*. On the one hand, the daily contact with teenagers gives me ideas and inspiration. On the other hand, it keeps me realistic about what actually works in the classroom.

If you don't know *Gateway* already, the course is designed to lead teenage students to success in exams, particularly school-leaving exams. It's also designed to prepare students for further study and the world of work.

In *Gateway 2ⁿᵈ Edition* we've kept many of the features that have made *Gateway* so popular. Each unit has a clear, logical structure. The whole approach to grammar and vocabulary and to the development of the four skills is carefully staged to be both teacher- and student-friendly. Each level offers a wide range of strategies that will help students pass their exams.

But *Gateway 2ⁿᵈ Edition* has several exciting new features. Firstly there are the **Flipped classroom videos**, which bring grammar points from the Student's Book to life.

Then there is a whole new focus on **Life skills**, with a special section in each unit preparing teenagers for many, varied facets of life, complete with its own tailor-made video featuring British teenagers.

Meanwhile *Gateway 2ⁿᵈ Edition* offers brand-new, up-to-date texts to motivate you and your students. Reading texts include **Critical thinking** questions to get students reflecting on what they've just read. And for all these features, new and old, we've refreshed the design and made it even clearer and easier to use.

With *Gateway 2ⁿᵈ Edition* we want to support you in the classroom and in your professional development. Via the **Gateway Facebook page**, you can keep in direct contact with me and the *Gateway* team and with other teachers from around the world. We have news, teaching tips and occasional competitions, plus access to teaching videos and webinars. You can also find out about any upcoming *Gateway* talks in your part of the world. So far I've spoken in over 20 countries and hope to continue being able to share activities and ideas with you all.

I hope you and your students enjoy teaching and learning with *Gateway 2ⁿᵈ Edition*!

Dave

f www.facebook.com/macmillangateway

Key concepts of *Gateway 2ⁿᵈ Edition*

1 Preparation for school-leaving exams

Gateway 2ⁿᵈ Edition prepares secondary school students for both international and school-leaving exams. Throughout the units there are plenty of exam-style activities and preparation tasks as well as **Exam success** tips. These tips lead the students to more in-depth help in the Exam success section at the end of book. After every two units there are **Gateway to exams** pages which revise the exam techniques they have learnt and give them more practice in doing typical exam tasks. *Gateway 2ⁿᵈ Edition* is closely mapped to the CEFR and the course comes with both a **Test generator** and **printable tests**.

2 Content-based material and critical thinking

Gateway 2ⁿᵈ Edition provides material which helps to develop other areas of knowledge, as well as English-language skills. The most important criteria for choosing texts is that they should be genuinely interesting and appealing to students of the age group. Texts are then used to provide a realistic and meaningful context for the grammar and vocabulary to be studied within the unit. Students are also encouraged to think critically about what they have read, to question the content and personalise the topic of the text.

3 Life skills

We now have two pages at the heart of each unit which prepare students for life outside the classroom. We help students in areas as wide-ranging as personal and physical well-being, citizenship, social skills, money and finance, and the world of work. Each Life skills section has a motivating video with British teenagers demonstrating the topic and ends with students performing a **Life task**, an activity that has direct relevance to the students' lives outside the classroom.

4 The active role of the learners

Students are encouraged to participate actively in their own learning throughout the course. Here are just some of the ways this is done:

Exam success boxes in the Student's Book and **Study skills** boxes in the Workbook encourage students to reflect on the best way to learn before they are guided to the suggestions at the back of the book.

Students hypothesise about grammar rules before they are directed to the relevant information in the **Grammar reference** section at the end of each unit.

Students are invited to express personal reactions and/or think critically after reading or listening.

On the **Gateway to exams** pages which appear after each two units there is a **'Can do' progress check** where students evaluate their own progress and decide what steps to take next to maximise their learning.

5 Grammar in context

The target grammar in each unit is given meaningful context through the reading and listening texts. The approach is one of guided discovery. Students are then directed to the **Grammar reference** section at the end of the unit to check their hypotheses.

An alternative approach to grammar presentation is now offered by the **Flipped classroom videos**.

After the grammar presentation stage, the students work through carefully graded exercises which help them to internalise the grammar, starting with exercises where students simply identify correct usage and ending with exercises where students use the grammar in active, oral communication.

The Grammar reference section appears directly at the end of the unit, providing a useful ch ckpoint for students when reviewing the unit. **Grammar revision** exercises facing the Grammar reference section make this part of the Student's Book interactive and ideal for self-study, for example for revision and self-testing before exams.

6 The Flipped classroom

In the traditional classroom, the teacher explains new content in the class and students do practice at home. The Flipped classroom refers to students learning new content outside the classroom, via video presentations, and then doing practice in the class. This makes it easier for the teacher to give more personalised help and attention during the practice stage. It also means students can go at their own speed during the presentation stage.

In *Gateway 2nd Edition* we have created a series of **Flipped classroom videos** to help you to find more time in lessons and to add variety to your teaching. The videos are short grammar presentations linked to one of each unit's **Grammar guides**. Students can watch the presentation at home, as many times as they want. There are interactive

tasks in the *Gateway 2nd Edition* Online Workbook or printable worksheets on the Resource centre to help the students to check that they've understood, and for you to check that they have actually watched the video.

The videos are a flexible teaching tool and can also be used for revision, or when students miss a class, or with the whole class in lesson-time, for variety. The Flipped classroom videos have the added bonus that they encourage students to take responsibility for their own progress and become independent learners.

7 Developing vocabulary

The course revises, extends and practises the most important lexical sets connected to typical topics that appear in school-leaving and international exams, so that students can talk and write about these topics with ease and will have less difficulty reading or listening to texts dealing with these topics. The course also develops the students' active vocabulary unit-by-unit by looking at 'systems' of vocabulary, such as word formation, collocation, phrasal verbs, and dependent prepositions. This approach is a key factor in helping students with Use of English tasks.

8 Developing skills

The emphasis of *Gateway 2nd Edition* is very much on developing the skills, not just testing them. In terms of speaking and writing, the approach taken is step-by-step preparation for the final, exam-style task at the end of the activity. Initial exercises are more receptive, working on a model text or dialogue. Students then analyse the words and expressions used and have guided, controlled practice of these before creating their own texts or performing their own dialogues. Words and expressions that are useful to complete these tasks successfully are highlighted in the **Speaking bank** and **Writing bank**. **Pronunciation**, an integral part of developing oral skills, is integrated into each unit at the most appropriate stage.

With reading and listening, there is attention to the strategies that help students to understand texts more easily. To develop reading and listening in a comprehensive way, there is a wide variety of text genres and task types.

The *Gateway 2nd Edition* Student's Book offers ten Grammar and Vocabulary reference and revision sections in the Language checkpoint at the end of each unit. Exam-style activities appear throughout, with consolidation and practice every two units in the Gateway to exams pages.

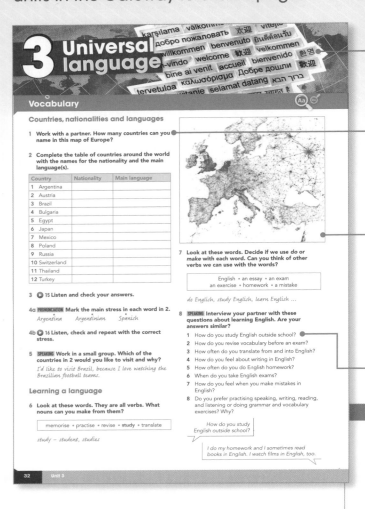

Unit themes and topics are designed to appeal to teenagers, and are introduced clearly at the beginning of each unit.

The first exercise gives students the opportunity to test their prior knowledge by introducing topic-related vocabulary.

Original, memorable and engaging images enhance students' learning experience.

Vocabulary is brought to life with skills activities, allowing students to personalise the language.

Reading tasks focus on stimulating topics using recognisable and relevant contexts.

Typical reading tasks include exam-style comprehension questions such as multiple-choice, True/False or inserting sentences into a text.

The **Critical thinking** activity embedded in every Reading lesson goes beyond traditional comprehension exercises to guide students towards the use of higher-order thinking skills. It also gives students the opportunity to develop analytical skills and use them in an authentically communicative way.

Grammar in context

some, any, much, many, a lot (of), a few, a little

1a Look at the words. Are they countable or uncountable?

1 country   3 money   5 area
2 time   4 colour   6 language

1b Look at these sentences. The words in bold all express quantity. Answer questions a–e about the words.

1 **Some** countries are almost invisible.
2 He needed **some** time to collect the data.
3 They couldn't see **any** good explanations for this.
4 Did Fischer make **any** money from the maps?
5 There aren't **many** different colours.
6 He didn't need **much** time.
7 There are **a lot of** different ways to communicate.
8 It doesn't take **a lot of** time.
9 There are **a few** areas where different languages co-exist.
10 They had **a little** knowledge of Tagalog, but not much.

a Which words do we use with uncountable nouns?
   some, any, much, a lot of, a little
b Which words do we use with plural, countable nouns?
c Which words usually appear in negative sentences and questions?
d Which words do we use to talk about large quantities?
e Which words do we use to talk about small quantities?

GRAMMAR REFERENCE ➤ PAGE 42

2a Complete the dialogue with *some* or *any*.

Jamie: Brad, I'm going shopping this afternoon. What do we need to get? Have we got (a) _____ bananas?

Brad: Yeah, we've got (b) _____ bananas but we haven't got (c) _____ tomatoes or potatoes.

Jamie: What about sugar? Have we got (d) _____ sugar?

Brad: No, we haven't got (e) _____ sugar, but we have got (f) _____ chocolate. And we need to get (g) _____ biscuits too.

Flipped classroom: watch the grammar presentation video.

Jamie: OK. Listen. I think I'll get (h) _____ burgers for dinner tonight.

Brad: Good idea. In that case, get (i) _____ tomato ketchup, too. We haven't got (j) _____ at the moment. And get (k) _____ yoghurt for dessert!

2b All the words above in bold are types of food, but they all have something else in common. Can you guess what it is?

3 Choose the correct alternative.

Nobody knows exactly how (a) *much/many* words there are in total in the English language but there are (b) *a lot/a lot of*. One reason why there are so (c) *many/much* is that English takes words from (d) *much/many* other languages. Look at the words for food in exercise 2, for example. There may be (e) *a few/a little* words there that come from your language. (f) *Some/Any* of the words come from South America – potato, tomato and chocolate. There aren't (g) *any/many* from Chinese in the English language, but ketchup is one of them. Originally, ketchup was the name for a type of fish sauce in China. Teenagers in the UK don't eat (h) *many/much* fish sauce but they do eat (i) *lots/lots of* burgers. There is (j) *some/any* confusion about the origin of the word burger, but (k) *a lot of/much* people think that it comes from German. Because the UK and France are neighbours it is normal that there are (l) *a few/a lot of* French words in English – hundreds in fact. Biscuit is just one example. On the other hand, (m) *a lot of/many* fruit travels a long way to get to the UK. That explains why the word banana comes from an African language. There are also (n) *a few/a little* words from Turkish, like yoghurt. And, finally, if you ask for (o) *a few/a little* sugar in your coffee, you're using two Arabic words. Just by being in an English kitchen you can travel to (p) *much/many* countries!

34 Unit 3

Developing vocabulary

4 Work with a partner. Complete these sentences about your language. Use the words in the box for ideas. You may complete each sentence with two or three different ideas.

> English/French/German/Russian words
> irregular past forms • phrasal verbs • prefixes
> prepositions • present tenses • words beginning with Z
> words with more than 12 letters

1 There are some *French words and some German words.*
2 There are a lot of _____
3 There aren't any _____
4 There aren't many _____
5 There are a few _____

5a Work individually. Look at the photos and choose a country. Make notes about things that there are or aren't in this country. Use the ideas in the box.

> animals • bicycles • food • fruit
> modern/old buildings • monuments • mountains
> offices • people • snow • tourism • trees • water

Japan

Brazil

Switzerland

Egypt

5b SPEAKING Work in pairs. You need to discover your partner's country by asking questions with any, much, many, a few, a little, a lot (of). Your partner can only answer 'Yes' or 'No'.

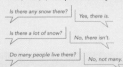

Is there any snow there? / Yes, there is.
Is there a lot of snow there? / No, there isn't.
Do many people live there? / No, not many.

5c SPEAKING Now choose different countries not in the photos and repeat.

Negative prefixes un-, in-, im-, ir-, il-

1 Look at the words in the box. What do they have in common? What is the opposite of each word?

> illegal • impossible • incorrect
> informal • invisible • irregular
> unhappy • unusual

2 Choose the correct alternative.

1 Many common English verbs, such as *go, do* and *make*, have *a regular/an irregular* past form.
2 People aren't usually *happy/unhappy* when somebody reads their private messages.
3 'A books' is *correct/incorrect* English.
4 You couldn't see the message. It was *visible/invisible*.
5 'Dear Sir or Madam' is a *formal/informal* expression.
6 It is *legal/illegal* to steal data.
7 It is *possible/impossible* to read hundreds of messages in just two minutes.

3a PRONUNCIATION ▶ 17 Listen to the words in 1. Underline the syllable we stress in each word. Do we stress the prefix in each word?

3b ▶ 17 Listen again and repeat the words with the correct stress.

4a Think of an example of something (for example, a word or a situation) for each word in 1.

4b SPEAKING Work with a partner. Say one of your words or situations. Can your partner guess the word?

Climbing Everest in a day.
Impossible.

Unit 3 35

Gateway to life skills lessons equip students with the necessary transferable skills for life beyond the classroom. Each unit has a Life skills lesson that allows students both controlled and freer language practice, using what they have learnt in previous lessons in a cumulative way.

The Life skills lesson is introduced to students with clear objectives.

Students are shown the key concepts of the Life skills lesson in a clear and concise form and have the chance to explore issues of universal interest and importance.

Engaging video activities show real teenagers talking about the Life skills topic in the form of street interviews, presentations and vlogs.

Students have many opportunities to give and share their opinions.

The Life skills lesson culminates in a productive **Life task** such as giving a presentation, creating a poster or making a plan. It gives students the opportunity to use language in an authentic and collaborative context while practising a useful and transferable Life skill.

Macmillan Life Skills winner of the ELTon award for Innovation in teacher resources!
Go to macmillanenglish.com/life-skills/resources to explore our collection of Life Skills resources.

Listening

Danke Gracias Merci Gracias Tha...
...nte Thank you Спасибо 감사합니다
Dziękuję Ευχαριστώ Kiitos Tak Dz...
有り難う Obrigado 謝謝 Hvala 有り難...
...ack חן Merci Danke Terima kas...
Grazie Thank you Gracias ขอบคุณ
...がとう 감사합니다 شکراً 謝謝 Спасиб...
Mulţumesc Спасибі Спасибо Dankon...
...вала Благодаря Asante Děkuju Obr...
شكراً ありがとう Teşekkür ederim
شكراً Köszönöm Obriga...

1 SPEAKING Work with a partner. Look at the five different languages below. What, if anything, do you know about each one? Do you think they are easy or difficult to learn? Why?

a Spanish   c French   e Klingon
b Esperanto   d Japanese

2 LISTENING ● 19 Listen to four speakers. Match each speaker to the language in 1 that they are learning now. There is one language you don't need.

Speaker 1 _____   Speaker 3 _____
Speaker 2 _____   Speaker 4 _____

3 ● 19 Listen again and match the speakers and the correct information. There are two pieces of information for each speaker.

A was not very successful with the first foreign language they learned.
B is learning a language because they like the idea behind the language.
C wants to learn a language to understand more about the people who speak it.
D is learning a language because it helps them professionally.
E started learning a language because of one special person.
F tells people they meet interesting facts about the language they are learning.
G was interested in a language from a TV programme before they started learning a real language.
H knows three or more languages.

Speaker 1 _____   Speaker 3 _____
Speaker 2 _____   Speaker 4 _____

4 SPEAKING What about you?

Choose one of the languages to learn. Give reasons.

Grammar in context

Relative pronouns

1a Look at these sentences.

1 Mexico and Argentina are two countries where I do a lot of business.
2 Zamenhof was the man who created Esperanto.
3 It was a TV series which made me want to learn Klingon.
4 He's the character (that) I like the most.
5 That was when I decided to start learning Japanese.
6 They're comics that come from Japan.
7 I don't know whose idea it was.

Which words in bold refer to:

a people? *who* _____ and _____
b things? _____ and _____
c possessions? _____
d places? _____
e times? _____

1b Look at sentences 4 and 6 in 1a and choose the correct alternative.

We *can/cannot* omit who, which or that when a noun or pronoun comes immediately after.

GRAMMAR REFERENCE ➤ PAGE 42

2 Look at the relative pronouns in these sentences. In which sentences can you omit the relative pronoun?

1 *The Big Bang Theory* was the series which made him famous.
2 That's the language that I want to learn.
3 English is a language which millions of people speak.
4 A linguist is a person who studies and speaks a lot of languages.
5 He is the teacher who taught me French.
6 She's the person that helped me to speak Italian.
7 The first person who I met at the hotel was Spanish.
8 She never forgot the people who helped her to learn English.

Jim Parsons from *The Big Bang Theory*

> Students listen to a wide variety of realistic types of recording which include dialogues, radio programmes, adverts and interviews.

> The second **Grammar in context** lesson functions in the same way as the previous one allowing students to discover grammar rules for themselves.

> There is a wide variety of listening tasks, all of which appear in listening exams, such as True/False, completing notes and matching.

3 Match the sentence halves using appropriate relative pronouns.

Quebec is a part of Canada where they speak French.

1 ~~Quebec is a part of Canada~~
2 Javier Bardem is a Spanish actor
3 Summer is a time
4 JRR Tolkien was the writer
5 Latin was the language
6 Sushi, manga and bento are words
7 Captain Kirk and Mr Spock are characters

a a lot of people go to the UK to study English.
b makes films in English in the US.
c adventures appear in the *Star Trek* films.
d they speak French.
e books became a series of very popular films.
f come from Japanese.
g they spoke in Ancient Rome.

4a SPEAKING Choose six words from the Vocabulary sections in Units 1–3. Write definitions of the words using who, that, which, where, when, whose.

4b Read your definitions to your partner. Can they identify the words?

> It's a person who attacks you to take money or objects from you.
> *A mugger.*
> It's the stage of life when you're a child.
> *Childhood.*

5 Complete these sentences with true information about you.

1 _____ is a place where I'm usually happy.
2 _____ is an object which is really important to me.
3 _____ was a year when something special happened to me.
4 _____ is a person who is special to me.
5 _____ is a place where I want to go one day.
6 _____ is a language that I want to learn.
7 _____ is a film that I love.

6 SPEAKING Work with a partner. Compare your sentences in 5 and discuss your answers.

> Home is a place where I'm usually happy.
> Me too. But I wrote 'the swimming pool'. I go swimming every weekend. I love it.

✔ EXAM SUCCESS

You are going to do a multiple-choice cloze activity. You have a text with gaps. You must complete each gap with one of three or four words that they give you. Why is it a good idea to read the complete text first, without thinking about the gaps?

➤ EXAM SUCCESS page 144

7 Read about Emilia Clarke. Choose the best answer (A, B, C or D) to complete the text.

Emilia Clarke

Actors have a difficult job. One difficult thing (1) _____ they need to do is learn all their words. But imagine how difficult it is when they need to learn words in (2) _____ language which doesn't really exist! Emilia Clarke is a British actress (3) _____ speaks not one but two fictional languages in the TV series *Game of Thrones*. One of the languages is called Valyrian (4) _____ the other is Dothraki. David Peterson is the person who invented all the languages in the series. Peterson went to the University of California, San Diego. That was (5) _____ he studied a master's in linguistics. For *Game of Thrones*, he created a (6) _____ of words for each language. His wife Erin helped him to create at least one word. She was the person (7) _____ name he used to create the adjective for *kind* or *good* in Dothraki. It must be really hard for Emilia (8) _____ she needs to film in Dothraki. But there are a (9) _____ words that she doesn't need to learn in Dothraki. One of them is 'Thank you'. The Dothraki people are quite aggressive and never use it!

1 A that   B who   C whose   D when
2 A –   B a   C the   D some
3 A –   B which   C who   D whose
4 A and   B but   C because   D that
5 A that   B what   C where   D which
6 A lot   B lots   C many   D few
7 A that   B which   C who   D whose
8 A that   B what   C when   D which
9 A few   B little   C lot   D many

> Photos are used to engage students and bring the grammar to life.

> Students are given lots of opportunities to use new grammar in active, oral communication. This activity usually involves personalisation. Students work in pairs or small groups and find out new things about their classmates.

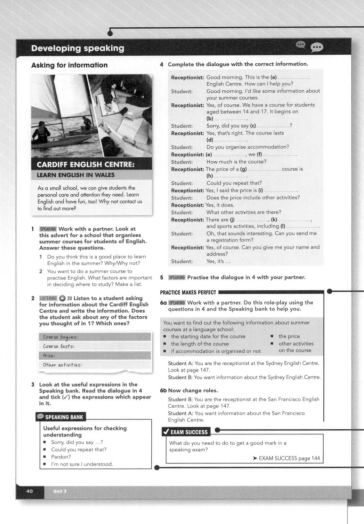

Developing speaking

Asking for information

CARDIFF ENGLISH CENTRE:
LEARN ENGLISH IN WALES

As a small school, we can give students the personal care and attention they need. Learn English and have fun, too! Why not contact us to find out more?

1 SPEAKING Work with a partner. Look at this advert for a school that organises summer courses for students of English. Answer these questions.

1 Do you think this is a good place to learn English in the summer? Why/Why not?
2 You want to do a summer course to practise English. What factors are important in deciding where to study? Make a list.

2 LISTENING 20 Listen to a student asking for information about the Cardiff English Centre and write the information. Does the student ask about any of the factors you thought of in 1? Which ones?

Course begins:
Course lasts:
Price:
Other activities:

3 Look at the useful expressions in the Speaking bank. Read the dialogue in 4 and tick (✓) the expressions which appear in it.

SPEAKING BANK

Useful expressions for checking understanding
- Sorry, did you say …?
- Could you repeat that?
- Pardon?
- I'm not sure I understood.

4 Complete the dialogue with the correct information.

Receptionist: Good morning. This is the **(a)** English Centre. How can I help you?
Student: Good morning. I'd like some information about your summer courses.
Receptionist: Yes, of course. We have a course for students aged between 14 and 17. It begins on **(b)**
Student: Sorry, did you say **(c)** ?
Receptionist: Yes, that's right. The course lasts **(d)**
Student: Do you organise accommodation?
Receptionist: **(e)** , we **(f)**
Student: How much is the course?
Receptionist: The price of a **(g)** course is **(h)**
Student: Could you repeat that?
Receptionist: Yes, I said the price is **(i)**
Student: Does the price include other activities?
Receptionist: Yes, it does.
Student: What other activities are there?
Receptionist: There are **(j)** , **(k)** , and sports activities, including **(l)** ,
Student: Oh, that sounds interesting. Can you send me a registration form?
Receptionist: Yes, of course. Can you give me your name and address?
Student: Yes, it's …

5 SPEAKING Practise the dialogue in 4 with your partner.

PRACTICE MAKES PERFECT

6a SPEAKING Work with a partner. Do this role-play using the questions in 4 and the Speaking bank to help you.

You want to find out the following information about summer courses at a language school:
- the starting date for the course
- the length of the course
- if accommodation is organised or not
- the price
- other activities on the course

Student A: You are the receptionist at the Sydney English Centre. Look at page 147.
Student B: You want information about the Sydney English Centre.

6b Now change roles.

Student B: You are the receptionist at the San Francisco English Centre. Look at page 147.
Student A: You want information about the San Francisco English Centre.

✓ EXAM SUCCESS

What do you need to do to get a good mark in a speaking exam?
➤ EXAM SUCCESS page 144

40　Unit 3

The **Developing speaking** lesson develops students' oral skills with a highly-structured and supportive approach to speaking.

Students are given extensive practice of the language they have learnt in the **Practice makes perfect** activity.

There are two **Exam success** boxes in each unit. They ask students to reflect on the best way to do a specific exam task. Students can discuss the question in pairs and they are then directed to a special section at the end of the book where useful strategies and tips are explained.

The **Speaking bank** highlights and analyses key language for students to refer to during the productive phase of the speaking task.

Developing writing

A language biography

1 SPEAKING Work with a partner. Look at the pictures. How can each one help you to learn English?

2 A language biography is a text where you describe your experiences of learning a different language. Read this language biography written by a student of English. What similarities are there between her experiences and yours?

We both started learning English at primary school.

My name is Celia Rojas and I'm 16 years old. I'm Mexican and my mother-tongue is Spanish. Apart from Spanish, I can speak English. I started learning English when I was at primary school. I was five years old. Primary school was where we listened to, and sang, a lot of songs in English. We also played games and read some stories. We didn't study a lot of grammar in primary school but we learned a lot of vocabulary and we practiced speaking. At the moment I'm studying English at secondary school. We study a lot of grammar and vocabulary, and we do a little speaking. We study vocabulary using an interactive wordlist. From time to time we do vocabulary tests. We don't do many translations in lessons, but we do lots of grammar exercises, sometimes on the computer. Outside school I don't really speak much English. For homework, we often read special English readers which our teacher gives us. When we finish them, we usually write summaries. I listen to a lot of English because I love English and American pop music and I also watch films in English, like The Hunger Games. That's my favourite. When I was thirteen I went to Canterbury to do a summer course. When I was there I met some great people. I'd like to go somewhere else in the UK, to London for example. I like learning English by doing activities and games in pairs. I make a few mistakes when I speak English, but I write the corrections down and revise them from time to time.

3 The text in 2 is not divided into paragraphs. Read it again and divide it into five paragraphs. Use the plan below to help you. When you finish, read the information in the Writing bank.

Paragraph 1: Basic personal information
Paragraph 2: Language-learning experiences at primary school
Paragraph 3: Language-learning experiences at secondary school
Paragraph 4: Language-learning experiences outside school, including trips
Paragraph 5: How you prefer to learn a language

4 Make notes for the paragraphs in 3 with information about yourself and your experiences of learning English.

✎ WRITING BANK

Paragraphs
We use paragraphs to group similar ideas and information together and express them more clearly. When you write a text in English, brainstorm your ideas and then group those ideas into logical paragraphs.
WRITING BANK ➤ PAGE 150

5 PRACTICE MAKES PERFECT Write your own language biography using your notes in 4. Organise your information into five clear paragraphs.

Unit 3　41

Students are given help in planning and organising the information they need to use in their writing activities. Model texts give students realistic examples of different genres of written texts.

The **Writing bank** highlights and analyses the key language of the writing task and gives help in planning and organising the information they need to include. Students refer to it during the productive stage.

The **Practice makes perfect** activity gives students further practice and refers them to the Writing bank at the end of the book for more extensive support and guidance.

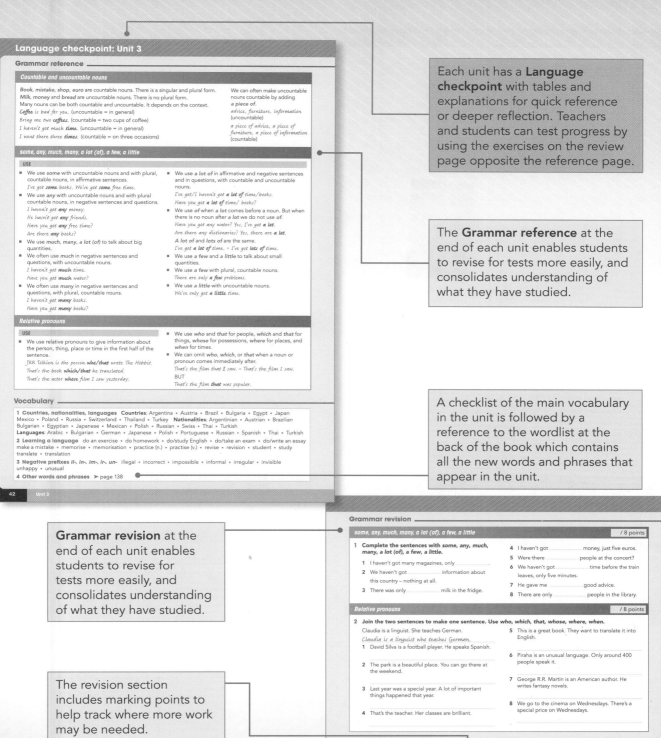

Language checkpoint: Unit 3

Grammar reference

Countable and uncountable nouns

Book, mistake, shop, euro are countable nouns. There is a singular and plural form. Milk, money and bread are uncountable nouns. There is no plural form. Many nouns can be both countable and uncountable. It depends on the context.

Coffee is bad for you. (uncountable = in general)
Bring me two *coffees*. (countable = two cups of coffee)
I haven't got much *time*. (uncountable = in general)
I went there three *times*. (countable = on three occasions)

We can often make uncountable nouns countable by adding *a piece of*.
advice, furniture, information (uncountable)
a piece of advice, a piece of furniture, a piece of information (countable)

some, any, much, many, a lot (of), a few, a little

USE

- We use *some* with uncountable nouns and with plural, countable nouns, in affirmative sentences.
  I've got *some* books. We've got *some* free time.
- We use *any* with uncountable nouns and with plural countable nouns, in negative sentences and questions.
  I haven't got *any* money.
  He hasn't got *any* friends.
  Have you got *any* free time?
  Are there *any* books?
- We use *much, many, a lot (of)* to talk about big quantities.
- We often use *much* in negative sentences and questions, with uncountable nouns.
  I haven't got *much* time.
  Have you got *much* water?
- We often use *many* in negative sentences and questions, with plural, countable nouns.
  I haven't got *many* books.
  Have you got *many* books?

- We use *a lot of* in affirmative and negative sentences and in questions, with countable and uncountable nouns.
  I've got/I haven't got *a lot of* time/books.
  Have you got *a lot of* time/ books?
- We use *of* when *a lot* comes before a noun. But when there is no noun after *a lot* we do not use *of*.
  Have you got any water? Yes, I've got *a lot*.
  Are there any dictionaries? Yes, there are *a lot*.
  A lot of and lots of are the same.
  I've got *a lot of* time. = I've got *lots of* time.
- We use *a few* and *a little* to talk about small quantities.
- We use *a few* with plural, countable nouns.
  There are only *a few* problems.
- We use *a little* with uncountable nouns.
  We've only got *a little* time.

Relative pronouns

USE

- We use relative pronouns to give information about the person, thing, place or time in the first half of the sentence.
  JRR Tolkien is the person *who/that* wrote The Hobbit.
  That's the book *which/that* he translated.
  That's the actor *whose* film I saw yesterday.

- We use *who* and *that* for people, *which* and *that* for things, *whose* for possessions, *where* for places, and *when* for times.
- We can omit *who, which, or that* when a noun or pronoun comes immediately after.
  That's the film that I saw. = That's the film I saw.
  BUT
  That's the film *that* was popular.

Vocabulary

1 **Countries, nationalities, languages Countries:** Argentina • Austria • Brazil • Bulgaria • Egypt • Japan • Mexico • Poland • Russia • Switzerland • Thailand • Turkey **Nationalities:** Argentinian • Austrian • Brazilian • Bulgarian • Egyptian • Japanese • Mexican • Polish • Russian • Swiss • Thai • Turkish **Languages:** Arabic • Bulgarian • German • Japanese • Polish • Portuguese • Russian • Spanish • Thai • Turkish
2 **Learning a language** do an exercise • do homework • do/study English • do/take an exam • do/write an essay • make a mistake • memorise • memorisation • practice (n.) • practise (v.) • revise • revision • student • study • translate • translation
3 **Negative prefixes il-, in-, im-, ir-, un-** illegal • incorrect • impossible • informal • irregular • invisible • unhappy • unusual
4 **Other words and phrases** ➤ page 138

42 | Unit 3

Grammar revision

some, any, much, many, a lot (of), a few, a little / 8 points

1 **Complete the sentences with some, any, much, many, a lot (of), a few, a little.**

1 I haven't got many magazines, only _____
2 We haven't got _____ information about this country – nothing at all.
3 There was only _____ milk in the fridge.
4 I haven't got _____ money, just five euros.
5 Were there _____ people at the concert?
6 We haven't got _____ time before the train leaves, only five minutes.
7 He gave me _____ good advice.
8 There are only _____ people in the library.

Relative pronouns / 8 points

2 **Join the two sentences to make one sentence. Use who, which, that, whose, where, when.**

Claudia is a linguist. She teaches German.
Claudia is a linguist who teaches German.
1 David Silva is a football player. He speaks Spanish.
2 The park is a beautiful place. You can go there at the weekend.
3 Last year was a special year. A lot of important things happened that year.
4 That's the teacher. Her classes are brilliant.
5 This is a great book. They want to translate it into English.
6 Pirahã is an unusual language. Only around 400 people speak it.
7 George R.R. Martin is an American author. He writes fantasy novels.
8 We go to the cinema on Wednesdays. There's a special price on Wednesdays.

Vocabulary revision

LEARNING A LANGUAGE / 8 points

1 **Complete the sentences with the words in the box. Use one word twice.**

do • exercise • make • practice
practise • revision • translation

1 Yesterday we read an English _____ of a Russian poem.
2 Before the exam, he did some _____
3 You need to _____ to speak English well.
4 Anybody can _____ a mistake.
5 Yesterday's exam was just a _____, it wasn't the real one.
6 Did you _____ the exercises yesterday?
7 This is the fourth _____ on this page.
8 At our school we _____ German.

COUNTRIES, NATIONALITIES AND LANGUAGES / 8 points

2 **Complete the sentences with the correct country, nationality or language.**

1 Thai people are from _____
2 In Brazil they speak _____
3 People from Turkey are _____
4 Austrians speak _____
5 _____ people are from Poland.
6 People from Argentina are _____
7 People from Egypt speak _____
8 People from Egypt are _____

NEGATIVE PREFIXES UN-, IN-, IM-, IR-, IL- / 8 points

3 **Complete the words.**

1 sad = un _____
2 wrong = in _____
3 you can't do it = im _____
4 relaxed and friendly = in _____
5 not follow the usual rules = ir _____
6 criminal = il _____
7 strange = un _____
8 you can't see it = in _____

Total: _____ / 40 points

Unit 3 | 43

Each unit has a **Language checkpoint** with tables and explanations for quick reference or deeper reflection. Teachers and students can test progress by using the exercises on the review page opposite the reference page.

The **Grammar reference** at the end of each unit enables students to revise for tests more easily, and consolidates understanding of what they have studied.

A checklist of the main vocabulary in the unit is followed by a reference to the wordlist at the back of the book which contains all the new words and phrases that appear in the unit.

Grammar revision at the end of each unit enables students to revise for tests more easily, and consolidates understanding of what they have studied.

The revision section includes marking points to help track where more work may be needed.

There is also a **Vocabulary revision** section. The revision sections can be used for self-study as well as in class.

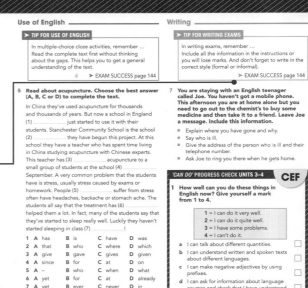

Every two units the **Gateway to exams** pages allow students to test their progress and at the same time develop their skills through targeted training tasks for exams.

Useful exam tips cover all of the skills – **Writing, Speaking, Listening, Reading** and give guidance for **Use of English** tasks, providing invaluable reminders and hints for students to approach their exams fully prepared.

Students are referred to the **Exam success** pages at the back of the book for more detailed exploration of the skills they have been learning and the best way to approach a specific exam task.

The '*Can do*' progress check empowers students by encouraging them to measure their own progress against a checklist of tasks they are able to do successfully after every two units. It also acts as a useful summary of the language topics and skills covered so far.

✓ Gateway to exams: Units 3–4

Reading

1 **SPEAKING** Work with a partner. Ask and answer these questions.

1 What do you think is good advice for somebody with a stomach virus?
2 How do you think speaking different languages can be good for your health?
3 Do you sometimes feel sick when you travel by car, plane or ship?

A *Health matters: This week's news*

SEASICK ON DRY LAND

Have you ever been on a boat or a ship? If you have, you probably know about seasickness, that terrible feeling caused by going up and down non-stop on the sea. But imagine feeling seasick when you're not at sea. Mrs Jane Houghton has been seasick since 2001. She was at sea for three days. When she got off the boat, she started to feel seasick and she has never recovered. One unusual thing about her illness is that she only feels OK when she is moving in a car, boat or aeroplane. It's difficult for Mrs Houghton to work because when she sits at her computer she feels terrible. Mrs Houghton has created a website with information about her illness. She wants people to know about it. Perhaps one day doctors will be able to help her.

B STAY AT HOME

A large number of people have a stomach virus called norovirus at the moment. This virus can cause stomach ache, high temperatures and pains in your arms and legs. Doctors have told patients to stay at home for two days after the illness has gone. They are also recommending that patients take paracetamol, drink lots of water and, most importantly, that they wash their hands regularly. The Health Protection Agency has said that this year there are twice as many people with the virus as last year. There are between 600,000 and one million cases of norovirus in the UK each year.

C BEING BILINGUAL IS GOOD FOR YOUR BRAIN

A recent study says that speaking two languages can help old people to stay mentally active. Dr Ellen Bialystok and her team of scientists at York University in Canada did experiments with 104 people between the ages of 30 and 88. They came to the conclusion that being bilingual can help old people to think quickly. Half of the people who did the tests came from Canada and only spoke English. The other half came from India and could speak English and a language called Tamil. The scientists tested vocabulary skills and maths ability. They also checked how fast they did the tests. The ones who could speak two languages did the exercises quickly and well. The people who spoke only one language weren't so good. The British Alzheimer's Society was very interested in the discoveries.

2 **Read these newspaper articles. Match each question in 1 with one of the three articles.**

1 _____ 2 _____

▶ TIP FOR READING EXAMS

In matching activities, remember … Read all the text once quickly to get a general understanding. Then read the information that you need to find. Look for the section of the text where you think this information appears and look at it again in more detail.
▶ EXAM SUCCESS page 144

3 **Which article …**

1 talks about an illness which is very bad when the patient isn't moving? _____
2 talks about action that can help older people? _____
3 recommends taking a type of drug? _____
4 mentions one person with problems at work? _____
5 talks about quick answers to questions? _____
6 mentions a new discovery in the world of medicine? _____
7 talks about the usual number of people who suffer a specific illness? _____
8 talks about an unusual illness? _____
9 mentions personal hygiene? _____

4 **SPEAKING** What about *you*?

How serious do you think the different illnesses mentioned in the text are? Why?

Use of English

▶ TIP FOR USE OF ENGLISH

In multiple-choice cloze activities, remember … Read the complete text first without thinking about the gaps. This helps you to get a general understanding of the text.
▶ EXAM SUCCESS page 144

5 **Read about acupuncture. Choose the best answer (A, B, C or D) to complete the text.**

In China they've used acupuncture for thousands and thousands of years. But now a school in England (1) _____ just started to use it with their students. Stanchester Community School is the school (2) _____ they have begun this project. At this school they have a teacher who has spent time living in China studying acupuncture with Chinese experts. This teacher has (3) _____ acupuncture to a small group of students at the school (4) _____ September. A very common problem that the students have is stress, usually stress caused by exams or homework. People (5) _____ suffer from stress often have headaches, backache or stomach ache. The students all say that the treatment has (6) _____ helped them a lot. In fact, many of the students say that they've started to sleep really well. Luckily they haven't started sleeping in class (7) _____!

	A	B	C	D
1	A has	B is	C have	D was
2	A that	B who	C where	D which
3	A give	B gave	C gives	D given
4	A since	B for	C at	D on
5	A –	B who	C when	D what
6	A yet	B for	C at	D already
7	A yet	B ever	C never	D in

Speaking

▶ TIP FOR SPEAKING EXAMS

In speaking exams, remember … It's important to know what the examiners want to hear. Find out how many marks there are and what you need to do to get a good mark.
▶ EXAM SUCCESS page 144

6 **SPEAKING** Work with a partner. Student A: Look at photo A on page 147. Student B: Look at photo B on page 148. Take it in turns to talk about your photos using the questions below.

1 Where are the people and what are they doing?
2 Who are the people and what are they wearing?
3 What else can you see?
4 How do you prefer to learn a language?

Writing

▶ TIP FOR WRITING EXAMS

In writing exams, remember … Include all the information in the instructions or you will lose marks. And don't forget to write in the correct style (formal or informal).
▶ EXAM SUCCESS page 144

7 **You are staying with an English teenager called Joe. You haven't got a mobile phone. This afternoon you are at home alone but you need to go out to the chemist's to buy some medicine and then take it to a friend. Leave Joe a message. Include this information.**

- Explain where you have gone and why.
- Say who is ill.
- Give the address of the person who is ill and their telephone number.
- Ask Joe to ring you there when he gets home.

'CAN DO' PROGRESS CHECK UNITS 3–4   CEF

1 **How well can you do these things in English now? Give yourself a mark from 1 to 4.**

> 1 = I can do it very well.
> 2 = I can do it quite well.
> 3 = I have some problems.
> 4 = I can't do it.

a I can talk about different quantities. ☐
b I can understand written and spoken texts about different languages. ☐
c I can make negative adjectives by using prefixes. ☐
d I can ask for information about language courses and check that I have understood. ☐
e I can write a text about my experiences of learning a language. ☐
f I can report general and recent experiences in the past using the present perfect. ☐
g I can talk about activities which continue up to now using the present perfect with for and since. ☐
h I can discuss health problems and illnesses. ☐
i I can describe scenes in photos and pictures using fillers. ☐
j I can write basic notes and messages. ☐

2 **Now decide what you need to do to improve.**

1 Look again at my book/notes.
2 Do more practice exercises.
▶ WORKBOOK Units 3 and 4
3 Ask for help.
4 Other: _____

Course components
Digital Student's Book

The *Gateway 2nd Edition* Digital Student's Book offers a content-rich interactive learning experience for your students, facilitating dynamic and engaging lessons.

Contains:

 Interactive Student's Book activities

 Complete class audio

 Integrated video

 Note-taking function

 Automated marking

 Gradebook

Students can work through interactive versions of the Student's Book exercises, developing their language skills through collaborative or individual learning.

Enhanced Student's Book pages are easy to navigate, and contain embedded audio and video, as well as interactive activities.

The Notes functionality enables students to put language into meaningful written practice, take presentation notes, or even add links for further research.

Completed exercises will be automatically marked and grades synced to your teacher Gradebook when online.

Course components
Presentation Kit

Bring *Gateway 2nd Edition* to life in the classroom with your complete presentation and teaching tool.

Contains:

Interactive Student's Book activities

Complete class audio

Integrated video

Additional vocabulary presentation tool

Answer key feature

Note pad feature

Pages contain interactive versions of many of the Student's Book exercises with automated marking offering instant feedback.

Class audio and video can be played at the click of a button.

The built-in tools allow you to annotate and customise your presentations in advance.

The interactive vocabulary presentation tool provides additional support for presenting the Student's Book core vocabulary.

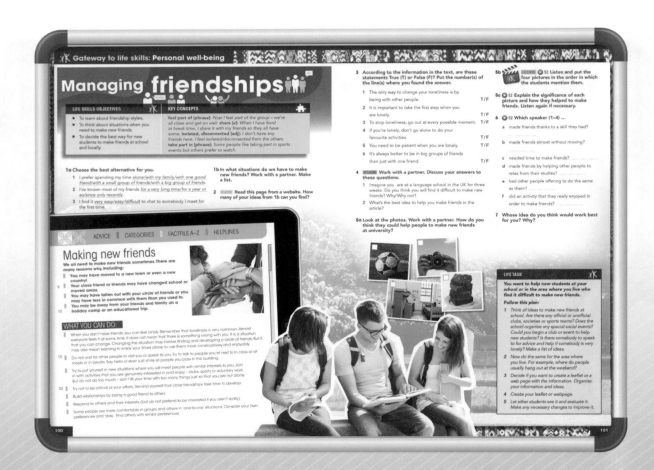

Course components
Videos

Gateway *2nd Edition* offers a Flipped classroom grammar presentation video and a Life skills video in each unit. These integrate effectively into Student's Book lesson stages to enrich classes.

Use in class or for self-study

Flipped classroom videos

David Spencer, the author of *Gateway 2nd Edition*, delivers engaging grammar presentations that accompany one Grammar in context section for each unit. The presentations take a visual approach, introducing concepts and making new structures accessible through examples, timelines and diagrams.

Flipped classroom approach

By presenting the grammar outside the class, Flipped classroom allows more time for in-class practice. To find out more about the Flipped classroom approach, go to macmillangateway2.com

Flexible tool

The videos are a versatile and efficient resource for teachers which can also be used flexibly as a useful tool for mixed-ability groups or for revision.

Life skills videos

The Life skills videos form part of the Life skills lessons. They show British teens demonstrating or discussing the Life skills topic in a way that has direct relevance to all students' lives. There are comprehension tasks on the Student's Book page and further exploitation exercises and activities for the video in the Resource Centre. The video formats are fun and appeal to teens, featuring:

- vlogs
- school projects
- street interviews

After watching the video, students complete the Life task – a project or presentation in which they can apply what they have learnt during the Life skills lesson.

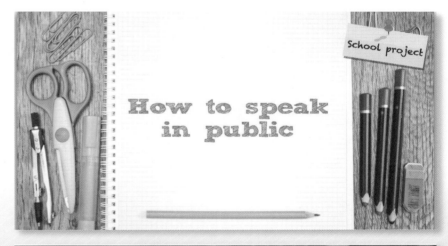

The Workbook offers consolidation of the core language in the Student's Book, with extra listening, Study skills and a special cumulative Revision page in each unit.

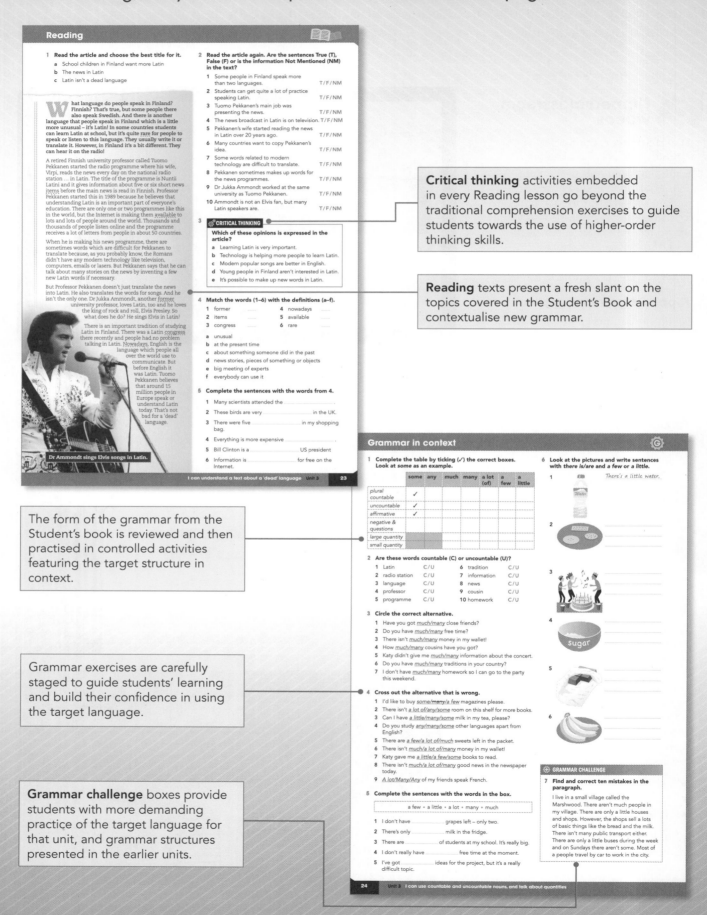

Critical thinking activities embedded in every Reading lesson go beyond the traditional comprehension exercises to guide students towards the use of higher-order thinking skills.

Reading texts present a fresh slant on the topics covered in the Student's Book and contextualise new grammar.

The form of the grammar from the Student's book is reviewed and then practised in controlled activities featuring the target structure in context.

Grammar exercises are carefully staged to guide students' learning and build their confidence in using the target language.

Grammar challenge boxes provide students with more demanding practice of the target language for that unit, and grammar structures presented in the earlier units.

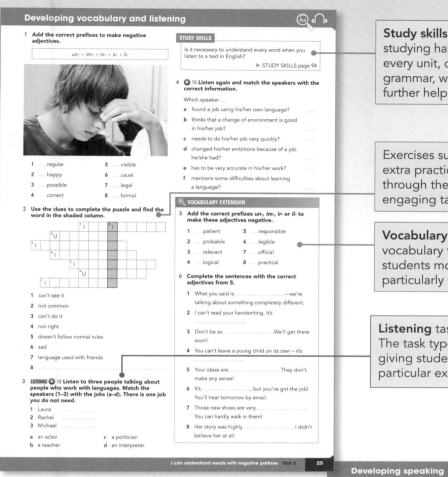

Study skills boxes help students to improve their studying habits. Two Study skills boxes appear in every unit, offering guidance on reading, listening, grammar, writing, speaking and vocabulary, with further help at the back of the book.

Exercises support the Student's Book and give extra practice in developing vocabulary, often through the use of images, puzzles and other engaging tasks.

Vocabulary extension boxes expand on the vocabulary taught in the Student's Book, offering students more challenge. These activities are particularly valuable in mixed-ability classes.

Listening tasks recycle the vocabulary of the unit. The task types match those in the Student's Book, giving students further opportunity to develop particular exam skills.

Describing pictures sections form part of each **Developing speaking** page and provide students with carefully staged practice of exam-style image description.

The audio model gives students examples of useful language and provides guidance on how best to tackle an exam-style task. There is then another image on the same theme, which they can describe using the model to help them.

Pronunciation boxes help students really focus on an aspect of pronunciation relevant to that speaking topic, heightening their awareness of the common sounds, intonation and stress of English and providing them with an audio model.

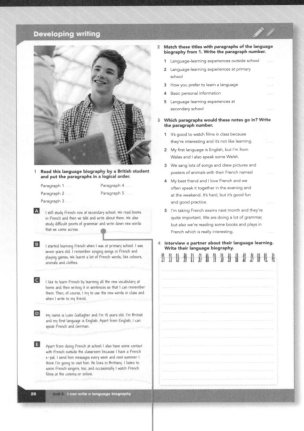

Cumulative revision pages provide essential recycling of language from not only the preceding unit but also earlier units in the book.

Further analysis and highlighting of key language for the same type of writing task as is covered in the Student's Book.

Gateway to exams pages appear every two units, offering Reading, Listening, Use of English and Writing tasks. The topics and tasks reflect what has been covered in the preceding two units, providing students with the opportunity to further develop their exam skills, while recycling key grammar and vocabulary.

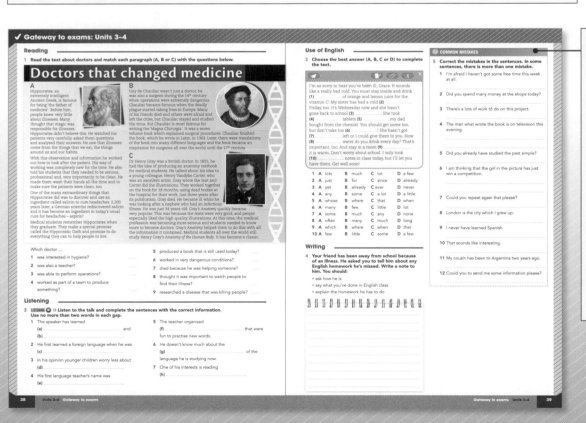

Common mistakes boxes provide error correction practice, with the focus on the language of the preceding two units. They highlight mistakes often made by students at this level, giving them the opportunity to recognise and reflect on any such errors they may be making in their own work.

Course components
Online Workbook

For students
PLUS
Gradebook
for teachers

All the printed Workbook content and more in a fully-interactive format for flexible self-study.

Contains:

Interactive
Workbook activities

Complete
Workbook audio

Integrated
video

Automated marking
for instant feedback

Gradebook

Multiple classes and levels can be managed in a single location, and the content-locking feature gives you control over how you set tasks for your students.

Detailed feedback on activity scores and progress all help to create a highly-personalised self-study environment.

Multiple attempts keep students motivated, allowing them to consolidate what they have learned in class in an engaging way. Students can also access the Flipped classroom videos and activities on the Online Workbook, making this an excellent tool for developing independent learning.

The messaging and notification features allow you to correspond with your students, send homework reminders and notify your classes when results are available.

Results are automatically collated in the Gradebook and displayed in an easy-to-read, easy-to-compare way. Learner progress can be monitored at a glance, highlighting areas where students may require additional support or assistance.

Course components
Teacher's and Student's Resource Centres

The Online Resource Centres contain a wealth of downloadable worksheets, multimedia assets and additional resources to support your *Gateway 2nd Edition* core course content.

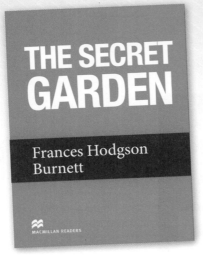

THE SECRET GARDEN

Frances Hodgson Burnett

MACMILLAN READERS

Student's Resource Centre

For students, the Student's Resource Centre provides complementary materials to consolidate learning and encourage independent study including:

- Teen-focused culture worksheets to inspire a broader cultural perspective
- A graded Macmillan Reader, with extra activities and extended reading support
- Study skills materials to encourage students to take control of their learning
- Life skills video worksheets and Flipped classroom video worksheets provide additional support for students to use with the videos

Teacher's Resource Centre

The Teacher's Resource Centre is your go-to place for resources to deliver dynamic lessons for homework assignments and to support you in the classroom. The flexible content includes:

- Audio and video files and scripts
- Complete answer keys
- Teacher tips and videos
- Extra grammar worksheets and communication activities
- Everyday English worksheets
- Optional CLIL and literature lessons
- Teacher notes and guides to accompany all material

Sounds: The Pronunication App

This award-winning app helps students practise and play with pronunciation wherever they are. Carefully selected wordlists from the *Gateway 2nd Edition* course are now available to download within the app.

Course components
Testing and assessment materials

For teachers

Extensive resources for assessing your students' progress and preparing them for international and school-leaving examinations.

Test Generator

The Test Generator allows you to create customised tests from an extensive database of exercises.

- Aligned closely to CEFR learning outcomes
- Includes a range of reading, writing, speaking and listening tasks typical of international and school-leaving exams
- Comes with the option to save tests in progress and to preview before printing
- Allows for maximum flexibility in choosing the test content
- Teacher-version of tests complete with answer keys

Printable tests

A comprehensive range of Printable tests are available on the Teacher's Resource Centre in both PDF and editable Word format. Tests matched to the course level can be selected and then customised to meet the specific needs of your school and classes.

- One diagnostic test per level
- Ten Unit tests, three Review tests and one End-of-year test for tracking progress
- Aligned closely to CEFR learning outcomes and international and school-leaving exams
- Complete answer keys, audio and audioscripts for all tests
- Two levels of difficulty for each test

Teacher support
Dave's top teaching tips

Here are some great teaching tips to help you throughout the year. These tips give you strategies for classroom management, planning and student training that you can use again and again to improve your students' results and get the best out of your teaching.

💬 USING ENGLISH IN THE CLASSROOM

At the beginning of the school year, students may be shy about using English. Be a good model for your students by making simple and natural comments in English, e.g. *Really? That's a good idea, Sylvie. What do you think, Jacob?* Use a small range of comments and use them consistently. At first, you can use gestures alongside the comments (e.g. thumbs up when you are saying something positive) to reinforce the idea of what you are saying. In time, students will start to imitate you and you can establish an English-only environment.

It is also useful to teach expressions that students can use for pair and groupwork. Put these expressions on posters around the classroom, or have them saved on a file that you can bring up on the IWB at relevant times and refer to them to remind students to always use English.

Pairwork: *Do you have a partner yet? Let's work together for this activity. Are you ready? I'll start. I'll be A and you be B.*

Groupwork: *We need one more person in our group. Can I join your group? Who wants to go first?*

Comparing answers: *What did you get for number 1? I got … for number 1. How about you? I have the same/a different answer. I didn't get that one.*

Finally, teach a few expressions that students can use to ask for meaning, pronunciation, spelling, repetition or clarification: *Could you say that again, please? Can you speak more slowly, please? How do you say … in English/Japanese? How do you pronounce/say this word? What does … mean? How do you spell …?*

✔ CHECKING ANSWERS

Using different ways to check answers makes the feedback stage more fun and changes the pace of the lesson. Some ideas include:

- Give the students an Answer Key or put the Answer Key on the wall or the board. Students can work in pairs: one student runs to the wall to check the answer and goes back to tell their partner.
- Give half the answers to one student in a pair and half the answers to the other student. They share their information like an information gap activity.
- One student has the Answer Key and plays the teacher.
- Get students to write their answers on the board.
- Get one student to read out his/her answers – the rest of the class see if they have the same.
- Students nominate each other to say the answer.
- Do it as a competition and award points for correct answers.

🎧 HOW TO DO LISTENING ACTIVITIES

- Always give students a clear purpose for listening to motivate them. For example, if students know they have to do a speaking exercise on the same topic as the listening, they will probably pay more attention.
- Make sure the context is clear (describe the situation and topic) and encourage students to predict content from Key words in the questions, visual clues, etc.
- Give students time to read the questions before they listen and ask if there is any vocabulary they don't understand.
- With less confident students, it is a good idea to play the listening in short sections. After each section, ask students to discuss what they have understood in pairs or groups. Discussion in pairs is motivating, makes listening activities less threatening and gives you more information about how much students have understood.

💬 WORD STRESS

Word stress is like a golden key to speaking and understanding English. It means that one syllable in each word is stressed, i.e. it is pronounced longer, louder and stronger than others, e.g. photograph, photographer, photographic.

This happens in all words with two or more syllables and the stress is always on a vowel. The syllables that are not stressed are weak. Native speakers of English listen for the stressed syllables, not the weak syllables. Show students how stress is indicated in dictionaries and either use this notation in class, or develop one of your own (e.g. putting a cross over the stressed syllable) and use it whenever you teach new vocabulary. By working on word stress with students, you will improve their pronunciation and comprehension.

🔍 KEEPING A VOCABULARY RECORD

Encourage students to keep a vocabulary notebook, organised in a way that is meaningful to them, e.g. by topic area, and with pronunciation and stress patterns also noted. Visual learners may like to draw a vocabulary tree to record the new words from this lesson, adding in vocabulary from the unit as they go. A vocabulary tree starts with the name of the vocabulary category in the trunk, e.g. TV. Next, students draw 'branches' off the central theme and entitle them, e.g. TV programmes, adjectives to describe TV programmes, etc. Students list the vocabulary on these branches and add other branches as they move through the unit.

✏️ USING THE BOARD

Using the board (or the interactive whiteboard) is an important teaching skill. Ideally, you should plan in advance how you are going to use the board during the lesson. By the end of the lesson, it should look well-organised and the student at the back of the room should be able to see everything on it. (Keep in mind that, in many classrooms, students find it difficult to see the bottom third of the board, or the far right or left.)

By modelling good organisation, you are also fostering students' note-taking skills. Take the time to reorganise your board while students are working on an activity. Always ask your students first before you erase anything. Use different colours and illustrations where possible. Remember that students like to 'play teacher' and also enjoy using the board.

Many teachers divide the board into three parts:

Key pad:	Active pad:	Note pad:
Write a summary of key points here (including key lexical and grammar points).	Use this section for any necessary notes during the lesson, e.g. explanations, answers, pronunciation notes, etc.	At the beginning of the lesson, note the aims of the class and today's main activities. At the end of the class, write the homework.

💬 ERROR CORRECTION

Accuracy

Before pointing out errors, encourage students to recognise and correct their own mistakes. You can do this by asking a student to repeat what he/she has said, or by echoing what the student said and placing emphasis on the error. You can also reformulate the sentence and repeat it correctly. Students could create an 'Errors' list in their notebooks to remind themselves of the errors they should try to avoid.

Fluency-based activities

Unlike accuracy activities, fluency-based activities require less error correction. Correcting individual errors on the spot may discourage students and make them feel inhibited, so it is preferable for correction to take place at the end of the activity. Be on hand during the activity to help with any language difficulties and note down both good use of language and problem areas. A chart with the following headings can be useful when monitoring: Grammatical errors, Vocabulary errors, Pronunciation errors, Good use of language, etc.

Go through the errors at the end of the activity, without mentioning who made each one. Praise students who made good use of language and invite the class to give opinions or ask questions.

Dave's top teaching tips

✔️ SELF-ASSESSMENT

In preparation for future examinations, it is important that students are aware of their own strengths and weaknesses. Self-assessment is a good way to raise students' awareness of the areas they need to work on. After a speaking activity, you could give students a pro-forma like the one shown below to fill in. They can assess both their own performance and/or their partner's performance.

☺ ? (Positive points)

😐 ? (Neutral comment)

☹ ? (Negative points)

⟫ FAST FINISHERS

If you have students who always finish before everyone else, look at their answers and tell them how many they have got wrong, but not which ones. This is a good way to keep a fast finisher busy for a little while longer while the others catch up. It's also a good way to get students to look at their answers again, which is a useful exam strategy.

🔍 USING DICTIONARIES IN THE CLASSROOM

Devoting time to dictionary use and training is beneficial for students and should regularly feature in their lessons. Ideally, the Macmillan Dictionaries should always be available. In this way, learners get used to looking up an unknown word or finding the verb that collocates with a particular noun for a writing exercise, as well as researching the pronunciation or word stress.

Dictionaries can be used in vocabulary lessons where learners are required to find the meanings of a set of words or to find examples of how they are used. However, you should also try to encourage students to work out the meanings of new words from their context in the first instance.

Teacher support
Teacher development tips index

There are a number of methodological and practical tips which are strategically placed within the Teacher's notes in the *Gateway 2nd Edition* Teacher's Book to be of most use to the teacher not just during planning, setting up and evaluating activities, but also helping 'on the spot' in certain language or pronunciation areas.

CLASSROOM TIPS AND PLANNING

Using English in class	p20	Managing discussions in class	p41	Using news stories in class	p82
How to do listening activities	p20	Pairwork	p45	Choral drilling	p89
Using the board	p21	Monitoring	p48	Checking answers	p92
Error correction	p21	A language biography	p61	Setting up a class debate	p99
Fast finishers	p22	Pyramid discussions	p65	Simulating a phone conversation	p111
Recorded reading texts	p30	How to teach text register	p72	Teaching reading skills	p116
How to teach articles	p35	Promoting debate	p78	Assessment guidelines	p145
Using spoken model texts	p36	Mingling	p80		

LANGUAGE

Actions vs states	p31	Past simple vs present perfect	p71	Modal verbs of obligation, prohibition and advice	p106
Present tense usage	p31	Separable phrasal verbs	p76		
Suffixes	p32, 118	Comparatives and superlatives	p79	Using conditionals	p110
Articles	p35	Adjectives ending in -*ing* and -*ed*	p80	*could* vs *can*	p111
Past tense forms	p43	*Less…than* and *not as…as*	p83	The past perfect	p117
Phrasal verbs	p44, 76, 130	Making suggestions	p84	Expressions of time	p118
Past continuous	p47	Future forms	p91	Gerunds and infinitives	p121
do and *make*	p54	*get*	p93	Reporting past events	p123
Countable or uncountable	p55	Zero conditional	p96	*say* vs *tell*	p130
Quantifiers	p55	Expressing agreement	p97	Reported speech	p131
Negative prefixes	p57	First conditional	p97	Reported speech – questions	p134
Defining relative clauses	p59	Present continuous for arrangements	p98	Active to passive	p140
Contractions	p66			Passive questions	p144
for and *since*	p67	Linkers and connectors	p99		
yet and *already*	p70	*job* vs *work*	p105		

STUDENT TRAINING

Using dictionaries in the classroom	p22	Using conversation fillers	p72	Listening outside class	p122
Keeping a vocabulary record	p21	Oral examinations	p85	Developing exam skills	p124
Self-assessment	p22	Key word transformations	p92	Missing sentence activities	p129
Describing a photo	p34	Writing stories	p94	Learning phrasal verbs	p131
Key information	p40	Writing in exam conditions	p100	Predicting missing words	p133
Asking for information	p60	True/false activities	p105	Guessing words from context	p140
Writing paragraphs	p61	Multiple-choice tasks	p109	Giving a presentation	p142
Revision techniques	p64	Exam preparation	p121	Cloze activities	p144

PRONUNCIATION

Word stress	p21	Word stress and nationalities	p53	Pronouncing *will*	p91
Connected speech	p29	Silent *k* and *ch* as *k* sound	p64	*be going to*	p92
Stressed and unstressed articles	p35	Sound/spelling relationships	p64	Sentence rhythm	p96
Intonation in questions	p36	Vowel sounds	p77	Chanting and backchaining	p97
The /θ/ sound	p40	Sentence stress and weak forms	p79, 91, 128	Teaching intonation	p98
Voiced and voiceless sounds	p43			The contraction *'d*	p117
Stressed and unstressed forms of *was*	p47	Weak form of *the*	p80	Word stress in nouns and verbs	p138
		Pronouncing -*ed*	p80		

The Common European Framework of Reference (CEFR) is a widely used standard created by the Council of Europe. *Gateway 2nd Edition* is carefully mapped to the CEFR helping teachers identify students' actual progress and helping them to set their learning priorities.

Gateway 2nd Edition offers a wide range of teaching materials in various components which give teachers the opportunity to develop all aspects of their students' language ability. The CEFR can be used to track their progress.

On pages 25–27 are the B1 descriptors (description of competences) covered in the B1 level of *Gateway 2nd Edition*. A2 descriptors are also available in the Gateway A2 Teacher's Book.

A basic level of confidence with the A2 descriptors is expected as students start using *Gateway 2nd Edition* B1 and, by the end of the course, students should be competent with the B1 level.

In the Teacher's Resource Centre you will also find a list of unit-by-unit CEFR descriptors with suggested targets which can be used for self-assessment. Students can use these at any point to get a detailed picture of their own individual progress.

WHAT IS A EUROPEAN LANGUAGE PORTFOLIO (ELP)?

The European Language Portfolio (ELP) was developed by the Language Policy Unit of the Council of Europe

- to support the development of learner autonomy, plurilingualism and intercultural awareness and competence;
- to allow users to record their language learning achievements and their experience of learning and using languages.

If you are using portfolios as a way of evaluating your students' coursework over the year, you will find a wide variety of opportunities within each *Gateway 2nd Edition* unit to provide material for the dossier.

A portfolio is a means to document a person's achievements. Artists, architects or designers collect samples of their work in portfolios and students are encouraged to do the same. Most of the time, these samples will be texts created by the students, but they could also include photos of classroom scenes, wall displays, audio recordings and videos. All these documents provide evidence of a student's performance, e.g. during a discussion, an oral presentation or a role-play.

Within each unit, there are several opportunities for students to practise speaking and record their conversations for the dossier in their portfolio. Students could record their conversations, date them and include them in their portfolio. They then assess their performance in each speaking activity and give themselves a mark according to the following self-assessment criteria:

CONTENT (1–5)

Did I say what I wanted to say? Was I interesting? Did I speak in English for a long time? Did I hesitate a lot?

VOCABULARY AND GRAMMAR (1–5)

Did I use different words? Did I use words I've learned recently? Were my sentences well constructed? Did I make a lot of errors?

COOPERATION (1–5)

Did I listen to my partner? Did we help each other if we had problems? Did we both speak for approximately the same length of time?

IN ENGLISH! (1–5)

When I didn't know how to say something, did I use English to solve my problem? Did we use English to talk about whose turn it was to speak?

The portfolio consists of three parts: the **Language Passport** with information about a student's proficiency in one or more languages, i.e. qualifications; the **Language Biography** where students reflect on their learning process and progress and say what they can do in their foreign language(s); and the **Dossier**, which is a collection of materials and data put together by students to document and illustrate their learning experiences.

Although it may be a demanding task to set up in the beginning, the overall aim is for students to be involved in planning, collecting and evaluating their own work, thereby taking responsibility for their own learning. This in turn may lead to increased participation and autonomy on the part of the learner.

	1	**2**	**3**	**4**	**5**	**6**	**7**	**8**	**9**	**10**
Listening	page number									
B1 — I can follow clearly articulated speech directed at me in everyday conversation, though I sometimes have to ask for repetition of particular words and phrases.						75		109	118	
B1 — I can generally follow the main points of extended discussion around me, provided speech is clearly articulated in standard dialect.	14	32	38	50	64	76	84	101 104 109	116	122 127 130 135
B1 — I can listen to a short narrative and form hypotheses about what will happen next.				50				109		
B1 — I can understand the main points of radio news bulletins and simpler recorded material on topics of personal interest delivered relatively slowly and clearly.	12	24	37		58 63	76 82	90	101 102	110 115 116 118	127 128 135
B1 — I can catch the main points in videos on familiar topics when the delivery is relatively slow and clear.	11	23	37	49	63	75	89		115	127
B1 — I can understand simple technical information, such as operating instructions for everyday equipment.										122

	1	**2**	**3**	**4**	**5**	**6**	**7**	**8**	**9**	**10**
Reading	page number									
B1 — I can understand the main points in short newspaper articles about current and familiar topics.			33	45	62	75		100		123 126 127 135
B1 — I can read columns or interviews in newspapers and magazines in which someone takes a stand on a current topic or event and understand the overall meaning of the text.		30	37			71 74	85			123 134
B1 — I can guess the meaning of single unknown words from the context thus deducing the meaning of expressions if the topic is familiar.	7		33	56	59 62 65	71 74 75	91	97 108		123 124 126 127
B1 — I can skim short texts (for example news summaries) and find relevant facts and information (for example who has done what and where).	7	19 30	37	45 56	59	75	85 88	97 108	111 114	123 126 128 134
B1 — I can understand the most important information in short simple everyday information brochures.							92	102		
B1 — I can understand simple messages and standard letters (for example from businesses, clubs or authorities).						79				
B1 — In emails, letters and blog posts I can understand those parts dealing with events, feelings and wishes well enough to correspond regularly with a pen friend.	15	27			67		85		111	
B1 — I can understand the plot of a clearly structured article or story and recognise what the most important episodes and events are and what is significant about them.			41	48 49			88 89	96 97	114	134

Speaking: Spoken Interaction

		1	2	3	4	5	6	7	8	9	10
		page number									
B1	I can start, maintain and close simple face-to-face conversation on topics that are familiar or of personal interest.	12	24	32	45	58	83	91	99 103	110 118	127 130
B1	I can maintain a conversation or discussion but may sometimes be difficult to follow when trying to say exactly what I would like to.			38	52	65	73 76 83	92	101	116	125 127
B1	I can deal with most situations likely to arise when making travel arrangements through an agent or when actually travelling.	*Gateway 2ⁿᵈ Edition A2 Student's Book*									
B1	I can ask for and follow detailed directions.	*Gateway 2ⁿᵈ Edition A2 Student's Book*									
B1	I can express and respond to feelings such as surprise, happiness, sadness, interest and indifference.			39		66	76	85	96 101 105	116	134
B1	I can give or seek personal views and opinions in an informal discussion with friends.	12	19 22 23	32 33 40	52 56	58 61 66	70 73 83	90 91	99 104	110 113 116 118	123 135
B1	I can agree and disagree politely.		22		63	64 66	71 79		104	110 113	123 130

Speaking: Spoken Production

		1	2	3	4	5	6	7	8	9	10
		page number									
B1	I can narrate a story.								96	119	
B1	I can give detailed accounts of experiences, describing feelings and reactions.	7			51	61			104	118	
B1	I can describe dreams, hopes and ambitions.						77				
B1	I can explain and give reasons for my plans, intentions and actions.			40		59	72 77 78	84		114	
B1	I can relate the plot of a book or film and describe my reactions.									114 115	
B1	I can paraphrase short written passages orally in a simple fashion, using the original text wording and ordering.		19	37		62 63	73 78	87	104	113	

Speaking: Strategies

		1	2	3	4	5	6	7	8	9	10
		page number									
B1	I can repeat back part of what someone has said to confirm that we understand each other.			40							
B1	I can ask someone to clarify or elaborate what they have just said.			40	51						
B1	When I can't think of the word I want, I can use a simple word meaning something similar and invite "correction".			37	57	58 63	78 82				127

		1	2	3	4	5	6	7	8	9	10
Vocabulary: Language Quality		page number									
B1	I can keep a conversation going comprehensibly, but have to pause to plan and correct what I am saying – especially when I talk freely for longer periods.	14							104	118	
B1	I can convey simple information of immediate relevance, getting across which point I feel is most important.		23	35	45 51		73	84	105	114	130
B1	I have a sufficient vocabulary to express myself with some circumlocutions on most topics pertinent to my everyday life such as family, hobbies and interests, work, travel, and current events.	15	22	33 34 42 43		58 59 68	70 75 82	84	96 101	113 116	127 128
B1	I can express myself reasonably accurately in familiar, predictable situations.		23	33 35	44	67	72	84 85 87 90	96 100 104	112 113 118	130 131

		1	2	3	4	5	6	7	8	9	10
Writing		page number									
B1	I can write simple connected texts on a range of topics within my field of interest and can express personal views and opinions.	31		35	57 63		76 79	87	105	113 119	131
B1	I can write simple texts about experiences or events, for example about a trip, for a school newspaper or a club newsletter.			41					101	119	
B1	I can write personal letters to friends or acquaintances asking for or giving them news and narrating events.	15	27		53		82				
B1	I can write a simple review of a TV programme.					67					
B1	In a letter I can express feelings such as grief, happiness, interest, regret and sympathy.					67	76 79 82				
B1	I can reply in written form to advertisements and ask for more complete or more specific information about products (for example a car or an academic course).							92	108		
B1	I can convey – via fax, e-mail or a circular – short simple factual information to friends or colleagues or ask for information in such a way.	31				67			105		
B1	I can write my CV in summary form.							93			

1 Family life

KEY LEARNING OUTCOMES

CEF

Students will be able to:

- understand a text about teenagers and responsibility
- talk about ages and family life using the present simple, present continuous and articles
- ask for and give personal information
- talk about family life and problems
- write an informal email

UNIT OVERVIEW

Vocabulary
Ages and stages of life
The family

Reading
Problem letters
CRITICAL THINKING Thinking of good advice for disagreements with parents

Grammar in context
Present simple and present continuous

Developing vocabulary
Noun suffixes -ment, -ion, -ence

Life skills
Autonomy: Contributing to family life

Listening
Family dinners

Grammar in context
Articles
PRONUNCIATION Different pronunciation of the word *the*

Developing speaking
Asking for personal information
PRONUNCIATION Intonation in questions

Developing writing
An informal email

Exam success
Reading: Multiple-choice activities
Speaking: Information role-plays

DIGITAL OVERVIEW

Presentation Kit

- ▶ **Flipped classroom video Unit 1:** Present simple and present continuous
- ▶ **Life skills video Unit 1:** Our special responsibilities
- ▶ v **Vocabulary tool:** Ages and stages of life
- ▶ **Interactive versions of Student's Book activities**
- ▶ **Integrated audio and answer key for all activities**
- ▶ **Workbook pages with answer key**

Teacher's Resource Centre

- ▶ **Flipped classroom video Unit 1:** Present simple and present continuous
- ▶ **Life skills video Unit 1:** Our special responsibilities
- ▶ **Grammar communication activity Unit 1:** Let's risk it
- ▶ **Worksheets for this unit, including:**
  - Grammar Practice worksheet Unit 1
  - Flipped classroom video worksheet Unit 1: Present simple and present continuous
  - Literature worksheet Units 1 and 2
  - Culture worksheet Unit 1
  - Life skills video worksheet Unit 1
  - Everyday English worksheet Unit 1

Student's App

Gateway 2nd Edition wordlist for the award-winning Sounds App (available for download)

✓ TESTING AND ASSESSMENT

Resources for exam preparation and measuring student progress

- ▶ Test Generator Unit 1
- ▶ Printable test Unit 1
- ▶ Gateway to exams Units 1 and 2 (end of Unit 2)

Vocabulary p6

Talking about the ages and stages of life and the family

>>> **FAST TRACK**

You could ask students to write the sentences in exercise 9 at home. They can then discuss their sentences in pairs at the next lesson.

WARMER

Ask what ideas and themes connected to the family they think they might study in this unit. Elicit ideas from around the class and write vocabulary/phrases that students suggest on the board.

[V] Ages and stages of life

1 Before students start, draw attention to the example. In pairs, students match the photos to the words and write down what ages (approximately) go with each stage of life.

Suggested answers

All ages are approximate.
a child, 4–12   **d** middle-aged (man/woman), 35–64
b senior citizen, 65+   **e** baby, 0–3
c teenager, 13–19   **f** young adult, 20–34

2 Check students understand the meaning of *stage*. Then look at the example *birth*. Ask students to work again in pairs to put the rest of the stages of life in order.

3 ▶ 01 Play the track for students to check their answers. Play it again and ask them to repeat the words. Give extra attention to any sounds students may find difficult, for example the /ə/ 'th' in *birth*, and the /tʃ/ 'ch' in *childhood*. See p149 for the audioscript for this exercise.

Answers

| birth | childhood | adolescence |
| middle age | old age | death |

TEACHER DEVELOPMENT: PRONUNCIATION

Connected speech

When a word ending in a consonant is directly followed by a word beginning with a vowel sound, the two words are often pronounced as one word. Write *old age* and *young adult* on the board and drill the pronunciation.

The family

4 Ask students to write the three headings (*Male*, *Female*, *Male or Female*) in their notebooks and write each word under the relevant heading. Check answers by asking different students.

Answers

Male: brother-in-law, grandfather, grandson, nephew, stepfather, uncle
Female: aunt, niece, wife
Male or Female: cousin

>>> **FAST FINISHERS**

Ask students to add other family words they know to the lists encouraging them to look at the patterns in the words to see if they can work out female equivalents (e.g. *stepmother, sister-in-law*, etc.). Allow them to use the Macmillan Online Dictionary to find additional words (e.g. *sibling, spouse, twin*, etc.). Write the column headings on the board, and nominate students to give their words. Ask other students to write down any words they didn't have so all students have complete lists.

5 Students read the descriptions and match them to the words from exercise 4.

Ask students to check their answers in pairs, then nominate different students to give their answers.

Answers

2 uncle   **3** stepfather   **4** niece   **5** grandson
6 brother-in-law

6 SPEAKING In pairs, students look at the other words in exercise 4 (and also the words added to the list by the Fast finishers if applicable) and take it in turns to define a word for their partner to guess. Draw attention to the model dialogue and/or practise the activity in open pairs before they begin.

7 Draw attention to the words in the box, then ask students to complete the sentences with the correct words. Ask them to compare their answers in pairs before you check as a class.

Answers

1 single   **2** only child   **3** partner   **4** divorced
5 one-parent   **6** born

8 LISTENING ▶ 02 Tell students they are going to listen to three people talking about themselves and their families. Draw students' attention to questions 1–3 and give them time to read through them. Play the track. Monitor students to see whether you need to play the track again. Ask students to check their answers first with a partner, then nominate different students to share their answers with the class.

Tell students they are going to listen again and ask some of the following comprehension questions (depending on the level of your students): *How old is Joshua? How many brothers and sisters does he have? Who is very special to Joshua and why? How old is Olivia? What's the name of Olivia's cousin? How old is Jessica? How many children has she got? When did she get married?* See p149 for the audioscript for this exercise.

Answers

1 a child, big
2 a teenager, small, father, cousin
3 twelve, married

9 SPEAKING Put students in pairs and ask them to tell each other about their family using the vocabulary from the lesson.

EXTRA ACTIVITY

Ask students to draw a family tree with illustrations and write a short paragraph underneath explaining how they are related to each person, e.g. *Sarah is my mother's sister so she's my aunt.*

HOMEWORK

Assign students page 4 in their Workbook or the relevant sections of the Online Workbook.

Reading p7

Skimming and scanning for global and specific information

>>> FAST TRACK

You could ask students to do exercise 7 at home so that less confident students can take the necessary time to look up the vocabulary in the Macmillan Online Dictionary.

TEACHER DEVELOPMENT: CLASSROOM TIPS

Recorded reading texts

The reading texts are recorded so students can listen to them as they read. The track numbers are indicated in the activity notes below. This recorded material provides exposure to correct pronunciation, stress, accent and sentence rhythm. For less confident students, use the audio to help support them as they read the text. For more confident classes you could use the audio to check answers to comprehension questions, asking students to raise their hands when they hear the part of the track with the answer.

WARMER

Write this statement on the board: *Parents should know everything about their teenage children's lives.* Divide students into small groups of three to four and choose half of the groups to be *for* and the other half to be *against* the statement. Give students five minutes to come up with some arguments, then pair each *for* group with an *against* one and ask them to have a mini-debate on the subject. Circulate and monitor to ensure that all students have the chance to talk.

Example answers

Arguments for: Parents need to know their children are safe. If there is a family emergency, parents need to know where to find their child. It's good for parents to take an active interest in their children's lives so they have things to talk about. Parents need to know that the friends of their children are a good influence.

Arguments against: Teenagers need to have their own lives, separate from their parents and some things are private. Teenagers need to learn to be independent and take responsibility for their own safety. Parents should trust their teenagers. Parents might not understand parts of their life and worry unnecessarily.

---

1 Check that students understand the verb 'to argue' (to disagree or to fight verbally, but never physically). In pairs, ask students to think of things that teenagers often argue about with their parents. Focus their attention on the two examples given and ask them to continue the list. Check answers as a class.

Suggested answers

going out with friends, make up, watching TV, chores

2 Set a time limit of two minutes for students to read the text quickly for gist. Ask students to check if any of their answers from exercise 1 were mentioned.

3 Put students in pairs and ask them to think of good advice to give to Zoe. You could model a few ideas with the class first. Nominate different pairs to give their suggestions.

4 Students read the advice from the expert. When they've finished ask them if any of their ideas from exercise 3 were mentioned. You could extend the exercise by discussing which ideas the expert had that they hadn't thought of. Do your students think these would work?

✓ EXAM SUCCESS Exercise 5 is a multiple-choice activity. Put students in pairs and give them two minutes to think of ways they could approach this type of exercise if they were unsure of the answers. Then brainstorm strategies together as a class. Refer students to Exam Success page 144 (Reading: Multiple-choice activities) to compare their answers.

5 Students complete exercise 5, keeping in mind the strategies they have discussed. Check answers in open class, asking students to identify the part of the text that helped them reach their answer if necessary.

Answers

1 b **2** a **3** a **4** c **5** b

6 ⚙ **CRITICAL THINKING** Ask students to think about good advice for young people when they disagree with their parents. Encourage students to think as objectively as they can, and to respect multiple points of view. Nominate different students to give their answers.

Example answers

Teenagers could write how they feel in a letter or email to their parents – this way they won't shout or argue. Teenagers and parents could each have five minutes to say how they feel – this way they don't interrupt each other. Teenagers and parents could agree a 'contract' or set of rules each month together.

7 Focus students' attention on the underlined words in the text. Ask them to guess what they mean and make notes in their notebooks. Remind them to look at the words before and after the key word, to look at what part of speech the key word is, and to think if it is similar to any words in their own language – these are all useful strategies for guessing unknown vocabulary. Then ask students to check the meanings in their dictionaries.

Answers

interrupts = stops someone by disturbing them
turn my music down = make music less loud
loud = not quiet
switch it off = stop an electronic device
realise = to become aware of something
convenient = the right one because it suits your timetable
make sure = plan and check
reasonable volume = not too loud

⟫⟫ FAST FINISHERS

Ask students to write eight sentences using the words and phrases from exercise 7.

8 SPEAKING Students look at the questions in exercise 8 and think of their answers. If appropriate, ask students to share their answers with the class, but keep in mind this could be a sensitive subject.

HOMEWORK

Assign students page 5 in their Workbook or the relevant sections of the Online Workbook.

Grammar in context pp8–9

Using the present simple and present continuous

⟫⟫ FAST TRACK

You could ask students to do exercise 2 at home. You could then go through the answers with the whole class at the beginning of the next lesson, inviting individual students to contribute their answers and writing them on the board.

Test before you teach: Flipped classroom
Set the Flipped classroom video and tasks for homework <u>before the lesson</u>. You can check the students' Flipped classroom video answers on the Flipped classroom video worksheet which you can give them to complete while watching the video or in the Online Workbook. This will allow you to assess the needs of the students before the class. Students can then move on to the relevant grammar practice activities.
Talk to students about this change in the classroom model. Go over the guidelines for watching the videos and discuss the procedure in class. After the students have completed their first Flipped classroom lesson, encourage students to evaluate if they think the learning video has been effective and helpful.

1a Give students 2–3 minutes to read the sentences and identify the tense.

Answers

1 present continuous **2** present simple **3** present simple **4** present simple

1b Read uses a–d as a class and provide further explanation and examples if necessary. Ask students to match sentences 1–4 from exercise 1a to the four uses.

Answers

1 d **2** b **3** c **4** a

TEACHER DEVELOPMENT: LANGUAGE

Actions vs states

State verbs (*love, like, hate, think, believe, know, understand, want, need*) are not usually used in the present continuous because they describe states not actions. However, verbs such as *think* are commonly used both ways. For example, in the sentence *I think teenagers don't have enough freedom these days*, *think* is a state verb (have an opinion) so must appear in the present simple. However, *think* can also describe a mental process, e.g. *I'm thinking about going to Paris next week*, and then it is used in the present continuous. Other common verbs that can describe actions or states, depending on their context and use, include:
be: *I'm being silly.* (action) *I'm French.* (state)
see: *I'm seeing Tom tomorrow.* (action) *I see what you mean.* (state)
have: *He's having a shower.* (action) *He has two sisters.* (state)

1c Remind students of the rules with verbs ending in 'y' then ask them to complete the sentences for the present simple and the present continuous.

Answers

Present simple: doesn't study; Does … study?
Present continuous: is studying; isn't studying; Is, studying?

TEACHER DEVELOPMENT: LANGUAGE

Present tense usage

Highlight the need for *do/does* for questions in the present simple and *don't/doesn't* for negatives. Remind students of the spelling rule for verbs ending in -y, i.e. the -y changes to -ies in the third person.
Students may get confused because in their language they use the present simple to ask about a particular moment. Ask students to translate *Where are you going?* and *What are you doing here?* to point out this difference.

2 Draw students' attention to the picture of the family and the example sentence and ask them to use the words in the box to write sentences about the members of the family using the present continuous form. Monitor and help with any vocabulary as necessary. Check answers as a class. Check that students have the correct spelling of *sitting* and review the spelling rules in present continuous if necessary.

Suggested answers

The dad is reading a book.
The mum is watching TV.
The grandfather is sleeping.

3 Students read through the dialogue in exercise 3, then complete the gaps using either the present simple or present continuous. For less confident students, you could work through initially as a class to identify which of the tenses should be used, then allow students to work individually to write the answers in the correct form. Check the answers together as a class, asking students at regular intervals to give reasons for their choice of tense to consolidate usage.

Answers

a are, doing **b** go **c** Are, watching **d** is watching
e watches **f** Is, crying **g** Does, cry **h** doesn't
i Do, know **j** is doing **k** don't **l** is listening
m hates **n** is sleeping **o** sleeps

>>> **FAST FINISHERS**

Ask students to write four extra lines to continue the dialogue.

✚ **EXTRA ACTIVITY**

Put students in pairs and have them practise the dialogue together (allow boys to change the names to masculine ones if they wish). Model some of the sentences first, asking students to pay attention to intonation. Choose a few pairs to act their dialogue out together in front of the class.

4 Students find the words and phrases in the dialogue in exercise 3, and identify which tense is used with each. Allow students to check their answers in pairs, before checking as a class.

Answers

2 never = present simple **3** normally = present simple
4 on Wednesdays = present simple **5** now = present continuous **6** right now = present continuous
7 usually = present simple

5 Students complete the sentences with the present simple or the present continuous form of the verbs in the box. Check answers in open class. Ensure students have spelled *lying* correctly.

Answers

1 'm helping **2** are, shouting **3** works
4 don't understand **5** Do, need **6** is lying

6 Draw students' attention to the example question in exercise 6. Remind them of the word order for questions: **QASV** (**Q**uestion word, **A**uxiliary, **S**ubject, main **V**erb). Ask students to write questions for the answers 2–6, paying attention to the tense they should use. Allow students to check their answers in pairs, before nominating students to give their answers.

Answers

2 What's your mum doing at the moment? **3** Where do your uncle and aunt live? **4** Is your cousin studying at university? **5** What do your grandparents do in the mornings? **6** What do your family (usually) do at the weekend?

7 SPEAKING Put students in pairs and ask them to use the questions in exercise 6 to interview their partners, swapping over when they have finished. Ask them to add any questions they can think of. Monitor as they do

the task and make a note of any pronunciation issues to work on at the end of class.

Refer students to the Grammar reference on page 16 if necessary.

HOMEWORK

Assign students page 6 in their Workbook or the relevant sections of the Online Workbook.

Developing vocabulary p9

Using noun suffixes -ment, -ion, -ence

>>> **FAST TRACK**

You could ask students to do exercise 2 at home before the class so that less confident students can take the necessary time to look up the vocabulary in the Macmillan Online Dictionary.

1 Students look at the words from the text on page 7. Tell students that the parts in **bold** are called suffixes and ask them to look at the examples and explanation in exercise 1. Provide further explanation/examples if necessary.

TEACHER DEVELOPMENT: LANGUAGE

Suffixes

A suffix is a letter or group of letters added to the end of a word to make a different kind of word. A good knowledge of English prefixes and suffixes will help students develop vocabulary and reduce the need to check their dictionary.

2 When you are happy that students understand the concept of suffixes, ask them to complete the table. Once they have finished, they can check their answers by looking the words up in the Macmillan Online Dictionary.

Answers

2 movement **3** improvement **4** retire
5 concentration **6** inform **7** description **8** discuss
9 different **10** adolescent **11** independent
12 confidence

3a Students choose the correct alternative in the sentences, referring to the table in exercise 2 where necessary. Choose students to read out their answers.

Answers

1 improve **2** independent **3** confidence
4 differences **5** discussions

>>> **FAST FINISHERS**

Ask students to write more sentences using nouns and adjectives from exercise 2. They then read them out to the class without saying the noun or adjective. The other students try to guess the missing word.

3b SPEAKING In pairs, ask students to ask and answer the questions in exercise 3a. Monitor and help with pronunciation where necessary.

Gateway to life skills pp10–11

Contributing to family life

To think about rights and responsibilities in a family, to learn about different ways of helping with family life and to decide positive steps to take to contribute to family life.

≫ FAST TRACK

You could ask students to answer the questions in exercise 1 at home before the class, before comparing their answers with a partner at the beginning of the lesson.

ⓘ BACKGROUND INFORMATION

Learning to do things independently is a crucial part of growing up, and during adolescence the progress towards autonomy accelerates quickly.

The ability to make decisions and act on them is an important skill for teenagers both at home where they are likely to be going out more often without parents and at school where independent study becomes essential.

In further education and in the workplace, decisiveness, independence and being able to manage oneself and one's workload are all vital qualities for success.

It is important that students learn when to make decisions independently and when to work with other people. This lesson focuses students on autonomy within the family, encouraging them to look at areas where they can take initiative.

WARMER

Focus students' attention on the photo on page 10. In pairs, ask them to think of three adjectives to describe the teenager in the photo. After two minutes, ask students for their suggestions.

Suggested answers
tidy, helpful, happy

Before you move to exercise 1, ask students to read through the Key concepts of the lesson. To check they understand the meaning of the words, ask students to come up with one more example sentence for *rights*, *responsibility*, *respect* and *independent*.

1a Put students in pairs to ask and answer the questions.

1b Students count up how many times they answered *I do* in 1a. Have a show of hands to see who in the class does the most and the least.

2 READING Students read through the titles a–c. Then ask them to read the text and choose the best title for it. Nominate a student to give their answer, giving their reasoning if possible.

Answer
a

3 SPEAKING Students look at the questions in exercise 3 and answer them. When they are finished, they can compare their answers with a partner. Then nominate a few students to give their answers.

4 LISTENING ▶ 03 Tell students they are going to listen or watch a video about three teenagers. Ask them to look at the table to check what information they need to listen for, then play the video or track. Monitor to see whether you will need to play it for a second time. Ask students to check their answers in pairs, before checking in open class. See p149 for the videoscript/audioscript for this exercise.

Answers

Grace:	She looks after her younger brother until her mother comes home from work.
Louis:	He takes the dog for walks every evening.
Jessica:	She visits her grandmother every day.

5 ▶ 03 Ask students if they can remember who says each of these sentences. If they are struggling to remember, play the video or track again, pausing after the necessary information.

Answers
1 Louis **2** Louis **3** Grace **4** Grace **5** Louis
6 Jessica

6a Ask students to work in pairs to look at the list of jobs in the table and check they know the meanings.

6b SPEAKING Students interview their partners using the questions in the table, and then write their own responses in the second column. Focus students on the example question to remind them how to form questions.

6c SPEAKING Students look at the example question, checking they remember that 'how often' relates to frequency. Then ask them to find out how often their partner does each chore. Nominate a few students to give their partner's answers.

LIFE TASK

Tell students they are going to think about how they can help out more at home and make a timetable.

- **Step 1**

  Divide the class into groups of three or four and ask students to read the instructions. Students start by discussing ideas for how they can help out more at home and making a note of them. If students have access to the Internet, they can search for other ideas, either in class or at home.

- **Step 2**

  Students work individually to think about their own family and situation at home and what they could do to make more of a contribution.

- **Step 3**

  Draw an example timetable on the whiteboard and explain to students that they are going to use their ideas to make their own timetable in their notebooks. Walk around and monitor while students are making their timetables. Help them with any suggestions or language difficulties.

- **Step 4**
  Students work with their group to compare their timetables. Monitor to ensure all students are given the chance to speak.
- **Step 5**
  Encourage students to take their timetables home and show their parents.

Listening p12

Listening for specific information

WARMER

Ask students to think about their favourite meal. Write these questions on the board: *What is it? How do you make it? Who usually makes it for you or do you make it yourself? When do you eat it? Where do you eat it? Who do you eat it with? What things affect your choices?* In pairs, students ask and answer the questions. Ask different pairs to report back to the class.

1 SPEAKING Give students two minutes to look at the photos and make notes. Then ask them to work in pairs and talk about what they see. Ask students to share their ideas with the class.

TEACHER DEVELOPMENT: STUDENT TRAINING

Describing a photo

For oral examinations, students are often asked to describe a photo. It is useful to give them a framework of fixed expressions and prepositional phrases that they can memorise. They should also remember to always move from the general to the specific, starting with a general description of the situation before giving more precise details.

General: *This is a photo of a/some … , In this photo I can see … , The photo shows … , There is/are …*

Prepositional: *At the top/bottom of the photo … , In the foreground/background … , On the left/right/in the centre of the picture … , Behind/In front of/Between/Next to the … we can see …*

Other things to think about: *Who can you see? What are they doing and what do they look like? Where are they? How are the people feeling and why? When was this photo taken?*

Personal reactions: *I think … , I imagine … , It seems to me that … , If you ask me, …*

EXTRA ACTIVITY

To prepare students for the listening topic, put students in pairs and ask them to discuss the following questions: 1 *What time do you usually have dinner?* 2 *Where do you usually have dinner?* 3 *Who do you usually have dinner with?* 4 *What do you usually do when you have dinner – talk, watch TV, listen to music … ?*

2 LISTENING ▶ 04 Play the track for students to listen to a radio programme about family dinners and match the people to the situations. Tell students that there are two extra situations. Play the track again if necessary, before checking answers.

Then ask some comprehension questions to check students' understanding: *What's Mike's job? How many children has he got? What does Chris usually eat? Why do Sally and her sister have dinner late? Why does she think family dinners are important? How many people are there in Alice's family? Why is Jennifer eating alone tonight? Why doesn't anybody talk in Daniel's house at dinnertime?* See p149 for the audioscript for this exercise.

Answers

1 D **2** G **3** E **4** A **5** F **6** B

3 LISTENING ▶ 04 Students answer the questions. Play the track again if necessary.

Answers

1 70
2 All over the country
3 Whatever's in the fridge
4 Quite late (in the evening)
5 Two children and three grandchildren
6 At the weekend
7 At a school meeting
8 The TV is always on and nobody says anything

4 SPEAKING What about *you*? Students look at the questions and think how they would answer them for themselves. Then ask them to discuss their answers with a partner.

HOMEWORK

Assign students page 7 in their Workbook or the relevant sections of the Online Workbook.

Grammar in context pp12–13

Using articles

》》 FAST TRACK

You could ask students to do exercise 5 at home and then compare their answers with a partner before the next class.

Test before you teach

Write the following gapped sentences on the board:
1 I can't find .... the book I bought last week.
2 I can't find .... good book to read.
Ask which sentence requires *a* and which *the*, and elicit the reason (sentence 1 refers to a specific book, whereas sentence 2 doesn't). Ask students when *an* is used instead of *a* (before a vowel sound). If students seem to be familiar with the use of articles, then move through the Grammar guide exercises quickly in open class.

1 Students look at the sentences from the listening and complete rules 1–5 with *a/an*, *the* or *no article*. Check answers as a class.

Answers

2 a/an   **3** the   **4** the   **5** a/an

TEACHER DEVELOPMENT: LANGUAGE

Articles

Remind students that we use *an* before a vowel sound, not just a vowel. For example, *university* starts with the same sound as *yacht* and so takes the article *a*.

TEACHER DEVELOPMENT: CLASSROOM TIPS

How to teach articles

Some general rules can be helpful for students, i.e. *a/an* = one (of several/many); *the* = you know the thing, or you are talking about something that is common knowledge.

Note that we use *a* the first time something is mentioned and *the* when something has already been mentioned. However, there are exceptions and teachers should encourage students to write new words with the article if appropriate, e.g. *the President of the United States* rather than just *President*.

In class, you could do a quick activity to practise when to use *a/an* and when to use *the*. Put a few objects (e.g. cups, phones, books, pens) around the classroom. Make sure you have more than one of each object type. Chorally drill two simple contrasting sentences with the students e.g. *Could you pass me the book please?* and *Could you pass me a cup, please?* Whenever they say *the* they have to point at the specific thing they want. When they use *a* they lift both hands in a general *anything* gesture. The listener now gives them what they asked for (either a specific cup or any cup). This student then makes a new request.

2a PRONUNCIATION ▶ 05 Students look at the words in List A and List B. Play the track for students to listen and note the difference in pronunciation depending on whether *the* is stressed or unstressed. Play the track again if necessary and ask students which one they think is stressed. See if students can spot any patterns in List A and List B for themselves before confirming the rule. See p149 for the audioscript for this exercise.

Answers

The is pronounced with a schwa (/ə/) before words beginning with consonants (List A) and with the /ɪː/ sound before words beginning with vowels and proper nouns (List B). When *the* is stressed, it also has the /ɪː/ sound.

TEACHER DEVELOPMENT: PRONUNCIATION

Stressed and unstressed articles

Remind students that there are also two pronunciations for *a*: /eɪ/ when it is stressed and /ə/ when it is unstressed. Point out that to make the stressed sound, the mouth is wide open and the jaw and the back of the tongue are down. Also, let students know that the stressed and unstressed pronunciations for *an* are /æn/ and /ən/.

2b ▶ 05 Play the track again for students to listen and repeat.

3 Students write *the* in the sentences that need it. Refer them back to the rules in exercise 1 if necessary. Nominate different students to give their answers.

Answers

1 the, –   **2** the   **3** –   **4** –   **5** –   **6** the   **7** –, –

4 Ask students to read the text and choose the correct alternatives.

Answers

a A   **b** –   **c** The   **d** –   **e** An   **f** –   **g** –   **h** a   **i** The   **j** –

5 Refer students to the seven sentences and tell them there is a mistake in each one. Ask them to circle the mistake and then correct it. Check answers as a class and write the correct sentences on the board.

Answers

1 I'm a vegetarian. I never eat meat.
2 My mum is a doctor in a big hospital.
3 Could you pass me the potatoes?
4 I had a cat but the cat disappeared last month.
5 He's a student at the University of Edinburgh.
6 She's got a brother and a sister.
7 I haven't got a watch – can you tell me the time?

6a Students look through the questions, and add *a*, *an*, *the* or –. Allow students to check their answers in pairs, before nominating different students to give their answers.

Answers

1 –   **2** –, an   **3** –, –   **4** –, –   **5** –   **6** the   **7** the

6b SPEAKING Students use the questions in exercise 6a to interview each other. Draw students' attention to the model dialogue before they begin. This is another opportunity to monitor and assess students' oral ability.

>>> **FAST FINISHERS**

Ask students to write five sentences to describe what is happening in the family dinner cartoon on page 13 of the Student's Book.

➕ **EXTRA ACTIVITY**

Ask the questions in exercise 6a to the whole class and get students to vote *Yes* or *No* for each one. Write the results on the board, e.g. Question 1: *yes* – 16 students; *no* – 18 students. Ask students to copy the results into their notebooks and write them up for homework with full sentences to summarise what they found e.g. *18 students think family dinners are important.* Ask them to also include some visual representation of the results such as a bar chart or graph.

Refer students to the Grammar reference on page 16 if necessary.

Developing speaking p14

Asking for personal information

1 Tell students to complete the personal information file with information about either their brother(s), sister(s) or their best friend, and about themselves.

2 SPEAKING In pairs, ask students to look at the four personal information files and compare them to their own. Students should say which person they are most similar to and why. Draw their attention to the model sentence.

TEACHER DEVELOPMENT: CLASSROOM TIPS

Using spoken model texts

To give students practice with intonation patterns, drill small parts of text in a variety of ways. Ask students to repeat them in a choral drill first (all students repeat the sentence together) to build their confidence then an individual drill (you indicate which student should repeat the sentence). Drills can help students become formally accurate in their speech and learn a useful collection of phrases and sentences.

3 LISTENING ▶ 06 Tell students they are going to listen to two of the teenagers in exercise 2 meeting and talking at a party and they have to decide which two. Encourage them to think of what information and key words they are likely to hear. Play the track. Let students compare their answers in pairs before checking in open class. See pp149–150 for the audioscript for this exercise.

Answers

Emma and Liam

4 In pairs, students complete the dialogue with the correct questions. Refer them to the Speaking bank for help.

Answers

a Have you got any brothers or sisters?
b How old is he?
c Does he live at home?
d How often do you see him?
e What do you usually do at the weekend?
f What about you?

5a PRONUNCIATION ▶ 07 Draw attention to the diagrams showing two different kinds of intonation for questions. Play the track so students can check their answers to exercise 4 and listen to the question intonation. Ask them to match the questions to the diagrams. See p150 for the audioscript for this exercise.

Answers

Diagram A: a, c   **Diagram B:** b, d, e, f

5b ▶ 07 Play the track again for students to repeat the questions.

TEACHER DEVELOPMENT: PRONUNCIATION

Intonation in questions

There is a final rising pitch for a *Yes/No* question, e.g. *Is your name Anna?*, and a final falling pitch for a *Wh*-question, e.g. *What's your name?* Intonation helps us to communicate meaning, i.e. whether a situation is open (rising pitch) or closed (falling pitch). In students' own language the intonation range may be narrower, so it is important to practise this.

6 SPEAKING In pairs, students read the completed dialogue in exercise 4 aloud, paying attention to the question intonation. If you have a confident class, you could nominate one or two pairs to perform the dialogue.

PRACTICE MAKES PERFECT

7a SPEAKING Students work with a partner and read the task. Remind them to use the dialogue in exercise 4 and the Speaking bank to help them construct their dialogue. For students who are less confident, photocopy the model dialogue below, and either read it aloud yourself or alternate the roles with you and a strong student. Then instruct students to read aloud in pairs, alternating between roles A and B. Then ask them to read it again, changing the underlined information so it is true for them.

7b SPEAKING When they have finished, students change partners and repeat the role-play. If you have time you could ask pairs to perform their role-play for another pair or in front of the class.

Model dialogue

A: Hi there. It's a nice party, isn't it? What's your name?

B: Yes, it is. My name's <u>Sophie</u>.

A: Hi, <u>Sophie</u>. My name's <u>Jake</u>. I'm a friend of <u>Elliot's</u>.

B: Hi <u>Jake</u>. So, tell me something about your family. Have you got any brothers or sisters?

A: Yes, I have. I've got a <u>sister. She's 17</u>.

B: Me too. My <u>sister's 16</u>. I've got a <u>brother</u> too. <u>He's</u> <u>only nine</u>.

A: What do you usually do at the weekend?

B: I <u>go swimming</u> on Saturday morning and then I usually <u>go to the cinema with my friends</u>. What about you?

A: I <u>go out with my friends</u> on Saturday <u>nights</u>. I <u>go to a BMX bike park</u> on <u>Saturday mornings</u>.

B: What else do you do in your free time?

A: I <u>play football, play computer games with my friends and go running</u>.

B: Wow! You do a lot of things!

✔ EXAM SUCCESS Put students in pairs and ask them to think of ideas for keeping the conversation going in role-play activities. Elicit ideas and then ask students to check the answers on page 144 (Speaking: Information role-plays).

HOMEWORK

Assign students page 9 in their Workbook or the relevant sections of the Online Workbook.

Developing writing p15

Writing an informal email

▶▶▶ FAST TRACK

You could ask students to write the email in exercise 5 at home. They can then compare their email in pairs at the next lesson.

WARMER

Write the following situations on the board: *job application, email to friend, letter to a newspaper, comment on online forum for teenagers, instant messaging*. Then write the following words or phrases: *Hey, Yours sincerely, Dear, I've, ☺, Love from, XX, Sir/Madam*

Ask students to write two columns in their notebooks headed 'Formal' and 'Informal' and write the situations, words and phrases where they fit best (ask them to write words in both if they think they could be used in both formal and informal situations).

Answers

Formal: Yours sincerely, Sir/Madam

Informal: Hey, I've, Love from, XX, ☺

Both: Dear

1 Students read the advert and decide what Alanna wants. Ask students if they are interested in contacting her and to give reasons why or why not.

Answer

Alanna wants to find an international e-pal.

2 Students read the reply and decide if this person is a good e-pal for Alanna, giving reasons why or why not. Ask a few students for their suggestions.

Answers

She is a good e-pal for Alanna because they have a lot in common. She comes from a big family. She also likes music, reading and is interested in practising her English as much as possible.

3 Students look at the email and complete the information in the Writing bank. If necessary remind students of when they might use informal language (to a friend, family member, somebody their own age, etc.) and when they might need more formal language (in a job application, in a school essay, in a report, etc.).

Answers

Contraction: I've

Emoticon: ☺

Change of subject: anyway

Finishing an informal email or letter: all, back, wishes

4 Ask students to read the email again and match each paragraph to the descriptions of their content.

Answers

1 basic personal information

2 family

3 main interest or hobby

4 favourite subject at school

5 asking for a reply

PRACTICE MAKES PERFECT

5 Students write an email to a new e-pal using Isabel's email in exercise 2 as a model. Draw their attention to the information they need to include and recommend that they follow the paragraph plan in exercise 4. Remind students to include expressions and conventions from the Writing bank. For students who are less confident, photocopy the model text below for extra support during the writing task.

Model text

Hi Giovanni!

I'm Adriana. I'm from Barcelona in Spain. Let me tell you about myself.

I've got a sister. She's older than me, but we have a lot of similar hobbies. We go everywhere together. My mum is a doctor and my dad works at the airport.

I love listening to music, especially pop and electronic music. I like Ed Sheeran and the Vamps. Do you like them too? Right now, I'm listening to their latest song on my phone.

English is one of my favourite subjects ☺, but I also like maths and science. I like sports too – swimming, running, cycling.

Anyway, that's all for now. Write back soon if you want to be my e-pal.

Best wishes, Adriana ☺

Language checkpoint: Unit 1

Grammar revision p17

Present simple and present continuous

1 Students write both the third person singular present simple form and the *-ing* form of each verb in the table. Remind them to pay attention to spelling and any irregular verbs.

Answers

1 has, having **2** lies, lying **3** writes, writing
4 cries, crying **5** gets, getting **6** watches, watching
7 does, doing **8** sits, sitting

2 Students choose the correct word to complete the sentences.

Answers

1 c **2** c **3** d **4** d **5** c **6** a **7** d **8** b

Articles

3 Students read the sentences and choose the correct alternatives. Students record their score out of eight.

Answers

1 a, the **2** A, The **3** –, a **4** a, –

Vocabulary revision p17

AGES AND STAGES OF LIFE – THE FAMILY

1 Students read the text and fill in the blanks with suitable words.

Answers

a single **b** aged **c** only **d** cousin **e** birth **f** wife
g grandmother **h** grandson

NOUN SUFFIXES -MENT, -ION, -ENCE

2 Students read each sentence, choose an appropriate word from the box and, if necessary, adjust the word so that it fits the sentence.

Answers

1 improvement **2** description **3** concentration
4 excitement **5** differences **6** adolescents
7 information **8** independent

2 Who did it?

KEY LEARNING OUTCOMES

CEF

Students will be able to:

- talk about crime and detective work using the past simple and continuous
- understand a text about crime values
- apologise and discuss crime stories in newspapers
- write a blog post

UNIT OVERVIEW

Vocabulary	Crime stories Detective work
Reading	Newspaper stories about crime CRITICAL THINKING Evaluating the seriousness of two crimes
Grammar in context	Past simple PRONUNCIATION The -ed ending
Developing vocabulary	Phrasal verbs connected with investigating and finding
Life skills	Social skills and citizenship: Thinking about right and wrong
Listening	A detective programme
Grammar in context	Past continuous
Developing speaking	Apologising
Developing writing	A blog post
Exam success	Listening: True/False/Not Mentioned activities Writing: Knowing evaluation criteria

DIGITAL OVERVIEW

Presentation Kit

- ▶ **Flipped classroom video Unit 2:** Past simple
- ▶ **Life skills video Unit 2:** Thinking about right and wrong
- ▶ ⓥ **Vocabulary tool:** Crime and criminals, Detective work
- ▶ **Interactive versions of Student's Book activities**
- ▶ **Integrated audio and answer key for all activities**
- ▶ **Workbook pages with answer key**

Teacher's Resource Centre **TRC**

- ▶ **Flipped classroom video Unit 2:** Past simple and present continuous
- ▶ **Life skills video Unit 2:** Thinking about right and wrong
- ▶ **Grammar communication activity Unit 2:** Prison break
- ▶ **Worksheets for this unit, including:**
  - Grammar practice worksheet Unit 2
  - Flipped classroom video worksheet Unit 2: Past simple
  - Literature worksheet Units 1 and 2
  - Culture worksheet Unit 2
  - Life skills video worksheet Unit 2
  - Everyday English worksheet Unit 2

Student's App

Gateway 2nd Edition wordlist for the award-winning Sounds App (available for download)

✓ TESTING AND ASSESSMENT

Resources for exam preparation and measuring student progress

- ▶ Test Generator Units 1–2
- ▶ Printable test Unit 2
- ▶ Gateway to exams Units 1 and 2 (end of Unit 2)

Vocabulary p18

Talking about crimes and criminals

>>> FAST TRACK

You could ask students to do exercise 2 at home so that less confident students can take the necessary time to look up the vocabulary in the Macmillan Online Dictionary.

WARMER

Ask students to keep their books closed. Play a quick game of *Snowman* with words connected to the theme of the unit. Divide the class into two teams. Choose a word, e.g. *crime*, and draw a short line on the board for each letter in the word. The first team says a letter. If it is in the word, write the letter in all the places it occurs. If the word does not contain the letter, draw the first part of the snowman. Continue playing with the same team until they either guess the word, or the snowman drawing is complete. Then play again with the other team. Award a point for each correctly guessed word.

Ask students to open their books and look at the title of the unit *Who did it?* In pairs, ask students to discuss how they think this relates to crime and what things they think they may learn about in the unit (e.g. types of crime, punishments, etc.). Elicit or teach the word *criminal* as the person who commits/does a crime.

⊻ Crimes and criminals

1 Students work in pairs to complete the sentences with the words from the box. Allow them to use a dictionary if necessary. Nominate different pairs to give their answers, encouraging them to read the full sentence each time.

Answers

1 theft **2** burglary **3** robbery **4** Vandalism
5 Shoplifting **6** Piracy **7** Mugging **8** Fraud

2 Students work individually to complete the words. Allow students to check their answers in pairs before nominating students to give their answers.

Answers

1 burglar **2** mugger **3** fraudster **4** pirate
5 robber **6** shoplifter **7** thief **8** vandal

3 ▶ 08 Play the track for students to check their answers. Ask students to repeat the word after they hear each one. See p150 for the audioscript for this exercise.

✛ EXTRA ACTIVITY

Play the track again and ask students to underline the stressed syllables and circle the schwa /ə/ sounds.

TEACHER DEVELOPMENT: PRONUNCIATION

The /θ/ sound

Some students may have difficulty pronouncing the /θ/ sound in *thief* and *theft*. Tell students to put their finger on their lips. Their tongue should lightly touch their finger when they make this sound. Chorally drill the words.

4 LISTENING ▶ 09 Tell students they are going to listen to four radio news items. Ask them to listen for the crimes mentioned and make note of any vocabulary that helped them choose their answers. With a less confident class you may like to pre-teach these words: *pound* – a unit of money used in the UK; *arrest* – take someone to a police station because they have committed a crime. Play the track. Nominate students to give answers and elicit additional information about each crime, e.g. what happened, where it happened, who did it, how they did it, why they did it. See p150 for the audioscript for this exercise.

Answers

1 robbery **2** vandalism **3** piracy **4** shoplifting

TEACHER DEVELOPMENT: STUDENT TRAINING

Key information

News stories are full of information and are often difficult for students to follow. They are generally constructed around the key questions listeners will want to know the answers to, i.e. who, what, why, where, when and how. Encourage students to learn these six key question words as a framework that will help them pick out key information in all skills areas.

⊻ Detective work

5 Focus students' attention on the picture of the crime scene. Ask them what they think happens after a crime and elicit the word 'detective'. Ask students to read the expressions in the box and tell them that these are all things that detectives do after a crime. Ask students to complete the definitions with the expressions. Allow students to check in pairs, before nominating students to give their answers.

Answers

1 investigate a case **2** question a suspect **3** arrest a suspect **4** charge a suspect **5** accuse a suspect
6 collect evidence **7** prove something **8** analyse evidence

✛ EXTRA ACTIVITY

Ask students to work in pairs and put stages 1–8 in the order they think they would usually occur. Tell them there is not an exact order. Then ask them to pretend they are detectives and create a short story in the past simple using each of the headings.

6 Students look at the verbs in exercise 5 and write the noun form of each. Allow them to use their dictionaries if necessary.

Answers

arrest (v) arrest (n), charge (v) charge (n), collect (v) collection (n), investigate (v) investigation (n), prove (v) proof (n), question (v) question (n)

7 SPEAKING Put students in pairs and ask them to ask and answer the questions in exercise 7. Hold a class discussion to see what students think about the crime in their country.

TEACHER DEVELOPMENT: CLASSROOM MANAGEMENT

Managing discussions in class

Discussions can be a good way for students to use English spontaneously and in a way that engages them. However, it is a good idea to put some rules in place to prevent heated discussions turning into arguments. Remind students to use respectful language, and avoid personal attacks, to respect other students' perspectives even though they may disagree. Before or during a discussion or debate, try a role-reversal exercise and ask students to defend the position with which they disagree. Monitor groups whenever a discussion is taking place to ensure that students are all being given the opportunity to speak and that the rules are being adhered to.

✚ **EXTRA ACTIVITY**

Write these crimes on the board: *A rich woman stole from a department store. A driver hit someone crossing the street. A vandal drew graffiti on a shop.* Students work in groups to write a short description of what they think a detective should do in each situation, e.g. interview witnesses, analyse the graffiti style, look for the owner of the car, check CCTV, etc.

HOMEWORK

Assign students page 12 in their Workbook or the relevant sections of the Online Workbook.

Reading p19

Predicting content, reading for gist and detail

>>> **FAST TRACK**

You could ask students to do exercise 6 at home so that less confident students can take the necessary time to look up the vocabulary in the Macmillan Online Dictionary.

1 Students match the titles of the newspaper stories to the pictures.

Remind them there is one title they will not need. Ask students to compare their answers in pairs before you elicit the answers from the class.

Answers

1 c **2** b **4** a

2 In pairs, students discuss what they think each story is about by looking at the titles and the pictures. Help out with any unfamiliar terms such as *security guard* and *dummies.* Nominate a different pair to give their ideas for each picture. Tell students that looking at titles and pictures first can often help them understand a text.

3 Students read the stories and match the pictures, titles and texts. Set a time limit of two minutes to encourage them to read quickly and not worry about difficult vocabulary. Remind them that once they have the general idea of the whole text, they may find they can guess the meaning of new words much more easily.

In a less confident class, you may want to pre-teach some vocabulary for the reading texts: *surprising* – describes something unexpected or unusual; *disappear* – to go away completely so it isn't visible; *complicated* – difficult, not simple.

Answers

Story A: title 1, picture c
Story B: title 4, picture a
Story C: title 2, picture b

4 Students read the texts again and answer the questions in their notebooks using complete sentences. Monitor and provide help if necessary. Elicit answers from the class.

Answers

1 They pretended to be part of the fashion display. **2** One of them moved. **3** A bottle of melted Antarctic ice water. **4** An art thief took it or someone drank it or someone threw it away. **5** Banks don't usually open on Saturday afternoons in Britain. **6** Their son Oliver discovered the problem and they called the police. **7** They opened an account for him.

5 ⚙ **CRITICAL THINKING** Ask students to work individually and look back at the crimes in stories A and B and think how serious they are. Encourage students to think about victims, whether people are hurt, whether people lose business, etc. Ask them to make some notes and then share their ideas with the rest of the class. You may want to give students vocabulary such as *consequences*, *implications*, *punishment* to help them express themselves.

Example answers

The robbery in A is very serious because even though no one was hurt, there are implications for the shop's business. And the robbers had committed crimes before. The crime in B is less serious because it was just a bottle of water so the consequences aren't as bad and it might have been a mistake. The punishment for the crime in A should be much more serious than for the crime in B.

6 Students look at the underlined words in the text and try to work out what they mean. Remind them to look at the type of word and the context to help them. Ask them to check in their dictionaries.

Answers

luxury = expensive and high quality

smart = not casual, suitable for a special occasion, work or a party

worth = with a value of

display = arrangement of things for people to look at

melted = something solid that becomes liquid

unprotected = with nothing to keep them safe

lock = close with a key

account = a 'place' with a number where you put or save your money in a bank

⟫⟫ FAST FINISHERS

Ask students to write sentences for each of the new words in exercise 6.

✛ EXTRA ACTIVITY

Bring in some photos either from newspaper articles or just interesting photos you have. Put students in small groups of three or four and give them a photo each and ask them to write a headline for it. After a few minutes swap the photos over so each group has a new one. After each group has written one for each photo, put their ideas on the board and have the class vote on the best one for each.

7 Draw students' attention to the question in exercise 7 and ask them to think of their own answers, making notes if necessary. Ask a few students to share their ideas.

HOMEWORK

Assign students page 13 in their Workbook or the relevant sections of the Online Workbook.

Grammar in context pp20–21

Using the past simple

⟫⟫ FAST TRACK

You could ask students to do exercise 1a at home and check their answers at the start of the lesson.

WARMER

Ask students what they remember of the three stories from the last lesson. Then ask them to read the sentences in exercise 1a and match them to a news story from page 19.

Answers

a Story A   **b** Story B   **c** Story C   **d** Story B
e Story A   **f** Story C   **g** Story A   **h** Story B

🎬 **Test before you teach: Flipped classroom**
Set the Flipped classroom video and tasks for homework <u>before the lesson</u>. This will allow you to assess the needs of the students before the class. Students can then move on to the relevant grammar practice activities.

1a Students identify which tense the sentences are in: past simple or present simple.

Answers

a past simple   **b** past simple   **c** present simple
d past simple   **e** past simple   **f** present simple
g past simple   **h** past simple

1b Elicit from students when we use the past simple (to describe actions or situations that started and finished in the past). Then ask students to look at exercise 1a and find the sentences to match 1–6. Check answers in open class.

Answers

2 h   **3** a   **4** e   **5** b   **6** g

1c Students complete the sentences with the correct past simple forms of *be*, *walk* and *go*. Elicit the answers and write them on the board. Remind students that in negative and question forms of *be* in the past simple, we don't use *did/didn't*.

Answers

b wasn't/didn't walk/didn't go   **c** Was/Did/Did
d –/walk/go

✛ EXTRA ACTIVITY

Write these additional examples on the board:
Affirmative: They _____ on the phone last night.
Negative: They _____ on the phone last night.
Question: _____ they _____ on the phone last night?
Ask students to complete the sentences with the correct past simple forms of *be*, *talk* and *speak*.

Answers

Affirmative: were/talked/spoke

Negative: weren't/didn't talk/didn't speak

Question: Were they/Did they talk/Did they speak

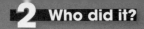
TEACHER DEVELOPMENT: LANGUAGE

Past tense forms

The major difficulty students have with the past tense is that negative and question forms use auxiliary verbs and infinitives. It may help to present this visually and explain that the -ed ending transforms into an auxiliary verb for negatives and questions:

Affirmative: He walked to school yesterday.

Negative: He didn't walk to school yesterday.

Question: Did he walk to school yesterday?

2a PRONUNCIATION Students practise saying the words in each list and decide on the pronunciation of the -ed ending in each list.

Answers

List A: /t/   List B: /ɪd/   List C: /d/

2b ▶ 10 Play the track for students to listen, check and repeat. See p150 for the audioscript for this exercise.

TEACHER DEVELOPMENT: PRONUNCIATION

Voiced and voiceless sounds

Teaching the past simple offers a great opportunity to teach students the difference between voiced and voiceless sounds. A simple explanation of voiced consonants is that they use the voice. Ask students to test this by putting their finger on their throat. If they feel a vibration, the consonant is voiced. Voiceless consonants do not use the voice. They are hard sounds and there is no vibration in your throat, just a short explosion of air as you speak.

Voiced: If the stem of the verb ends with a vowel sound or a consonant (-b, -g, -l, -m, -n, -th, -v or -z), the pronunciation of the -ed ending is /d/.

Voiceless: If the stem of the verb ends with a voiceless sound (-f, -p, -k, -s, -sh, -ch, -x or -h), the pronunciation of the -ed ending is /t/.

Remind students that the e of the -ed ending in both cases is silent. Tell students that the difference between /d/ and /t/ is very small and it is more important to remember when to pronounce /ɪd/.

2c Ask students to look at the list with the /ɪd/ ending and to decide which letters come before the -ed ending in this list.

Answers

List B: verbs that end in -t or -d

✚ EXTRA ACTIVITY

Write these past tense forms on the board: *missed, stayed, decided, talked, rained, turned, demanded, planted, played, worked, cooked, celebrated.* Ask students to look at and say the words and match them to the correct pronunciation of -ed (/t/, /d/ or /ɪd/). Confirm the answers with the class and drill each word.

Answers

/t/:   worked, talked, cooked, missed

/d/:   played, turned, stayed, rained

/ɪd/:   planted, demanded, celebrated, decided

3 Set a strict five-minute time limit. In pairs, students write an A to Z of irregular past simple forms with one verb for each letter. Warn students that it will be very difficult to think of irregular verbs for v, y and z. Elicit answers from different pairs. Refer to the irregular verb list on page 149 of the Student's Book.

4 Students complete the text with the past simple forms of the verbs in brackets.

Answers

a was **b** mugged **c** stole **d** ran **e** didn't know
f got **g** wasn't **h** took **i** emailed **j** printed
k went **l** found **m** arrested **n** had **o** were

5 Students complete the questions with the past simple form of the verbs. Remind them not to use the -ed ending for past simple questions. Check answers in open class.

Answers

1 did, mug **2** did, steal **3** Did, know **4** Was
5 did, do **6** Did, help **7** Was **8** did, end

6 SPEAKING In pairs, students take it in turns to ask and answer the questions in exercise 5. Nominate a different pair to give their suggestion to each question.

7a SPEAKING Draw students' attention to the photo and ask them if they know who it is and what his job was. (Sherlock Holmes the detective and Dr Watson his friend.) Students work in pairs. Ask Student A to look at the information on page 21 and Student B to turn to page 147. Tell them to prepare the questions they need to ask to find out the missing information. Draw attention to the example on page 21.

7b SPEAKING Students interview their partners. Monitor and make a note of any errors to correct at the end of the activity.

Answers

Student A:

When was Conan Doyle born? In 1859

What did Conan Doyle do? He was a doctor.

What was the title of the first Sherlock Holmes story? *A Study in Scarlet*

What was the name of Conan Doyle's teacher? Joseph Bell

How many novels did Sherlock Holmes appear in? Four

How old was Conan Doyle when he died? 71

Where does Sherlock Holmes continue to appear? Films, TV series and novels

Student B:

Where was Conan Doyle born? In Edinburgh, Scotland

When did he begin writing stories? When he was at university

When did Conan Doyle write his first Sherlock Holmes novel? In 1886

Which other interesting character did Conan Doyle create? Doctor Watson

How many short stories did Sherlock Holmes appear in? Over 50

What did Conan Doyle try to do in 1893? He tried to kill the character of Sherlock.

What happened in 1903? Conan Doyle started writing more Sherlock Holmes stories.

Refer students to the Grammar reference on page 28 if necessary.

Assign students page 14 in their Workbook or the relevant sections of the Online Workbook.

Developing vocabulary p21

Using phrasal verbs connected with investigating and finding

>>> FAST TRACK

You could do exercise 2 as a class activity, by inviting individual students to read a definition and the rest of the class to call out the correct answer. Make sure to give them time to reread the stories on page 19.

WARMER

To remind students what phrasal verbs are before starting the lesson, write the following two sentences on the board:

He _____ the piece of paper from the floor.

He _____ English very quickly.

Tell students that the same two words fill both gaps and ask for any suggestions.

Answer

picked/picks up

Write the answer on the board and elicit from students what two parts of speech make up a phrasal verb (a verb followed by a particle and/or preposition). Point out that phrasal verbs are either literal (as in the first example) or idiomatic (as in the second example).

1 Students look at the phrasal verbs and look at how they are used in the texts on page 19. Then ask them to match them to the definitions.

Answers

2 come across (non-separable)
3 work out (separable)
4 look for (non-separable)
5 find out (separable)
6 turn up (non-separable)

⁺⁺ EXTRA ACTIVITY

Tell students which of the phrasal verbs are separable (see Answers above) and ask students to write two sentences for each showing the two ways it can be used (e.g. *He worked the problem out; He worked out the problem*). Ask students for suggestions and write them on the board. Remind students that this can only be done with separable phrasal verbs.

TEACHER DEVELOPMENT: LANGUAGE

Phrasal verbs

Phrasal verbs are usually verbs + prepositions or verbs + particles. Students tend to sound more natural if they use phrasal verbs when they speak. Associating phrasal verbs with a topic can help students remember them more easily.

Point out that phrasal verbs are either separable or non-separable. A separable phrasal verb can have the object of the phrasal verb either in the middle of the phrasal verb or after it, e.g. *find something out* or *find out something*. With non-separable phrasal verbs, the object can only come after the phrasal verb, e.g. *Police are looking into the crime* **not** *Police are looking the crime into*.

2 Students rewrite each sentence using the correct form of a phrasal verb from exercise 1. Remind them that this kind of transformation exercise is very common in examinations. Nominate different students to give their answers.

Answers

2 The CIA began to look into the case.
3 They came across the keys by accident in the garden.
4 The shoe turned up in the garden.
5 Sherlock Holmes used logic to work out crimes.
6 After their investigation, they soon found out where the thief was.

3 In small groups, ask students to make as many sentences as they can with the words in the table in three minutes. Draw attention to the example sentence.

Answers

I looked for the answer. I looked for the identity of the criminal. I found out the answer.
I found out the identity of the criminal. I came across the key. I came across the answer. I came across the identity of the criminal. I worked out the answer. I worked out the identity of the criminal.

HOMEWORK

Assign students page 15 in their Workbook or the relevant sections of the Online Workbook.

Gateway to life skills pp22–23

Thinking about right and wrong

To consider what your values are, to give advice to people in difficult situations and to decide on the right way to behave.

ⓘ BACKGROUND INFORMATION

Teaching young people to distinguish right from wrong has always been important, and many of the 'moral dilemmas' facing teenagers today are not so different from those of the past. However, key cultural changes in the last two decades, varying from the advent of the Internet to the growth in multiculturalism and from the rise in celebrity culture to increased disposable income, have all necessitated a review of 'right' and 'wrong' in society.

Being able to make well-informed decisions of their own values, to maintain them, and to respect other people's differing values without compromising their own, are all crucial skills to being a good citizen and integrating into new situations such as living abroad, starting university and starting at a new workplace.

This lesson encourages students to consider their own values and to look at the consequences of making the wrong decisions. Students look at a variety of other situations and consider advice they would give.

>>> **FAST TRACK**

You could ask students to make notes on exercise 1 at home. They can then compare their notes in groups at the next lesson.

WARMER

If possible bring in a picture(s) of a peaceful demonstration (preferably with people holding banners with slogans) to class, or project one onto the whiteboard. In groups, ask students to look at the Key concepts and to make three or four sentences about the situation in the photo using some of the words. Encourage them to use their dictionaries if they need to find the verb or noun form of the words (e.g. *The people have strong beliefs. They believe in peace. They are standing up for victims of war.*).

1 SPEAKING Students work individually and look through the Values checklist and decide whether they agree with them or not. Then ask them to discuss their thoughts with a partner. Ask some students to share their thoughts with the rest of the class. Encourage them to say why they agree or disagree with the statements.

2 READING Students read through the explanations and match them to the ideas in 1.

Check answers as a class. Did any of the explanations match their own?

Answers

A 2 **B** 7 **C** 4 **D** 3 **E** 1 **F** 5 **G** 6

3 Students read through the explanations in exercise 2 again and answer the questions. Encourage them to use full sentences.

Answers

1 It's normal and we need to respect that right.
2 The world becomes a cold and difficult place.
3 Taking someone's things, copying other students and piracy
4 It brings more violence.
5 When we lie people lose confidence in us.
6 It belongs to all of us and we shouldn't damage it.
7 Never do things that you believe are wrong.

4a Draw students' attention to the photos on page 23. Ask students what they can see. Nominate one or two students to give their ideas about what has happened.

Suggested answers

Picture a: The girl is copying the answers. She didn't study for her exam.
Picture b: The window is broken. Someone kicked a football through the window.

4b LISTENING ▶ 11 Tell students they are going to listen or watch a video about two teenagers talking about a problem. Ask them to read through the values listed in exercise 1 again and to choose which one each teenager has a problem with in the video. Ask them to match each teenager to the photos above. Play the video or track. See p150 for the videoscript/audioscript for this exercise.

Suggested answers

James: Picture b, Value 1: Don't lie, always tell the truth.
Jessica: Picture a, Value 6: Stand up for what you think is right.

5 ▶ 11 Students read through the sentences before listening or watching the video again, so they know what information to listen out for. Play the video or track again. Allow students to check their answers in pairs before nominating individual students to give their answers.

Answers

1 his **2** mum **3** Oliver **4** friends **5** history
6 didn't **7** fair, teacher **8** Kayla

6a Students think what would be good advice to give to James and Jessica and to make notes.

6b Put students into groups of three or four and ask them to compare ideas. Have a feedback session as a class.

TEACHER DEVELOPMENT: CLASSROOM TIPS

Pairwork

Before a speaking activity, think carefully about how to group the students in order to best encourage speaking. You can either choose to have students of a similar level work together or to have students of different levels work together.

Similar levels: The benefit of this is that the students have similar needs and it is easier to address these if they work together.

Different levels: The benefit of this is that the higher-level students can help the lower-level students.

7 Students work with a partner and look at the two situations then answer the questions. Tell students that they don't necessarily have to agree with their partner on everything, but that they should listen to each other's point of view. Ask for feedback from students.

>>> **FAST FINISHERS**

For pairs who finish exercise 7 before others, ask them what they would do in situation 1 if the amount was a) 1 pound b) 50 pounds c) 150 pounds? Would their answers to the questions still be the same, and if not, why?

LIFE TASK

Tell students they are going to think of more difficult situations where they have to choose between right and wrong and give them to other students.

- **Step 1**

  Divide the class into groups of three or four and ask students to read the instructions. Give them a time limit and help them with inspiration for situations if necessary (e.g. You accidentally scratched your parents' car when you cycled past it; You found a website that generates answers to school essays for you; You get the bill in a restaurant and notice they missed two items so it's a lot cheaper than it should be).

- **Step 2**

  Help students pair up with other groups and monitor as they discuss their questions. Make a note of any errors to go over at the end of the task.

- **Step 3**

  Students discuss their findings and the questions with their initial group. Monitor to ensure all students are given the chance to speak.

- **Step 4**

  Ask students to nominate one person in each group to summarise and share what they have found with the class.

Listening p24

Listening for specific information and inferring

WARMER

To prepare students for exercise 1, ask them to work in pairs and give them one minute to label as many of the objects and people in the four pictures as possible. Check their answers as a class and help out with any vocabulary they don't know. Then ask them to write a sentence for each one describing what's happening. Remind them, or elicit from them, to use a continuous tense, e.g. *A teenage boy is watching TV, a man and woman are looking at a computer*, etc.

1 SPEAKING Tell students that they are going to use their vocabulary and sentences from exercise 1 to create a very short story that connects the four pictures.

✓ **EXAM SUCCESS** Ask students what they should do first in a True/False/Not Mentioned listening activity. Students turn to page 144 (Listening: True/False/Not Mentioned activities) to check their answers.

2 LISTENING 12 Play the track for students to listen to. Ask them how the pictures in exercise 1 are connected. See p150 for the audioscript for this exercise.

Suggested answer

Daniel was watching TV last night (picture a). He was watching a detective film (picture d) while his parents were doing something on the computer (picture c). The loud scary noise he heard was the cat (picture b).

3 LISTENING 12 Tell students they are going to listen again and have to decide if the statements are true, false or if the information is not mentioned. Play the track. With more confident students ask them to correct the false statements.

4 Ask students to compare their answers with a partner.

Answers

1 T
2 NM
3 T
4 F Daniel stopped watching because he heard a loud noise in the kitchen.
5 T
6 T
7 F The cat was 'crying' in the kitchen.
8 NM

HOMEWORK

Assign students page 15 in their Workbook or the relevant sections of the Online Workbook.

Grammar in context pp24–25

Using the past continuous

≫ FAST TRACK

You could ask students to write the sentences in exercise 6 at home. They can then compare their stories in pairs at the next lesson.

Test before you teach

Write some times on the board, e.g. 7 am, 8.15 am, 9.30 am, 1.30 pm, 5.00 pm, 7 pm, 11.30 pm. Ask students to write sentences about what they were doing at these times using the past continuous. Monitor to see if students are familiar with the form and use of the past continuous tense.

1a Point out to students that the sentences are from the listening activity. Ask students to look at sentences 1–4 and match them to the explanation of their uses (a–d).

Answers

1 c **2** d **3** a **4** b

✚ EXTRA ACTIVITY

If students find use *d* difficult to understand, give another example sentence and explain in more depth. Write this sentence on the board: *John was writing an email when the phone rang*. In this example, John started writing, and then the phone rang and interrupted his writing action.

Draw a timeline to illustrate this on the board using a long line to illustrate the past continuous action and an arrow to illustrate the past simple action:

(past) ——————……was writing……rang ————— (now)

Elicit another example sentence from students with the verbs *drive* and *see a friend in the street* (*John was driving when he saw a friend in the street.*). If students are having difficulty with any of the other uses, draw timelines using the same notation to help them.

TEACHER DEVELOPMENT: PRONUNCIATION

Stressed and unstressed forms of *was*

Remind students that the pronunciation of *was* changes according to whether it is stressed (at the beginning or end of a sentence) or unstressed (in the middle of a sentence). Write these examples on the board and chorally drill them:

Was he playing in the park? Yes, he was. /wɒz/
My friend was walking to school. /wəz/

Ask students to write four more sentences using *was* and to practise saying their sentences to a partner.

1b Ask students to complete the rule.

Answer

be

✛ EXTRA ACTIVITY

Ask students to tell you how to form the present continuous. Write an example sentence on the board in the present continuous, e.g. *I'm shopping.* Then ask them to change the sentence to the past continuous. Elicit from students that you only need to change *am/is/are* for *was/were*.

TEACHER DEVELOPMENT: LANGUAGE

Past continuous

- Some verbs are not often used in the past continuous because they are not normally action verbs, e.g. *believe, belong, depend, hate, know, like, love, mean, need, prefer, realise, suppose, want, understand.*

- *While*, *as* and *when* can introduce information related to time. They mean 'during the time that' and indicate that something was happening when another event occurred, e.g. *I was talking on the phone while I was getting dressed.*

- We use *when*, not *while*, to talk about something that interrupts a longer action or event, e.g. *I was sleeping when Joanna rang to say she wasn't coming home.*

- We also use *when*, not *while*, to talk about one event that happens immediately after another and to talk about periods of time in the past, e.g. *When the lights went out, everybody screamed. When I was a little boy, we didn't have a television.*

2 Ask students to look at the photo of the two girls and then draw their attention to the prompts in question 1. Nominate a student to say what the girls were doing yesterday at 6.30 pm. Remind students of the spelling rules for *-ing* endings that they learned for the present continuous. Check answers as a class.

Answers

1 Rachel and Kate were buying clothes.   **2** Joe's dad wasn't making the dinner.   **3** Kim was running in the park.   **4** We weren't watching TV.   **5** We were doing homework.   **6** Becky was swimming.   **7** Sam and Beth were sitting in the kitchen.

✛ EXTRA ACTIVITY

Ask students to write three sentences using the past continuous about what they were doing at 6.30 pm yesterday. Tell them that two sentences must be false and only one must be true. After they've finished writing, put students in pairs and ask them to read out their sentences for their partner to guess the true one.

3 Before doing the exercise, check that students are confident in forming questions and short answers in the past continuous. Remind them to look at the Grammar reference if they need to review the form.

Answers

1 Were Rachel and Kate swimming?
2 Was Joe's dad making the dinner?
3 What was Kim doing?
4 Was Becky swimming?
5 Where were Sam and Beth sitting?

1 No, they weren't.
2 No, he wasn't.
3 She was running in the park.
4 Yes, she was.
5 They were sitting in the kitchen.

4 Draw students' attention to the street scene and tell them they have two minutes to memorise the details. Then ask students to close their books and work with a partner to list all the things they remember. Set a time limit for this and ask students to write full sentences in the past continuous. Check answers in class, and see which pair had the most sentences.

Suggested answers

A (middle-aged) man was getting into a taxi, a man in a beret (with a moustache) was cycling with bread under his arm, a young woman was carrying two plastic bags full of shopping, a young man was jogging in sports clothes, an elderly man was looking at a shop window, a small boy was holding his mother's hand, he was eating an ice cream, she was drinking water from a small bottle, a teenage boy was making a call on his mobile phone, a teenage girl was texting

5 SPEAKING Put students in pairs and ask them to take it in turns to close their books and ask each other questions about the scene. Draw their attention to the model question on the page.

Suggested answers

What was the middle-aged man doing?
What was the man with a moustache (in a beret) doing?
What was he carrying?
What was the woman doing?
How many bags was she carrying?
What was the young man doing?
What was he wearing?

6 Students work individually and write answers to the questions in the mystery story. Tell them that there is no right or wrong answer and to be as creative as they like. Remind them to use both the past simple and past continuous in their answers.

7 SPEAKING Students read their stories to a partner, and then to answer the questions. Ask if any students want to volunteer to read their stories to the rest of the class and have other students vote on their favourite.

TEACHER DEVELOPMENT: CLASSROOM TIPS

Monitoring

It is important to monitor students while they are working, so you can answer any language difficulties, give advice on how to structure sentences in a more natural way, provide vocabulary that students are lacking and deal with individual needs, as well as noting common problem areas.

To monitor your students, you need to get physically close to pairs or groups and focus your attention on one pair or group at a time. Try to be as unobtrusive as possible and avoid eye contact. Make sure you have a notepad and a pen to write down both errors and good language use. Write common errors on the board at the end of the activity for the class to consider, correct or rephrase. Praise students who demonstrated good language use.

Refer students to the Grammar reference on page 28 if necessary.

HOMEWORK

Assign students page 16 in their Workbook or the relevant sections of the Online Workbook.

Developing speaking p26

Apologising

>>> **FAST TRACK**

You could ask students to prepare the dialogue in 7a and 7c at home. They can then present these in pairs at the next lesson.

WARMER

Elicit the word *sorry* by saying the following: *I forgot your birthday, I'm …* and asking students to complete the sentence. In pairs, give students one minute to think of as many situations as they can when you might say sorry. Nominate a few pairs to give their suggestions. Then ask if students know the word for the action of saying sorry. Elicit, or tell students, the verb *to apologise* and tell them they are going to look at ways of apologising and accepting apologies in the lesson.

1 SPEAKING In pairs, ask students to look at the pictures and describe what they can see. Ask them to focus on how the people feel, too. Ask a few students for their suggestions.

Example answers

Picture a: A woman standing on a teenager's foot by accident. The woman probably feels guilty or sorry. The teenager probably feels in pain.

Picture b: A teenager apologising to a teacher for arriving late. The teenager probably feels guilty or a bit scared. The teacher probably feels angry or annoyed.

Picture c: A teenager apologising to her mum and dad for breaking a plate. The teenager probably feels guilty, sorry and a bit scared. The parents probably feel annoyed or angry.

2 SPEAKING Students work in pairs and answer the questions. Nominate one or two students to give their answers to each question.

3 LISTENING ▶ 13 Tell students that you can either *accept* or *reject* an apology. Tell them they are going to listen to two short dialogues. They need to listen for the reason for the apology and whether the apology is accepted or rejected. Play the track. See pp150–151 for the audioscript for this exercise.

Answers

1 He drank the girl's bottle of water. Yes.
2 Dylan forgot to bring a book he borrowed in time for the next lesson. No.

4 ▶ 13 Draw students' attention to the sentences. Tell them they are going to listen again and complete the expressions with one word in each gap. For more confident students you could ask them to see what they remember from the first listening and ask them to complete the gaps in pencil, before you play the track again for checking.

Answers

1 sorry **2** doesn't **3** only **4** Let **5** make **6** last **7** feel

EXTRA ACTIVITY

Make copies of the audioscript and hand them out to pairs. Ask them to practise reading them in pairs, before swapping roles. Then, model some of the key sentences from the dialogues (e.g. *Oh no. I'm sorry. Was it yours? I'm really, really sorry. I feel terrible.*) and show students how differences in intonation and emphasis can make an apology sound more or less sincere. Ask them to read the dialogues again, paying attention to how sincere they sound.

5 Students look at the Speaking bank and complete the gaps with expressions from exercise 4.

Answers

Making apologies: expressions 1, 4, 5, 7
Responding to apologies: expressions 2, 3, 6

6 In pairs, ask students to read through the situations 1–3 and to add two more to the list.

PRACTICE MAKES PERFECT

7a In the same pairs, ask students to choose one of the situations from exercise 6 and create a dialogue from it using expressions from the Speaking bank.

7b SPEAKING Students practise their dialogue. Circulate and help with pronunciation if necessary. Then ask pairs to act their dialogue out to the class. Ask the class if any of them have been in these situations in real life.

7c SPEAKING Students repeat the process with another situation from exercise 6 and create another dialogue. For variation, you could ask students to write a dialogue where the apology is rejected this time.

HOMEWORK

Assign students page 17 in their Workbook or the relevant sections of the Online Workbook.

Developing writing p27 ✏️ ✏️

Writing a blog post

»» FAST TRACK

You could ask students to write the blog post in exercise 5 at home. They can then compare their blogs in pairs at the next lesson.

WARMER

To introduce the lesson topic and to recycle the past simple tense, prepare a set of 'lost' cards for half the class, each with a lost item on it (e.g. *keys, a passport, a mobile phone*), a place (e.g. *in the street, at the cinema, at school*) and a time (e.g. *Saturday evening, Thursday morning*). Prepare an identical set of 'found' cards, preferably on a different colour card. Hand out a card to each student and ask the two groups to mingle asking each other questions using the past simple tense until they find their partner e.g. '*I lost my keys on Saturday.' 'Where did you lose your keys?' 'At the cinema.' 'Sorry, I don't have them.'* etc. Check students have found the correct partners.

1 SPEAKING Students work in pairs and look at the photos from a newspaper and decide what they think happened. Nominate a few students to give their answers.

2 Students read the blog post and say whether their ideas in exercise 1 were correct.

3 Students look at the words and expressions in the Writing bank and explain when we use them if necessary. Do a choral drill of the words before asking students to go back to the text and tick the ones that appear.

Answers

At first, then, Suddenly, In the end

EXTRA ACTIVITY

Ask students to choose four of the words or expressions from the Writing bank and write four sentences for what they have done that day using the expressions. Nominate two or three students to read out their sentences.

4 Students imagine they found something unusual last week. You may want to help them with some initial ideas. Ask them to read the questions and make notes answering them.

PRACTICE MAKES PERFECT

5 Students look at the task and write a blog post using their words from 4 and the expressions in the Writing bank. Remind students to check they have included the necessary information given in the box.

Set students a time limit, and encourage them to check their writing when they have finished.

Model text

Lara's London Life

A theatrical evening!

Yesterday morning I was walking along the street with my uncle, when we saw a hat in the middle of the pavement. When we got closer we saw that it was a 'helmet' – the type of hat soldiers wear. At first, we thought it was very old; my uncle said it was possibly from World War II. We knew there was a museum nearby and asked them if they knew anything about the helmet. They said it looked very new. Then they looked inside the helmet and saw an address for the local theatre. We went to the theatre and explained what we found. A few minutes later an actor came to meet us and said it was his helmet. He dropped it in the street while he was running to work. He was very happy and gave us two tickets to see the show which was about World War II. It was excellent!

✓ EXAM SUCCESS Ask students to discuss what they feel are the criteria for getting good marks in English writing exams. Write their ideas on the board. Then ask students to turn to Exam Success on page 144 (Writing: Knowing about evaluation) and read through the section. Add anything students hadn't thought of to the list.

HOMEWORK

Assign students page 18 in their Workbook or the relevant sections of the Online Workbook.

Language checkpoint: Unit 2

≫≫ FAST TRACK

The extra support provided on the Grammar and Vocabulary reference sections makes the Grammar and Vocabulary revision sections ideal for setting as homework. You could get students to complete the whole revision page or just certain exercises for homework.

Grammar revision p29

Past simple

1 Students change the sentences from present simple to past simple.

Answers
1 Richard and I were students at this school.
2 What was the problem?
3 We left school at five o'clock.
4 She caught the bus at that stop.
5 What time did you finish work?
6 She didn't teach English.
7 Running made me tired.
8 They had a problem.

Past continuous

2 Students complete the sentences with the past continuous form of the appropriate verb from the box. Tell them they will need to use affirmative, negative and question forms.

Answers
1 was reading   2 were, listening   3 wasn't writing
4 Were, sleeping   5 was tidying   6 weren't waiting
7 were, sitting   8 was crying

Past continuous and past simple

3 Students choose the correct alternatives.

Answers
1 was travelling, rang
2 stole, was looking
3 was driving, remembered
4 broke, ran

Vocabulary revision p29

CRIMES AND CRIMINALS

1 Students complete the sentences with the words in the box. Tell them there are more words than sentences, so there are some words they don't need.

Answers
1 mug   2 steal   3 Thief   4 Burglary   5 vandal
6 piracy

DETECTIVE WORK

2 Students choose the correct alternatives to complete the sentences.

Answers
1 accusation   2 proof   3 analyse   4 questioned

PHRASAL VERBS CONNECTED WITH INVESTIGATING AND FINDING

3 Students to complete the sentences with prepositions.

Answers
a for   b up   c across   d into   e out   f out

HOMEWORK

Assign students page 19 in their Workbook or the relevant sections of the Online Workbook.

Reading p30

1 Students look at the picture and answer the question.

Answers

In an emergency, for a fire, an accident or a crime

2 Ask students to read the text and write a title for it.

Suggested answers

Only in a real emergency!
911 in the US for emergencies only

3 Students read the questions and put an X next to answer options that they think are definitely not correct.

4 Students read the text again and choose the best answers. Check answers as a class.

Answers

1 b **2** c **3** a **4** a **5** b

Listening p31

5 LISTENING ▶ 14 Give students time to read the questions and encourage them to predict the topic and vocabulary. Play the track for students to listen and decide if the statements are true or false. Elicit answers from students. See p151 for the audioscript for this exercise.

Answers

1 F The popular name is MI6. **2** T **3** F The director is called 'C'. **4** T **5** F It is next to the River Thames. **6** T **7** F There is a secret tunnel under the River Thames.

6 ▶ 14 Students correct the false sentences. Play the track again if necessary. Check answers as a class and write the correct answers on the board.

Speaking p31

7 Tell students to look at the situation and make a list of questions that they can ask. Draw students' attention to the example questions.

Suggested answers

Where are you from? Have you got any brothers or sisters? Which member of your family is special to you? What is special about this person? How are you related to him/her? What do you do in your free time?

8 SPEAKING In pairs, students act out the role-play using their questions and notes if necessary. In a less confident class, you could ask students to do the role-play the first time with their notes, then swap pairs and do the role-play a second time without their notes.

Writing p31

9 Students write an informal email to an e-pal about a good friend at school. Ask them to read the paragraph plan before they begin and remind them to use typical words and expressions. For students who are less confident, photocopy the model text below.

Model text

Hi Max,

It's me again. How are you? Let me tell you about Lucia in my class. She's a good friend. She's from São Paulo, Brazil. She's 14 like me.

She's got two brothers and a sister. Her dad is a teacher and her mum is a doctor. She has lots of cousins, but I don't know them very well.

We've got lots in common, too. She loves listening to music, especially pop, and she always has the latest songs on her MP3 player. She likes climbing and skiing and she also likes hanging out with her friends.

Her favourite subject is maths. I don't like maths ☹ so she helps me with my homework. She's really clever and she's good at most subjects.

Anyway, that's all for now. Write back soon and tell me about one of your friends!

Best wishes,

Sasha

HOMEWORK

Assign students pages 20–21 in their Workbook or the relevant sections of the Online Workbook.

'CAN DO' PROGRESS CHECK p31

1 Ask students to mark from 1–4 how well they can do the things on the list in English.

2 Ask students to look at their marks and decide which things on the list they can do to improve. Elicit suggestions on how to improve their work and ask them to write these in the *Other* category.

KEY LEARNING OUTCOMES

CEF

Students will be able to:

- understand a text about world languages
- talk about countries, nationalities and languages
- ask for and give information
- write a language biography

UNIT OVERVIEW

Vocabulary
Countries, nationalities and languages
Learning a language
PRONUNCIATION Word stress

Reading
Mapping the world's languages
CRITICAL THINKING Discussing a Twitter map of your town, city, region or country

Grammar in context
some, any, much, many, a lot (of), a few, a little

Developing vocabulary
Negative prefixes *un-, in-, im-, ir-, il-*
PRONUNCIATION Contrastive word stress

Life skills
Social skills: Public speaking

Listening
Languages

Grammar in context
Relative pronouns

Developing speaking
Asking for information

Developing writing
A language biography

Exam success
Use of English: Multiple-choice cloze activities
Speaking: Knowing evaluation criteria

DIGITAL OVERVIEW

Presentation Kit

- ▶ **Flipped classroom video Unit 3:** *some, any, many, a lot (of), a few, a little*
- ▶ **Life skills video Unit 3:** How to speak in public
- ▶ Ⅴ **Vocabulary tool:** Learning a language
- ▶ **Interactive versions of Student's Book activities**
- ▶ **Integrated audio and answer key for all activities**
- ▶ **Workbook pages with answer key**

Teacher's Resource Centre
TRC

- ▶ **Flipped classroom video Unit 3:** *some, any, much, many, a lot (of), a few, a little*
- ▶ **Life skills video Unit 3:** How to speak in public
- ▶ **Grammar communication activity Unit 3:** Bingo pairs
- ▶ **Worksheets for this unit, including:**
  - – Grammar practice worksheet Unit 3
  - – Flipped classroom video worksheet Unit 3: *some, any, much, many, a lot (of), a few, a little*
  - – Literature worksheet Units 3 and 4
  - – Culture worksheet Unit 3
  - – Life skills video worksheet Unit 3
  - – Everyday English worksheet Unit 3

Student's App

Gateway 2nd Edition wordlist for the award-winning Sounds App (available for download)

✓ TESTING AND ASSESSMENT

Resources for exam preparation and measuring student progress

- ▶ Test Generator Units 1–3
- ▶ Printable tests Unit 3 and Review (Units 1–3)
- ▶ Gateway to exams Units 3 and 4 (end of Unit 4)

Vocabulary p32

Talking about countries, nationalities and learning a language

>>> FAST TRACK

You could ask students to do exercise 2 at home and check their answers at the start of the lesson.

WARMER

In pairs, students discuss the meaning of the unit title *Universal language* and what they think the unit is going to be about. Elicit ideas from the class.

Suggested answers

The word 'universal' suggests something that unites us all. This unit could look at all the languages of the world and how they are related, the importance of communication and learning other languages as well as the idea of having one language for everyone.

Countries, nationalities and languages

1 Students work with a partner and name as many countries as they can on the map. If possible, you could project the map onto the board and ask students to come up to the board and label it.

2 Students complete the table with the correct nationality or language. Remind students that, in English, countries, nationalities and languages always begin with a capital letter. Tell students that although German is the language spoken by the largest proportion of the Swiss population (approx. 65%) they also speak French, Italian and Romansh in Switzerland.

>>> FAST FINISHERS

Students think of a famous person from each country. They then read out the names of the famous people for the other students to say where they come from and which language they speak.

3 ▶ 15 Play the track for students to listen and check their answers. See p151 for the audioscript for this exercise.

Answers

1 Arge<u>ti</u>na Arge<u>tin</u>ian <u>Spa</u>nish
2 <u>Au</u>stria <u>Au</u>strian <u>Ger</u>man
3 Bra<u>zil</u> Bra<u>zil</u>ian Portu<u>guese</u>
4 Bul<u>gar</u>ia Bul<u>gar</u>ian Bul<u>gar</u>ian
5 <u>E</u>gypt E<u>gyp</u>tian <u>A</u>rabic
6 Ja<u>pan</u> Japa<u>nese</u> Japa<u>nese</u>
7 <u>Mex</u>ico <u>Mex</u>ican <u>Spa</u>nish
8 <u>Po</u>land <u>Po</u>lish <u>Po</u>lish
9 <u>Russ</u>ia <u>Russ</u>ian <u>Russ</u>ian
10 <u>Swit</u>zerland <u>Swiss</u> Ro<u>man</u>sh/I<u>tal</u>ian/<u>Ger</u>man/<u>Fre</u>nch
11 <u>Thai</u>land <u>Thai</u> <u>Thai</u>
12 <u>Tur</u>key <u>Tur</u>kish <u>Tur</u>kish

4a PRONUNCIATION Students say the words from the table aloud and mark the stress on each one.

4b ▶ 16 Play the track for students to listen, check and repeat with the correct stress (see p151 for the audioscript for this exercise and Answers in 3 for answers).

TEACHER DEVELOPMENT: PRONUNCIATION

Word stress and nationalities

- Most nationalities end in -*(i)an*, e.g. *Argentinian, Brazilian, German, Italian*. The stress comes before the -*(i)an* sound.
- A lot of nationalities end in -*ish*, e.g. *British, English, Irish, Scottish, Spanish*. These are generally two-syllable words and the stress is on the first syllable.
- A few nationalities end in -*ese*, e.g. *Chinese, Portuguese, Japanese*. The stress is always on the -*ese* sound.
- There are also a few exceptions, e.g. *French* (from France), *Welsh* (from Wales), *Dutch* (from the Netherlands), *Arabic* (from many Arabic countries).
- The word for the language is often the same as for the nationality, e.g. *German, Portuguese, Japanese, Spanish*.

5 SPEAKING Put students in small groups and tell them to answer the question giving their reasons. Draw students' attention to the example answer. After everyone has had the chance to speak, have a class vote on the most popular country to visit.

v | Learning a language

6 Students change the verbs in the box into nouns. For less confident students you could allow the use of dictionaries to check.

Answers

memorise – memory; practise – practice;
revise – revision; translate – translation, translator

>>> FAST FINISHERS

Ask students to make a sentence using each of the nouns from exercise 6.

7 Students look at the words and decide if they use *do* or *make* with each word. Tell them to think of other verbs they can use with these words.

Suggested answers

English: *do* (also *study, learn, speak, write, listen to*)
an essay: *do* (also *write, compose, check, read*)
an exam: *do* (also *sit, take, pass, fail, study for, revise for*)
an exercise: *do* (also *try, repeat, complete*)
homework: *do* (also *start, finish, hand in, mark, forget*)
a mistake: *make* (also *correct, notice, apologise for*)

TEACHER DEVELOPMENT: LANGUAGE

do and make

Students can find it difficult to know when to use *do* or *make* as main verbs. The best way to remember is for students to memorise expressions. Students may appreciate a general explanation, but point out that there are many exceptions.

do is used when someone performs an action, activity, task or some kind of work. It is also used with the words *something, nothing, anything, everything,* etc. to describe an action without saying exactly what the action is, e.g. *I'm not doing anything today.*

However, *make* is used when someone is constructing, building or creating something, or preparing food.

8 **SPEAKING** Students use the questions to interview their partners and find out if their answers are similar. Draw attention to the model dialogue. You may want to ask students to write their answers first. Ask different students to share their answers with the class and compare techniques and ideas about learning English.

✚✚ EXTRA ACTIVITY

Ask students to **make** a list of ten different ways to study English outside the classroom. It could be a list of study ideas or favourite English websites. Students could compare their ideas at the start of the next class and **make** a Top Ten Techniques list which you could display in the classroom.

HOMEWORK

Assign students page 22 in their Workbook or the relevant sections of the Online Workbook.

Reading p33

Reading for gist and for specific information

⟫⟫ FAST TRACK

You could do exercise 1 as a class activity, by choosing a colour and inviting the class to call out their suggestions.

WARMER

Write the following sentences on the board about languages of the world. Put students in small groups and see if they know the answers. Tell the students the answers (reminding them that the figures are approximate and according to the majority of studies) and ask them if they were surprised by any.
1 The number of languages in the world.
2 The language with the most native speakers.
3 The language with the most non-native speakers.
4 The oldest written language that still exists.
5 The country with the most languages spoken by native inhabitants.

Answers
1 Around 7,000 languages in the world, with approximately 500 nearly extinct   **2** Mandarin   **3** English   **4** Chinese or Greek   **5** Papua New Guinea (with over 800 living languages)

1 Students look at the map on page 32 and see if they can guess what language is represented by each colour. Ask some students for suggestions, but don't confirm answers yet.

2 Students read the text and answer the two questions. Nominate students to give their answers.

Answers
They used data collected from a social network.
A map of London.

3 Now ask the students to read the whole text in detail. They should decide if each piece of information is true (T), false (F) or not mentioned (NM). Check answers as a class, asking students to say which part of the text helped them find the answer.

Answers
1 NM   **2** T   **3** T   **4** F   **5** T   **6** NM   **7** NM   **8** T

⟫⟫ FAST FINISHERS

Ask students to correct the false sentences.

4 **⚙ CRITICAL THINKING** Ask students to think about what a Twitter map of their own town, city, region or country would show. Ask them to make some notes and then put students in small groups to discuss their ideas. Hold a class discussion to see what different groups thought.

Example answers
A Twitter map would show how many people were in each area of the town and the types of things they tweeted about.

5 Students look at the underlined words in the text and guess their meanings. You could nominate students to share their ideas with the class at this point. Then ask students to check in their dictionaries. Ask students to make a note of the meanings, and what type of word (noun, verb, adverb, adjective, etc.) it is.

Answers
fascinating (adj) = very interesting to look at or learn about
closely (adv) = in a careful way
co-exist (verb) = live or be there together in the same place at the same time
concentrated (adj) = all together, mostly
detailed (adj) = with a lot of information

Write the following gapped sentences on the board:

1 The population in England is more _____ in the south.
2 The scientist studied her results _____.
3 The painting was very _____; you could see all the different people's faces.
4 In Wales, the English and Welsh languages _____.
5 I thought the documentary last night was _____; I learnt so much!

Students use the words from 5 to complete the sentences.

Answers

1 concentrated **2** closely **3** detailed **4** co-exist
5 fascinating

6 SPEAKING **What about *you*?** Students think about their own answers to the questions, then discuss with a partner. Ask some pairs to share their thoughts with the class.

HOMEWORK

Assign students page 23 in their Workbook or the relevant sections of the Online Workbook.

Grammar in context pp34–35

Using some, any, much, many, a lot (of), a few, a little

⟫⟫ FAST TRACK

If students are familiar with the vocabulary, you could ask them to complete 1a and 1b at home and then check their answers at the start of the lesson.

 Test before you teach: Flipped classroom
Set the Flipped classroom video and tasks for homework underline before the lesson. This will allow you to assess the needs of the students before the class. Students can then move on to the relevant grammar practice activities.

1a Students look at the words and decide if they are countable or uncountable.

Answers

1 countable **2** uncountable **3** uncountable
4 countable **5** countable **6** countable
Both *time* and *colour* can be countable or uncountable.

TEACHER DEVELOPMENT: LANGUAGE

Countable or uncountable

Students often learn basic quantifiers within the context of food, so this is a good opportunity to show students they need to think about nouns and how to quantify them in a wider context. Write on the board: *advice, furniture, information, news*, and ask if they are countable or uncountable. Remind students that they can make each word countable by adding *a piece of* before the noun, e.g. *a piece of news, advice*, etc. When you teach new vocabulary, make a habit of telling students which words are countable and uncountable, and, if the latter, which word (e.g. *piece, slice, cup*) usually goes before it to make it countable.

1b In pairs, give students two minutes to read the sentences and answer questions a–e about the words in bold. Remind students that some words will be correct for more than one question.

Answers

b some, any, many, a lot of, a few   **d** much, many, a lot of
c any, many, much, a lot of   **e** a few, a little

TEACHER DEVELOPMENT: LANGUAGE

Quantifiers

Remind students of some key rules for using quantifiers:
a with singular countable nouns
some/any with plural countable and uncountable nouns
some in affirmative sentences
any in negative sentences and questions
many/much mainly in negative sentences and questions
a lot of mainly in affirmative sentences
much/a little with uncountable nouns
many/a few with plural countable nouns
a lot of with uncountable and countable nouns (point out that *lots of* is also used and has the same meaning)

2a Students complete the dialogue with *some* or *any*.

Answers

a any **b** some **c** any **d** any **e** any **f** some
g some **h** some **i** some **j** any **k** some

⟫⟫ FAST FINISHERS

Ask students to work in pairs and role-play the dialogue.

✚ EXTRA ACTIVITY

If students are still finding the concept of *some/ any* difficult, write some more food items on the board. Then ask students to re-enact the dialogue substituting different food items.

2b Students look at the words in bold in the dialogue and guess what they have in common, apart from the fact that they are all types of food.

Answers

All these words have been taken from other languages to become part of the English language.

3 Students read the text and choose the correct alternatives.

Answers

a many **b** a lot **c** many **d** many **e** a few
f Some **g** many **h** much **i** lots of **j** some
k a lot of **l** a lot of **m** a lot of **n** a few **o** a little
p many

ⓘ CULTURAL INFORMATION

One distinctive aspect of the English language is its tendency to absorb foreign words and this has been happening for the last 1600 years. It began with the migration of the Jutes, Angles and Saxons from Germany and Denmark to Britain in the fifth and sixth centuries. Later, the Norman Conquest of 1066 brought many French words into English. In the late 15th century, Greek and Latin words began to enter into the English language.

⁺✛ EXTRA ACTIVITY

Ask students to categorise nouns from exercises 1b and 2a as countable or uncountable.
Countable – colours, languages, burgers, biscuits, bananas, tomatoes, potatoes, countries, explanations, maps, areas, ways
Uncountable – chocolate, sugar, yoghurt (in this context), tomato ketchup, data, time (in this context), knowledge, money

⁺✛ EXTRA ACTIVITY

In pairs, give students five minutes to write an A to Z of food and drink items with one noun for each letter, except u, x and z. Allow students to use dictionaries if you think this may be too challenging without. When the five minutes are up, elicit food nouns for each letter and ask if they are uncountable or countable. You could develop this into a discussion about which foods are healthy/unhealthy and why.

Suggested answers

apple, banana, coffee, doughnut, egg, fish, grape, hamburger, ice cream, jam, ketchup, lentil, milk, nut, orange, potato, quiche, rice, sugar, tea, vanilla, walnut, yoghurt

4 In pairs, ask students to complete the sentences about their own language using the words in the box for ideas. You may like students to complete the sentences individually first as a writing activity before they work in pairs. Nominate students to give their answers. You could ask students to do further research and find specific examples for homework.

Answers

Students' own answers

5a Students look at the photos and elicit some ideas about what they know about these countries in general. Individually, students choose a country and make notes about things that there are or aren't in this country. Tell them to use the ideas in the box. For less confident students, you could write the example answer (below) on the board, and then ask them to choose one of the other countries for their answer.

Example answer

(Egypt) There aren't many animals. There isn't any snow and there isn't much water. There's a lot of tourism and there are a lot of monuments.

5b SPEAKING In pairs, students ask each other questions with *any, much, many, a lot of, a few, a little* to find out which country their partner chose. Drill the model dialogue as an example for students. Monitor and provide help if necessary. Note down common errors to go over in a feedback session after the activity.

Suggested answers

Is there any snow there? Is there a lot of snow? Are there any animals? Do many people live there? Are there many monuments/modern buildings/old buildings/offices? Are there a lot of mountains? Is there a lot of water? Is there a lot of tourism?

5c SPEAKING Students choose a country that is not in the photos and to repeat exercises 5a and 5b. For variety, you could ask individual students to come to the front of the class and have the rest of the class ask questions.

Refer students to the Grammar reference on page 42 if necessary.

HOMEWORK

Assign students page 24 in their Workbook or the relevant sections of the Online Workbook.

Developing vocabulary p35

Using negative prefixes un-, in-, im-, ir-, il-

⫸ FAST TRACK

You could ask students to write their examples for 4b at home. They can then guess the words in pairs at the next lesson.

WARMER

To introduce students to the lesson's focus, write the following clues on the board and give students 30 seconds to work in pairs and guess the words:
1 If the law says you can do something, it is l............... .
2 I smile when I feel h............... .
3 My teacher does a ✓ when the answer is c............... .
Answers
1 legal **2** happy **3** correct

Elicit from students that these are all positive words. Tell students that they are going to look at ways they can make these words negative.

1 Students look at the words and decide what they have in common. Ask them to write down what the opposite of each word is in their notebooks.

Answers

They are all negative words with prefixes. By removing the prefix, you can make the opposite word: illegal – legal; impossible – possible; incorrect – correct; informal – formal; invisible – visible; irregular – regular; unhappy – happy; unusual – usual.

TEACHER DEVELOPMENT: LANGUAGE

Negative prefixes

Un- is the most common negative prefix, but there are few hard and fast rules for which prefix students should use (except words that start with the letter *m* always take the prefix *im-*). Advise them to consult the Macmillan Essential Dictionary if they have doubts.

Tell students that the main stress is usually on the original word, e.g. *unnatural*, but there is often a secondary (smaller) stress on the prefix. Point out that prefixes can be added to verbs, nouns and adjectives.

2 Students read the sentences and choose the correct alternatives. Check answers as a class.

Answers

1 an irregular **2** happy **3** incorrect **4** invisible
5 formal **6** illegal **7** impossible

3a PRONUNCIATION ▶ 17 Play the track and ask students to underline the stressed syllable in the words from 1. See p151 for the audioscript for this exercise.

Answers

il<u>le</u>gal imp<u>os</u>sible inco<u>rrect</u> in<u>for</u>mal in<u>vis</u>ible ir<u>reg</u>ular un<u>happy</u> un<u>us</u>ual

The main stress isn't on the prefix.

3b ▶ 17 Play the track again for students to listen again and repeat the words, paying attention to the correct stress.

4a Ask students to think of an example of something for each word in exercise 1. Circulate and help any students with ideas if necessary.

4b SPEAKING Draw students' attention to the model dialogue and then ask them to work in pairs and read out their examples from exercise 4a for their partners to guess the word. If some pairs finish early, ask them to swap partners and work through exercise 4b again with their new partner.

HOMEWORK

Assign students page 25 in their Workbook or the relevant sections of the Online Workbook.

Gateway to life skills pp36–37

Public speaking

To consider the importance of body language, to learn useful tips for public speaking and to practise giving a talk to the class.

⟫⟫ FAST TRACK

You could ask students to write their answers to exercise 3 at home. They can then compare their answers in pairs at the next lesson.

ⓘ BACKGROUND INFORMATION

Speaking in public can be a daunting task even for adults, but teenagers can be particularly uncomfortable speaking in front of others. However, there are many situations where being able to speak confidently in public is a distinct advantage such as giving a presentation in the workplace or at university, delivering a speech at a social event, or even talking in front of the class. It is normal to feel nervous, but students need to learn how to control nerves and not be overcome by them.

A good public speaker delivers his or her message clearly and confidently without distracting behaviour or too much additional or unnecessary information.

There are various statistics for how much body language contributes to the efficacy of delivering a message, but some experts think that nonverbal communication contributes significantly more than the verbal part. It is important, therefore, that students are also made aware of the importance of body language and gestures and this is the focus of the lesson.

WARMER

Think of a very simple sentence (e.g. *My name is Mrs Jones and I come from London.*)

Tell students you are going to say the same thing in many different ways and ask them to note down what sort of person they think you are after each one. Then, repeat the sentence four or five times, each time varying the confidence and volume of your voice, your body language, the speed at which you talk, etc.

Ask students what affected what they wrote down and elicit the term *body language*.

Ask students to read through the Key concepts and see if they can apply any of these words to the ways you delivered the sentence (e.g. *You were very insecure the first time, you were very confident the second time, you used a lot of gestures the third time*).

1a Ask students to look at the photos of different body language. In pairs, ask students to choose which description best fits the person. Nominate a few students to give their answers, encouraging them to give their reasons why.

1b Ask students to turn to page 147 for the expert's answers.

Answers

1 B **2** A **3** A

1c Students note whether they agreed or disagreed with the expert's opinions and if so, why. Nominate a few students to give their answers. Then, as a class discuss which body language is impolite in the students' country.

2 READING Students read the text and choose the best title. For less confident students, you could break up the reading into paragraphs, and stop after each paragraph to ask questions to check they have understood before they move on.

Answer

2

3 Students read the text again and answer the questions, using full sentences. Allow students to check their answers in pairs, before nominating different students to give their answers.

Answers

1 Gestures do not mean the same thing in every country.
2 We can understand a lot without words.
3 Because they are lying.
4 Good. It is a sign of sincerity and confidence.
5 Because they use different gestures to other countries.
6 In some countries it's good, and in some countries it makes people uncomfortable.
7 You can learn and practise it.

✚ **EXTRA ACTIVITY**

Ask students to work in pairs and write four to five 'body language' tips for when foreigners come to their country (e.g. shake hands when you meet people; don't fold your arms, etc.) If you have more time, students could put together a leaflet or poster with this advice to be displayed in the classroom.

4 Draw students' attention to the main photo. Ask them to think of one word that describes her body language (e.g. *good, secure, confident*). In pairs, ask students to imagine they are going to talk to a group of people and to write down some ideas for good body language. Remind them to look at the photos for some ideas. Elicit some suggestions from different pairs.

5 LISTENING ▶ 18 Tell students they are going to listen to or watch a video of two students giving advice on speaking in public. Play the video or track. Ask students if any of their ideas from exercise 4 were mentioned. Ask students if they heard any additional ideas. See p151 for the videoscript/audioscript for this exercise.

6 ▶ 18 Students read the checklist and complete each piece of advice. Play the video or track again if you feel students need it. Ask different students to read out their answers.

Answers

1 Stand 2 hands 3 up 4 Don't 5 stopping
6 interested 7 prepare

⟫ **FAST FINISHERS**

Ask students to add an extra piece of advice to the checklist.

7 Ask students to work individually and think about their answers to the questions. Then nominate a few students to share their thoughts with the class.

LIFE TASK

Tell students they are going to prepare and give a short talk to the class.

■ *Step 1*
Ask students to work individually and read the instructions. Circulate as they do this and help with any necessary vocabulary or structures.

■ *Step 2*
Students prepare their talks individually. If you feel your students are confident enough, ask them to deliver their talks to the whole class. Otherwise put students in smaller groups.

■ *Step 3*
Remind students to look at the advice in 6 before they do their talk. Students give their talks to the class or their groups while other students make notes for feedback.

■ *Step 4*
Ask other students in the group or class to give their feedback, but ensure that it is positive or constructive criticism. Encourage students to think of one thing they did well and one thing they can work on next time.

Listening p38

Identifying key words for gist

WARMER

In pairs, ask students to think about their experience of learning English. Do they think it's an easy language or difficult language? Which things do they find difficult? What things do they think make a language easy or difficult? Nominate a few pairs to give their answers.

1 SPEAKING Students work with a partner and look at the languages a–e. Ask them to make notes about what they know about each one and to decide whether they think it's a difficult or easy language to learn, giving their reasons. Ask a few students to give their opinions.

Example answers

Spanish is a European language. People in Spain and many people in South America speak it. It's a Latin or romance language. It's quite difficult.

Esperanto is a made up language. It was supposed to become a universal language.

French is a European language. People speak it in France and in other parts of the world. It's quite difficult.

Japanese is a very difficult language. It uses symbols not words. People in Japan speak it. It's a little bit like Korean.

Klingon is the language of the Klingons from the Star Trek series.

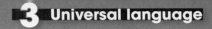

2 LISTENING ▶ 19 Tell students they are going to listen to four speakers and to write down the language each one is learning. Pre-teach any necessary vocabulary. Remind them there is one language they don't need. Play the track. Check answers as a class. See pp151–152 for the audioscript for this exercise.

Answers

Speaker 1: Esperanto   **Speaker 3:** Japanese
Speaker 2: Spanish   **Speaker 4:** Klingon

3 ▶ 19 Students listen to the track again and match the speakers to the correct information. Give students time to read through the statements before playing the track. Nominate different students to give their answers.

Answers

1 B, H   **2** A, D   **3** C, G   **4** E, F

4 SPEAKING What about *you*? Students discuss which language they would choose to learn and why. Then have a show of hands in class to see which is the most popular language to learn.

HOMEWORK

Assign students page 25 in their Workbook or the relevant sections of the Online Workbook.

Grammar in context pp38–39

Using relative pronouns

⟩⟩⟩ FAST TRACK

You could ask students to write their answers to exercise 5 at home. They can then compare their answers in pairs at the next lesson.

Test before you teach
Start the class by giving students names of people, places and things on slips of paper (*Lionel Messi, London, a pencil,* etc.) In pairs, students define the word on their slip of paper for their partner to guess, e.g. *He's a footballer who plays for Barcelona. It's the city where you can see Big Ben.* Monitor to see how comfortable students are with using relative pronouns in their definitions.

1a Students read the sentences and then decide what each word in bold refers to. Ask them to answer questions a–e. Check students' answers and make sure they have copied the correct information into their notebooks.

Answers

a who, that   **b** which, that   **c** whose   **d** where   **e** when

1b Students look at sentences 4 and 6 and decide why it is possible to omit *that* in sentence 4 but not in sentence 6.

Answer

We *can* omit *who, which* or *that* when a noun or a pronoun comes immediately after.

TEACHER DEVELOPMENT: LANGUAGE

Defining relative clauses
Relative clauses contain necessary information that defines the person, thing, place or time that comes in the first half of the sentence. Because it is necessary information, there are no commas before or after the relative clause.

✛✛ EXTRA ACTIVITY

Ask students to write one more example sentence for each relative pronoun. Ask several students to write their sentences on the board and ask the class if they are correct.

2 Focus students' attention on the photo. Ask them if they know the programme or the character. Then ask students to look at the relative pronouns in the sentences and decide in which sentences the relative pronoun can be omitted.

Answers

The relative pronoun can be omitted in sentences 2, 3 and 7.

✛✛ EXTRA ACTIVITY

Divide the class into two teams. Draw a three by three grid on the board and write the relative pronouns in the spaces with a question mark (?), plus sign (+) or minus (–) sign depending on whether you want them to form interrogative, affirmative or negative sentences.

To win a square, the teams take turns to choose a square and make a correct sentence with the relative pronoun in the correct form. A team must win three squares in a horizontal, diagonal or vertical row to win the game.

3 Students match the sentence halves and link them using appropriate relative pronouns. Draw students' attention to the example sentence.

Answers

2 b (who)   **3** a (when)   **4** e (whose)
5 g (which/that/–)   **6** f (which/that)   **7** c (whose)

4a SPEAKING Students choose six words from the Vocabulary sections in Units 1–3 and write definitions of these words using *who, that, which, where, when, whose.*

4b In pairs, students read the definitions they wrote in exercise 4a for their partner to identify the words. Ask a pair to read out the model dialogue first.

5 Students complete the sentences with true information about themselves. Complete the first two sentences for you as a model, e.g. *The beach is a place where I'm usually happy. My wedding ring is an object that is really important to me.*

6 SPEAKING In pairs, students compare the sentences they wrote in exercise 5 and discuss their answers. Draw attention to the model dialogue before they begin and encourage students to ask follow-up questions to find out more about their partner's answers. Ask volunteers to share information from their discussion with the class.

Ask students to read the instructions for the task and elicit why it is a good idea to read (skim) the text first, without thinking about the gaps. Refer students to page 144 (Use of English: Multiple-choice cloze activities) to check their answers.

7 Focus students' attention on the picture of Emilia Clarke. See if any of your students can give you a sentence about the photo using a relative pronoun (e.g. *She's the actress who's in* Game of Thrones). Ask students to read the text and choose the best answer A–D. Allow students to check their answers in pairs, before nominating students to give their answers in class.

Answers

1 A 2 B 3 C 4 A 5 C 6 A 7 D 8 C 9 A

Refer students to the Grammar reference on page 42 if necessary.

HOMEWORK

Assign students page 26 in their Workbook or the relevant sections of the Online Workbook.

Developing speaking p40

Asking for information

≫≫ FAST TRACK

You could ask students to prepare their answers to exercises 6a and 6b at home. They can then present their answers at the next lesson.

WARMER

Put students in pairs and ask them to think of some advantages and disadvantages of learning English at a summer school in an English-speaking country.

Example answers

(advantages) you can hear the language all day, you can meet people from other countries, you won't just meet people who speak your language, you will be able to practise English with native speakers; (disadvantages) you may be homesick, you may want to go sightseeing, it's expensive

Ask them if they could choose an English-speaking country to go to for summer school, where would they go? Nominate some students to give their answers.

1 SPEAKING Students look at the advert and answer the questions in pairs. Elicit answers from different pairs asking students to give reasons for their choices.

Suggested answers

1 I think it's a good place to learn English in the summer because it's a small school so they can give students personal care. It looks as if there are fun activities to do.

2 Some important factors are: course dates, cost, age of students, quality of teaching, other activities, size of school, distance to nearest town, accommodation, food.

2 LISTENING ▶ 20 Tell students they are going to listen to a student asking for information about the Cardiff English Centre. Ask them to write the information that the receptionist gives. Play the track. Check answers as a class. See p152 for the audioscript for this exercise.

Answers

Course begins: 10th July   **Course lasts:** two weeks
Price: £815
Other activities: excursions, discos, sports activities including sailing

3 Students read the dialogue in exercise 4 and note which useful expressions from the Speaking bank appear in it.

Answers

Sorry, did you say …? Could you repeat that?

TEACHER DEVELOPMENT: STUDENT TRAINING

Asking for information

Elicit the key strategies the student in the audio uses to make sure he gets the information he needs:

- He states the objective of his call immediately, e.g. *I'd like some information about summer courses.*
- He is polite, e.g. *I'd like … , Could you … ?*
- He checks information, e.g. *Sorry, did you say … ? Could you repeat that?*
- He has prepared a list of questions (date, length, accommodation, etc.).
- He concludes the conversation with an action that will get him more information (asking for a registration form).

4 Students complete the dialogue with the correct information. Play the track again if necessary.

Answers

a Cardiff   **b** the 10th of July   **c** the 10th of July
d two weeks   **e** Yes   **f** do   **g** two-week   **h** £815
i £815   **j** excursions   **k** discos   **l** sailing

5 SPEAKING In pairs, ask students to practise the dialogue in exercise 4, paying attention to pronunciation and intonation. When students have finished, ask them to swap roles and read through again.

✚✚ EXTRA ACTIVITY

Ask students to extend the dialogue by writing two extra lines for each person. Then ask them to practise the new part with a partner.

PRACTICE MAKES PERFECT

6a SPEAKING Divide the class into two teams: A and B. All students from Team A find someone from Team B to be their partner. When the students are in their pairs, explain the role-play. Student As play the role of the receptionist and look at the information about Sydney English Centre on page 147. Student Bs play the role of the student and look at the information on page 40. Students Bs use the questions in exercise 4 and expressions from the Speaking bank to help them. Monitor and help with any difficulties as students perform their role-plays.

6b When they have finished, Student B looks at the information about the San Francisco English Centre on page 147 and Student A plays the role of the student. At the end of the activity, ask volunteers to perform one of their role-plays for the class.

✓ EXAM SUCCESS Ask students to think about what they need to do to get a good mark in a speaking exam. Exchange ideas and ask students to check their answers on page 144 (Speaking: Knowing about evaluation).

➕ EXTRA ACTIVITY

Ask students to create their own advertisement for a language school or find one on the Internet. They work in pairs and role-play a phone conversation in which one student asks for information about their partner's language school. You could ask students to create or find an advert for homework and do the speaking activity as a warmer in the next class.

HOMEWORK

Assign students page 27 in their Workbook or the relevant sections of the Online Workbook.

Developing writing p41

Writing a language biography

⟫⟫ FAST TRACK

You could ask students to write the language biography in exercise 5 at home. They can then compare their language biographies in pairs at the next lesson.

WARMER

In pairs, ask students to tell each other about when they first started learning English or another foreign language, and different language-learning experiences in and outside school. Ask them not just to think about dates, but about materials they used, the teachers, when they improved the most. You could model some sentences of your own experience learning English or another language first.

1 **SPEAKING** Students work with a partner and look at the pictures and say how each one of them can help to learn English.

Suggested answers

a You can visit London and speak English with native speakers in shops and restaurants.
b *The Hunger Games* DVD is good if you have the subtitles on – you can hear natural English and it's enjoyable.
c You can listen to songs in English on your MP3 player and download the lyrics.
d You can chat to an e-pal in English online, or surf sites in English on the Internet.
e The reader is good for people who like literature – you learn lots of interesting words in a different context.
f An English course helps you study grammar and vocabulary, and all the skills you need.

2 Students read the explanation of what a language biography is and then to read the text. Ask them to find as many similarities as they can between her experiences and their own. Direct students' attention to the model sentence. Elicit answers from different students.

TEACHER DEVELOPMENT: CLASSROOM TIPS

A language biography

In this lesson, students write a language biography. The Europass Language Passport was developed by the Council of Europe as part of the European Language Portfolio which consists of three documents: the Language Passport, the Language Biography and the Dossier.

The Language Biography compiles an overview of a student's most important language-learning experiences. He/She identifies personal learning objectives, monitors progress, reflects on the learning process and documents learning activities.

3 Students read the text again and mark where each new paragraph should begin using the plan to help them. When they have finished, direct their attention to the Writing bank.

Answers

Paragraph 1: My name is Celia … I can speak English.
Paragraph 2: I started learning English … and we practised speaking.
Paragraph 3: At the moment … sometimes on the computer.
Paragraph 4: Outside school … to London for example.
Paragraph 5: I like learning English … revise them from time to time.

TEACHER DEVELOPMENT: STUDENT TRAINING

Writing paragraphs

The topic of one paragraph should follow logically from the topic of the previous paragraph and should lead on to the topic of the next paragraph. In general, the purpose of a paragraph is to express one point, idea or opinion. This main idea is expressed through three sections of a paragraph:

Beginning – Introduce your idea.
Middle – Explain your idea.
End – Make your point again and transition to the next paragraph.

4 Individually, students make notes about their own experiences of learning English for each paragraph in exercise 3. Remind them to use information from the Warmer. Monitor and provide help with vocabulary.

5 **PRACTICE MAKES PERFECT**
Students write their own language biography using their notes from exercise 4. Remind them to look at the Writing bank and to organise their information into five clear paragraphs. For students who are less confident, photocopy the model text below for extra support during the writing task.

Model text

My name is Sebastian Kosowski and I'm 15 years old. I'm Polish and my mother tongue is Polish. Apart from Polish, I can speak English and German.

I started learning English when I was at primary school. I was eight years old. We learnt a lot of vocabulary, but we didn't study a lot of grammar – just the present simple. We sang songs and played games to make it fun. I loved my English lessons! The teacher was really kind, too.

Now I am studying English at secondary school. We study a lot of grammar and it is much more difficult than at primary school. The lessons are still fun and I'm learning a lot. I like speaking and reading English, but I'm not so good at listening and writing. Sometimes our teacher gives us tests and I usually do OK.

Outside school, I try to speak English as much as possible, but it's not easy because no one in my family can speak it. I have an English friend who I met on holiday last summer. We send each other emails almost every week. He likes all the same things as I do like football and films. I like watching films in English with Polish subtitles. That helps me to learn new words. Last year, I went on a school trip to England with my class. It was great! I stayed with an English family – they were very friendly and kind. They helped me a lot with my English.

I like learning a language by talking to native speakers and listening to real English on TV or on the radio. It's the best way to learn quickly and speak naturally. I hope I can live and work in England one day. That's definitely the best way to learn a language!

✚ EXTRA ACTIVITY

Ask students to make a mind map with words that refer to learning a language. They could divide their mind map into verbs and nouns.
Verbs: *do/study English, do an essay, do homework, do an exercise, do an exam, make a mistake, memorise, practise, revise, translate*

HOMEWORK

Assign students page 28 in their Workbook or the relevant sections of the Online Workbook.

Language checkpoint: Unit 3

⟫⟫ FAST TRACK

The extra support provided on the Grammar and Vocabulary reference sections makes the Grammar and Vocabulary revision section ideal for setting as homework. You could get students to complete the whole revision page or just certain exercises for homework.

Grammar revision p43

some, any, much, many, a lot (of), a few, a little

1 Students complete the sentences with *some, any, much, many, a lot (of), a few, a little*. Let them know that more than one answer is sometimes possible.

Answers
1 a few **2** any **3** a little **4** much **5** many/any/a lot of **6** much **7** some/a lot of **8** a few

Relative pronouns

2 Students read the two sentences and join them to make one sentence using *who, which, that, whose, where, when*. Direct attention to the example sentence. Elicit in which sentences we can omit the relative pronoun (5 and 6).

Answers
1 David Silva is a football player who speaks Spanish. **2** The park is a beautiful place where you can go at the weekend. **3** Last year was a special year when a lot of important things happened. **4** That's the teacher whose classes are brilliant. **5** This is a great book which/that they want to translate into English. **6** Piraha is an unusual language which/that only around 400 people speak. **7** George R.R. Martin is an American author who writes fantasy novels. **8** We go to the cinema on Wednesdays when there's a special price.

Vocabulary revision p43

LEARNING A LANGUAGE

1 Students complete the sentences with the words from the box. Remind them they need to use one word twice.

Answers
1 translation **2** revision **3** practise **4** make **5** practice **6** do **7** exercise **8** do

COUNTRIES, NATIONALITIES AND LANGUAGES

2 Students complete the sentences with the correct country, nationality or language.

Answers
1 Thailand **2** Portuguese **3** Turkish **4** German **5** Polish **6** Argentinian **7** Arabic **8** Egyptian

NEGATIVE PREFIXES *UN-, IN-, IM-, IR-, IL-*

3 Students read the definitions and complete the words.

Answers
1 unhappy **2** incorrect **3** impossible **4** informal **5** irregular **6** illegal **7** unusual **8** invisible

HOMEWORK

Assign students page 29 in their Workbook or the relevant sections of the Online Workbook.

KEY LEARNING OUTCOMES

CEF

Students will be able to:

- understand a text about teen health tips
- talk about parts of the body using the present perfect
- talk about health tips and problems
- describe photos
- write notes and messages

UNIT OVERVIEW

Vocabulary	Parts of the body Health problems and illnesses
Reading	Why learn first aid? Teen health tips CRITICAL THINKING Discussing why young people have an obsession with suntans
Grammar in context	Present perfect with *ever* and *never* Present perfect with *for* and *since*
Developing vocabulary	Compound nouns connected with health and medicine PRONUNCIATION Word stress in compound nouns
Life skills	Physical well-being: Learning some basics of first aid
Listening	Action scenes
Grammar in context	Present perfect with *just, yet, already* Present perfect and past simple
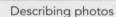 **Developing speaking**	Describing photos
Developing writing	Notes and messages
Exam success	Reading: Matching activities Writing: Content and style

DIGITAL OVERVIEW

Presentation Kit

- ▶ **Flipped classroom video Unit 4:** Present perfect with *ever* and *never*
- ▶ **Life skills video Unit 4:** The recovery position
- ▶ ⓥ **Vocabulary tool:** Parts of the body; Health problems and illnesses
- ▶ **Interactive versions of Student's Book activities**
- ▶ **Integrated audio and answer key for all activities**
- ▶ **Workbook pages with answer key**

Teacher's Resource Centre TRC

- ▶ **Flipped classroom video Unit 4:** Present perfect with *ever* and *never*
- ▶ **Life skills video Unit 4:** The recovery position
- ▶ **Grammar communication activity Unit 4:** A perfect player
- ▶ **Worksheets for this unit, including:**
  - – Grammar practice worksheet Unit 4
  - – Flipped classroom video worksheet Unit 4: Present perfect with *ever* and *never*
  - – Literature worksheet Units 3 and 4
  - – Culture worksheet Unit 4
  - – Life skills video worksheet Unit 4
  - – Everyday English worksheet Unit 4

Student's App

Gateway 2nd Edition wordlist for the award-winning Sounds App (available for download)

✓ TESTING AND ASSESSMENT

Resources for exam preparation and measuring student progress

- ▶ Test Generator Units 1–4
- ▶ Printable test Unit 4
- ▶ Gateway to exams Units 3 and 4 (end of Unit 4)

Vocabulary p44

Talking about parts of the body, health problems and illnesses

>>> **FAST TRACK**

You could ask students to do exercise 4 at home so that less confident students can take the necessary time to look up the vocabulary in the Macmillan Online Dictionary.

WARMER

In pairs, students discuss the meaning of the unit title *Health watch* and what they think the unit is going to be about. Elicit ideas from different students.

> **Suggested answers**
>
> The unit is probably about health and medicine, and taking care of ourselves. The word *health* means how we feel in mind and body.

v Parts of the body

1a In pairs, ask students to look at the picture and point to the parts of the body. Check answers as a class.

1b Students match the words to numbers 1 to 16.

2 ▶ 21 Play the track for students to listen, check and repeat. See p152 for the audioscript for this exercise.

> **Answers**
>
> **1** forehead **2** cheek **3** chin **4** throat **5** back
> **6** wrist **7** thumb **8** neck **9** shoulder **10** chest
> **11** elbow **12** hip **13** thigh **14** knee **15** heel
> **16** ankle

TEACHER DEVELOPMENT: STUDENT TRAINING

Revision techniques

Drawings and notes are good memory triggers for when students return to a topic for revision purposes. Ask students to sketch a body in their notebooks and label the body parts, including pronunciation notes where applicable. Tell them to use this same page in their notebook to record other new vocabulary from the unit.

v Health problems and illnesses

3 In pairs, ask students to complete each phrase with three parts of the body. Elicit the meaning of *ache* (to feel a continuous, but not very strong, pain in part of your body) and compare this to an *injury*, e.g. breaking a bone (physical harm caused in an accident or an attack). Point out that we use *hurt* to describe pain somewhere in our body. Check answers with the class.

> **Answers**
>
> **1** arm, ankle, leg, finger, toe, wrist, neck
> **2** ear, (a) head, stomach, back **3** any part of the body
> **4** any part of the body

>>> **FAST FINISHERS**

Ask students to write a short dialogue between a parent and a teenager, with question 2 as the first line.

TEACHER DEVELOPMENT: PRONUNCIATION

Silent *k* and *ch* as *k* sound

Highlight the pronunciation of *stomach* /'stʌmək/ and the silent *k* in *knee*. Elicit other words with the silent *k*: *know*, *knock*, etc. Wordlist in the Student's Book, page 138.

4 Students complete the texts with the correct form of the words. They can use the Macmillan Essential Dictionary if necessary. Monitor while students are carrying out the task and make a note of common problems to feed back on.

> **Answers**
>
> **a** flu **b** coughs/is coughing **c** sore **d** temperature
> **e** pain **f** virus

TEACHER DEVELOPMENT: PRONUNCIATION

Sound/spelling relationships

Highlight the irregular pronunciation of *cough* /kɒf/ (rhymes with *off*) and *temperature* /'temprɪtʃə(r)/.

5 LISTENING ▶ 22 Play the track and ask students to decide what illness each of the four people has. Tell students to note down key words which help them decide on their answer as they listen. Check answers and elicit what question people ask if there is something wrong (*What's the matter?*). See p152 for the audioscript for this exercise.

> **Answers**
>
> **1** stomach ache **2** a (bad) cough **3** a headache
> **4** toothache

6 SPEAKING Students work with a partner and discuss the questions. Nominate a few students to summarise their partner's answers.

++ EXTRA ACTIVITY

Ask students if they think they are healthy at the moment, and what they think they could do to improve their health. Ask them to compare their ideas with a partner.

HOMEWORK

Assign students page 30 in their Workbook or the relevant sections of the Online Workbook.

Reading p45

Reading for gist and specific information

WARMER

Put students in two teams, and give each team a set of Post-it® notes. Draw an outline of two bodies, one on each side of the board. Each team has to stand in a line at the back of the class. The first person in each team has to write the name of a body part on a note and then run (or walk, depending on space) to the board and stick it in the right place then go back to his/her team, where the second person then has to start writing the next body part. Tell students they can't start writing until the person before them is back. Time two minutes and then award a point for each Post-it® note with a correctly-spelled body part in the correct place.

1 Students work in pairs. Ask them to look only at the titles and the photos and predict what the articles are about. Nominate a few pairs to give their ideas.

✔ EXAM SUCCESS Ask students to read the text and brainstorm good ways to do matching activities. Ask students to turn to page 144 (Reading: Matching activities) to compare their ideas.

2 Students match the articles to the sentences. Elicit the meaning for *insufficient* (not enough), if necessary. Allow students to compare their answers in pairs, before checking together as a class.

Answers

1 C **2** A **3** B **4** A **5** C **6** B **7** A **8** C

3 **⚙ CRITICAL THINKING** Ask students to work individually to think about the question and make notes. Then have a class discussion and encourage students to share their ideas.

Example answer

Because some people think it looks better to have a tan and shows you have been on holiday somewhere hot. Also, lots of popular celebrities have tanned skin.

4 Students guess the meaning of the underlined words in the text. Allow them to use a dictionary to check their answers.

Answers

increase = there will be more than usual, the number will grow

skin = this is the material or substance that covers our bodies

bandage = a long piece of cloth you wrap around an injured part of your body

tight = the opposite of *loose*, holding with pressure or strength

obsession = feeling very strongly that something is important and wanting it in a desperate way

remedy = a cure or solution that makes you better

get rid of = make go away or disappear

✚ EXTRA ACTIVITY

In pairs, ask students to choose 3–4 of the words from exercise 4 and write a short dialogue between a patient and a doctor including these words. Circulate and monitor to check that the new vocabulary is being used correctly. Ask a few pairs to perform their dialogues for the class.

5 **SPEAKING** What about *you*? Students look at the questions and think about their own answers. Then have them ask the questions to a partner. Hold a class discussion and encourage students to give their opinions. Ask students if they have ever used the RICE method or if they think any other traditional remedies work.

TEACHER DEVELOPMENT: CLASSROOM TIPS

Pyramid discussions

Give students plenty of time to think and prepare in pairs before you build an activity into a whole-class discussion. A technique called a pyramid discussion is often useful. First, ask students to write down their own ideas individually. Next, ask them to share these with a partner. Then, ask them to discuss their ideas with another pair in groups of four. This gives students plenty of practice and develops not only content, but also allows them to focus on how they express their ideas when participating in the whole-class discussion.

HOMEWORK

Assign students page 31 in their Workbook or the relevant sections of the Online Workbook.

Grammar in context pp46–47

Using the present perfect with ever, never, for, since

⟫⟫ FAST TRACK

If students are familiar with the vocabulary, you could ask them to complete exercise 1a at home and then check their answers at the start of the lesson.

WARMER

Play *Past participle bingo*. Write the infinitives on the board and elicit the past participles: *do – done; have – had; see – seen; catch – caught; be – been; meet – met; go – gone; take – taken; sleep – slept; know – known; wear – worn; break – broken; fall – fallen; ride – ridden; eat – eaten; find – found.*

Ask students to draw a three by two grid in their notebooks and write a past participle in each of the six squares. You then call out the infinitives in a random order and students cross out the corresponding past participles as they hear them. The first student to cross out all six past participles shouts *Bingo!*

Test before you teach: Flipped classroom

Set the Flipped classroom video and tasks for homework <u>before the lesson</u>. This will allow you to assess the needs of the students before the class. Students can then move on to the relevant grammar practice activities.

Present perfect with ever and never

1a Students look at the sentences and match them to the explanations of their uses in a–c.

Answers

1 a **2** c **3** b

1b Students read and complete the rule.

Answers

past participle

1c Students complete the sentences with the present perfect forms of *see* and *visit*. Nominate students to give their answers.

Answers

Affirmative: has seen/visited
Negative: hasn't seen/visited
Question: Has … seen/visited

1d Students look and choose the correct alternatives. Check answers in open class.

Answers

1 ever **2** never

1e Students look at the sentences and choose the correct alternatives.

Answers

1 Ever **2** Never **3** before

✚ EXTRA ACTIVITY

Ask students to write two more example sentences like those in exercise 1d in their notebooks.

2 Students complete the sentences with the present perfect form of the verbs. Draw their attention to the example. Remind students to check for irregular verbs.

Answers

2 has met **3** have studied **4** haven't had
5 Has, worked **6** has become

3 Students complete the sentences by adding *never* or *ever* in the correct place.

Answers

1 Have you ever had hot soup to stop a cold?
2 I've never felt sick in a car.
3 She's never taken antibiotics.
4 Has your dad ever helped anyone in an accident?
5 Sam and I have never written a story about doctors.
6 Have you ever done first aid?

TEACHER DEVELOPMENT: LANGUAGE

Contractions

Draw students' attention to the contracted verb forms in exercise 3: *'s* and *'ve*. Point out to students that *'s* is the contraction for both *has* and *is*. If necessary, drill the pronunciation of the weak form of 'have'. Remind students that we don't use contractions in short answers.

4 Students write questions using *ever* to ask their partner using the prompts. Draw students' attention to the example and do the first one together as a class. Nominate different students around the class to say their questions.

Answers

1 Have you ever stayed in bed because of flu?
2 Have you ever had a very high temperature?
3 Have you ever slept in a hospital?
4 Have you ever made soup?
5 Have you ever taken medicine that tastes really bad?
6 Have you ever visited a friend in hospital?
7 Have you ever broken your arm?
8 Have you ever watched a hospital drama on TV?

5a SPEAKING Ask the first question from exercise 4 to elicit the short answers *Yes, I have./No, I haven't*. Ask students to add one extra piece of information to their answers. Ask them to prepare their answers first as a writing activity before they ask and answer the questions in pairs.

5b SPEAKING Students swap partners and tell the new student about their previous partner. Draw attention to the model sentence and elicit model exchanges from open pairs across the classroom. Remind students that they should use *has/hasn't* in this activity.

Present perfect with *for* and *since*

6a Students look at the sentences and decide when we use *for* and *since*. Discuss the answer as a class. Remind students that *for* and *since* go just before the time expression.

Answers

a since   **b** for

for and *since*

We tend to use *since* when we want to be exact, e.g. *since December 2006*, and *for* when approximating time, e.g. *for ages, for a long time*. Highlight that the important thing for students to learn is that the present perfect is used with *for* and *since* to show how long a situation has continued until now.

6b Students look at the question and answer, and decide if we use *How long* to ask about frequency or duration. Discuss the answer as a class.

Answer

duration

7 Ask students to look at the time expressions and decide if they are used with *for* or *since* and put them in the correct column.

Answers

For: an hour, five years, ten seconds, three days
Since: 6 o'clock, 7th February, 2014, Friday, the age of five, the day I met you

>>> **FAST FINISHERS**

Have students create two columns in their notebooks headed *for* and *since*. Dictate additional time expressions, or elicit from students, for the whole class to categorise. Check students have written them under the correct column.

✚ EXTRA ACTIVITY

Dictate additional time expressions for students to categorise under *for* (e.g. *ever, a long time, three months, weeks*) or *since* (e.g. *January, I was 15, last year, we were kids*). Check students have written them under the correct column.

8 Students complete the sentences with information about themselves. Remind students to use the correct form of the present perfect and a time expression. Focus their attention on the example sentence. Monitor and help with any language difficulties.

Example answers

1 have known, three years
2 have lived, 2004
3 have had, nine months
4 have been, I was six
5 have lived, two months

9a Individually, students guess their partner's answers in exercise 8 and write them in their notebooks.

9b SPEAKING In pairs, students ask and answer questions with *How long* to find out if their guesses were correct. Ask a pair to read out the model dialogue before they begin.

Refer students to the Grammar reference on page 54 if necessary.

HOMEWORK

Assign students page 32 in their Workbook or the relevant sections of the Online Workbook.

Developing vocabulary p47

Using compound nouns connected with health and medicine

>>> **FAST TRACK**

You could do exercise 1 as a class activity. First, write the words from column A and column B on the board, and invite individual students to come up and join them to make a compound noun. Then, for the second part of the exercise, read a definition aloud and invite the rest of the class to call out the correct answer.

1 Tell students that we make compound nouns by joining two nouns or an adjective and a noun. Draw their attention to the example then ask them to join the words to make compound nouns. They then match the compound nouns to the definitions. Have dictionaries available.

2 ▶ 23 Play the track for students to check their answers. See p152 for the audioscript for this exercise.

Answers

2 heart attack (e)
3 health centre (d)
4 waiting room (a)
5 food poisoning (f)
6 first aid (c)

3a PRONUNCIATION ▶ 24 Play the track for students to listen to the pronunciation of the compound nouns and decide if the stress is on the first or second word. Elicit answers from different students. See p152 for the audioscript for this exercise.

Answers

In nouns 1–5 (noun + noun), the first word is stressed, e.g. painkiller, heart attack. In noun 6 (adjective + noun), the second word (the noun) is stressed, e.g. first aid.

3b Drill the words with the correct stress. Then ask students to practise saying the words in pairs.

4 Students complete the sentences with the compound nouns in exercise 1.

Answers

1 health centre   **2** waiting room   **3** food poisoning
4 heart attack   **5** first aid   **6** painkiller

Gateway to life skills pp48–49

Learning some basics of first aid

To think about why first aid is important, to learn when and how to put somebody in the recovery position and to check understanding of the basics of first aid.

ⓘ BACKGROUND INFORMATION

According to St John's Ambulance (a well-known, UK-based first aid charity), tens of thousands of lives could be saved every year with some basic knowledge of first aid. A survey, conducted by the charity showed that nearly two-thirds of people wouldn't feel confident enough to administer first aid and almost a quarter would not do anything in a situation and wait for an ambulance to arrive. These statistics show the need for everyone, including the younger generation, to appreciate the importance of first aid and to make the effort to learn practical skills.

The ability to be calm and give first aid in both minor and severe cases makes a person a useful and valuable member of the community.

This lessons looks in particular at prevention of accidents in the home.

1a Focus students' attention on the picture. Pre-teach any vocabulary they may need and then ask students to work in pairs and find the dangers in the scene. Ask different pairs to give their answers.

Answers

broken plate, hot water, wet floor, sharp knife balanced near the edge of the table top

1b Students imagine they are alone and they find someone in the situation in exercise 1a. Ask them to make a list of things they need to do. Allow them to compare lists with a partner, before nominating students to give their ideas.

Answers

1 Switch off the cooker. **2** Move the saucepan of hot water. **3** Carefully move the knife. **4** Clean the water from the floor. **5** Look after the boy. **6** Call the emergency services.

2 READING Students read the text and answer the questions. Check answers as a class.

Answers

1 Because it helps you to help somebody.
2 Students' own answers

3 Check students understand the words in the box and drill pronunciation. Then ask students to complete the gaps with the words. Nominate different students to give their answers. It's worth reminding students that we should only move a person into the recovery position if it's certain there's no spinal injury.

Answers

1 dangers **2** 999 **3** conscious **4** breathing
5 airway **6** recovery **7** ambulance

4 SPEAKING Put students in pairs and ask them to choose whether they are A or B and then to act out the situation. Circulate while students are acting out the role-play, then nominate a few pairs to perform theirs for the rest of the class.

5 Draw students' attention to the pictures and ask them if they know the name for what the first-aider is doing (putting a person in the recovery position). Ask students to work with a partner to put the pictures in the right order. Don't check the answers yet.

6 Students read though the descriptions and match them to the pictures and steps. Explain the meanings of *right angle* and *flat* if necessary. Nominate a few students to give their answers, but don't confirm them at this point.

7 25 Tell students they are going to listen or watch a video showing how to put someone in the recovery position. Play the video or track and ask students whether their answers to exercises 5 and 6 were correct. See p152 for the videoscript/audioscript for this exercise.

Answers

Exercise 5
2 e **3** c **4** a **5** b

Exercise 6
1 a **2** b **3** d **4** e **5** c

8 Students answer the two questions. Play the video again if necessary.

Answers

1 No, it isn't.
2 Before putting them in the recovery position.

LIFE TASK

Tell students they are going to prepare a quiz to test other students' knowledge of putting a person in the recovery position.

- **Step 1**
  Divide the class into pairs and ask students to read the instructions. Students start by looking again at the information on pages 48 and 49.

- **Step 2**
  Students prepare their quizzes with their partner using the different question types. Give them a time limit and circulate to help with any necessary vocabulary or structures. For less confident students you could give an example of each question type.

- **Step 3**
  Ask students to swap their quiz with another pair. When they have finished completing the quizzes, students discuss and feed back on answers.

✚ EXTRA ACTIVITY

Ask students to work in pairs and research another first aid process (e.g. what to do if somebody is burnt or if someone has broken their arm). Ask them to produce a step-by-step guide for a person performing first aid including illustrations, similar to the instructions in exercises 5 and 6.

Listening p50

Listening for specific and general information

WARMER

Play a quick game of *Snowman* (see Warmer on page 40) with the words 'James Bond'. Then ask students if they like James Bond films and if they can name any of the actors who have played James Bond (Sean Connery, Timothy Dalton, Roger Moore, George Lazenby, Pierce Brosnan and Daniel Craig). Elicit that James Bond films are action films and tell students that these types of films often contain something called *stunts*, and ask if they know what this is (something dangerous, for example jumping from a building, that is done to entertain people, often as part of a film). Tell students they are going to learn about actors doing stunts and action scenes in the lesson.

1 SPEAKING In pairs, ask students to look at the photo(s) and answer the questions. Elicit answers from different students. Try to elicit vocabulary that will come up in the listening.

2 LISTENING ▶ 26 Play the track for students to listen to the interview and make a note of which two actors are mentioned and why. See pp152–153 for the audioscript for this exercise.

Answers

Jackie Chan and Daniel Craig because they do their own stunts.

3 ▶ 26 Play the track again for students to decide if the sentences are true or false. Tell students to read the sentences before you play the listening. Elicit the answers and ask students to correct the false sentences.

Answers

1 T **2** F (He has injured himself making lots of films.)
3 T **4** F (He hit his head on a rock.) **5** T
6 F (He does some of the stunts.)
7 F (He has broken a finger.) **8** T

4 SPEAKING **What about *you*?** Students look at the questions and think about their own answers. Ask students to share their opinions with the class.

HOMEWORK

Assign students page 33 in their Workbook or the relevant sections of the Online Workbook.

Grammar in context pp50–51

Using the present perfect with just, yet, already and comparing it to the past simple

⟫⟫ FAST TRACK

You could ask students to answer the questions in exercises 3a and 3b at home. They can then use these to interview their partner at the next lesson.

WARMER

Individually, students write three sentences in the present perfect about things that they have done (two should be true and one false), e.g. *I have ridden an elephant.* In pairs, they read each other's sentences and ask questions to guess which sentence is false, e.g. *When did you ride an elephant? What was the elephant's name?* They can lie in their answers to questions about the false sentence. Monitor to check that they are using the present perfect correctly and resolve any issues before you start the lesson.

Test before you teach

Ask students to look at their timetable for this week and write sentences using *just, yet* and *already*, e.g. *I have just had a science class. I haven't done any sports yet this week. I have already done my English homework.* If students seem confident with these structures, move through the exercises in the Grammar guide quickly as a class.

Present perfect with just, yet, already

1a Students look at the sentences and complete rules 1–3 with *just, yet* or *already*.

Answers

1 just **2** yet **3** already

1b Students choose the correct alternative in each sentence.

Answers

1 negative **2** before

TEACHER DEVELOPMENT: LANGUAGE

yet and *already*

Yet and *already* may not be easy concepts for students to understand as they may use the same word in L1. You could explain that they are words which add emphasis. There is not much difference between *I haven't done it* and *I haven't done it yet*, but yet emphasises the idea that you are going to do it in the future.

✚ EXTRA ACTIVITY

Tell students that these are the Martin family's plans for their holiday to Spain and write them on the board:
Monday am: Seville; Monday pm: travel to Córdoba;
Tuesday: Córdoba; Wednesday am: Arrive in Granada;
Thursday: Madrid; Friday am: Fly to Barcelona
Now tell students it's midday on Wednesday. Ask if these sentences are true or false:
The Martin family have already been to Barcelona. (False)
The Martin family have not been to Madrid yet. (True)
The Martin family have just arrived in Granada. (True)

2 Students write at least one sentence to describe what has just happened in each photo. Refer students to the example sentences in exercise 1.

Suggested answers

1 He's just hurt himself. He's just had an accident. He's just fallen off his skateboard.
2 She's just run a race. She's just done some exercise.
3 He's just won the lottery. He's just become rich. He's just become a millionaire.
4 He's just broken his racket. He's just lost the match.

3a Students write six sentences about themselves, using *already, yet* and *just*. With less confident students, you may like to brainstorm a few ideas together as a class and write the key words on the board. Direct attention to the example sentence before they begin.

3b Students change their sentences into questions and write them in their notebook. Draw attention to the example question. Nominate a few students to read out their first question to check they are forming questions properly.

3c SPEAKING Students interview their partner with their questions.

✚ EXTRA ACTIVITY

Draw a three by three grid on the board and divide the class into two teams: X and O. Write *for, since, ever, never, yet, just, already* and *How long* (x 2) in the squares. The teams take turns to choose a square and make a sentence/question in the present perfect using the word in the square. If the sentence is correct, they can put their symbol in the square (X or O). For a more confident class you could give them an irregular verb which they need to use. When they win three squares in a horizontal, diagonal or vertical row, they win the game.

Present perfect and past simple

Test before you teach
Put these two sentences on the board and elicit the difference between them: *Charles Dickens wrote some good books.* (He is dead, so he no longer writes books.) *J.K. Rowling has written some good books.* (She's still alive, so she could write more books in the future.) If students seem comfortable with the difference, you may wish to go through the Grammar guide exercise quickly as a whole class.

4   Students look at the dialogue and answer questions 1–4.

Answers
1 present perfect   **2** general experience   **3** past simple
4 a specific moment in the past

✚ EXTRA ACTIVITY
Write another mini-dialogue on the board and go through questions 1–4 in the Grammar guide a second time.
A: *Have you seen the new Hunger Games film?*
B: *Yes, I've seen it.*
A: *Oh, when did you see it?*
B: *I saw it on a plane.*

TEACHER DEVELOPMENT: LANGUAGE

Past simple vs present perfect
The past simple is used to talk about actions in the past that have finished. It talks about then and excludes now. The present perfect is used to look back on actions in the past with a link to the present. It always includes now. The present perfect is often used to talk about someone's experiences or about something in the past which is relevant to the immediate present.

5   Students complete the dialogue by putting the verbs in the correct form of the present perfect or past simple.

Answers
a Have, broken   **b** have   **c** went   **d** broke
e have, broken   **f** have had   **g** have crashed
h Did, fall   **i** didn't   **j** fell

6   SPEAKING In pairs, students ask each other if they have ever done the things in the pictures and then ask follow-up questions in the past simple to find out more details. Write the six question words on the board (*what*, *why*, *when*, *how*, *where* and *who*) to help them. Ask a pair of students to read out the model dialogue as an example. Ask different pairs to tell the class about one experience.

Answers
a Have you ever broken your arm?   **b** Have you ever ridden a motorbike?   **c** Have you ever met a famous person?   **d** Have you ever visited the UK?   **e** Have you ever swum in the sea?   **f** Have you ever been in a race?

Suggested follow-up questions
Have you ever broken your arm? Yes, I have. How did it happen? Have you ever met a famous person? Yes, I have. Who did you meet? Have you ever visited the UK? Yes, I have. When did you go?

Refer students to the Grammar reference on page 54 if necessary.

HOMEWORK
Assign students page 34 in their Workbook or the relevant sections of the Online Workbook.

Developing speaking p52

Describing photos

⟫⟫ FAST TRACK
You could ask students to complete exercise 5 at home. They can then present their descriptions to the class at the next lesson.

1   SPEAKING In pairs, students look at the scenes in the photos and decide what the connection is between them. Elicit answers from different pairs.

Suggested answer
The connection is people being ill or injured and how to help them.

2a LISTENING ▶ 27 Play the track for students to listen and decide which photo the girl is describing. See p153 for the audioscript for this exercise.

Answers
Photo b

2b ▶ 27 Students listen to the track again and tick the questions the girl answers. Nominate students to give their answers.

Answers
1, 2, 3, 4 (only man), 5, 6 and 9.

3   SPEAKING In pairs, ask students to compare their answers and try to remember what information the boy gives. They then practise describing the same photo.

4 ▶ 27 Students read about fillers. Play the track again for students to listen again and tick the fillers in the Speaking bank that the boy uses.

Answers
Errr …   Well …   The thing is … I'm not really sure but …   Maybe …   I think …   I imagine that …

TEACHER DEVELOPMENT: STUDENT TRAINING

Using conversation fillers

Fillers perform important linguistic functions: they help you maintain control of the conversation, rather than leaving a pause where someone else could start talking; they give you extra time to decide what to say next; they can soften or weaken what you're saying (*I'm, you know, kind of worried about him.*); or they can emphasise or strengthen a point (*I'm really worried about him, you know?*).

PRACTICE MAKES PERFECT

5 SPEAKING Students read the task and make notes. In pairs, students take it in turns to describe photo a or b using the questions in exercise 2b and the words and expressions from the Speaking bank.

✚ EXTRA ACTIVITY

In pairs, students write the conversation fillers from the Speaking bank on small pieces of paper. They then divide the pieces of paper between them. Each student must tell their partner a story about an accident they had (it can be true or invented) and use their conversation fillers as quickly as possible. The other student times their partner. The student who is the quickest to use all their conversation fillers wins the game.

HOMEWORK

Assign students page 35 in their Workbook or the relevant sections of the Online Workbook.

Developing writing p53

Writing notes and messages

⟫⟫ FAST TRACK

You could ask students to write the message in exercise 4a at home. They can then write the reply to their partner at the next lesson.

WARMER

In pairs, ask students to think of abbreviations they know in English and their meanings. Write some abbreviations that students may be familiar with on the board to start the activity: OK – alright; 'cause/'cos – because; min. – minimum; max. – maximum; esp. – especially.

1 Students read the three notes and messages and write two sentences to explain the situation in each one. Elicit sentences from students and together try to create three 'perfect' brief summaries to explain the notes and messages.

2 Students look at the notes and messages in exercise 1 again and complete the information in the Writing bank.

Answers

asap; sorry to hear that; Get well soon!

---

3 Students match the abbreviations to their meanings. If students are interested in terms and abbreviations used in text messages for mobile phone calls and emails, you could direct students to a useful website such as the Macmillan Online Dictionary.

Answers

2 e.g. = for example   **3** NB = please pay special attention   **4** asap = as soon as possible
5 i.e. = that is, this is exactly what I mean
6 etc. = and other things of the same type

PRACTICE MAKES PERFECT

4a Students look at the task and leave a message for a friend. Remind them to use expressions from the Writing bank and the abbreviations in exercise 3. For students who are less confident, photocopy the model text below for extra support during the writing task.

4b In pairs, students swap messages and write a reply to their partner's message.

Model text

(Note)

Joe

I've just been to your house 'cos you disappeared, but your mum says you've just gone to the doctor. How are you? What have you done in the last two days? You haven't missed much at school. We've learnt about the present perfect in English etc., and we've finished the science project . Jane's had a sore throat and has also been at home and Sammy hasn't come to football practice this week 'cause he hurt his ankle.

Get well soon!

Mike

PS Don't worry, I've taken notes for you in class!

(Answer)

Thanks, Mike. I've broken my toe and I can't walk. I think I can go to school next week. Thanks for taking notes and coming round.

See you soon! Joe

TEACHER DEVELOPMENT: CLASSROOM TIPS

How to teach text register

Students need to know how to write formal and informal texts for examinations. You could discuss when formal/informal register is appropriate, e.g. formal: a letter asking for information, an accompanying letter to a CV; informal: notes and messages, an email to a friend. Elicit a list of common features in formal and informal texts.

Formal: Latin-based words, uncommon words, full words, passive constructions, noun phrases, complex sentences

Informal: Anglo-Saxon words, phrasal verbs, common words, abbreviations, contractions, active constructions, verb phrases, simple sentences

✓ **EXAM SUCCESS** Students look at the instructions for the writing task in exercise 4 and decide if they can write in whatever style they like and if the style of the text is important. Tell them to turn to page 144 (Writing: Content and style) to compare their answers.

HOMEWORK

Assign students page 36 in their Workbook or the relevant sections of the Online Workbook.

Language checkpoint: Unit 4

>>> **FAST TRACK**

The extra support provided on the Grammar and Vocabulary reference sections makes the Grammar and Vocabulary revision section ideal for setting as homework. You could get students to complete the whole revision page or just certain exercises for homework.

Grammar revision p55

Present perfect (ever, never, for, since)

1 Students look at the sentences and choose the correct alternatives.

Answers

1 taken **2** Have **3** since **4** ever eaten **5** never **6** for **7** long

Present perfect (already, yet, just)

2 Students look at the list of Lily's jobs and write sentences with *already*, *yet* and *just*.

Answers

1 She's just washed the dishes.
2 She's already bought the bread.
3 She hasn't taken the rubbish out yet.
4 She hasn't rung her mum at work yet.
5 She's just made the beds.
6 She's already made something for dinner.

Present perfect and past simple

3 Students decide if the sentences are grammatically correct and rewrite the incorrect sentences.

Answers

1 x Danny went to Bulgaria last year.
2 x Did you see the Eiffel Tower when you were in Paris?
3 x Has your sister ever ridden a horse?
4 [correct]
5 x My brother's 18. He's been to the US three times.
6 [correct]

Vocabulary revision p55

PARTS OF THE BODY

1 Students label the parts of the body.

Answers

1 cheek **2** chin **3** throat **4** shoulder **5** elbow **6** thumb **7** wrist

HEALTH PROBLEMS AND ILLNESSES

2 Students look at the pictures and identify the health problems.

Answers

1 temperature **2** broken **3** sore **4** virus

COMPOUND NOUNS CONNECTED WITH HEALTH AND MEDICINE

3 Students complete the compound nouns with the correct words.

Answers

1 waiting **2** aid **3** poisoning **4** pain **5** health **6** attack

HOMEWORK

Assign students page 37 in their Workbook or the relevant sections of the Online Workbook.

Reading p56

> ➤ **TIP FOR READING EXAMS**
>
> Ask students to read the tip and then look at Exam Success on page 144 for more ideas.

1 **SPEAKING** In pairs, ask students to answer the questions. Elicit possible answers from different students.

2 Ask students to read the newspaper articles and match them to the questions in exercise 1. Check answers as a class.

Answers

1 B **2** C **3** A

3 Students read the text again and match the descriptions 1–9 to the texts A–C. Remind students to use the reading strategy from the Tip for Reading Exams.

Answers

1 A **2** C **3** B **4** A **5** C **6** C **7** B **8** A **9** B

4 **SPEAKING** What about *you*? Students read the question and think of their own answers. Then ask them to discuss their thoughts in pairs or small groups.

Use of English p57

> ➤ **TIP FOR USE OF ENGLISH**
>
> Ask students to read the tip about multiple-choice cloze activities and to look at Exam Success on page 144 for more ideas.

5 Students complete the text by choosing the correct option: A, B, C or D to fill each gap. Check answers as a class.

Answers

1 A **2** C **3** D **4** A **5** B **6** D **7** A

Speaking p57

> ➤ **TIP FOR SPEAKING EXAMS**
>
> Ask students to read the tip for speaking exams and to look at Exam Success on page 144.

6 **SPEAKING** Put students in pairs. Ask one of them to be Student A and turn to page 147 and the other to be Student B and turn to page 148 and describe their photos using the questions given.

Writing p57

> ➤ **TIP FOR WRITING EXAMS**
>
> Ask students to read the tip and then to look at Exam Success on page 144 for more ideas.

7 Students read the task instructions and write a message to Joe. For students who are less confident, photocopy the model text below for extra support during the writing task.

> **Model text**
>
> Joe,
> I'm not at home 'cos I've gone to the chemist's to buy some medicine for Lily. She isn't well. I haven't got my mobile so ring me at Lily's when you get back – her address is 17 Duniston Drive & her no. is 617 565555. Anyway, hope you're OK. See you later!
> Ethan

> **HOMEWORK**
>
> Assign students pages 38–39 in their Workbook or the relevant sections of the Online Workbook.

'CAN DO' PROGRESS CHECK p57

1 Ask students to mark from 1–4 how well they can do each thing in English.

2 Ask students to look at their marks and decide which of the things they can do to improve. Elicit other suggestions on how they can improve their work.

5 TV addicts

KEY LEARNING OUTCOMES

Students will be able to:

- understand texts about TV and fame
- talk about TV using comparative and superlative adjectives
- ask and give opinions about film and TV
- talk about fame and negotiate plans
- write a review of a film or TV programme

UNIT OVERVIEW

Vocabulary	Television Adjectives describing TV programmes PRONUNCIATION Word stress
Reading	Slow TV CRITICAL THINKING Giving opinions about whether reality shows show the real world
Grammar in context	Comparative and superlatives PRONUNCIATION Sentence stress and weak forms
Developing vocabulary	Adjectives ending in -ing and -ed
Life skills	Personal well-being: Thinking about fame
Listening	TV today
Grammar in context	less … than, (not) as … as too and (not) enough
Developing speaking	Negotiating
Developing writing	A review
Exam success	Listening: Identifying the speaker activities Speaking: Negotiating

DIGITAL OVERVIEW

Presentation Kit

- ▶ **Flipped classroom video Unit 5:** Comparatives and superlatives
- ▶ **Life skills video Unit 5:** Would you like to be famous?
- ▶ **⟨v⟩ Vocabulary tool:** Television
- ▶ **Interactive versions of Student's Book activities**
- ▶ **Integrated audio and answer key for all activities**
- ▶ **Workbook pages with answer key**

Teacher's Resource Centre

- ▶ **Flipped classroom video Unit 5:** Comparatives and superlatives
- ▶ **Life skills video Unit 5:** Would you like to be famous?
- ▶ **Grammar communication activity Unit 5:** Just ten questions
- ▶ **Worksheets for this unit, including:**
  - Grammar practice worksheet Unit 5
  - Flipped classroom video worksheet Unit 5: Comparatives and superlatives
  - Literature worksheet Units 5 and 6
  - Culture worksheet Unit 5
  - Life skills video worksheet Unit 5
  - Everyday English worksheet Unit 5

Student's App

Gateway 2nd Edition wordlist for the award-winning Sounds App (available for download)

✓ TESTING AND ASSESSMENT

Resources for exam preparation and measuring student progress

- ▶ Test Generator Units 1–5
- ▶ Printable test Unit 5
- ▶ Gateway to exams Units 5 and 6 (end of Unit 6)

Vocabulary p58

Talking about television and TV programmes

>>> FAST TRACK

You could do exercise 5 as a class activity, by inviting individual students to read an adjective and the rest of the class to call out the correct name. Some words, such as *scary*, could be seen as both positive and negative. You might like to take a poll, asking students to raise their hands to see which is the most popular choice.

WARMER

Write this short text on the board:
Most teenagers in the UK have one of these in their bedroom. Some people really want to appear on it. Doctors say it can cause health problems. Some people think it is a bad influence on young people. What is it?
Ask students to read and guess what the object is (TV). Elicit some vocabulary associated with watching TV, including the following words which come up in this lesson: *switch on/off, turn on/off, channel, programme, series, remote control, live* (as adjective).

[v] Television

1 In pairs, students match the photos to the words in the box. You could elicit definitions of new words before they begin: *chat show* – a programme where people talk about themselves and their work; *reality show* – a programme, often a competition, involving ordinary people and real events; *documentary* – a programme that shows real people and events, often to highlight serious issues; *drama* – a play for TV; *game show* – a programme in which people play games or answer questions in order to win prizes; *the news* – a programme that gives you information about important recent events.

You could also share the following information about the vocabulary with students:
The news looks like a plural, but it is never used with a plural verb and cannot be used with *a*. We often say *on the news*, e.g. *What's on the news tonight?*
In British English we write *programme*, but in US English the spelling is *program*.
Advert (*commercial* in the US) is the short form of *advertisement* and *ad* is also a common abbreviated form.

Answers

a sports programme   **b** cookery programme
c documentary   **d** chat show   **e** drama/film/soap
f the news

2 Students think of one or two examples for each programme in exercise 1. Allow them to compare answers with a partner and then elicit some ideas from the class.

3a **PRONUNCIATION** Students mark the stressed syllable on the words in exercise 1. Draw their attention to the example.

Answers

advert, car<u>too</u>n, <u>chat</u> show, <u>com</u>edy, <u>cook</u>ery <u>pro</u>gramme, docu<u>men</u>tary, <u>dra</u>ma, film, <u>game</u> show, re<u>al</u>ity show, <u>soap</u>, <u>sports</u> programme, the <u>news</u>

>>> FAST FINISHERS

Ask students to find and mark the schwa (/ə/) sound in the words.

3b ▶ 28 Play the track and ask students to listen, check and repeat the words. See p153 for the audioscript for this exercise.

++ EXTRA ACTIVITY

Ask students to think of their favourite type of programme and their least favourite. Ask them to predict which types will be the most and least popular in the class, before asking for students to vote by raising their hand as you read out each programme type. Write the results on the board, and discuss with students if they're as they expected or not.

4 **SPEAKING** Students look at the words in bold in the sentences and check they understand them. Remind them of strategies they have learnt before for guessing unknown vocabulary. Elicit the meanings and write them on the board: *live* – happening now, not pre-recorded; *series* – a set of television or radio programmes that are all about a particular subject, person, or group of people; *channel* – a television station and the programmes that it broadcasts; *presenter* - the person who introduces a television or radio programme; *turn on* – to make a piece of equipment start working by pressing a button or moving a switch; *switch off* – if you switch off something such as a light or a machine, it stops working; *remote control* – a piece of equipment that you use for controlling a machine, such as a television or stereo system, from a short distance away. Then ask students to use the questions to interview their partner. Nominate students to give their partner's answers.

TEACHER DEVELOPMENT: LANGUAGE

Separable phrasal verbs

Turn (something) *on/off* and *switch* (something) *on/off* are synonyms. Both are examples of separable phrasal verbs, i.e. we can put another word between the two parts of the verb. Remind students of the rules:

- If we use a noun, we can construct a sentence in two different ways: *James turns on the TV./James turns the TV on.*
- If we use a pronoun, we can only construct a sentence in one way: *James turns it off.*

Adjectives describing TV programmes

5 Students look at the adjectives and decide whether they have a positive or negative meaning. Let students know that there isn't necessarily always a right or wrong answer here, and to decide for themselves. Nominate students to give their answers.

Answers

awful (–) boring (–) cool (+) exciting (+) funny (+)
informative (+) interesting (+) moving (+) popular (+)
scary (+/–)

6 Students match some of the words in exercise 5 to
the explanations. Draw their attention to the example.
Nominate students to give their answers.

Answers

2 scary **3** awful **4** popular **5** funny **6** moving

>>> FAST FINISHERS

Ask students to think of definitions for the remaining
words in exercise 5. Then ask them to see if a partner
can guess the words.

TEACHER DEVELOPMENT: PRONUNCIATION

Vowel sounds

Elicit the pronunciation of *moving* /ˈmuːvɪŋ/ and remind
students how to pronounce *awful* /ˈɔːf(ə)l/ (they saw this
word in Unit 2). Draw attention to the vowel sound /ʌ/
in *funny* and elicit the stress pattern in *interesting* and
informative.

7 **LISTENING** ▶ 29 Play the track for students to listen to the
five people talking about TV programmes. Tell students
to decide what type of programme each person is
talking about. Ask students to note down key words that
helped them decide on their answer as they listen (for
suggestions, see underlined words in the audioscript).
They can add these words to their vocabulary record,
e.g. *episode, characters, presenter, contestant*. In less
confident classes, you could pause the track after each
speaker for students to check their answer in pairs and
then discuss as a class. See p153 for the audioscript for
this exercise.

Answers

1 documentary **2** cartoon **3** sports programme
4 chat show **5** game show

8a Individually, students think of things or people for each
adjective in exercise 5 and write them down in their
notebooks. Draw their attention to the example.

8b **SPEAKING** Students work with a partner and compare their
ideas. Ask a pair to read the model dialogue first.

✚ EXTRA ACTIVITY

Try to develop a class discussion about TV
programmes. Write the ten adjectives from exercise 5
on the board and ask students to share their opinions
from exercise 8, e.g. *I think Big Brother is awful.*
Write the students' suggested programmes for each
adjective on the board and then vote to find which
programme the class thinks is most suited to each
adjective.

HOMEWORK

Assign students page 40 in their Workbook or the
relevant sections of the Online Workbook.

Reading p59

Reading for gist and specific information

>>> FAST TRACK

You could ask students to do exercise 6 at home so
that less confident students can take the necessary
time to look up the vocabulary in the Macmillan Online
Dictionary.

WARMER

Without opening their Student's Book, ask students
to write down as many of the adjectives to describe
TV programmes as they can remember in one minute.
Allow them to compare their lists with partners,
then elicit the words to write up on the board. Ask
students to come up with a sentence using each
word, to check they remember the meanings (e.g.
*The comedy made me laugh as it was very funny; I
learnt lots when I watched the documentary about
dolphins; it was very informative*, etc.).
Ask students which three things are most important
to them when they choose what to watch on TV. Elicit
some ideas.

1a Students work in pairs and look at the TV screens. Ask
them to say which programme they would prefer to
watch and why. Remind them to use the adjectives they
revised in the Warmer. Nominate students to give their
answers.

Suggested answers

I would prefer to watch the music programme because
it's popular and sometimes it's funny. I love music, too.
The programme about the train is boring.
I would prefer to watch the programme about the train
because it's informative.

1b Students guess what Slow TV is. Nominate students to
give their ideas, but don't confirm answers yet.

2 Students read the text and check their predictions in
exercise 1b. Set a strict time limit of three minutes to
encourage students to read quickly. Remind them not to
read every word.

ℹ CULTURAL INFORMATION

Slow TV is a genre of television that shows an ordinary
(and sometimes typically mundane) event in its
entirety. The programmes are often longer than usual
programmes, and the pace is often slower than the
majority of programmes.
The concept is said to have originated with Andy Warhol's
movie *Sleep* in 1963, but the genre has been revitalised
by the Norwegian Broadcasting Corporation in recent
years. Slow TV programmes have included a 12-hour
programme on a log burning and a 7-hour broadcast on
knitting. People put the genre's success in Norway down
to its almost hypnotic appeal with its slow pace being an
antidote to the speed of more usual programmes.

3 Students read the text again and choose the best answers. Nominate students to give their answers.

Answers

1 b **2** c **3** a **4** b **5** a

✚ EXTRA ACTIVITY

Ask students to cover the text and write the following numbers on the board: 2009, 20%, 11, 1963.

Ask students to work in pairs and see if they can remember what the numbers referred to in the text. If they are finding it difficult, give them some extra clues.

Answers

In 2009 the programme about the railway was on TV; 20% of Norwegians watched the programme; 11 cameras filmed the coast of Norway; Andy Warhol made the film *Sleep* in 1963.

4 Students answer the questions. Allow students to discuss their answers in pairs, before nominating pairs to give their answers.

Answers

1 Because it was the 100th anniversary of the train route. **2** Slow TV is more relaxing than modern programmes. It makes people feel in contact with nature. **3** *Sleep* showed a man sleeping for six hours. It was also Slow TV.

5 **⚙ CRITICAL THINKING** Students think of their own ideas about the statement. Then have a class discussion. Ensure that all students are given an opportunity to contribute.

Example answers

I agree because the people who go on reality shows sometimes just want to be famous. Sometimes they just have young people or loud people so it's not really like real life. I disagree because some people on reality TV forget there's a camera there so they act as they do in real life. Reality TV shows show all parts of life now: airports, hotels, shops, so you can see how things really are.

TEACHER DEVELOPMENT: CLASSROOM TIPS

Promoting debate

Make a statement that students can either agree or disagree with, e.g. *TV is a bad thing*. Ask students who agree to go to one side of the room and students who disagree to go to the other side. Students form small groups with people who share their opinion and prepare a list of arguments to support their view. Then ask one group to start the debate by explaining their point of view to the class. Encourage students from the other debating side to ask questions and say why they disagree, and students from the same side to provide additional arguments.

6 Students look at the underlined words in the text and guess their meaning. Then allow them to check in their dictionaries.

Answers

railway = metal track that trains travel on

cheap = not expensive

ended up = found yourself in a situation

wool = thick hair that grows on sheep

burning = on fire

stressful = causing a lot of worry

editing = make changes or corrections to a programme

7 **SPEAKING** **What about *you*?** Students think about their answers to the questions, then to discuss with a partner.

✚ EXTRA ACTIVITY

You could conduct a class survey at the end of this speaking activity to find out how many hours students spend in front of the TV on weekdays and at the weekends. You could extend the survey to cover what types of programme the students watch the most. Then ask students to put together an infograph to represent the data.

HOMEWORK

Assign students page 41 in their Workbook or the relevant sections of the Online Workbook.

Grammar in context pp60–61

Using comparatives and superlatives

⟩⟩⟩ FAST TRACK

If students are familiar with the vocabulary, you could ask them to complete exercise 1a at home and then check their answers at the start of the lesson.

WARMER

Ask students to work in small groups and race to see if they can think of an adjective for every letter of the alphabet (except x and z). Set a time limit of four minutes. The group with the most correct adjectives wins the game. Ask students if they know the comparative/superlative forms of any of the adjectives.

Suggested answers

awful, boring, clever, dull, exciting, funny, green, happy, interesting, jealous, kind, loud, mean, nice, open, popular, quiet, real, scary, tall, unusual, violent, wet, young

Test before you teach: Flipped classroom

Set the Flipped classroom video and tasks for homework <u>before the lesson</u>. This will allow you to assess the needs of the students before the class. Students can then move on to the relevant grammar practice activities.

1a Students look at the comparative and superlative form of the adjectives and match the adjectives to the rules.

Answers

a 4 **b** 2 **c** 3 **d** 1 **e** 5

1b Students use the rules in exercise 1a to write the comparative and superlative forms of the adjectives. Allow students to compare their answers before nominating students to give their answers.

Answers

1 crazier, the craziest **2** worse, the worst
3 more boring, the most boring **4** shorter, the shortest
5 sadder, the saddest

>>> **FAST FINISHERS**

Ask students to choose three superlatives and three comparatives from exercise 1b and write six sentences.

1c Students look at the sentences and complete them with the correct words. Elicit the correct answers from students.

Answers

1 than **2** in

2a **PRONUNCIATION** ▶ 30 Students look at the sentences and notice two different colours. Ask them to read the questions and see if they can guess the answers after reading the sentences aloud to themselves. Then play the track for them to check. See p153 for the audioscript for this exercise.

Answers

1 red **2** content words, i.e. nouns, main verbs, adverbs and adjectives **3** function words, i.e. auxiliary verbs, prepositions, articles, etc.

2b ▶ 30 Ask students to listen again and repeat the sentences. Play the track.

TEACHER DEVELOPMENT: PRONUNCIATION

Sentence stress and weak forms

Sentence stress is when the accent is on certain words within a sentence. Most sentences have two types of word: content words and function words.

Content words are the key words of a sentence. They are the important words that carry the meaning or sense and they are usually stressed.

Function words are not very important words. They are small, simple words that make the sentence correct grammatically. If you remove the function words from a sentence, you will probably still understand the meaning.

Words that are usually unstressed are: *a, am, an, and, are, as, at, be, been, but, can, could, do, does, for, from, had, has, have, he, her, him, his, just, me, must, of, shall, she, should, some, than, that, the, them, there, to, us, was, we, were, who, would, you.*

A technique that helps students recognise the importance of word stress is to listen to a sentence and count the number of words. This, along with sentence dictations, can help raise awareness of weak forms.

✛ EXTRA ACTIVITY

Write these sentences up on the board and elicit the weak forms:

I went to my friend's house for the evening. We watched a film and then a game show. The film was more interesting.

Then ask a student to come to the front and find and circle all the schwa /ə/ sounds (*to, for, the, a, and, a, was*). Point out that most of the unstressed words are pronounced with the schwa sound.

TEACHER DEVELOPMENT: LANGUAGE

Comparatives and superlatives

We use the comparative and superlative forms to compare and contrast different objects. Tell students that, in spoken English, people don't always apply these rules strictly and *more* + adjective is sometimes preferred to adjective + *er* with some two-syllable adjectives, e.g. *more clever* instead of *cleverer*, *more friendly* instead of *friendlier*.

3a Remind students to always use *than* with comparative sentences. Ask them to complete the sentences using the comparative form and the words in brackets. Elicit answers from students.

Answers

1 more interesting than **2** better than **3** worse than
4 more exciting than **5** funnier than

3b Students work in pairs and say which of the sentences they agree with. Nominate a few students to give their partner's answers.

4 Students look at the words we use to modify comparative adjectives. Check students understand the words and then ask them to choose the correct alternatives.

Answers

1 far **2** slightly **3** a lot **4** a bit

5 **SPEAKING** Students complete the sentences logically. Then ask them to compare their sentences with a partner.

Suggested answers

2 Jennifer Lawrence is a lot younger than Meryl Streep.
3 *House* is slightly more popular than *CSI*.
4 *The Simpsons* is far funnier than *South Park*.
5 The BBC news is much more informative than CNN.
6 Spiders are a bit scarier than snakes.

✛ EXTRA ACTIVITY

In pairs, students take turns to compare objects in their bags or on their desks with those of their partner, using a different comparative adjective each time, e.g. *My folder is slightly messier than yours. My lunchbox is a bit smaller than yours*, etc.

6a SPEAKING Students write sentences comparing the appearance of Justin Timberlake in the two photos. Draw attention to the adjectives in the box. Encourage students to use the words from exercise 4 if they can.

Suggested answers

He looks more/less attractive in photo b.
His hair is darker in photo b.
He looks better/worse in photo b than in photo a.
He looks older in photo b, and his clothes are smarter.
His hair is curlier in photo a.

6b In pairs, ask students to compare the two photos. Draw attention to the model dialogue and ask a pair to read it out to the class. Elicit comparative sentences from different pairs.

6c SPEAKING Ask students to imagine themselves as a seven year old. Ask them to think about what they looked like and their character, too. Then ask them to tell a partner. Allow less confident students to make notes first, but encourage them not to write out full sentences – this way they will still have some practice at speaking spontaneously.

7 Students complete the questions with the superlative form of the adjectives, as in the example answer. Nominate students to give their answers.

Answers

2 the most difficult **3** the funniest **4** the happiest
5 the best

8a SPEAKING Students stand up and mingle so they can interview different people in the class using the questions from exercise 7. Ask them to note down the name of the student and the answer given.

TEACHER DEVELOPMENT: CLASSROOM TIPS

Mingling

Mingling means 'to move around and socially interact'. In this fluency-based activity, students get up and interview different people in the class. The objective is to get students talking and forming sentences in a relaxed environment. It is helpful to play music so students feel less inhibited. You could also stop the music to indicate when students must move on and find another partner. Monitor the activity and note down any errors that you can go through with the class later.

8b SPEAKING Ask students for some of the interesting answers they had from other students.

TEACHER DEVELOPMENT: PRONUNCIATION

Weak form of *the*

Highlight the weak form of *the* in superlative statements: /ðə/.

Refer students to the Grammar reference on page 68 if necessary.

HOMEWORK

Assign students page 42 in their Workbook or the relevant sections of the Online Workbook.

Developing vocabulary p61

Using adjectives ending in -ing and -ed

>>> **FAST TRACK**

You could ask students to make notes on exercise 4a at home. They can then compare their notes with a partner at the next lesson.

1 Students look at the examples and choose the correct alternative. Nominate students to give their answers.

Answers

1 exciting, excited **2** interesting, interested
To describe how somebody feels, we use the *-ed* ending.

2 Students write the *-ing* or *-ed* forms of the words in the box. Provide dictionaries for students to check their answers.

Answers

bored, confused, disappointed, embarrassing, excited, frightening, interested, moved, relaxing, surprising, tiring

✚✚ EXTRA ACTIVITY

Give students two more examples and ask them to compare the two sentences and compare the differences in meaning:
My friend is bored. (My friend feels bored.)
My friend is boring. (My friend is a boring person.)
I am confused. (I don't understand something.)
I am confusing. (I will cause you to be confused.)

TEACHER DEVELOPMENT: LANGUAGE

Adjectives ending in *-ing* and *-ed*

You could point out to students that adjectives ending in *-ing* usually describe things rather than people, although they also describe the effect that something has on your ideas and feelings.
Like other adjectives, *-ing* and *-ed* adjectives can be used in front of a noun and modified by adverbials, such as *quite*, *really* and *very*. They can also be used in the comparative and superlative forms, e.g. *This is one of the most boring books I've ever read.*

TEACHER DEVELOPMENT: PRONUNCIATION

Pronouncing *-ed*

Most adjectives are based on a verb that can be changed into an adjective by adding either *-ed* or *-ing*. Remind students that *-ed* adjectives follow the same pronunciation rules as they saw in Unit 2 (Student's Book, page 20) for *-ed* endings in the past tense: /d/ after a voiced sound, e.g. *surprised*; /t/ after an unvoiced sound, e.g. *relaxed*; /ɪd/ after t or d, e.g. *excited*. Chorally drill the *-ed* adjectives in exercise 1 to practise the pronunciation.

3 Students complete the sentences with the correct ending. Check answers as a class, asking students to read out full sentences.

Answers

1 surprised **2** embarrassing **3** confusing **4** moved
5 disappointed **6** boring **7** relaxing

4a Students look at the topics in the box and make notes about their opinions on each one. They should try to use adjectives ending in -ing and -ed. Draw attention to the example before they begin.

Suggested answers

pop music = moving, makes me feel relaxed
reading = interesting, makes me feel relaxed
spiders = frightening, make me feel scared
sport = boring, makes me feel tired
theme parks = exciting, make me feel a bit frightened
watching documentaries = interesting, makes me feel moved

4b SPEAKING Students discuss their ideas in pairs. Ask a pair to read out the model dialogue. Tell students they should refer to their notes but speak in full sentences.

HOMEWORK

Assign students page 43 in their Workbook or the relevant sections of the Online Workbook.

Gateway to life skills pp62–63

Thinking about fame

To think about the consequences of wanting to be famous, to consider different opinions and attitudes to fame, and to give advice to somebody who wants to become famous.

>>> FAST TRACK

You could ask students to make notes on exercise 7 at home. They can then compare their notes with a partner at the next lesson.

ⓘ BACKGROUND INFORMATION

A recent survey found that the top three career aspirations for 5-to-11-year-olds in Britain were sports star, pop star and actor, compared with teacher, banker and doctor 25 years ago. Reality shows like X Factor and Britain's Got Talent present a quick fix route to stardom which appeals to many young people who see it as an easy way to money and fame and in doing so may neglect their studies or other ambitions. What these shows don't always present are the downsides to fame: the potential failure, the pressures, the loss of privacy to name a few.

There are, of course, plus sides to celebrity culture: young people having a good role model to look up to, or emulating celebrities who promote good causes can be beneficial.

This lesson weighs up all aspects of celebrity culture, looking at different things to be famous for and the consequences of fame and encourages students to give advice to another young person seeking fame.

WARMER

Ask students to look at both the title of the lesson and the headline of the article and discuss in pairs what they think about *fame* and *being famous*. Elicit some positive and negative opinions from pairs. Ask students to read through the objectives and the Key concepts for the lesson and help with any vocabulary they don't understand before starting the lesson.

1 SPEAKING In pairs, ask students to discuss the questions. Elicit answers from students. For question 2, have a show of hands for who wants to be famous and who doesn't. Ask the question again at the end of the lesson to see whether anyone has changed their views.

2 READING Students read the text quickly and then write one or two sentences to summarise the message of the text. Nominate a student to give his/her summary and see if the rest of the class agree or if they can add anything.

Answers

It's about a boy called Murat. He is quite clever, but he doesn't always go to school because he believes one day he will be famous. Lots of students in the UK believe this. They don't want to study because being famous will make them rich.

3 Students read the text again and answer the questions. Allow students to check their answers with a partner, before nominating individual students to give the answers.

Answers

1 He doesn't mind; he wants to be a model, a singer or an actor. **2** He goes to Turkey to have an operation on his nose. **3** The chances are 30 million to one.
4 They want to let everyone know who they are and they want to appear attractive. **5** They have money but no qualifications. **6** She enjoyed being clever and always going to school.

4a Students work with a partner and complete the statements with the correct words. If you have more confident students, ask them to try to complete them from memory before checking in the text.

Answers

1 reality show **2** attractive **3** enjoy, celebrity
4 money, qualifications **5** study

4b Students consider their own opinions of the statements in exercise 4a.

4c SPEAKING Have a class discussion, encouraging all students to talk and to give reasons for their opinions.

✚ EXTRA ACTIVITY

Ask students to imagine what celebrity culture was like a generation ago, and ask them to write three to four sentences comparing then with now, e.g. *I think in the past, celebrities were less important than now. I think celebrities had more privacy in the past because there was no Internet.*

5 **LISTENING** ▶ 31 Tell students they are going to watch or listen to four people talking about fame. Ask them to read the questions. Play the video or track then elicit answers from students. See p153 for the videoscript/audioscript for this exercise.

Answers

Molly:	Yes. A singer and songwriter.
Kieran:	Yes. An actor.
George:	No. A doctor.
Amelia:	No. A writer.

6a ▶ 31 Tell students that they're going to watch the video or listen again and need to answer the questions. Give them time to read the questions before playing it again. Play the video or track.

6b Put students in small groups and ask them to compare their ideas. Encourage them to give their reasons. Ask one person from each group what most people in their group thought.

7 Students read the text about a teenage boy. Nominate a few students to say what they think of his plans.

LIFE TASK 🤾

Tell students they are going to create a video or an email giving Eddie advice about his plans.

- **Step 1**
  Divide the class into groups of three or four and ask students to read the instructions. Ask them to imagine that Eddie in exercise 7 is a friend of theirs and ask them to follow the steps to prepare a video message or email for him. Remind students that this is a collaborative task, so everyone needs to contribute.

- **Step 2**
  Students work with their group to think of comments about Eddie's plan to become a footballer. Encourage students to be constructive in their comments, not just critical. Monitor to ensure all students are given the chance to speak.

- **Step 3**
  Students discuss their opinions and prepare suggestions about Eddie's idea to leave school before doing his exams. Circulate to help with any necessary vocabulary or structures.

- **Step 4**
  When students have finished, ask one student from each group to read out the email, or if you have the facility you could film their video messages.

Listening p64

Identifying key words and listening for gist

WARMER

Ask students what ways there are to find out the news, other than the TV (*newspapers, magazines, the Internet, radio*, etc.). Ask students how often they listen to the radio, and what type of programme they usually listen to. Tell students they are going to listen to a radio programme in the UK, and pre-teach the vocabulary *phone-in* and *caller*.

1 **SPEAKING** In pairs, ask students to discuss the questions. Then nominate different pairs to share their answers.

2 **LISTENING** ▶ 32 Play the track and ask students to match the speakers to the types of programmes. Remind students there are two options they do not need. See pp153–154 for the audioscript for this exercise.

Answers

1 f **2** d **3** e **4** a

✓ **EXAM SUCCESS** Students read about the next activity where they will have to identify the statements the speaker makes. Ask students to think about the question in the Exam Success box and then compare their answers with the information on page 145 (Listening: Identifying the speaker activities).

3 ▶ 32 Give students time to read through the statements before playing the track again. Ask students to identify the correct speaker, reminding them that their names are written in exercise 2. Play the track and nominate students to give their answers. See pp153–154 for the audioscript for this exercise.

Answers

1 Harry **2** Olivia **3** Lily **4** Tyler **5** Lily **6** Harry
7 Olivia **8** Tyler

4 **SPEAKING** **What about *you*?** Students work in pairs to discuss their opinion of TV in their country. Open it out into a class discussion.

TEACHER DEVELOPMENT: CLASSROOM TIPS

Using news stories in class

With careful selection, authentic news reports can become accessible to students of all levels. Encourage students to visit sites, such as BBC or CNN, and to listen to news programmes in English. CNN also provides transcripts for most of its shows.

If you choose to watch or listen to a news report in class, make sure it is fairly short (can be read, watched or listened to in three to four minutes) and something students are likely to have some prior knowledge of. Students feel more comfortable with content that is familiar. Give students a headline and ask them to predict what the news story might be about and give them questions to answer so their listening is focused.

Grammar in context pp64–65

Using less ... than, (not) as ... as, too and (not) enough

>>> **FAST TRACK**

If students are familiar with the vocabulary, you could ask them to complete exercise 2 at home and then check their answers at the start of the lesson.

Test before you teach

Draw a picture of three weights on the board – one small weight of 500 g and two large weights, both 1 kg. Label them A, B and C. Then write: *A is _____ heavy _____ B and C. B is _____ heavy _____ C.* Ask students to look at the pictures and complete the sentences. Monitor and check their knowledge of *less ... than* and *as ... as.*

Answers

Weight A is less heavy than/not as heavy as weights B and C. Weight B is as heavy as weight C.

less ... than, (not) as ... as

1a Students read sentences 1–3. Point out to students that the sentences are from the listening. Ask if they agree with the statements and to give reasons why or why not. Remind students that *than* /ðən/ and *as* /əz/ are usually unstressed in spoken English. Practise these sounds by chorally drilling the sentences.

1b Students decide if the statements are true or false. Nominate students to give their answers.

Answers

1 T **2** T **3** T

TEACHER DEVELOPMENT: LANGUAGE

Less ... than and *not as ... as*

For adjectives which form the comparative with *more*, both *less ... than* and *not as ... as* can be used to negatively compare quantity and quality, e.g. *Reality shows are less interesting than/not as interesting as documentaries.*

For one-syllable adjectives which form the comparative with *-er*, we only use *not as ... as*, e.g. *Amsterdam is not as big as Paris.*

2 Students rewrite the sentences, but with the same meaning. Draw attention to the example sentence. Monitor students to see if they have understood the grammar point. Elicit answers from different students.

Answers

2 Game shows are as exciting as soaps.
3 TV programmes are less popular than/not as popular as computer games with today's teenagers.
4 Football programmes on the radio are as exciting as they are on TV.
5 Watching horror films at home is not as scary as/less scary than watching them in the cinema.
6 TV documentaries are less informative than/not as informative as books.

3 SPEAKING In pairs, students decide if they agree with the opinions in exercise 2. Ask a pair to read out the model dialogue before they begin.

too and (not) ... enough

Test before you teach

Draw pictures on the board, for example, a small girl standing next to an adult bicycle or a short man trying to reach a book on a high shelf, and ask: *What's the problem? Why can't she ride the bike? Why can't he reach the book?* Elicit: *It's too big. She's too small. He's too short. He's not tall enough.* If students are familiar with *too* and *enough,* you could go through the Grammar guide together as a class.

4a Students look at the sentences. Point out that they are sentences from the listening on page 64.

4b Students match the first and second halves of the rules, using the sentences in exercise 4a to help them deduce the answers.

Answers

1 c **2** a **3** b

4c Students look at the word order in exercise 4a and answer the questions.

Answers

1 *too* comes before the adjective
2 *enough* comes after the adjective
3 *enough* comes before the noun

5 Focus students' attention on the photo and ask if they know anything about the characters in the picture. If not, ask if they can guess what type of TV programme it is and what the telephone box could be used for. Then, ask students to complete the text with the words in the box. Allow students to compare their answers in pairs before checking answers as a class.

Answers

a as **b** too **c** enough **d** not **e** as **f** than
g young **h** serious

>>> **FAST FINISHERS**

Ask students to write comprehension questions to ask other students, e.g. *What type of programme is Doctor Who? Is it less popular than big American series? How old is the series? How many actors have played Doctor Who? Were they all popular?*

ⓘ CULTURAL INFORMATION

Doctor Who is a British TV series which started in 1963. It's largely science fiction, and features a man who travels through time in a machine called a TARDIS (made to look like a British telephone box). It has something of a cult following in the UK, and the Guinness Book of Records lists it as the longest-running science fiction series of all time.

6 Students complete the sentences with the verb *to be* and *too* or *not ... enough* plus the adjective. Draw attention to the example sentence before they begin. Nominate students to give their answers.

Answers

2 is too easy   **3** isn't original enough   **4** isn't good enough   **5** is too hot   **6** is too confusing   **7** wasn't scary enough

✚ EXTRA ACTIVITY

Ask students to draw pictures similar to the ones in Test before you teach and ask their partner to think of two sentences with *too* and *enough* to describe the picture.

7a Students look at the questions and make notes for their answers, using *too* and *enough* and the adjectives in the box.

Suggested answers

1 too young/not old enough/not serious enough/hair's too long

2 fast enough/too slow/legs aren't long enough/healthy enough/fit enough

3 clever enough/too lazy/not serious enough

7b SPEAKING In pairs, students discuss their answers with a partner. Ask a pair to read out the model dialogue as an example for the class.

Refer students to the Grammar reference on page 68 if necessary.

HOMEWORK

Assign students page 44 in their Workbook or the relevant sections of the Online Workbook.

Developing speaking p66 💬 💬

Negotiating

≫ FAST TRACK

You could ask students to prepare for exercise 6 at home in pairs. They can then present their role-play to the class at the next lesson.

WARMER

Start by describing what you saw on TV last night. Mention a couple of programmes and say if you enjoyed them. Grade your language to suit the level of your class. Then ask students in the class: Did you watch TV last night? What did you see? How do you decide what to watch? Have you got a TV in your bedroom?

1 SPEAKING In pairs, ask students to look at the TV Guide and decide which programmes they would like to watch and why. You could ask two confident students to have a conversation in open class as a model for other students.

Example answer

A: *What's on TV tonight?*

B: *There's a new science fiction drama series at 9 pm and a game show at 8 pm where you can get rich.*

A: *I'd like to see the drama series. Game shows are too boring.*

2a LISTENING 33 Play the track for students to listen to two people deciding what to watch on TV tonight. Ask students to tick the types of programmes they hear in the conversation. Next, students put another tick next to the programme the speakers decide to watch. Ask students to compare their answers in pairs before you check answers with the class. See p154 for the audioscript for this exercise.

Answers

(✓) drama series, documentary
(✓✓) cookery programme

2b Ask students what the two girls think about different types of programme. Play the track again if necessary. Check answers as a class and ask students if they agree or disagree with the opinions.

Answers

drama: one of the girls doesn't like drama and especially not science fiction
documentaries: too serious and too scary, not relaxing
cookery programmes: a bit boring

3 33 Play the track again for students to listen to and tick the expressions they hear. Ask more confident students if they remember the full sentences.

Answers

✓ Shall we ...?, OK., Why don't we ...?, Let's ...?, I know what you mean, but ..., Fine.

TEACHER DEVELOPMENT: LANGUAGE

Making suggestions

Remind students that *Why don't we ...?/Shall we ...?* are followed by the infinitive without *to*, e.g. *Shall we go out to dinner?* A common answer to *Shall we ...?* is *Yes, let's* not *Yes, we shall.*

How about ...?/What about ...?, on the other hand, are followed by the gerund, e.g. *How about watching a DVD?*

4 SPEAKING In pairs, students take it in turns to suggest watching a programme from exercise 1 and responding to the suggestion. Draw attention to the model dialogue.

5 In pairs, students look at the photos and think of good and bad things about each way to spend an evening. Elicit ideas from different students. Then ask students to vote for their favourite way to spend an evening.

Suggested answers

a watching a film/DVD at home
  Good: cheap, stop the film when we want, talk if we like
  Bad: don't get to talk much, screen is small

b playing computer games
  Good: entertaining, makes you think
  Bad: gets boring, too repetitive, not healthy

c going to the cinema
  Good: watch a film on big screen/in 3D, eat popcorn, see new film
  Bad: expensive, difficult to find a film everyone likes

d going bowling
  Good: competition is good, keeps you fit
  Bad: expensive, difficult to get to a bowling alley

e dancing
  Good: keeps you fit, listen to good music
  Bad: tiring, music is loud so you can't talk

f eating out
  Good: chat with friends, try different food
  Bad: cheap fast food is usually bad for you, some restaurants are expensive

PRACTICE MAKES PERFECT

6 **SPEAKING** Students read the task individually before they get into pairs. Then, using their ideas in exercise 5 and the expressions in the Speaking bank, students follow the instructions and act out the role-play. Draw attention to the example and ask a pair of students to read it out.

For students who are less confident, photocopy the model dialogue below, and either read it aloud yourself or alternate the roles with you and a strong student. Then instruct students to read aloud in pairs, alternating between roles A and B. Then ask them to read it again, changing the underlined information so it is true for themselves.

Model dialogue

A: Hi there. How are you? What are you doing tonight?

B: Nothing much. Why don't we go to the cinema?

A: I'm not sure. There aren't any good films on at the moment.

B: You're right. Shall we go bowling?

A: No, I don't think bowling is fun with only two people. I prefer dancing. There's a new street dance class that's open on Thursday evenings for teenagers.

B: But I'm not very good at dancing. How about texting Jake and Ellie and going to that new burger place?

A: Great! We can go back to my place afterwards and watch a film.

B: Good idea. Let's text them now.

✓ EXAM SUCCESS Students read about negotiating and think about what they can do in an exam if they can't think of anything to say. Brainstorm ideas and ask students to turn to page 145 (Speaking: Negotiating) to compare their answers.

Oral examinations

Tell students that in oral examinations they should always ask for clarification if they are not sure, e.g. *Could you repeat that please?* Students should also learn several expressions to help them interact spontaneously, such as phrases to agree or disagree. 'Hesitation devices', such as *in my opinion* or *let me see*, will allow them time to think about what they want to say.

Remind students that examiners are trained to keep their body language neutral and may not smile. They may interrupt or ask *Why?* after an initial answer because they want the student to say more.

HOMEWORK

Assign students page 45 in their Workbook or the relevant sections of the Online Workbook.

Developing writing p67

Writing a review

>>> FAST TRACK

You could ask students to write the review for exercise 6 at home. They can then compare with a partner at the next lesson.

WARMER

In pairs, ask students to discuss the best and worst films they've seen this year, giving as many reasons as they can. Ask them to give each film a mark out of ten. Nominate students to share their partner's opinions. Elicit the word *review* from students, and ask what type of things you would expect to have reviews for (films, restaurants, hotels, etc.).

1 Students read the review of the British TV programme and answer the questions. Nominate different students to give their answers.

2a Students read the text again and match the information to the paragraphs.

Answers

Paragraph 1: title, channel, time and day
Paragraph 2: a description of the programme
Paragraph 3: why the writer likes the programme
Paragraph 4: a recommendation to watch/not to watch the programme

2b Students write basic notes on the information the writer gives. Remind them not to write full sentences in this case.

Answers

2 BBC1 with repeat on BBC3 **3** on Saturdays at 7 and on Sundays **4** Four famous singers choose a voice for their team then they compete to find the winner.
5 Likes the programme because the writer likes music, game shows and reality shows. *The Voice* is fairer because you can't see the singers.

---

3 Students read the review again and complete the expressions in the Writing bank.

Answers

In my opinion, think, would recommend, far as I'm

4a In pairs, students make a list of TV programmes that are popular in their country.

4b SPEAKING Students then tell their partners their opinion of the programmes, using expressions from the Writing bank.

5 Students make notes about their favourite TV programme. Refer them back to the information in exercise 2a.

PRACTICE MAKES PERFECT

6 Students read the task and write a review with information about their favourite TV programme. Remind them to follow the paragraph plan in exercise 2a and to use the expressions from the Writing bank, as well as their information from exercise 5.

For students who are less confident, photocopy the model text below for extra support during the writing task.

Model text

Sherlock

Sherlock is on BBC1 every Saturday evening at 7.30 pm. It's a drama series set in London about a detective called Sherlock Holmes and his assistant, Dr Watson. The series is based on the stories by Arthur Conan Doyle. Sherlock investigates unusual cases which the police cannot solve. He is really intelligent and a brilliant detective, but he is very bad at talking to people and making friends. This means that the other characters sometimes get really annoyed with him and it is very amusing.

As far as I'm concerned, *Sherlock* is the best thing on TV because each episode is a mystery and it's always very interesting and funny. I always want to watch the next episode to find out what will happen.

I would recommend *Sherlock* to anybody who likes mysteries and detectives!

HOMEWORK

Assign students page 46 in their Workbook or the relevant sections of the Online Workbook.

Language checkpoint: Unit 5

>>> FAST TRACK

The extra support provided on the Grammar and Vocabulary reference sections makes the Grammar and Vocabulary revision section ideal for setting as homework. You could get students to complete the whole revision page or just certain exercises for homework.

Grammar revision p69

Comparatives and superlatives

1 Students correct the mistakes in the sentences.

Answers

1 My school is bigger than this school.
2 You look thinner than the last time I saw you.
3 Some people think that watching sport is more boring than playing it.
4 The Volga is the longest river in Europe.
5 Ethan is much worse at German than Jake.
6 Do you think this exercise is the most difficult in the book?
7 That's the silliest thing you've said today.

less … than, (not) as … as

2 Students make true sentences using *as … as, not as … as* or *less … than.*

Answers

1 Spain isn't as big as the US./Spain is less big than the US.
2 A kilo of sugar is as heavy as a kilo of iron.
3 To become a doctor, philosophy is less important than anatomy./philosophy isn't as important as anatomy.
4 Jamie isn't as old as Brad./Jamie is less old than Brad.
5 I'm less good at maths than my best friend./I'm not as good at maths as my best friend.
6 Playing tennis is less dangerous than parachuting./isn't as dangerous as parachuting.

too, (not) … enough

3 Students write sentences using *too* or *(not) … enough.*

Answers

1 It's too high.
2 He isn't old enough.
3 My legs aren't strong enough.
4 I haven't got enough money.
5 She's too young.
6 It isn't warm enough.
7 It's too slow.

Vocabulary revision p69

1 Students read the descriptions and name the types of TV programmes.

Answers

1 the news   **2** chat show   **3** game show/quiz show
4 documentary   **5** advert   **6** reality show

ADJECTIVES DESCRIBING TV PROGRAMMES

2 Students complete the adjectives with vowels. They then decide if each one is positive or negative.

Answers

1 awful (–)   **2** boring (–)   **3** cool (+)   **4** informative (+)
5 moving (+)   **6** popular (+)   **7** relaxing (+)
8 scary (+/–)

ADJECTIVES ENDING IN *-ING* AND *-ED*

3 Students complete the sentences with the words in the box. Remind them they do not need to use all the words.

Answers

1 disappointed   **2** surprising   **3** embarrassing
4 frightened   **5** relaxed   **6** tired

HOMEWORK

Assign students page 47 in their Workbook or the relevant sections of the Online Workbook.

6 Planet Earth

KEY LEARNING OUTCOMES

Students will be able to:

- understand texts about conservation and environment
- talk about geography and the environment using *be going to* and *will*
- talk about the future and ecology
- make arrangements
- write a formal letter

UNIT OVERVIEW

Vocabulary

Geographical features
The environment

Reading

Is this the most important building in the world?
CRITICAL THINKING Discussing the importance of a building and identifying plants to protect

Grammar in context

be going to and *will*
will, may, might
PRONUNCIATION Sentence stress

Developing vocabulary

Different uses of *get*

Life skills

The world around you:
Reducing our ecological footprint

Listening

Sustainable energy

Grammar in context

Zero conditional
First conditional

Developing speaking

Making arrangements
PRONUNCIATION Intonation – showing enthusiasm

Developing writing

A formal letter

Exam success

Use of English: Sentence transformation activities
Writing: Exam conditions

DIGITAL OVERVIEW

Presentation Kit

- ▶ **Flipped classroom video Unit 6:** *be going to* and *will*
- ▶ **Life skills video Unit 6:** How we reduced our school's carbon and water footprint
- ▶ **V Vocabulary tool:** Geographical features, The environment
- ▶ **Interactive versions of Student's Book activities**
- ▶ **Integrated audio and answer key for all activities**
- ▶ **Workbook pages with answer key**

Teacher's Resource Centre

- ▶ **Flipped classroom video Unit 6:** *be going to* and *will*
- ▶ **Life skills video Unit 6:** How we reduced our school's carbon and water footprint
- ▶ **Grammar communication activity Unit 6:** Sets of three
- ▶ **Worksheets for this unit, including:**
  - Grammar practice worksheet Unit 6
  - Flipped classroom video worksheet Unit 6: *be going to* and *will*
  - Literature worksheet Units 5 and 6
  - Culture worksheet Unit 6
  - Life skills video worksheet Unit 6
  - Everyday English worksheet Unit 6

Student's App

Gateway 2nd Edition wordlist for the award-winning Sounds App (available for download)

✓ TESTING AND ASSESSMENT

Resources for exam preparation and measuring student progress

- ▶ Test Generator Units 1–6
- ▶ Printable tests Unit 6 and Review (Units 4–6)
- ▶ Gateway to exams Units 5 and 6 (end of Unit 6)

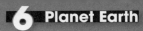

Vocabulary p70

Talking about geographical features and the environment

>>> **FAST TRACK**

You could ask students to research and complete their answers for exercise 7 at home. They can then ask and answer with a partner at the next lesson.

WARMER

Draw a circle on the board representing the sun, and then eight other circles in a line next to it. In pairs, see if students can label the eight planets in the correct order (using English names if possible). Give students the correct words and order: *Mercury, Venus, Earth, Mars, Jupiter, Saturn, Uranus, Neptune*. Model and practise the pronunciation of *Earth* and ask students if they know any of the big differences between the planets. Elicit a few, e.g. *Earth has life, the others don't, Mercury and Venus don't have any moons, the four outer planets are much bigger.*

[v] Geographical features

1 **SPEAKING** In pairs, ask students to name a famous example for each of the geographical features in the box. Allow students to use a dictionary if necessary. Elicit answers, and see if any students had answers that no-one else had.

Example answers

Miami Beach, Gobi Desert, The Black Forest, North/South Pole, Easter Island, Amazon jungle/rainforest, Lake Michigan, Mont Blanc, The Alps, The Mediterranean Sea, The Pacific Ocean, The River Thames, Death Valley

2 ▶ 34 Play the track for students to listen and repeat. Point out the different pronunciation and stress for these three words: *desert* (v meaning to leave) /dɪˈzɜː(r)t/; *desert* (n a dry and arid region) /dezə(r)t/; *dessert* (n the sweet course at the end of a meal) /dɪˈzɜː(r)t/. See p154 for the audioscript for this exercise.

3 Play a game with the class. Ask a student to come to the board and draw one of the words from exercise 1 for the rest of the class to guess. Repeat until all the words have been used. You could make this a team game, awarding a point to the team who guesses each word first.

[v] The environment

4 In pairs, ask students to match the words to the definitions. Remind them there are more words than they need in the box. You may like to provide dictionaries for this task. Check answers by asking different students. Ask students to underline the stressed syllables in the words. Drill any difficult pronunciations (see Answers below).

Answers

1 <u>green</u>house effect /ˈɡriːnˌhaʊs ɪˈfekt/
2 melt /melt/
3 drought /draʊt/
4 <u>o</u>zone layer /ˈəʊzəʊn ˈleɪjə(r)/
5 po<u>ll</u>ution /pəˈluːʃ(ə)n/
6 flood /flʌd/
7 <u>g</u>lobal <u>war</u>ming /ˈɡləʊbəl ˈwɔː(r)mɪŋ/
8 <u>nu</u>clear di<u>sas</u>ter /ˈnjuːklɪə(r) dɪˈzɑːstə(r)/
9 oil spill /ɔɪl spɪl/

+ EXTRA ACTIVITY

Ask students to write definitions of other words related to the environment. They then read their definitions for the class to guess the word, e.g. *waste, save, recycle, ecology, deforestation, acid rain,* etc.

TEACHER DEVELOPMENT: CLASSROOM TIPS

Choral drilling

Choral drilling involves you giving an oral model of a word or phrase for the whole class to repeat. It is particularly useful for less confident students, so they can get used to saying the words in a group before they attempt on their own. Use choral drilling to practise new words or phrases, especially phrases that will be useful in future communicative activities.

5 **SPEAKING** Students look at the photos and describe what they see in pairs. Draw attention to the example sentence. With a less confident class, elicit key words to describe the photos before they begin, e.g. *recycle, ozone layer, sun, drought, flood,* etc.

Suggested answers

a You can recycle bottles here. It's good for the environment.
b This is a flood. It has rained a lot.
c This is the ozone layer. It protects us from the sun's rays.
d There is a drought in this place. It is very dry.

6 **LISTENING** ▶ 35 Play the track and ask students to match the four short recordings to the photos in exercise 5. Tell students to note down key words which help them decide on their answer as they listen. You may like to pre-teach these words: *sort out rubbish* – to get rid of things you don't need; *bin* – a container for putting rubbish in; *ultraviolet radiation* – rays from the sun which are harmful to humans. Check answers with the class. See p154 for the audioscript for this exercise.

Answers

1 b **2** c **3** a **4** d

7 **SPEAKING** In pairs, ask students to ask and answer the questions. Circulate and help with any vocabulary. Nominate a few students to give their answers.

Suggested answers

1 very hot summers, less rain, some areas becoming desert

2 floods in low-lying and coastal areas in spring and autumn, droughts in the summer

3 have baths instead of showers, leave lights and the TV on

4 switch off the tap when I brush my teeth, switch off lights, TV and computer when not using them

5 plastic, glass, cans, food waste and clothes

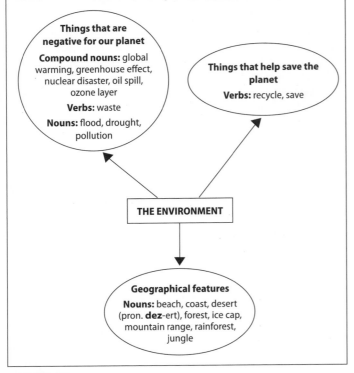
HOMEWORK

Assign students page 48 in their Workbook or the relevant sections of the Online Workbook.

Reading p71

Skimming and scanning for global and specific information

WARMER

Write the following words in two columns on the board:

switch off	*less*
turn off	*school*
fly	*lights*
recycle	*more*
walk to	*taps*

Ask students to work in pairs and match the words to make phrases. Then ask them to say what the phrases relate to (being green/protecting the environment). Ask students if they try to do any of these things.

Answers

switch off lights, turn off taps, fly less, recycle more, walk to school

1a Focus students on the photos. Ask them to work with a partner and talk about what they can see. Ask students what they think the connection is between the photos. Elicit answers from different students.

Answer

They both contain seeds.

1b Students look at the title of the text and the photos. Ask what they think the title refers to and why. Nominate different students to give their suggestions.

2 Tell students they have three minutes to read the text and check if their prediction was correct. Remind students not to worry about understanding every word of the text.

Answer

The Svalbard Global Seed Vault is the most important building in the world because it stores seeds and protects our food source for the future.

3 Students read the sentences and choose the correct alternatives. Tell them to write the paragraph where they found their answer.

Answers

1 don't pay (D) **2** won't (E) **3** the altitude will keep the seeds dry (E) **4** wide variety (C) **5** doesn't have (C) **6** possible environmental disasters (B) **7** might (A)

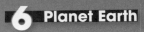

Ask students to write two or three sentences to explain why they keep different seeds in the Svalbard Global Seed Vault. Encourage students to use their own words. Ask a few students to read out their sentences.

4 ⚙ **CRITICAL THINKING** Students read through the questions and consider their own responses. Put students in pairs to discuss their thoughts before opening up the discussion to the whole class.

| **Example answer**

Yes, I think it's the most important building in the world, because in the future we will need a lot more food. Without this, people will starve.

5 Students look at the underlined words in the text and guess their meaning. Allow students to check in their dictionaries. Confirm answers as a class.

| **Answers**

impact = effect, cause problems
vault = a safe place to keep or store things
survive = stay alive in difficult circumstances
peas = a small round green vegetable like a small bean
level = how high or low something is
remote = far away and difficult to reach

Ask students to choose three of the words from exercise 5 and write a gapped sentence for each, e.g. *I think my English* .... *is improving (level), It takes a long time to travel to the island. It is very* ....
(remote), etc. They then read out their sentences for their partner to guess the word that fits the gap.

6 SPEAKING **What about** *you*? Students think about their answers to the questions, then have a class discussion. Have a show of hands to see how many people are optimistic about the planet's future, and how many are pessimistic.

HOMEWORK

Assign students page 49 in their Workbook or the relevant sections of the Online Workbook.

Grammar in context pp72–73

Using be going to, will, may, might for future predictions

⟩⟩⟩ FAST TRACK

You could ask students to complete their answers for exercises 4 and 5 at home. They can then compare with a partner at the next lesson.

 Test before you teach: Flipped classroom
Set the Flipped classroom video and tasks for homework <u>before the lesson</u>. This will allow you to assess the needs of the students before the class. Students can then move on to the relevant grammar practice activities.

be going to and will

1a Students look at the sentences with *be going to* and *will*.

1b Tell students to match the explanations to the example sentences in exercise 1a.

| **Answers**

2 b **3** a **4** e **5** d

TEACHER DEVELOPMENT: LANGUAGE

Future forms

Explain to students that the key difference between *will* and *be going to* is that if you make a decision at the moment you speak, you use *will*, e.g. *Do you want to go to the cinema tonight? Sure. I'll see you there at 8 pm.* You could also tell students that *shall* can be used as an alternative to *will*, but it is much less common. The contracted forms of *shall not* and *will not* are *shan't* and *won't*. They are both used to make predictions about what will happen in the future, e.g. *We shan't be there before 5 pm. I won't see Sarah at the party. Shall* and *shan't* are used only with first person pronouns, *I* and *we*.

TEACHER DEVELOPMENT: PRONUNCIATION

Pronouncing *will*

In normal everyday speech, *will* is rarely used; the contraction *'ll* is much more common. Encourage students to use the contracted form rather than the full form, unless they are speaking in more formal situations. If they use the full form, remind them not to stress it unless they have a very strong intention to do something. *'ll* is pronounced with the dark /l/ sound, i.e. it sounds like the *ull* in *full* rather than the *l* in *light*. Chorally drill the pronunciation.

Write these problems on the board:
1 *I can't decide what to do after school today.*
2 *I don't know what to buy my friend for his birthday.*
3 *I don't know what to wear to the party tonight.*
4 *I'm tired of being a teacher, but I don't know what job to do.*
Ask students to call out a decision on how to solve each problem using *I know! I'll …*
e.g. 1 *I know! I'll read a book. I know! I'll play football with my friends,* etc.

2a PRONUNCIATION Students look at the sentences and decide why some of the words are marked in bold.

Answer

The words in bold are stressed because they are the content words. The other words are unstressed because they are function words.

TEACHER DEVELOPMENT: PRONUNCIATION

Sentence stress

Remind students that information/content words are the ones that are usually stressed. These are words you hear more clearly when someone speaks to you. The unstressed words are heard much less clearly and sometimes hardly at all. Words that are usually unstressed are articles, conjunctions, prepositions and auxiliary verbs.

2b PRONUNCIATION ▶ 36 Play the track and ask students to answer the questions. See p154 for the audioscript for this exercise.

Answer

The words in bold are pronounced longer and louder and have a higher pitch. The pronunciation of *be going to* is unstressed and the words are contracted.

TEACHER DEVELOPMENT: PRONUNCIATION

be going to

Write the stressed and unstressed forms of *am/are going to* on the board:

	Stressed	Unstressed
am	/æm/	/əm/
are	/ɑː(r)/	/ə(r)/
to	/tuː/	/tə/

Chorally drill *am going to* and *are going to* in the stressed and unstressed forms. Remind students of the popular spoken form of *going to*: *gonna*. They hear this form in film and TV dialogues and in songs.

2c ▶ 36 Play the track again for students to repeat with the correct stress.

3 Students complete the sentences with the correct form of the verbs, plus *will* and *be going to*.

Answers

1 will disappear **2** 's going to be **3** 'll open **4** will be
5 are going to write **6** will cause **7** 'll come

✛ EXTRA ACTIVITY

Ask students to underline the stressed words in the sentences in exercise 3 and practise saying the sentence using correct sentence stress.

4 Students write about six different plans or intentions they have for the future. Tell them to write about the six areas listed. Draw their attention to the example sentence. Nominate students to read out their sentences, reminding them which words to stress.

Example answers

2 I'm going to decorate my bedroom.
3 I'm going to apply for work experience at the local radio station.
4 I'm going to play in a football match on Friday.
5 I'm going to visit my cousins this weekend.
6 I'm going to go out with my friends after school.

5 Students write about six different predictions they have for the future. Tell them to write about the six areas listed. Draw their attention to the example sentence.

Nominate students to read out their sentences, reminding them which words to stress.

Example answers

2 I think there will be more reality TV programmes.
3 I think green politicians will win the next election.
4 We will see new products made from recycled materials.
5 France will win the next World Cup.
6 We will find a cure for Aids in the near future.

6 SPEAKING Students compare their plans and predictions with a partner. Elicit any predictions that the pairs found interesting or have in common.

will, may, might

7a Students look at the sentences and give an approximate percentage for certainty for each expression in bold. Students could compare their answers in pairs before you elicit answers from the class.

Suggested answers

2 100% certain **3** 50% certain **4** 50% certain
5 50% certain **6** 50% certain **7** 70% certain
8 100% certain

TEACHER DEVELOPMENT: CLASSROOM TIPS

Checking answers

Asking students to check their answers together with a partner before open-class feedback gives students confidence and a chance to confirm their answers. Give them useful language for this task: *I think … What do you think about … ? I think so too./Me too. I don't agree.*

7b Ask students what they notice about the position of the adverbs *definitely* and *probably* in sentences 1 and 2 and sentences 7 and 8.

Answers

In sentences 1 and 2 the adverbs come after *will*.
In sentences 7 and 8 the adverbs come before *won't*.

✓ EXAM SUCCESS Students read the instructions for exercise 8 and decide what is important for them to check when they finish this activity. Tell them to turn to page 145 (Use of English: Sentence transformation activities).

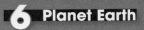

Key word transformations

Key word transformations are popular in Use of English exam papers. Remind students always to use the key word in their answer and to keep the meaning of the original sentence and the tense form. Students should read each sentence very carefully so they do not miss any information and check the number of words they have used. Tell them that contractions count as one word, e.g. *I'll, it's,* etc.

8 Students rewrite the sentences keeping the same meaning. Remind them that they must not change the word given and they can only use between two and five words. Draw their attention to the example sentence.

Answers

2 will definitely become
3 The consequences will perhaps be
4 definitely won't end
5 probably won't change their
6 It's possible that the situation

9 Students write sentences with the expressions in exercise 8 to say how certain they are about the predictions. Note down errors to go over with students before the speaking activity.

Example answers

1 I think summers will definitely get hotter.
2 In my opinion, polar bears will probably become extinct.
3 From my point of view, cars of the future definitely won't use petrol.
4 I'm pretty sure that we won't have another ice age.
5 I think it's possible that natural disasters will become more common.
6 I think the south of Europe might become a desert one day.

10 SPEAKING In pairs, students compare their answers in exercise 9. Ask a pair to read out the model dialogue before they begin. Elicit opinions from different students and try to develop a class debate.

Refer students to the Grammar reference on page 80 if necessary.

HOMEWORK

> Ask students to write a magazine article about the future of the Earth. They should include imaginary interviews with someone who thinks we have no hope and someone who thinks the Earth will survive forever.
>
> Assign students page 50 in their Workbook or the relevant sections of the Online Workbook.

Developing vocabulary p73

Exploring the different uses of get

>>> **FAST TRACK**

You could ask students to write their story for exercise 4a at home with a partner. They can present their story to the class at the next lesson.

1 Students look at the different uses of *get* in the sentences and match each one to the correct meaning (a–e).

Answers

1 c **2** e **3** d **4** a **5** b

get

The verb *to get* has many different meanings in English. It is also part of many phrasal verbs. When we use *get* with a direct object (a noun or pronoun), it often means *receive, obtain, bring, catch, give* or something similar, e.g. *I got your email yesterday, Last week she got a book about pollution. Can you get me that pen that's on the desk?* When we use *get* before an adjective, it often means *become*, e.g. *Summers are getting very hot.* These usages of *get* are generally more informal than the alternatives.

Get often means *travel* and when we use it before a word like *up, out, to,* or *away*, it usually refers to a movement of some kind, e.g. *Are you going to get away this summer?*

2 Students complete the sentences with the words and decide what the meaning of *get* is in each sentence. Tell students that it is the same for 1–6.

Answers

1 red **2** thin **3** ready **4** worse **5** late **6** dark
get means *become* in each sentence.

>>> **FAST FINISHERS**

> Ask students to write two more sentences using the word *get*, with the meaning of *become*.

3 Students read the situations and write sentences with *get* and the words in the box to say what usually happens in each case.

Answers

2 You get tired. **3** You get presents. **4** You get home late. **5** You get bread. **6** You get an email with news.

4a In pairs, students write a story using *get* as many times as possible. Draw attention to the example sentence in exercise 4b before they begin. With a less confident class, you could brainstorm other uses of *get* and write the suggestions on the board for students to use in their stories, e.g. *get up, get dressed, get ill, get bored, get on, get over, get under, get a shock*, etc.

Writing stories

When writing stories, students need to think about these three main points:

characters: *Who?*;

setting: *Where? When?*;

plot: *What happens? How?* and *Why?*

Encourage students to discuss each of these aspects in pairs and make a visual story map (a graphic organiser that maps out the story) before they start writing.

4b SPEAKING Students tell their story to the class. Ask two students to count the number of times *get* is used correctly in each story. The pair with the most correct uses is the winner.

HOMEWORK

Assign students page 51 in their Workbook or the relevant sections of the Online Workbook.

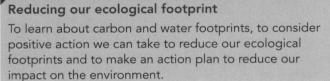

Gateway to life skills pp74–75

Reducing our ecological footprint

To learn about carbon and water footprints, to consider positive action we can take to reduce our ecological footprints and to make an action plan to reduce our impact on the environment.

>>> FAST TRACK

You could ask students to write their answers to the questions in exercise 2 at home. They can discuss their answers with a partner at the beginning of the lesson.

ⓘ BACKGROUND INFORMATION

The apparent consequences of environmental damage in recent years have been dramatic: from forest fires to melting ice caps. These problems are largely caused by humans, so it is up to humans to reverse them or at least try to prevent further damage.

Looking at the idea of a 'footprint' can help students realise the impact an individual can have on the environment – both in negative and positive terms. The lesson looks in detail at carbon footprints, water footprints, the greenhouse effect and global warming and students work in groups to put together an environmental plan for their school.

WARMER

Ask students to keep their books closed. On the board draw a footprint, the symbol for recycling and a greenhouse. Ask students to work in pairs and see if they can think of ways that these connect to environmental issues. After two minutes, nominate pairs to give their ideas. Then allow students to open their books to page 74 and read through the Life skills objectives and the Key concepts and see if they can add any extra information.

Answers

We use the word *footprint* to describe an individual's impact on the environment through their use of water or carbon (carbon footprint, water footprint). The symbol refers to recycling – the process where materials are reused, not thrown into landfill. If we burn fossil fuels, the greenhouse gases in the atmosphere increase, leading to the 'greenhouse effect' and global warming.

1 Students look at the pictures and work with a partner to say whether they think they are bad for the environment. For less confident students, teach them necessary vocabulary (e.g. *fuel, packaging, high-speed, by hand*) so they can give their opinions. Elicit some suggestions from students, but don't confirm answers yet.

2 READING In pairs, ask student A to read text A and student B to read text B, then answer the questions about their texts.

Answers

Text A:

1 It is the impact each person has on the environment when they create greenhouse gases.

2 The things you are directly responsible for are the primary footprint (electricity and travelling). The things you are indirectly responsible for are the secondary footprint (emissions from factories that make the things we buy).

3 Yes, packaged food and travelling by plane are bad for the environment. The text also mentions that travelling by train is three times more fuel-efficient than travelling by plane.

4 They can use less electricity, e.g. watch less TV, switch off the lights, unplug phones or play outside.

Text B:

1 The amount of water we use every day.

2 The primary footprint is the water we use directly, e.g. for washing and drinking, and the secondary footprint is the water we use indirectly, e.g. the water used for growing food or making things.

3 Yes, meat and washing dishes. They are bad for the environment because they need a lot of water.

4 The text says the food we eat makes a difference.

3 SPEAKING Students explain to their partner what carbon/ water footprints are. For more confident students, you could ask them to answer the questions about their partner's text, following their explanation, to check how much they have understood.

4 In small groups, ask students to make a list of ideas for how the school could reduce its carbon and water footprints.

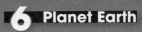

Example answers

Collect water from the sinks in the bathrooms.
Sell special food in the school canteen.
Use less paper.
Try to use less electricity.
Grow our own vegetables.
Travel to school by train or coach in big groups instead of using cars.

5 ▶ 37 Tell students they are going to listen to or watch a video about students talking about ideas for reducing carbon and water footprints at their school. Play the video or track. Ask students if any of their ideas from exercise 4 were used. See p154 for the videoscript/audioscript for this exercise.

6 ▶ 37 Students complete each sentence with one or two words. For more confident students, see if they can complete them from memory first and then play the video or track again to check.

Answers

1 recycling **2** 11 **3** cans, plastic bottles **4** paper
5 little **6** forgot **7** 12

7 Ask students how many things in exercises 5 or 6 they already do in the school. Ask the class what other things in exercises 5 or 6 they think the school could do, if it doesn't already.

LIFE TASK

Tell students they are going to make a video or poster about how to reduce your carbon footprint.

- **Step 1**

  Divide the class into groups of three or four and ask students to read the instructions. Students start by discussing ideas for how they can reduce their ecological footprint at school and making a note of them. If students have access to the Internet, they can search for other ideas, either in class or at home. Remind students of the importance of allowing everyone in the group to have a chance to speak and voice opinions. Circulate to check that everyone is contributing.

- **Step 2**

  Students decide whether they want to make a poster or, if you have the facility, a video.

- **Step 3**

  Encourage students to structure their ideas logically, whether they are making a poster or a video. Remind them that they are trying to make other students change their habits so they need to be persuasive.

- **Step 4**

  Students create their poster or video. Monitor to help with any necessary vocabulary or structures.

- **Step 5**

  When groups present their video or poster, encourage other students to say what they thought was successful about the presentations and to give constructive criticism. You could extend the task so students pass on their ideas for changes to the school to reduce its ecological footprint.

Listening p76

Listening for gist and specific information

WARMER

Write these words on the board: *layer, warming, level, greenhouse, sea, climate, disaster, global, ozone, carbon, cap, change, nuclear, ice, footprint, effect*. Give students two minutes to make eight compound nouns using the words.

Answers

global warming, greenhouse effect, ozone layer, nuclear disaster, carbon footprint, climate change, ice cap, sea level

1 SPEAKING In pairs, students discuss what they can see in the photo. Elicit ideas from students.

Suggested answer

A white corridor with students walking; two girls sitting on the floor reading.

1b Students look at the words and check they understand what they mean. For less confident students, write the words on the board within sentences so they have some context. Ask students if they can think how the words could be connected.

2 LISTENING ▶ 38 Tell students they are going to listen to a science programme on the radio. Ask them to listen for the words in exercise 1b and say why they appear. Play the track then elicit answers. See pp155 for the audioscript for this exercise.

Answer

There is a corridor in a school which produces sustainable energy. When students run in the corridor it produces enough energy to charge mobile phones.

3 ▶ 38 Students read the sentences. Play the track again for students to decide whether the sentences are true or false. Check answers as a class.

Answers

1 T **2** F **3** F **4** T **5** F **6** F **7** T

4 Students look at the false sentences and say why they are false. Ask them to use full sentences in their answers.

Answers

2 The idea came from someone who used to study at the school. **3** They could charge one mobile for two and a half years. **5** He had the idea when he was watching people at Victoria Station. **6** He used the technology at a dance festival and at the Paris Marathon and in an underground station in London during the Olympic Games.

5 SPEAKING **What about *you*?** Students consider their own answers to the questions and then to discuss them with a partner.

Grammar in context pp76–77

Using the zero conditional and the first conditional

>>> FAST TRACK

You could ask students to write their answers to the questions in exercise 3a at home. They can discuss their answers with a partner at the beginning of the next class.

Test before you teach

Write these two half sentences on the board and ask students to complete them so they are true for them:

If/When I have a shower, ...

If/When I leave a room, ...

Monitor to see if students have a good grasp of the form and use of the zero conditional.

Suggested answers

When I have a shower, I try to be as quick as possible.
When I leave a room, I switch off the lights.

Zero conditional

1a Students look at the sentences in the zero conditional and choose the correct alternative to complete the rule.

Answer

things that are generally true

1b Students look again at the sentences in exercise 1a and answer the questions.

Answers

1 present tense, present tense   **2** No. It can come second with no difference in meaning.   **3** We use a comma when *if* is in the first part of the sentence.

EXTRA ACTIVITY

Write these prompts on the board:
I/eat/too much chocolate/I/get/sick
You/not/do/homework/your/teacher/angry
Ask students to use the prompts to write sentences in the zero conditional. Remind them they need to use *if* or *when*.

Answers

If/When I eat too much chocolate, I get sick.
If/When you don't do homework, your teacher gets angry.

TEACHER DEVELOPMENT: LANGUAGE

Zero conditional

We often use the zero conditional to talk about scientific facts and general truths. It is useful to point out to students that there are other words and phrases which have a similar meaning to *if*, e.g. *when*.

2 Students complete the sentences with the verb in the correct form. Elicit answers from different students.

Answers

1 go   **2** doesn't rain   **3** are   **4** die   **5** is   **6** shines

TEACHER DEVELOPMENT: PRONUNCIATION

Sentence rhythm

Ask students to underline the stressed words in the sentences in exercise 2. Then get students to practise saying them, exaggerating the stressed words and saying the unstressed words quickly, and contracting where necessary. Chorally drill the sentences, reading out either the first or second part of each sentence in a random order:
Teacher: *People often go to the beach …*
Students: *… if it's sunny.*

3a Students write sentences to make general statements in the zero conditional. Draw attention to the example sentence. Ask different students to give their answers.

Suggested answers

2 your eyes get sore
3 you feel tired in the morning
4 my parents argue
5 I listen and participate
6 I get good marks at school

>>> FAST FINISHERS

Ask students to think of alternative ways they could have completed the sentences.

3b SPEAKING In pairs, students compare their sentences in exercise 3a to see if they are the same or different. Elicit sentences from different students.

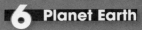

Expressing agreement

Remind students that we can express agreement or say we have similar views by saying: *Me too. So do I. I do, too. Do* can also be replaced by another auxiliary verb, e.g. *have, am,* etc.

If the verb we are agreeing with is negative, we need to use a different structure to show our agreement: *No, me neither. Neither do I. I don't either.*

First conditional

Test before you teach

Ask students the following question: *What would you do if you won 100,000 euros?* Ask them to write a sentence to answer the question. Tell them that their sentence should begin: *If I won 100,000 euros …*

Monitor to check they are able to form first conditional sentences. Ask a few students to read their sentences aloud and gently correct any errors.

4a Students look at the sentences in the first conditional and choose the correct alternative to complete the rule. Nominate a student to give the answer.

Answer
possible

First conditional

When we use the first conditional, we're talking about a particular situation in the future and the result of this situation. There is a real possibility that this condition will happen.

4b Students look at exercise 4a again and choose the correct alternatives.

Answers
1 present simple **2** *will* or *won't*

✛✛ EXTRA ACTIVITY

Introduce the idea of Murphy's law: the opposite of what you want/expect is what usually happens. Ask students to complete the following sentences using the first conditional and thinking about the concept of Murphy's law:

1 If I bring an umbrella, ...
2 If I don't bring an umbrella, ...
3 If I study hard for the test, ...

Suggested answers
1 it won't rain   **2** it will rain   **3** I'll be ill that day

Chanting and backchaining

Chant some first conditional sentences with students to practise rhythm in conditional sentences. Say these chunks in turn and ask students to repeat each one after you: *If; If he comes; If he comes, we will go; If he comes, we will go to the party.*

You could also choose to backchain. This means you start with the last word and work backwards through the sentence. Again, say these chunks in turn for students to repeat: *party; we will go to the party; If he comes, we will go to the party.*

5 Students choose the correct alternatives. Nominate different students to give their answers.

Answers

1 don't, will need   **2** cut, will disappear   **3** will be, disappear   **4** are, will become   **5** will die, becomes

6 Students put the verbs in the correct tenses using the first conditional. Allow students to check answers with a partner before nominating individuals to give their answers.

Answers

a don't do   **b** will create   **c** continues   **d** will need
e won't be   **f** don't have   **g** forget   **h** will use

7 SPEAKING Students work in groups and take turns to say a first conditional sentence. Each sentence must begin with the second half of the previous sentence as shown in the model dialogue. Ask three students to read out the model dialogue and continue it in open class to demonstrate the activity.

Refer students to the Grammar reference on page 80 if necessary.

HOMEWORK

Assign students page 52 in their Workbook or the relevant sections of the Online Workbook.

Developing speaking p78

Making arrangements

⟫⟫ FAST TRACK

You could ask students to prepare their dialogue for exercise 7a at home with a partner. They can present their dialogue to the class at the beginning of the next lesson.

WARMER

Play the game *Snowman* (see Warmer on page 40) with some key words from the unit.

1 SPEAKING In pairs, students answer the questions about the photos. Ask a few pairs to share their ideas.

2 LISTENING ▶ 39 Play the track for students to listen to two people making arrangements for the weekend and answer the questions. Ask different students to give their answers. See p155 for the audioscript for this exercise.

Answers

1 They're going to go to the beach.
2 They're going to meet at 11 o'clock at the station.
3 They're going to bring some sandwiches.
4 They will go somewhere else.

3 ▶ 39 Students complete the dialogue. Play the track again if necessary.

Answers

a good **b** beach **c** 11 o'clock **d** station
e sandwiches **f** have lunch on the beach **g** rains
h ring on your mobile **i** Liz too **j** 11

4 Students tick the expressions in the Speaking bank that appear in the dialogue.

Answers

Are you up to anything at the weekend? Do you fancy verb + -ing?
What time shall we meet? Why don't we meet at …?
Sure./OK./Fine./Good idea. Not really.

✦ EXTRA ACTIVITY

Suggest a few activities to different students in the class and ask them to accept or reject them using a phrase from the Speaking bank.

TEACHER DEVELOPMENT: LANGUAGE

Present continuous for arrangements

Ask students to read the reminder at the bottom of the Speaking bank regarding the use of the present continuous for talking about future arrangements. English teachers often call the present continuous future form the 'diary form' because you can use it for anything you write in your diary, e.g. *On 23rd September, I'm seeing the dentist.*

5a PRONUNCIATION ▶ 39 Play the track again for students to listen and decide how the speakers use their voices to show enthusiasm.

Answer

To show enthusiasm, the voice starts high, then goes down and then goes up again.

5b SPEAKING In pairs, ask students to practise the first six sentences of the dialogue. Remind them to show enthusiasm using intonation. Ask for volunteers to perform the dialogue to the rest of the class.

TEACHER DEVELOPMENT: PRONUNCIATION

Teaching intonation

Intonation can be described as the movements or variations in pitch which affect the level (high/low) and tone (falling/rising) of our voices. Rising intonation means the pitch of the voice increases; falling intonation means that the pitch decreases. Intonation can be difficult to teach. However, students can easily learn the key functions of intonation:

■ Linguistic form-based: grammatical, e.g. the intonation of *Yes/No* or *Wh-* questions; lexical, e.g. intonation on modifiers like *really* or *absolutely.*
■ Attitudinal or interpersonal, e.g. *sounding enthusiastic, interested, polite,* or *showing disbelief.*
■ Accentual, especially in contrasts, e.g. *special stress, emphasising, correcting.*
■ Conversation management, e.g. *asking someone to repeat something, disagreeing strongly.*

6 SPEAKING Students work in pairs and look at the places to go. Ask students to say if they like them and when is best to go. Elicit answers from different students.

PRACTICE MAKES PERFECT

7a SPEAKING Students work with a partner to prepare a dialogue using the diagram. Ask students to choose one part of the dialogue and follow the prompts. Remind them to use the expressions in the Speaking bank. Allow less confident students time to prepare or hand out copies of the model dialogue below for them to base theirs on.

7b SPEAKING Students swap roles and do the dialogue again. Ask for pairs to volunteer to perform their dialogue for the rest of the class.

Model dialogue

A: Hi, Lucy.
B: Hi, Jack.
A: What are you up to at the weekend?
B: Nothing, why? What are you up to?
A: We're playing football in the park if it's sunny. Do you fancy playing, too?
B: Great. What time are we meeting?
A: How about 2 pm?
B: Sure. Shall we meet at the park entrance?
A: Yes, good idea.
B: What if it's raining?
A: Hmm … if it rains we'll go to the cinema.
B: Okay. See you tomorrow.
A: See you!

HOMEWORK

Assign students page 53 in their Workbook or the relevant sections of the Online Workbook.

Developing writing p79

Writing a formal letter

>>> **FAST TRACK**

You could ask students to write their letter for exercise 6b at home. They can then compare with a partner at the next lesson.

WARMER

Elicit the word *evidence*. Ask students if they know of any evidence that some people believe there is for climate change. Write their ideas up on the board (e.g. *hotter summers, melting ice caps*). Elicit or teach the word *coincidence* (when events are seemingly unconnected) and ask students if they think their ideas could be a coincidence and not connected.

1 Students read the newspaper article about climate change and decide what the writer thinks about it and why. You could ask students to compare in pairs before you elicit the answers.

Answers

Harry Macdonald thinks climate change is real. He thinks there is evidence with colder winters and hotter summers.

2 SPEAKING In pairs, students note down their opinions on climate change. Ask them to write whether they agree or disagree with Harry Macdonald, giving their reasons. Nominate different pairs to give their answers, or if you have time, have a short class debate on climate change.

TEACHER DEVELOPMENT: CLASSROOM TIPS

Setting up a class debate

Ask students to find a partner who shares their opinion on climate change. Set a time limit for students to plan their arguments. Then put pairs with opposing opinions together in groups of four and ask them to have a small debate. You could write some key structures on the board to help them: *In my/our opinion, …; If you ask me, …; This is my/our point of view: …; That doesn't make sense.; I understand what you're saying, but I don't agree.; Let me explain, …; Here's why I don't agree with you: …*

Once students have practised their arguments in small groups, you can ask them to share their opinions with the class and develop a whole-class debate.

3 Students read the letter to the editor of a newspaper and decide if the reader agrees or disagrees with Harry Macdonald. Ask students if any of their ideas from exercise 2 are in the letter.

Answer

The reader agrees with Harry Macdonald.

4 Students look at the words in bold in the letter and put them in the correct place in the Writing bank.

Answers

Sequence: *Next, Finally*
Addition: *What is more*
Contrast: *Nevertheless*

>>> **FAST FINISHERS**

Ask students if they know any other linkers and to add them to their lists, e.g. *then, besides, in addition, on the other hand, moreover*, etc.

TEACHER DEVELOPMENT: LANGUAGE

Linkers and connectors

Linkers (sometimes called connectors) are words that join simple and complex sentences with others. Some frequent connectors are: *and, but, or, so*. Linkers have different functions (in this unit students see connectors which express sequence, addition and contrast). Remind students that a logical argument needs few linkers and they should not overuse them.

Point out that *nevertheless* is slightly more formal than *however*. *However* and *nevertheless* are normally placed at the beginning of a sentence when contrasting two ideas. They can also come in the middle or at the end. *Furthermore* is quite formal and *what's more* has the same meaning, but is more idiomatic.

5 Students complete the sentences with the linkers from the Writing bank. Ask students to check in pairs before you elicit answers from the class.

Answers

1 What is more/Furthermore **2** Firstly, Finally
3 However/Nevertheless

PRACTICE MAKES PERFECT

6a Students look at the task and make notes with their ideas about the topic in preparation for writing their letter.

6b Students write a letter using the one in exercise 3 as a model. Remind them to use the notes they have made and include the linkers from the Writing bank. You could do this activity as an exam simulation. For students who are less confident, photocopy the model text below for extra support during the writing task.

Model text

Dear Editor,

I am writing in response to your article about young people and the environment, which appeared in your newspaper last week. Personally I disagree with you and I will explain why.

Firstly, while it's true that *some* young people don't do anything to protect the environment, this isn't true for all young people.

At my school we have Green Club, where we discuss environmental issues and what we can do to make a difference. Moreover, we have already made differences in our community: our school now recycles paper and, in addition, we have a 'Walk to school day' every week where we ask people to walk, not drive, to school.

I agree that young people can do more to help the environment. However, I think that older people can do more, too.

Finally, I think it would be useful if you wrote more positive articles about what young people are doing.

Yours faithfully,

Sofia Shorter, Lincolnshire

✓ EXAM SUCCESS Students read about writing in exam conditions. Discuss what they can do if they are not sure of a word or a specific grammar structure. Tell them to turn to page 145 (Writing: Exam conditions) and compare their answers.

TEACHER DEVELOPMENT: STUDENT TRAINING

Writing in exam conditions

Students need a lot of practice to write confidently in exam conditions, so it is a good idea to do some writing activities as exam simulations. Tell students that their letter should be 100–150 words. Set a time limit of 20 minutes and give regular updates on the time. Make sure students only have the things that they are allowed in a real exam and that their bags are closed.

If you can, move the desks in some way to simulate exam conditions. If you can't move the desks, ask students to change their usual seating positions. Give all the students blank paper to make notes and write their letter on.

Mark strictly and take marks off for things such as bad handwriting, too many words, spelling, not following the task, etc. Give students exactly the same kind of results and feedback they would get in an exam. Give back the corrected letters in the next lesson and discuss particular difficulties they had, as well as tips on dealing with real exam conditions.

HOMEWORK

Assign students page 54 in their Workbook or the relevant sections of the Online Workbook.

Language checkpoint: Unit 6

>>> FAST TRACK

The extra support provided on the Grammar and Vocabulary reference sections makes the Grammar and Vocabulary revision section ideal for setting as homework. You could get students to complete the whole revision page or just certain exercises for homework.

Grammar revision p81

be going to, will

1 Students correct the mistakes in these sentences.

Answers
1 The students are going to go on an excursion.
2 What are your plans? What are you doing/going to do tomorrow?
3 They say it's going to rain next week.
4 I can't meet you tomorrow because I am going to do an exam.

will, may, might

2 Students complete the sentences with the words in the box.

Answers
1 definitely 2 may 3 Perhaps 4 probably 5 won't
6 will

Zero conditional

3 Students answer the questions with complete sentences.

Suggested answers
1 If you mix blue and yellow, you get green.
2 If you study hard for an exam, you get a good mark.
3 If you never brush your teeth, they go bad and fall out.
4 If you eat too much, you feel sick.

First conditional

4 Students complete the sentences with the correct form of the words.

Answers
1 shines 2 finishes 3 'll get 4 comes 5 is
6 won't bring

Vocabulary revision p81

GEOGRAPHICAL FEATURES

1 Students look at the names and write the geographical features.

Answers

1 desert   **2** rainforest   **3** mountain range   **4** beach
5 lake   **6** ice cap   **7** island

THE ENVIRONMENT

2 Students to complete the text with the words.

Answers

a Global warming   **b** ozone layer   **c** floods
d droughts   **e** waste   **f** save   **g** recycle

DIFFERENT USES OF *GET*

3 Students decide on synonyms for *get* in these sentences.

Answers

1 bought   **2** arrive   **3** bring   **4** receive   **5** became
6 received

HOMEWORK

Assign students page 55 in their Workbook or the relevant sections of the Online Workbook.

Listening p82

> **TIP FOR LISTENING EXAMS**

Ask students to read the tip and look at Exam Success on page 145.

1 SPEAKING In pairs, students look at the photos and discuss with a partner which way of finding out the news they prefer and why.

2 LISTENING ▶ 40 Play the track for students to listen and match the speakers to their preferences. Remind them that there is one option that they do not need. See p155 for the audioscript for this exercise.

Answers

1 E 2 B 3 A 4 D

3 ▶ 40 Students listen again and choose the correct speaker.

Answers

1 Dan 2 Amanda 3 Jerry 4 Sarah 5 Dan

Writing p82

> **TIP FOR WRITING EXAMS**

Ask students to read the tip and ask them to look at Exam Success on page 145 for more ideas.

4 SPEAKING Students work with a partner and read through the topic then discuss their ideas. Encourage them to give their reasons.

5 Tell students to read the instructions carefully and write a letter to a newspaper expressing their opinion on the topic. For students who are less confident, photocopy the model text below for extra support during the writing task.

Model text

Dear Editor,

I read about Brad Pitt's environmental foundation in your newspaper. He's a great actor and also a campaigner for the environment. I am writing to you because I want to highlight Leonardo DiCaprio's charity work. In my opinion his foundation also does lots of good work, including a campaign to stop people using plastic bags. He also donated $1 million to victims of the earthquake in Haiti. I love Leonardo DiCaprio because he's an amazing actor and a very generous person, and I would like to see more publicity for his charity work in the newspapers.

Yours faithfully,

Kate

Use of English p83

> **TIP FOR USE OF ENGLISH**

Ask students to read the tip and think of any other ideas they can. Ask them to look at Exam Success on page 145 for more suggestions.

6 Students rewrite the sentences keeping the same meaning. Remind students to use between two and five words including the word given in bold.

Answers

1 isn't as hot as 2 is not as important as
3 will be too cold 4 is more serious than
5 may become 6 will definitely die
7 things will probably get

Speaking p83

> **TIP FOR SPEAKING EXAMS**

Ask students to read the tip and think of other fillers they can remember. Ask them to look at Exam Success on page 145 for more ideas.

7 In pairs, students make a list of different ways to make and respond to suggestions.

Suggested answers

Making suggestions:

Why don't we … ? Do you fancy … ? Let's …
How about … ? Shall we … ?

Responding to suggestions:

Sure/OK/Fine/Great/Good idea; Not really/Sorry, I can't/ I prefer …

8a In pairs, students look at the TV guide and read what programmes are on tonight.

8b SPEAKING Students work with a partner and make and respond to suggestions about what to watch. Set a strict time limit of three minutes, after which students have to make a decision.

HOMEWORK

Assign students pages 56–57 in their Workbook or the relevant sections of the Online Workbook.

'CAN DO' PROGRESS CHECK p83

1 Ask students to mark from 1–4 how well they can do each thing in English.

2 Ask students to look at their marks and decide what they need to do to improve. Elicit other suggestions.

7 Job hunting

UNIT OVERVIEW

 Vocabulary
Jobs and work
Personal qualities

 Reading
Do you have an unusual job?
CRITICAL THINKING Evaluating whether certain jobs are important for society

 Grammar in context
Modal verbs of obligation, prohibition and advice
PRONUNCIATION Silent letters

 Developing vocabulary
Compound adjectives
PRONUNCIATION Stress in compound adjectives

 Life skills
The world of work:
Assessing your transferable skills

 Listening
Film and TV extras

 Grammar in context
Second conditional

 Developing speaking
Making polite requests

 Developing writing
A letter of application and CV

✔ **Exam success**
Reading: True/False activities
Listening: Multiple-choice activities

DIGITAL OVERVIEW

Presentation Kit

- ▶ **Flipped classroom video Unit 7:** Modal verbs of obligation, prohibition and advice
- ▶ **Life skills video Unit 7:** Transferable skills
- ▶ v **Vocabulary tool:** Jobs and work
- ▶ **Interactive versions of Student's Book activities**
- ▶ **Integrated audio and answer key for all activities**
- ▶ **Workbook pages with answer key**

Teacher's Resource Centre

 TRC

- ▶ **Flipped classroom video Unit 7:** Modal verbs of obligation, prohibition and advice
- ▶ **Life skills video Unit 7:** Transferable skills
- ▶ **Grammar communication activity Unit 7:** Problem solving
- ▶ **Worksheets for this unit, including:**
  – Grammar practice worksheet Unit 7
  – Flipped classroom video worksheet Unit 7: Modal verbs of obligation, prohibition and advice
  – Literature worksheet Units 7 and 8
  – Culture worksheet Unit 7
  – Life skills video worksheet Unit 7
  – Everyday English worksheet Unit 7

Student's App

Gateway 2nd Edition wordlist for the award-winning Sounds App (available for download)

✔ TESTING AND ASSESSMENT

Resources for exam preparation and measuring student progress

- ▶ Test Generator Units 1–7
- ▶ Printable test Unit 7
- ▶ Gateway to exams Units 7 and 8 (end of Unit 8)

Vocabulary p84

Talking about jobs, work and personal qualities

>>> FAST TRACK

You could do exercise 4 as a class activity, by reading a category and inviting the rest of the class to call out matching jobs.

WARMER

Elicit different ways of asking about someone's job: *What do you do? What is your job? What do you do for a living?* In pairs, students discuss the meaning of the unit title *Job hunting* and what they think the unit is going to be about. Elicit ideas from around the class.

Suggested answer

In English, *job hunting* is often used to mean actively looking for a job. The unit will look at ways of finding a job.

Jobs and work

1 SPEAKING In pairs, ask students to look at the four photos and name the jobs they can see. Refer students to the words in the box and check that they understand all of them.

Answers

a vet **b** plumber **c** fashion designer **d** receptionist

2 ▶ 41 Play the track for students to listen, check and repeat. See p156 for the audioscript for this exercise.

++ EXTRA ACTIVITY

Ask students to underline the stressed syllable in each word. Play the track again if necessary.

3a In pairs, ask students to think of a job for each letter of the alphabet. Refer students to the example, but see if they can find new ones for A, B and C. You can check by going round the class asking the first pair for the letter A, the second for letter B, etc.

3b Ask students if there are any letters they couldn't find jobs for. Give some suggestions if possible.

Suggested answers

architect, babysitter, baker, chef, dentist, doctor, editor, fashion designer, firefighter, graphic designer, helicopter pilot, IT consultant, judge, kindergarten teacher, librarian, manager, mechanic, nurse, office manager, painter, pharmacist, reporter, researcher, salesperson, taxi driver, teacher, umpire, vet, web designer, writer, zoo-keeper

++ EXTRA ACTIVITY

Play a game to practise job-related vocabulary. Ask for a volunteer to step outside the classroom. While he/she is outside, the other students choose a job for him/her. When he/she returns to the classroom, he/she has to guess his/her profession by asking the class questions, e.g. *Do I work with people? Do I work in an office? Do I play sport?* When he/she guesses correctly, ask another student to go out and repeat the process.

4 In pairs, students think of two or three jobs for each different category. Students can use the Macmillan Online Dictionary to help them in this task. Draw attention to the example before they begin. Check answers by asking different students.

Suggested answers

2 gardeners, farmers, builders
3 lawyers, office workers, immigration officers
4 miners, carpenters, plumbers
5 waiters/waitresses, flight attendants, hairdressers
6 bankers, accountants, tax inspectors

>>> FAST FINISHERS

Ask students to order the jobs in exercise 1 from least to most stressful and from worst to best paid. Then ask them to compare with another student.

Personal qualities

5 Students complete the sentences with words from the box. Focus attention on the example sentence. Students may also use their dictionaries for this task. With a less confident class, you may wish to pre-teach the following words: *carefully* – thinking about what you do so that you avoid problems; *force* – physical strength or energy; *depend on someone* – trust someone to do something/rely on somebody; *effort* – an attempt to do something that involves hard work.

Answers

2 caring, sensitive, patient, calm   **6** sociable
3 fit, strong   **7** confident
4 clever/bright, creative   **8** ambitious
5 reliable, hard-working

>>> FAST FINISHERS

Ask students to match the adjectives to the jobs in exercise 1.

6 LISTENING ▶ 42 Play the track for students to decide which four jobs are being described. Tell students to note down key words which help them decide on their answers. With a less confident class, pause the audio after each person for students to check their answers in pairs. Check the answers and elicit any other information students remember about each job and the adjectives the people used. See p156 for the audioscript for this exercise.

Answers

1 builder **2** fashion designer **3** receptionist
4 shop assistant

7 SPEAKING In pairs, students use adjectives from exercise 5 to describe themselves. Draw their attention to the example sentence.

++ EXTRA ACTIVITY

In pairs, students race to form as many nouns as they can from the adjectives in exercise 5, e.g. *ambition, organisation, care, fitness*, etc.

HOMEWORK

Assign students page 58 in their Workbook or the relevant sections of the Online Workbook.

Reading p85

Skimming and scanning for global and specific information

>>> FAST TRACK

You could ask students to do exercise 4 at home so that less confident students can take the necessary time to look up the vocabulary in the Macmillan Online Dictionary.

WARMER

Ask students to brainstorm jobs that they think would be boring and jobs that they think would be fun. Write the suggestions on the board and ask the class to vote for the most boring and the most fun jobs.

TEACHER DEVELOPMENT: LANGUAGE

Job vs *work*

Job and *work* have the same meaning. *Job* is countable and *work*, in most cases, is uncountable. Therefore, *work* rarely comes after *a* or a number, and it is rarely used in the plural.

1 Focus students' attention on the photos. Ask students if they can predict what the text might be about. Ask students to read the blog and then answer the questions. Elicit answers from different students.

Answers

A Ryan O' Connor. This person prepares people for bungee-jumps. (1)
B Grace Simmons. She's a 'mystery shopper'. (3)
C Gavin Henderson. He's a rickshaw driver. (2)

✔ EXAM SUCCESS Ask students to think what they should do after reading a text quickly to get the general idea. Ask them to talk to a partner, then compare their ideas with the information on page 145.

TEACHER DEVELOPMENT: STUDENT TRAINING

True/False activities

- Write *True* or *False* (or T/F), and not *Yes* or *No*.
- When in doubt, guess. You have a 50% chance of being correct.

2 Students read the blog again and decide if the sentences are true or false. Nominate different students to give the answers.

Answers

1 T **2** F **3** T **4** T **5** T **6** F **7** F **8** T **9** F
10 F

>>> FAST FINISHERS

Ask students to correct the false sentences in exercise 2.

3 ⚙ **CRITICAL THINKING** Students consider the jobs in exercise 3 and think whether they are important for society. Ask them to compare their answers with a partner before discussing with the class.

Example answers

I think a rickshaw driver is important for society as he helps people travel around quickly and also helps tourists. Rickshaws are better for the environment than cars. Preparing people for bungee jumps isn't an important job for society, because bungee jumping isn't necessary and doesn't help other people.

4 Students write the meaning of the underlined words in the text. Nominate students to give their answers.

Answers

equipment = objects needed to do a specialised activity
heights = high places like the top of buildings, mountains or bridges
sorts = different types or varieties
spy = a person who watches and gathers important information secretly
treat = way of behaving towards another person
mixture = combining more than one thing
shout at = speak loudly, rudely and aggressively to people

5 **SPEAKING** What about *you*? In pairs, students discuss the questions. To facilitate and give structure to students' discussions, write these key areas for evaluating a job on the board: *good work conditions (hours, pay and holidays)? any other extra benefits? includes special training? possibilities for promotion? interesting? challenging?*

✚ EXTRA ACTIVITY

Divide the class into small groups and ask them to discuss these questions: What kind of work do you want to do in the future? What would your dream job be? What do you need to do in order to get this job? Which jobs wouldn't you like to do? Why not? What was your dream job when you were a child?

HOMEWORK

Assign students page 59 in their Workbook or the relevant sections of the Online Workbook.

Grammar in context pp86–87

Talking about obligation, prohibition and advice using modal verbs

⟫ FAST TRACK

You could ask students to complete their answers for exercise 3 at home. They can then compare with a partner at the next class.

 Test before you teach: Flipped classroom
Set the Flipped classroom video and tasks for homework <u>before the lesson</u>. This will allow you to assess the needs of the students before the class. Students can then move on to the relevant grammar practice activities.

1a Students read the sentences. Point out that most are from the text in the previous lesson.

1b Tell students to decide which sentence(s) express obligation, no obligation, prohibition and advice/recommendation. Nominate different students to give their answers.

Answers
2 a **3** d **4** c, f

1c Elicit which type of word comes after *must, mustn't, should, shouldn't, have to, don't have to*.

Answer
a verb in the infinitive (without *to*)

TEACHER DEVELOPMENT: LANGUAGE

Modal verbs of obligation, prohibition and advice

should/shouldn't for giving advice:
Should/shouldn't are used when we want to give a strong opinion, telling someone the best thing to do. We can request advice by saying *Do you think I should … ?* or *Should I … ?*

have/has to for obligation:
have/has to and *must* mean the same when we are talking about rules and obligations. We can also say *I have got to …* and this has the same meaning.

don't/doesn't have to for no obligation:
Make it clear that this is not the same as *mustn't*, which is used for prohibition. *Don't/doesn't have to*, on the other hand, means it is not necessary to do something, but you can do it if you wish.

must/mustn't for obligation or prohibition:
Must is not very common in question forms; we usually say *Do I have to … ?* instead.

2a **PRONUNCIATION** Draw students' attention to the silent letter 'l' in *should*. Tell students to read the sentences and cross out the silent letters. You could also provide dictionaries for this task.

2b ▶ 43 Play the track for students to listen, check and repeat (the letters in bold below are silent). Ask students to compare their answers in pairs before you elicit the answers and write them up on the board. See p156 for the audioscript for this exercise.

Answers
1 Firefigh**t**ers should be calm.
2 You mus**t**n't ta**l**k to the bus driver.
3 Disciplin**e** can be important.
4 My s**c**ience tea**c**her comes to s**c**hool at ha**l**f past eigh**t**.
5 Fashion designers shou**l**dn't copy other peo**p**le's designs.
6 He works as a g**u**ide at the cas**t**le on the is**l**and.

⟫ FAST FINISHERS

Write these words on the board: *climb, foreign, Wednesday, knee*. Students find the silent letter in each word. They also think of one more to add to the list and ask the class to identify the silent letter.

3 Students look at the pictures and the sentences, and use *should* or *shouldn't* to give advice to the people. Ask students to think what people will need to know to do their jobs or what things they will need.

Elicit answers from the class, paying special attention to correct pronunciation.

Suggested answers
1 You should learn French and English/foreign languages.
   (You should read about other countries.)
2 You should practise cooking at home.
   (You should do the cooking for your family.)
3 You should study a lot/work really hard.
   (You should do a first aid course.)
4 You shouldn't play computer games all the time.
   (You should get a science kit.)

4 Students choose the correct alternatives. Remind them they can choose both alternatives if they think they are correct.

Answers
1 must/have to **2** don't have to **3** mustn't
4 have to **5** must/have to **6** has to
7 doesn't have to **8** deal

5 Students rewrite each sentence using a modal verb of obligation, prohibition or advice. Draw students' attention to the example sentence. Elicit answers from students, paying attention to the correct pronunciation of the modal verbs. Ask different students to write the correct answers on the board.

Answers
2 Builders must/have to wear hard hats here.
3 Frank should work in the summer.
4 In our school, teachers mustn't wear jeans.
5 You shouldn't wear informal clothes for a job interview.
6 Our receptionists don't have to speak French.
7 Karen has to/must be calm in her job.

6a SPEAKING Ask students to look at the photos and identify the jobs (doctor/nurse, police officer, football player, teacher, model).

Individually, students choose one of the jobs and make a note of the things they *have to/don't have to/must/ mustn't/should/shouldn't* do in this job.

Suggested answers

a **A doctor/nurse:** You have to be good at listening to people. You should be confident. You shouldn't get nervous in an emergency. You have to work as part of a team. You mustn't make mistakes.

b **A police officer:** You have to be fit. You must understand the law. You have to be honest. You should have good people skills. You must work as part of a team. You don't have to be tall. You shouldn't be impatient. You have to stay calm in difficult situations.

c **A football player:** You have to be brilliant. You must be fit and strong. You don't have to have any qualifications. You should be good at working in a team. You have to train a lot.

d **A teacher:** You should be calm and patient. You have to know your subject. You don't have to wear a suit to work. You mustn't shout at the children. You don't have to work in the summer.

e **A model:** You should be good-looking or beautiful. You have to wear special clothes.

6b Students describe the job they chose in exercise 6a for their partner to guess. Draw attention to the model dialogue and ask a pair to read it out. Monitor and provide help if necessary.

Refer students to the Grammar reference on page 94 if necessary.

HOMEWORK

Assign students page 60 in their Workbook or the relevant sections of the Online Workbook.

Developing vocabulary p87

Using compound adjectives

>>> FAST TRACK

You could do exercise 4 as a class activity, by reading aloud the definitions and inviting the rest of the class to call out matching compound adjectives.

1 Students look at the compound adjectives and point out that they are usually connected with a hyphen. Ask them to complete the compound adjectives in the definitions using the words in the box.

2 ▶ 44 Play the track for students to check their answers. See p156 for the audioscript for this exercise.

Answers

1 part   **2** easy   **3** badly   **4** full   **5** well
6 blue/brown/green   **7** right/left   **8** good
9 well   **10** well

3a PRONUNCIATION ▶ 44 Play the track again for students to listen to the pronunciation of the compound adjectives and decide where the stress is (see underlined words in audioscript). Point out that in compound adjectives the stress in on the second part, but in compound nouns the stress is on the first part (e.g. <u>fire</u>fighter).

3b Drill the words, practising the correct stress. Students can also drill each other in pairs.

4 Students write as many compound adjectives as they can to describe the three people. Ask them to tell their partner and then nominate students to share their answers with the class.

Suggested answers

1 I'm right-handed and easy-going.
2 My dad is left-handed and brown-eyed. He isn't easy-going!
3 He's left-handed, easy-going, well-paid, brown-eyed and good-looking.

✚ EXTRA ACTIVITY

Bring in some magazines or allow students to go online to look for pictures which illustrate compound adjectives from the lesson, e.g. *blue-eyed people, good-looking people, left-handed people, well-paid people*, etc. They could use their pictures to make a poster with a short description included.

HOMEWORK

Assign students page 61 in their Workbook or the relevant sections of the Online Workbook.

Gateway to life skills pp88–89

Assessing your transferable skills

To learn about transferable skills and their importance in finding a job, to consider practical examples of transferable skills in daily life and to assess and express your own transferable skills.

>>> FAST TRACK

You could ask students to do exercise 1 at home before the class and then compare their answers with a partner at the beginning of the lesson.

ⓘ BACKGROUND INFORMATION

Transferable skills are the abilities you have developed that are useful across a range of different jobs. They might be directly related to the job or more general. Transferable skills are increasingly valued by employers in the job market, and people are more likely these days to change careers throughout their working life, so it is important that students not only learn how to identify their own transferable skills but recognise how each skill could be useful across different situations. Students listen to three people talking and identify their transferable skills, before focusing on their own and the careers they could be suitable for.

Write on the board *I am good at maths* and ask students to recommend jobs that they think would be suitable for someone who's good with numbers, e.g. *maths teacher, banker, mathematician, engineer.* Encourage them to also think of less obvious jobs where numeracy skills are needed, too, e.g. *waitress, shop worker,* etc. Tell students that they are going to look at different types of skills and how these can be suitable for more than one type of job.

1 Students read through the Key concepts before drawing their attention to the two photos. Tell students that although they are quite different jobs, they both have skills in common. Ask them to read the two examples and then list skills and qualities they both would need. Elicit answers from different students.

Suggested answers

They both need to be hard-working. They both need to pay attention to detail. They both need to be good at working as a team and working individually. They both need to be good at communicating.

2 READING Students read the text and answer the questions. Ask different students to give their answers.

Answers

Transferable skills are skills that can be used in different jobs, not just one specific job. They are important because people change jobs and careers and employers want people with good transferable skills.

3 Students read the text again and answer the questions. Allow them to check with a partner before nominating students to share their answers.

Answers

1 Because people did the same job for life.
2 Everybody, because we use technology everywhere.
3 Good communication, teamwork and leadership, working well with others; creating a good personal impression is essential. **4** waiters, bankers and shop assistants **5** problem solving **6** ambitious people, to keep learning and improving the company

4 Students look back at their lists in exercise 1 and identify any transferable skills.

5a LISTENING ▶ 45 Tell students they are going to watch/listen to three people talking about what they do or did in their free time. Ask students to tick the transferable skills that are part of what they did. Play the track. Check answers as a class. See p156 for the videoscript/audioscript for this exercise.

Suggested answers 5a and 5b

		Amelia	Kieran	Molly
1	Friendly and caring	✓ The girls like her. She wants to know how they feel.	✓ People like the fact he's patient.	
2	Good communication skills		✓ I want people to understand what I'm telling them.	
3	Good at motivating others	✓ They enjoy coming; she tries to motivate them.		
4	Good at organising others	✓ I've made a timetable, for training sessions and matches.		
5	ICT skills		✓ A computer expert	
6	Leadership	✓ I help train our youngest team.		✓ I had an idea.
7	Maths and money			✓ I had an idea to get some money. We had a raffle and a lottery.
8	Patience		✓ I'm good at staying calm and explaining as many times as necessary.	
9	Problem solving		✓ usually know what to do	✓ There were some problems. I helped to find solutions.
10	Teamwork	✓ I enjoy being with the girls and I think I've got a good relationship with them.		✓ I really like working with others.

5b 45 Students listen or watch again and add notes to the table to justify their answers.

6 Put students in small groups and ask them to compare their answers in exercise 5. Ask them to add any extra examples to their table if they didn't already have them.

LIFE TASK

Tell students they are going to evaluate and write a description of their transferable skills.

- **Step 1**
  Ask students to work individually and read the instructions. Students start by looking at the list of transferable skills on page 147 and giving themselves a mark for each from 5 to 1. Encourage them to add any further skills they feel they have to the list. Circulate as they do this and help with any necessary vocabulary.

- **Step 2**
  Students think of as many examples of their skills as they can. Remind them they can think of their hobbies and interests as well as their academic skills.

- **Step 3**
  Students use their examples to write a description of their transferable skills. Walk around and monitor while students are writing their descriptions. Help them with any language difficulties and make a note of any errors to go over at the end of the task. When students have finished the task, you could nominate more confident students to read their descriptions to the class or go over any common errors. Remind students that they can use their descriptions in future when they are applying for a course or a job.

✚ EXTRA ACTIVITY

Ask students to work in pairs and read out their marks and examples from the Life task to their partner. Ask their partner to recommend jobs, based on their strengths.

Model a few sentences with a student so they are clear what to do, e.g. *You are friendly and caring and you have good communication skills. You should be a nurse.*, etc.

Listening p90

Listening for general and specific information

WARMER

Elicit from students which skills and personal qualities are important in the working world, e.g. *communication skills, honesty, teamwork, motivation, flexibility, computer skills, analytical skills, organisational skills,* etc. Ask students what makes a job interesting for them. Is it more important to have an interesting job or a well-paid job? Ask if they think you should do a job you don't really like just for the money.

1 SPEAKING Students look at the definition of an *extra*, then work with a partner to make lists of the good and bad things about the type or work. Divide the board into two columns and ask students to come and write suggestions.

Suggested answers

Bad: You don't get paid much money. You spend a lot of time standing around. You have to be really patient. It's probably boring.

Good: You see famous people. You can work in the film industry. You wear interesting costumes.

2 LISTENING ▶ 46 Tell the students they are going to listen to someone talking about being an extra and to tick their ideas from exercise 1 that are mentioned. Play the track. Ask students if there were any other ideas that were mentioned and add them to the board. See pp156–157 for the audioscript for this exercise.

TEACHER DEVELOPMENT: STUDENT TRAINING

Multiple-choice tasks

Multiple-choice questions usually include a phrase or stem followed by three to five options. Students should approach a multiple-choice task as follows:

- Read the directions carefully.
- Read the stem with each option. Treat each option as a true/false question and choose the truest option. If two alternatives seem correct, compare them for differences, then refer to the stem to find the best answer.
- Eliminate options they know to be incorrect.
- If there are two very similar options, one is probably correct. Choose the best, but eliminate choices that mean basically the same thing, and thus cancel each other out.
- If two options are opposites, the chances are one of them is correct.
- Be careful with 'second-guessing' original answers. Research indicates that our first instinct is more likely to be correct. Students should only change answers if they originally misread them or if they have found information that indicates that their first choice was incorrect.
- Always guess when there is no penalty for doing so.

✓ EXAM SUCCESS Students look at the Exam Success box and discuss the question with a partner. Then ask students to turn to page 145 and compare their ideas with the information there.

3 ▶ 46 Play the track for students to listen again and choose the correct alternatives. With a less confident class, you could pre-teach some of the more complex words from the listening. Either elicit the meaning of these words from students, or write them on the board and read out the definitions for students to call out the matching words: *autograph* – a signature from a famous person; *scene* – a small part of a play or film; *to take ages* – to take a long time. Give students time to compare in pairs before you elicit answers from the class. Then ask some follow-up questions: *Do you think Sarah should take the job? Do you think the conditions are good? Why/Why not?*

Answers

1 c 2 b 3 a 4 a 5 b

4 SPEAKING **What about *you*?** In pairs or small groups, students discuss the questions. You may like students to note down some ideas individually before they do this activity. Elicit ideas from the class.

HOMEWORK

Assign students page 61 in their Workbook or the relevant sections of the Online Workbook.

Grammar in context pp90–91 Ⓖ

Using the second conditional

≫≫ FAST TRACK

If students are familiar with the vocabulary, you could ask them to complete exercise 2 at home and then check their answers at the start of the lesson.

Test before you teach

Write these sentences on the board and ask students to finish them: *If I had a million pounds, …*; *If I could drive a car, …* Monitor as students write their sentences to see if they are comfortable with the second conditional. Ask different students to share their sentences with the class.

1a Students look at the sentences and then choose the correct alternatives in sentences a–c.

Answers

a possible and probable **b** the present or future
c give advice

1b Students choose the correct alternatives. Check answers as a class.

Answers

1 the past simple **2** *would(n't)* + infinitive **3** *can*

TEACHER DEVELOPMENT: LANGUAGE

Using conditionals

Remind students that we often use the contracted form of *would* (*'d*) when we speak and this makes it difficult to hear. The best way to hear if someone is using a first, second or third conditional is by focusing on the tense of the verb after *if*. Point out that, in the second conditional, the past simple clause always follows *if* (never in the *would* clause).

Remind students that when the *if* clause comes first, a comma is usually used. When the *if* clause comes second, there is no need for a comma, e.g. *You wouldn't be late if you got up earlier.*

2 Students look at the situations and write sentences using the second conditional. Focus students' attention on the example sentence first.

Answers

2 If he could see well, he would be a pilot.
3 She would repair computers if she knew how to.
4 If I was fast enough, I would be a professional athlete.
5 I would work as an interpreter if I spoke more languages.
6 If we were happy, we wouldn't want to leave this company.
7 She would take part in the concert if she could sing well.

✛ EXTRA ACTIVITY

Ask students to close their books. Then elicit the sentences from exercise 2 orally to see if they can remember them, e.g. *If I wasn't still at school (… I'd work).* Students continue testing each other in pairs, practising the contracted form of *would* (*'d*).

3 Draw students' attention to the photo and ask them what they think the person's job could be. Then ask students to complete the text with the correct form of the verbs in the box. Ask different students to read out answers.

Answers

a played **b** looked **c** ate **d** did **e** was **f** put

4a Individually, students make notes on the advice they would give somebody in each situation. For less confident students, model the first one so they can see the structure.

Example answers

1 If I were you, I'd get a part-time job. **2** I f I were you, I'd learn to speak English really well. **3** If I were you, I'd start recycling at home. **4** If I were you, I'd try going to bed earlier. **5** If I were you, I'd try yoga. **6** If I were you, I'd check your spelling in a dictionary.

4b SPEAKING In pairs, students ask for and give advice using *If I were you …* Focus attention on the model dialogue. You may like to do the first two situations with the class before students continue in pairs. Monitor to make sure students are using the correct form and pronunciation. When they have finished, elicit some ideas from students, review any errors you noted and give praise for good language use.

5a SPEAKING Students look at the situations and think about what they would do in each one. Ask them to make notes.

5b Students work with a partner and compare their ideas for each situation. Draw their attention to the model dialogue. Remind students that they can disagree with each other.

≫≫ FAST FINISHERS

Ask students to write another sentence for each situation saying what they *wouldn't* do, e.g. 1 *I wouldn't wear my slippers all day; it would be so embarrassing!*

Refer students to the Grammar reference on page 94 if necessary.

Developing speaking p92

Making polite requests

>>> FAST TRACK

You could ask students to prepare their dialogue for exercise 5a at home with a partner. They can present their dialogue to the class at the beginning of the next lesson.

WARMER

Ask students to think of three things they would want to know before applying for a job.

Example answer

I would want to know how many hours per week, how much money I would earn, and where the job is.

1a SPEAKING Students look at the adverts and think which job they would be interested in. Ask them to compare their answer with a partner. Have a quick vote in the class to see the most popular and least popular job.

1b Students work with their partner to choose a job and make a list of questions they would want to ask to find out more information. Draw attention to the example questions.

Suggested answers

Do I have to wear a uniform? Do I get a discount on clothes? Is there any training?

Do I need any special qualifications? What hours do I have to work?

Do you get any time to visit the country?

What sports do they do? How old are the children? How big are the groups?

2 LISTENING ▶ 47 Play the track for students to listen to a teenager calling about one of the adverts. Ask students to decide which advert she is calling about and if she asks any of their questions from exercise 1. See p157 for the audioscript for this exercise.

Answer

She is calling about the advert for a shop assistant in a clothes shop.

3 ▶ 47 Focus students' attention on the expressions in the Speaking bank. Play the track again for students to listen and put the polite requests in the order they hear them. Nominate a student to give their answers.

Answers

1 Could I ask for some information first?
2 Could you tell me if the job is full-time or part-time?
3 Can you tell me what the wages are?

✚ EXTRA ACTIVITY

Ask some follow-up comprehension questions about the listening: *Where does the girl see the advert?* (in the newspaper) *How many hours a week is the part-time job?* (24 hours per week) *Does she need any experience?* (no) *When is the job for?* (July and August) *How much are the wages?* (£140 per week) *What does she have to do to apply?* (send a letter and CV)

4 SPEAKING In pairs, students take it in turns to practise making polite requests for information using the phrases in the table. You could model this activity first with a pair of more confident students.

Answers

Could you tell me/Could I ask/Can you tell me …

… if you need experience?/what we have to do?/what the wages are?/when the job starts?/when I can apply?/how I can apply?/how much we have to do?/what sort of person you are looking for?

TEACHER DEVELOPMENT: LANGUAGE

Could vs *can*

Can …? is more direct than *Could …?* However, making polite requests also depends on intonation and students should always try to have a warm and friendly attitude when making requests.

PRACTICE MAKES PERFECT

5a SPEAKING Students read the task individually. Divide the class into pairs. Student A prepares questions to ask for information about the job at Cinerama Cinemas. Student B looks at page 148 to find the information they need to give their partner and invents any extra information. Students role-play the telephone conversation using words and expressions from the Speaking bank. Draw attention to the example before they begin.

For less confident students, photocopy the model dialogue on this page and instruct students to read aloud in pairs, alternating between roles A and B.

5b Then ask them to change roles and for student B to prepare questions about the job at Sports Star Camp and student A to turn to page 148 and look at the information about the role. Circulate as students speak and make a note of any errors to correct at the end of the task.

TEACHER DEVELOPMENT: CLASSROOM TIPS

Simulating a phone conversation

Telephone conversations are hard because there are no clues from body language. To duplicate these conditions, you can have students sit back to back so they can't see each other. This may be challenging for some students, so elicit what they can say if they do not understand or if they need their partner to speak more slowly: *Would you mind repeating that? Could you speak more slowly, please?*

Model dialogue

A: Good afternoon. I'm calling about your job offer in the newspaper yesterday.

B: Yes. What would you like to know?

A: Can you tell me if the job is for the whole of the summer, from June to September?

B: Yes, it's from the 20th of June to the 20th of September.

A: And do you have to work weekends?

B: Yes, but you don't have to work on Mondays.

A: Can you tell me what the wages are?

B: Yes, they're £7.80 an hour.

A: I see. And could you tell me if the job is part-time or full-time.

B: It's a part-time job.

A: Oh, I see. Could you tell me how many hours a week it is?

B: Yes, it's 24 hours a week.

A: What personal qualities do you need to do the job?

B: You need to be sociable and reliable, but you don't have to be an expert in films.

A: Do you need any experience of working in a cinema?

B: No, no experience is necessary.

A: OK, great.

B: Good. Any more questions?

A: Well, yes. Could you tell me how to apply?

B: Easy. Just email a letter and CV to me. That's Janet Doors at jdoors@cineramacinemas.co.uk.

A: Would you mind repeating that?

B: Sure, jdoors@cineramacinemas.co.uk.

A: Thank you very much.

B: Not at all. I look forward to getting your application. Bye.

A: Bye.

Developing writing p93

Writing a letter of application and CV

≫ FAST TRACK

You could ask students to write their letter of application for exercise 7a at home. They can then compare their application with a partner at the next lesson.

WARMER

Elicit what type of information students think would need to go in a CV. Tell them to open their books at page 93 and compare their answers to the CV they see there.

ⓘ CULTURAL INFORMATION

In the UK, a CV usually covers a maximum of two sides of A4. A covering letter accompanies a CV and this is where you should add any other relevant information which does not appear on the CV, e.g. availability, suitability for the job, etc. The covering letter should not be more than one side of A4.

1 Students read the letter of application and CV and decide which advert on page 92 the person is responding to and why. Elicit answers from the class.

Answers

US Au pairs, because she talks about experience with children and says she's patient and caring.

2 Students read the letter and CV again and decide where Diana gave each piece of information – in her letter, her CV or both. Allow students to compare in pairs before you elicit answers from the class.

Answers

1 letter **2** letter **3** both **4** CV **5** CV

3 Students read the letter and CV again and find the information listed in exercise 2. Draw attention to the example.

Answers

2 She is caring, patient and very hard-working.

3 34 Norton Road, Stoke, SO3 6HT, 0342 455 3212, 632 12 34 56, dhuxley@anynet.uk

4 cookery, surfing, computers

5 part-time teaching assistant at a kindergarten and a helper at a summer camp

4 Students write their own CV using exercise 1 as a model. Monitor, helping students with vocabulary or grammatical queries.

5 Students look again at the letter in exercise 1 and complete the information in the Writing bank. Check their answers as a class.

Answers

Ms, look forward, sincerely, contractions

6 Students work with a partner and think of what qualities, skills or experience would be useful for the job in the advert. Elicit ideas from the class.

Suggested answers

Qualities: friendly, hard-working, sociable
Skills: know how to prepare food, good people skills, able to work in a team, numeracy, responsible
Experience: previous jobs in another fast food restaurant

PRACTICE MAKES PERFECT

7a Students read the task and write their letter of application using the letter in exercise 1 as a model. Remind them to include expressions and conventions from the Writing bank. They should also include the ideas they had in exercise 6. For students who are less confident, photocopy the model text below for extra support during the writing task.

7b Students read each other's letters and decide who they would give the job to and why.

Model text

37 Wavertree Road
Southport
L76 3FP

3rd March 2015

Dear Mr Daly,

I am writing in response to your advertisement in the *Mersey Mirror*. I would like to apply for the job you advertised in the newspaper on 1st March.

I enclose a CV with information about myself, including education and work experience.

As you can see, I have experience working at a local fast food restaurant at the weekends and at the social club once a week. I've worked in the kitchen to help prepare food and I was also a waitress.

I think I am very sociable and hard-working. I play for a local football club, so I have a lot of experience working as a team.

I look forward to hearing from you soon.

Yours sincerely,

Scarlett Webster

HOMEWORK

Assign students page 64 in their Workbook or the relevant sections of the Online Workbook.

Language checkpoint: Unit 7

>>> FAST TRACK

The extra support provided on the Grammar and Vocabulary reference sections makes the Grammar and Vocabulary revision section ideal for setting as homework. You could get students to complete the whole revision page or just certain exercises for homework.

Grammar revision p95

must, mustn't, have to, don't have to

1 Students choose the correct alternatives. Remind them that if two alternatives are correct they can choose both of them.

Answers

1 mustn't **2** must/have to **3** don't have to
4 have to/must **5** mustn't **6** doesn't have to
7 mustn't

should, shouldn't, If I were you

2 Students choose the correct alternatives.

Answers

a look **b** Should I **c** would send **d** shouldn't
e would

Second conditional

3 Students write complete sentences in the second conditional.

Answers

1 If I saw a bear, I'd take a photo of it.
2 If my brother was angry, he would shout.
3 If my parents won the lottery, they'd give me a present.
4 If I didn't have a pen, I'd ask my friend for one.
5 If we didn't have a TV, we'd talk more.
6 If he wasn't very good at football, he wouldn't play in the first division.
7 If I lived in Italy, I'd speak Italian.
8 If we had wings, we'd be able to fly.

Vocabulary revision p95

JOBS AND WORK

1 Students complete the jobs with vowels.

Answers

1 journalist **2** builder **3** plumber **4** shop assistant
5 receptionist **6** vet **7** fashion designer **8** mechanic

PERSONAL QUALITIES

2 Students complete the sentences in a logical way.

Example answers

1 Alex is very ambitious because he wants to have his own company in five years.
2 He's very reliable. He is always on time.
3 She's very caring. Do you remember when she looked after you when you were ill?
4 Dean is very sociable. He always chats to people.
5 When you're creative, you have lots of great ideas.
6 If you are very bright, you can do your work easily.

COMPOUND ADJECTIVES

3 Students complete the compound adjectives with the appropriate word.

Answers

1 paid **2** going **3** known **4** handed **5** looking
6 time

HOMEWORK

Assign students page 65 in their Workbook or the relevant sections of the Online Workbook.

8 Best friends forever

KEY LEARNING OUTCOMES

Students will be able to:

- understand texts about friendship
- talk about friends and friendships using the past perfect
- discuss interests
- report a past event
- write an email giving advice

UNIT OVERVIEW

Vocabulary
Friendships
Feelings

Reading
A lesson in friendship
CRITICAL THINKING Evaluating and giving opinions about a message in a story

Grammar in context
Past perfect
used to
PRONUNCIATION The contraction *'d*

Developing vocabulary
Noun suffixes -*ness*, -*ship*, -*dom*

Life skills
Personal well-being: Managing friendships

Listening
Discover your secret self

Grammar in context
Gerunds and infinitives

Developing speaking
Reporting a past event

Developing writing
An email of advice

Exam success
Speaking: Reporting activities
Writing: Answering the question

DIGITAL OVERVIEW

Presentation Kit
- ▶ **Flipped classroom video Unit 8:** Past perfect
- ▶ **Life skills video Unit 8:** Making friends
- ▶ **Ⅴ Vocabulary tool:** Feelings
- ▶ **Interactive versions of Student's Book activities**
- ▶ **Integrated audio and answer key for all activities**
- ▶ **Workbook pages with answer key**

Teacher's Resource Centre
- ▶ **Flipped classroom video Unit 8:** Past perfect
- ▶ **Life skills video Unit 8:** Making friends
- ▶ **Grammar communication activity Unit 8:** One word at a time
- ▶ **Worksheets for this unit, including:**
  – Grammar practice worksheet Unit 8
  – Flipped classroom video worksheet Unit 8: Past perfect
  – Literature worksheet Units 7 and 8
  – Culture worksheet Unit 8
  – Life skills video worksheet Unit 8
  – Everyday English worksheet Unit 8

Student's App
Gateway 2nd Edition wordlist for the award-winning Sounds App (available for download)

✓ TESTING AND ASSESSMENT

Resources for exam preparation and measuring student progress

- ▶ Test Generator Units 1–8
- ▶ Printable test Unit 8
- ▶ Gateway to exams Units 7 and 8 (end of Unit 8)

Vocabulary p96

Talking about friendships and feelings

You could ask students to do exercise 2 at home so that less confident students can take the necessary time to look up the vocabulary in the Macmillan Online Dictionary.

WARMER

Ask students to think about the most important friendships in their lives. Ask students to talk about these friendships in pairs, saying why they are important. Ask them to include how they know their friend, why this person is special and to describe a memory they have of them, e.g. *My relationship with my best friend is important to me because I can tell him everything and he always gives me good advice. We met at primary school when we were six years old. I remember playing football with him on the first day we met.*

If students wish to do so, they can share some of their thoughts and ideas with the class.

Friendships

1 Students match the pictures to an appropriate phrase (a–j) in the story. Draw attention to the example before they begin. Ask students to compare in pairs before you check the answers with the class.

Answers

2 i **3** a/b

2 Students match the words and phrases in the story in exercise 1 to the definitions. Allow students to check their answers in pairs before you elicit answers from the class.

Answers

1 g **2** i **3** j **4** c **5** h **6** e **7** f **8** a **9** b **10** d

3 Students complete the sentences with the correct preposition. For less confident classes, write the prepositions they will need on the board (but in the wrong order). Nominate different students to give their answers, asking them to read out the full sentence.

Answers

1 of **2** to **3** with, up **4** out **5** in **6** on, with
7 out

4 SPEAKING Students use the completed questions in exercise 3 to interview their partner. Draw attention to the example dialogue. When students have finished ask them to swap roles.

[v] **Feelings**

5 Students write the words in two columns (nouns and adjectives) in their notebooks.

Answers

Adjectives: afraid, angry, bored, excited, happy, lonely, sad

Nouns: fear, anger, boredom, excitement, happiness, loneliness, sadness

>>> **FAST FINISHERS**

Students think of two more adjectives and corresponding nouns related to the theme of relationships or friendships, e.g. *loyal/loyalty, excited/excitement, jealous/jealousy*, etc.

6 ▶ 48 Play the track so that students can listen and repeat the words. See p157 for the audioscript for this exercise.

+ EXTRA ACTIVITY

Play the track again and ask students to mark the stressed syllable in each word.

7 LISTENING ▶ 49 Play the track for students to write down the feeling expressed by each speaker. See p157 for the audioscript for this exercise.

Answers

1 fear **2** boredom **3** excitement **4** anger
5 happiness

+ EXTRA ACTIVITY

Play the track again and ask students to note down where they think the speakers are in each listening, e.g. 1 *at a haunted house or fairground attraction* 2 *at the cinema or watching a DVD at home* 3 *at a football stadium* 4 *outside their house* 5 *at their birthday party.*

8 SPEAKING In pairs, students ask and answer questions about the adjectives in exercise 5. Draw attention to the model dialogue. Ask students to share their answers with the class.

HOMEWORK

Assign students page 66 in their Workbook or the relevant sections of the Online Workbook.

Reading p97

Skimming and scanning for global and specific information

>>> **FAST TRACK**

You could ask students to do exercise 5 at home so that less confident students can take the necessary time to look up the vocabulary in the Macmillan Online Dictionary.

1 Students look at the picture and predict what the story could be about. Ask students to read the text and answer the question.

Answer

Yes, they are.

TEACHER DEVELOPMENT: CLASSROOM TIPS

Teaching reading skills

For the first reading, students skim (quickly read) the text to get the main idea. They should start with the title and then read the topic sentence of each paragraph (usually the first sentence). When they read the text for a second or third time, they scan for the specific information required for the task.

2 Students read the text for a second time and put the events of the story in the correct order. Nominate a student to give the answer.

Answers

1 g **2** a **3** d **4** j **5** f **6** h **7** i **8** c **9** b **10** e

3 Students read the story again and answer the questions.

Answers

1 Sometimes they had arguments about school. **2** He was angry because Nadeem was talking about his mark in a test. **3** A part of the river bank broke because of the rain. **4** Nadeem couldn't swim. **5** A sharp stone **6** You should forget arguments, but you should remember kindness.

4 🔧 **CRITICAL THINKING** Ask students what they think the message of the story is and if they agree with it or not. Have a class discussion and ask students if they've had any similar arguments with friends.

Example answer

The message of the story is to forgive the bad things your friends do, but to remember the good things as these are more permanent and more important.

5 Students look at the underlined words in the text and guess their meaning. Then ask them to check in their dictionaries.

Answers

competitive = wanting to be better than other people
wet = the opposite of dry, the way the countryside looks when there is rain
kept on = continued doing something
slapped = hit hard with an open hand
shocked = very surprised because of an unexpected event
river bank = the sides of a river
safety = a place where there is no danger
sharp = pointed like a knife so that it can cut

6 **What about you?** Students consider their own answers to the questions, before discussing their ideas as a class.

Grammar in context pp98–99

Using the past perfect and used to

Test before you teach: Flipped classroom
Set the Flipped classroom video and tasks for homework <u>before the lesson</u>. This will allow you to assess the needs of the students before the class. Students can then move on to the relevant grammar practice activities.

Past perfect

1a Students look at the sentences and decide if the green or red actions happened first. Elicit the names of the tenses in red and green.

Answer

The actions in green (past perfect) happened before the actions in red (past simple).

1b Students choose the correct alternative to complete the information about the past perfect.

Answer

before

1c Students complete the rule.

Answers

have, past participle

✛✛ EXTRA ACTIVITY

> Ask students to write down what they have already
> done today with a time next to the action, e.g.
> *7.00: had a shower, 7.30: ate breakfast, 8.00: went
> to school*, etc. They then use their notes to write
> sentences about what they had already done by the
> time they did an action, e.g. *When I got to school,
> I had already eaten breakfast.* Students can ask and
> answer questions about their day in pairs, e.g. *Had
> you already had lunch when you went to the science
> lesson?*

TEACHER DEVELOPMENT: LANGUAGE

The past perfect

Draw the table below on the board and write the headings
in the left-hand column. Ask students to complete the
table with the past perfect form of the verb *to study*.

Affirmative	I had/'d studied.
Negative	I had not/hadn't studied.
Yes/No questions	Had I studied?
Short answers	Yes, I had. No, I hadn't.
Wh- questions	When had she studied?

Draw a timeline to explain the use of the past perfect.
Explain that the past perfect is used when we are already
talking about the past, and we want to go even further
back in time. It makes it clear that something happened
before another point in the past.

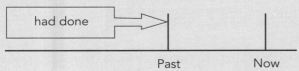

had done
Past   Now

Point out to students that sometimes native speakers
avoid the past perfect by using the words before and
after to make the order of actions clear, e.g. *After I did my
homework, I went to bed.* However, there are instances
when the past perfect is necessary. Point out, or mark on a
timeline, the differences between these sentences:
When I arrived, John left. (John left at the same time as I
arrived, i.e. the actions happened simultaneously.)
When I arrived, John had left. (John left before I arrived.)

2a PRONUNCIATION Students add *'d* only to the sentences that
should be in the past perfect.

2b ▶ 50 Play the track for students to listen and check their
answers. See p157 for the audioscript for this exercise.

Answers

1 He'd known him since he was five
2 They went to live in another town.
3 She'd gone to the shops.
4 We'd seen him that morning.
5 She took her phone with her.
6 I'd given him my pen.

2c ▶ 50 Play the track again for students to repeat the
sentences.

TEACHER DEVELOPMENT: PRONUNCIATION

The contraction *'d*

We use the contracted form of *had* in spoken language
because using the whole word can seem too emphatic.
Point out to students that we can spot the difference
between *'d = had* and *'d = would* by the context.
It can be difficult to hear the *'d* in spoken language,
especially when the next verb begins with a *t* or *d*,
e.g. *you'd told me* might sound like *you told me* or *I'd
danced with you* might sound like *I danced with you.*

3a Students match the sentences. Nominate students to
give their answers.

Answers

1 b 2 d 3 a 4 f 5 e 6 c

3b Students rewrite the sentences in exercise 3a as one
sentence, putting one verb in the past perfect and the
other in the past simple. Remind them to use *when* or
after as in the example sentence (they are both correct).
Monitor and then elicit answers from the class.

Answers

2 When/After she had finished the shopping, she carried
  it home.
3 When/After they had finished their lunch, they left the
  restaurant.
4 When/After he had got out of the pool, he dried
  himself with a towel.
5 When/After we had finished the test, we gave it to the
  teacher.
6 When/After I had found my keys, I opened the door.

✛✛ EXTRA ACTIVITY

> Drill the sentences in exercise 3b, paying special
> attention to correct pronunciation of the contracted
> form of *'d.*

4 Students complete the sentences in a logical way using
the past perfect. Draw their attention to the example.
Nominate different students to give their answers.

Example answers

2 I was feeling ill because I'd eaten too many sweets.
3 They were very happy because they had passed all
  their exams.
4 She was bored because her friends had gone on
  holiday.
5 We were angry because we had lost the football
  match.
6 He was feeling sad because he had had an argument
  with his girlfriend.
7 Yesterday I was excited because my friend had invited
  me to stay.
8 They were afraid because he had switched off all
  the lights.

5 Students complete the text with the past perfect. Nominate different students to give their answers.

Answers

a had learned/had learnt **b** had passed **c** had given
d hadn't made **e** had been **f** had met
g hadn't seen **h** had taken

6 SPEAKING Students find out which of the things in the list their partner had done by the age of seven. Ask a pair of more confident students to read out the model dialogue before they begin. Nominate different students to give their partner's answers.

Answers

1 Had you begun to learn English by the age of seven?
2 Had you travelled to a different country by the age of seven?
3 Had you learnt to read by the age of seven?
4 Had you swum in the sea by the age of seven?
5 Had you started to ride a bike by the age of seven?
6 Had you been on holiday without your parents by the age of seven?
7 Had you used a computer by the age of seven?

TEACHER DEVELOPMENT: LANGUAGE

Expressions of time

Go through the meaning of these expressions with the class:

By the age of seven = when I reached the age of seven, e.g. *By the age of seven, I could ride a bike with two wheels.*

By the time = when, at the time (of the event), e.g. *By the time I arrived, everyone else had left.*

As soon as = immediately after something happened, e.g. *We cleared up as soon as our guests had left.*

used to

7 Students look at the sentences and choose the correct alternatives. Nominate students to give their answers.

Answers

a habits **b** infinitive

8 Students look at the two photos and see if they can guess the locations (Spain and Manhattan). Tell them that Isabel lived in Spain in the past and now she lives in New York. Ask students to complete the sentences using *used to* or *didn't use to*. Elicit answers from different students.

Answers

1 used to **2** didn't use to **3** used to **4** didn't use to
5 used to **6** didn't use to

9a SPEAKING Students think about themselves when they were seven and complete the sentences with *used to* or *didn't use to*.

9b Students compare answers with a partner.

Refer students to the Grammar reference on page 106 if necessary.

HOMEWORK

Students write four true sentences and one false sentence about what they could do by the age of ten. In the next class, they read their sentences out to their partner. Their partner must try to identify the false sentence.

Assign students page 68 in their Workbook or the relevant sections of the Online Workbook.

Developing vocabulary p99

Using noun suffixes -ness, -ship, -dom

You could do exercise 4a as a class activity, by reading aloud the sentences and inviting the rest of the class to call out the matching suffix.

1 Students look at the words and decide which suffix they can add to them and if they need to change the spelling.

TEACHER DEVELOPMENT: LANGUAGE

Suffixes

In this activity, students work on word formation – the ways in which new words are built on the bases of other words.

The suffix *-ness* is perhaps the most productive in the English language and can be attached to many adjectives to make abstract nouns, e.g. *happiness, friendliness.*

The suffix *-ship* denotes a state or condition and is similar in meaning to *-dom.* Base words for *-ship* are usually connected to social groups, e.g. *friendship, relationship, apprenticeship.*

Remind students of the suffix *-hood,* which they have already seen, and elicit some abstract nouns with this suffix, e.g. *childhood, adulthood, motherhood.*

2 ▶ 51 Play the track for students to listen, check and repeat. Elicit the spelling rule: *y* changes to *i* in *happiness* and *loneliness.* See p157 for the audioscript for this exercise.

Answers

boredom, freedom, friendship, happiness, illness, kingdom, leadership, loneliness, madness, relationship, sadness, weakness

3 Students complete the sentences using the noun form of the words in exercise 1.

Answers

1 madness **2** Leadership **3** weakness **4** freedom
5 relationship **6** illness **7** happiness **8** boredom

4a Students complete the questions with the correct noun suffix.

Answers

1 ship **2** ness **3** dom **4** iness **5** dom **6** dom
7 ness

4b SPEAKING In pairs, students ask and answer the questions in exercise 4a.

Example answers

1 I think it's important to always tell the truth and be loyal.

2 I am quite impatient sometimes.

3 I think I have a lot of freedom. My parents let me stay out late and do what I want.

4 The secret of happiness is to enjoy the present and not worry about the future.

5 You can stop boredom if you always carry a good book with you.

6 Yes, I'd love to go there to study English in the summer.

7 Yes, I once bought a really expensive pair of jeans that I didn't really need.

✚ EXTRA ACTIVITY

Write these words on the board and ask students to change them to nouns by adding one of the three suffixes or prefixes from the lesson, *-ness, -ship, -dom*: wise, citizen, fit, ready, good, member. Students may use their dictionaries to help them.

Answers

wisdom, citizenship, fitness, readiness, goodness, membership

HOMEWORK

Assign students page 69 in their Workbook or the relevant sections of the Online Workbook.

Gateway to life skills pp100–101

Managing friendships

To learn about friendship styles, to think about situations when you need to make new friends and to decide the best way for new students to make friends at school and locally.

⟩⟩⟩ FAST TRACK

You could ask students to complete the questions in exercise 4 at home. They can then compare their answers with a partner at the next lesson.

ⓘ BACKGROUND INFORMATION

The friends we make at school can often become lifelong friends, and friendships are often a core part of a teenager's life. However, friendships can also be turbulent at this age and changing schools and classes can threaten stability. It's important for students to understand that different people look for different social set-ups and that some people may prefer a wider group of friends, some prefer to have a close group of a few people and some people value time on their own. Being able to make friends and manage friendships will make the transition from school to university or work smoother. This lesson looks at different situations where they're likely to meet new people and need to make friends and how best to approach this.

WARMER

Write the two words *lonely* and *alone* on the board and ask students if they know the difference. (*Lonely* usually has negative connotations; *alone* is a more neutral term.)

Tell students they are going to look at ways to make friends and avoid loneliness, and at ways to maintain good friendships.

1a Students look at the sentences and choose the best alternatives for themselves. Tell them that there are no right or wrong answers.

1b Students think about situations where we have to make new friends. Nominate different students to give their answers.

Example answers

When we change schools. When things aren't going well with old friends. When we move to a new town. When we join a club. When there is someone new at school or in the neighbourhood.

2 READING Students read the page from a university website and answer the question. Nominate students to give their answer, comparing their ideas.

3 Students go back to the text and say whether the sentences are true or false. Ask them to include the number of the line where they found their answers.

Answers

1 F, line 14 **2** T, line 15 **3** F, line 19
4 F, line 17 **5** T, line 20 **6** F, line 23

⟩⟩⟩ FAST FINISHERS

Ask students to correct the false sentences.

4 SPEAKING Students answer the questions for themselves then have a class discussion. Ask students who don't think such web pages and articles are helpful, what they think more helpful alternatives would be.

5a Students look at the pictures and work with a partner to say how they think these things could help people make friends at university. Help students with any vocabulary they might need (*brownies, football, photography, open door,* etc.).

Suggested answers

If you make cakes, you can share them.
If you do sports or team games, you will meet people when you play.
If you join a club, you will meet the other members.
If you leave your door open, people will come in.

5b 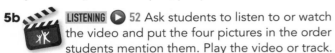 **LISTENING** ▶ **52** Ask students to listen to or watch the video and put the four pictures in the order students mention them. Play the video or track. Elicit the answer. See pp157–158 for the videoscript/ audioscript for this exercise.

Answers

1 open door   **2** brownies   **3** football   **4** photography

5c ▶ **52** Students explain how each thing in the picture helped the speakers to make friends. Play the video or track again if necessary.

Answers

1 He left his door open so that people would come and say hello.
2 Students came to eat her chocolate brownies.
3 He knocked on people's doors and asked them to play sports.
4 She joined the photographic society and met people with similar interests and met her best friend.

6 ▶ **52** Play the video or track again. Students choose the correct speaker for each sentence. Allow students to check with a partner then elicit answers from individual students.

Answers

a 2   **b** 1   **c** 4   **d** 3   **e** 2   **f** 4

7 Students think which idea would work best for them and why. Nominate a few students to share their ideas.

LIFE TASK   ✕⅄

Tell students they are going to create a web page to give advice to other teenagers about how to make new friends.

■ *Step 1*
Divide the class into groups of three or four and ask students to read the instructions. Students start by discussing possible ideas for the best ways to make new friends at school and making a note of them. Remind them to think about any clubs or teams that students can join or any social events organised by the school. Circulate as they do this and help with any necessary vocabulary.

■ *Step 2*
Students do the same for the local area. They can think of different places that teenagers enjoy going and spending time with their friends, or any special social events organised locally.

■ *Step 3*
Students decide if they want to create a leaflet or a web page. Make sure students have the materials they need to create both. Encourage them to make sure their ideas are organised and persuasive.

■ *Step 4*
Students create their leaflet or web page. Monitor to provide help with language difficulties where necessary.

■ *Step 5*
Students present their leaflet or web page to other students. Encourage other students to give their feedback, but ensure that it is positive or constructive criticism.

Listening p102

Listening for general and specific information

WARMER

Write the following words on the board: *perfectionist, romantic, thinker, leader.* Ask students to work in pairs and use their dictionaries to write a definition for each word. Then ask students to talk about which word best describes their character and explain why.

Suggested answers

perfectionist = someone who wants things to be done perfectly
romantic = someone who has an idealistic view of life
thinker = someone who thinks carefully about things
leader = someone who likes to take control and be in charge

Explain that the questionnaire will tell students what kind of person they are, and if their opinions from the Warmer were accurate.

1 **SPEAKING** Students read through the questionnaire and tick any statement that is true for them. Ask them to compare their results with a partner.

2 Students check in which section they have the most ticks and turn to page 148 to discover what personality type that section represents. Ask students to compare in pairs and decide if they agree with the results.

3 **LISTENING** ▶ **53** Play the track for students to listen and answer the questions. Ask students to read the questions carefully before you play the track. See p158 for the audioscript for this exercise.

Answers

1 section 4   **2** Jessica doesn't agree, but Jack does.

4 ▶ **53** Play the track for students to listen again and choose the correct alternatives. Give students time to compare in pairs before you elicit answers from around the class. Ask students to remember information from the text to justify their answers.

Ask follow up questions such as: Where did they go last week? (to the cinema) Which adjectives does Jack use to describe Jessica? (bossy, not very patient, angry) How long did Jack wait last week? (half an hour, according to him) What was wrong with the quality of the food? (the burger was still frozen in the middle)

Answers

1 what they saw   **2** waiting   **3** how long
4 doesn't agree   **5** quality of the food   **6** never

HOMEWORK

Assign students page 69 in their Workbook or the relevant sections of the Online Workbook.

Grammar in context pp102–103

Gerunds and infinitives

>>> FAST TRACK

You could ask students to complete the questionnaire in exercise 2 at home before the class. They can then compare their answers with a partner at the beginning of the lesson.

Test before you teach

Ask students to give you five gerunds and five infinitives and write them on the board. Next, ask them to write at least two sentences with gerunds and two with infinitives. When they have finished, elicit examples and ask the class to correct any errors.

1a Students look at the sentences and notice the use of gerunds and infinitives in each sentence. Ask students to look at the types of word that come before them and where the verbs are in the sentence.

1b Students put the rules in the correct column. They can refer to the sentences in exercise 1a to help them. After you have checked the answers, elicit which rules are exemplified in exercise 1a.

Answers

Gerund: 1, 5, 6, 7
Infinitive: 2, 3, 4

TEACHER DEVELOPMENT: LANGUAGE

Gerunds and infinitives

Gerunds and infinitives are both verbal forms that act as nouns. Gerunds end in -*ing*, e.g. *swimming, walking, laughing*. Infinitives are the basic verb form with the particle *to*, e.g. *to swim, to walk, to laugh*.

It can be hard for students to recognise whether an -*ing* word in a sentence is really a gerund, or if it is a participle (a verb form used as an adjective to modify nouns and pronouns). Below are some examples of different kinds of -*ing* words:

Gerund used in present continuous: *The girl is crying.*
Gerund used as an adjective: *We looked at the crying girl.*
Gerund used as a noun: *Crying is a sign of unhappiness.*

2 Students look at the statements and match each one to a rule in exercise 1b.

Answers

Section 5: 3, 7, 2, 4, 6
Section 6: 7, 5, 3, 1, 6

3 Individually, students tick the statements in exercise 2 which are true for them. They then see where they have more ticks and find out what that section means on the next page.

TEACHER DEVELOPMENT: STUDENT TRAINING

Exam preparation

Gerunds vs infinitives is one of the grammar areas that is often tested in exams so it is worth students spending time and effort here.

One way to help students succeed is to suggest that they pay close attention to what happens before or after a word, e.g. after *go*, most activities take -*ing* – *go swimming, go running*, etc. This is why it is important to write example sentences alongside any new vocabulary and to practise writing sentences using new words and phrases.

4 Students complete the texts with the gerund or infinitive form of the verbs in brackets.

Answers

a to make   **b** to make   **c** being   **d** to know
e showing   **f** falling   **g** to make   **h** to argue
i listening   **j** to hear   **k** doing   **l** accepting
m to spend   **n** Defending   **o** Getting

5 In pairs, students discuss their results and decide if they agree or not. Nominate different pairs to give their opinions.

6 Focus students' attention on the photo of Hanna and Barbera. Ask if any students recognise them. Ask students to read the text about them and to correct the eight mistakes in gerunds and infinitives. Elicit answers from different students, asking them what the correct answer should be and why.

Answers

William Hanna and Joseph Barbera were the creators of popular cartoons. They were responsible for <u>creating</u> Tom and Jerry, The Flintstones, and Scooby-Doo. Hanna and Barbera had different skills. Hanna, for example, liked singing and <u>playing</u> music. Barbera was very good at <u>thinking</u> of funny situations for the characters. Hanna used to go <u>walking</u> and he enjoyed <u>being</u> outdoors. Barbera relaxed by <u>going</u> to the beach. <u>Eating</u> good food was another of his hobbies. They had different personalities but they got on really well. They were always excited about <u>working</u> together. They remained partners and friends for over 60 years.

7 Individually, students finish the questions with a gerund or an infinitive. Focus attention on the example question. Monitor and help students with any language questions.

Example answers

2 going out with your friends
3 to live in another country
4 running
5 to start a conversation with someone new
6 to get a well-paid job
7 getting up early in the morning
8 shopping for clothes
9 chatting to people on the Internet
10 getting married and having children

8a SPEAKING In pairs, students take it in turns to ask their partner their questions from 7. Encourage students to ask follow-up questions to find out more information about their partner. Monitor students and assess oral ability. Note down any errors to go through with the class at the end of the lesson.

8b SPEAKING Students tell the class some things they discovered about their partner. Draw attention to the example. With a less confident class, you may want to give students a few moments to note down what they want to say in their notebooks.

TEACHER DEVELOPMENT: STUDENT TRAINING

Listening outside class

Encourage students to expose themselves to English as much as possible with the following suggestions:

- Listen and sing along to English language music.
- Watch English language films.
- Watch interviews online with their favourite English-speaking actors, sport stars, singers or politicians. They can pause and replay as often as they want.
- Download podcasts from the Internet. Podcasts are audio files featuring radio programmes, news reports, etc. that can be downloaded to an MP3 player. You can also sign up to a podcast, which means that each time a new episode is posted, it is automatically downloaded to your hard drive.
- Find audiobook versions of their favourite stories in English and listen to these. Students can listen alongside reading the book if they find it easier to follow.
- Visit websites that offer video resources.

Refer students to the Grammar reference on page 106 if necessary.

HOMEWORK

Assign students page 70 in their Workbook or the relevant sections of the Online Workbook.

Developing speaking p104

Reporting a past event

⟫⟫ FAST TRACK

You could ask students to complete their notes for the questions in exercise 4 at home. They can then discuss their answers with a partner at the next lesson.

WARMER

Brainstorm language students can use to describe a photo. (Refer to the Unit 1 Teacher development box, Describing a photo, page 34.) Elicit prepositional phrases (*at the top/bottom, in the background/ foreground,* etc.) and the six questions they should consider (*Who can you see? What are they doing? Where are they? How are the people feeling and why? When was this photo taken?*). Remind students they should always move from the general to the specific.

1a SPEAKING Students work with a partner and list the things they like doing with friends.

1b In pairs, students look at the photos and take it in turns to describe what they can see in each photo and say which event they prefer and why.

Suggested answers

Picture a: This picture shows friends at a sport event (probably a football match). They are all shouting and cheering for their team. I like doing active things with friends.

Picture b: This picture shows some boys at a barbecue/ party. In the background, there are some trees. The boys look relaxed and happy. I like parties with my friends because I always have a good time.

✚ EXTRA ACTIVITY

In pairs, students choose a photo to describe and time each other talking about it for a minute to simulate exam conditions. Remind them to use fillers to give themselves time to think, e.g. *Well, Umm, Let me see,* etc.

2 LISTENING ▶ 54 Play the track for students to listen to a conversation about a barbecue. Ask students to answer the questions. Elicit answers from different students. See p158 for the audioscript for this exercise.

Answers

1 Because he had passed his driving test **2** At his parents' holiday home in the country **3** It was one of the best parts of the party because one of Mike's friends was a DJ and he played really cool music. **4** About 50 **5** Joe's parents **6** Oliver

3 Students look at the sentences in the Speaking bank and match the verbs in bold to the name of the tense and its use. Elicit answers from different students.

Answers

1 c, ii **2** d, iii **3** b, iv **4** a, i

4 Individually, students look at the questions and make notes about an event with family or friends they went to. Monitor and help with any language difficulties.

PRACTICE MAKES PERFECT

5 SPEAKING Students read the task and then describe their event to their partner. Remind them to use their notes in exercise 4 and the sentences in the Speaking bank to help them. Tell students to be 'active listeners' and ask each other questions if their partner can't think of anything to say.

For students who are less confident, photocopy the model text below and instruct them to read it to their partner. Then ask them to read it again, changing the underlined information so it is true for themselves.

Model text

I went to a great party this weekend. It was <u>Dean</u>'s party, you know my friend from <u>karate</u>, and it was at his parents' house. He was celebrating because he <u>had passed all his exams</u>. I went with my <u>friend</u>. There were about <u>forty</u> people and we had a barbecue outside. His parents had prepared lots of food and the music was really cool. We danced a lot!

I don't usually like dancing, but it was all my favourite music. I met all my friends from the <u>karate club</u> and I knew almost everyone, which was really nice. We didn't leave until about <u>midnight</u>.

✦✚ EXTRA ACTIVITY

Ask students to swap pairs and repeat the activity with another partner. This time they should not refer to their notes.

✔ EXAM SUCCESS
Elicit from students what language is useful in tasks where they have to report past events. Ask them to go to page 146 (Speaking: Reporting activities) and compare their ideas.

TEACHER DEVELOPMENT: LANGUAGE

Reporting past events

When students report past events, they are giving information based on first-hand experience rather than telling a story. Remind students that they need to help their listener by signposting their discourse, e.g. *then, next, finally*, etc., as well as by using a variety of past tenses to clarify the sequence of events.

As in a narrative, a report consists of the following three elements: people, place and time. Students can use the past perfect to show a shift in temporal perspective. For this reason, the past perfect is sometimes referred to as a 'flashback tense'. Students will gain extra marks in oral exams if they use a variety of verb tenses, interesting words and expressions, as well as a careful linking of ideas.

HOMEWORK

Assign students page 71 in their Workbook or the relevant sections of the Online Workbook.

Developing writing p105

Writing an email of advice

⟫⟩ FAST TRACK

You could ask students to prepare their email for exercise 6 at home. They can present their email to the class at the beginning of the next lesson.

WARMER

Write the phrasal verb *to fall out* on the board and elicit the meaning. In pairs, ask students what they think the most common reasons to fall out with friends are. Elicit some ideas from students and ask which they think is the most and least serious reason.

1 Students read the email and answer the question.

Answer

She thinks she doesn't have anything in common with her best friend any more.

2 SPEAKING Students work with a partner and think what advice they would give Rachel.

Suggested answers

Rachel should talk to her friend and find things they still have in common. She should spend more time with her because they've been friends for a long time. She shouldn't lie to her friend.

3 Students read Sophie's reply and answer the questions. Nominate students to give their opinions.

4 Students look at the email again and find words to complete the Writing bank.

Answers

First of all, Next, After that, Lastly

5a Students read the email and answer the questions.

Suggested answers

Problem: He is worried about his friend.
Advice: Try talking to him. Call him and try to chat. Speak to his parents. Ask a teacher. Ask some of his other friends.

5b SPEAKING Students work with a partner and compare their ideas.

6 **PRACTICE MAKES PERFECT**
Students write an email giving advice to Dan. Remind them to use the email in exercise 3 and their ideas from exercise 5 to help them.

Model text

Dear Dan,

Thank you for your email.

I remember your friend Jonathan. I'm sorry you are having problems with him at the moment.

Firstly, I think you should talk to him. Tell him you don't need to see him all the time, but you still want to be friends. If he doesn't like basketball anymore, maybe you can suggest another sport or activity to do together.

I think you should be honest and tell him you are worried about him. If he doesn't listen to you and his marks are still getting worse, you should talk to a teacher.

I hope that helps you.

All the best,

Henry

+= EXTRA ACTIVITY

Ask students to swap emails and decide if their partner has addressed everything in the exam task.

TEACHER DEVELOPMENT: STUDENT TRAINING

Developing exam skills

Students need to develop exam strategies in order to gain competence and confidence under exam conditions. Some types of questions, such as the one in this writing task, require students to demonstrate a variety of tenses and vocabulary. You can train students to observe what grammatical structures or vocabulary a question might be trying to elicit.

If possible, show students representative samples of exam questions and get them used to working with time limits to improve their time management skills. Asking students to underline key words in questions encourages them to make sure they have fully understood the question before they answer.

HOMEWORK

Assign students page 72 in their Workbook or the relevant sections of the Online Workbook.

Language checkpoint: Unit 8

>>> FAST TRACK

The extra support provided on the Grammar and Vocabulary reference sections makes the Grammar and Vocabulary revision section ideal for setting as homework. You could get students to complete the whole revision page or just certain exercises for homework.

Grammar revision p107

Past perfect

1 Students complete the sentences in a logical way. Remind them to put one verb in the past perfect and the other in the past simple.

Answers

1 had finished, brushed   2 had done, said   3 dried, had washed   4 took, had had   5 arrived, had started   6 had written, sent   7 went, had bought

used to

2 Students write logical sentences about Andy using *used to* or *didn't use to*.

Answers

1 used to   2 didn't use to   3 didn't use to   4 used to

Gerunds and infinitives

3 Students choose the correct alternative and decide why we use the gerund or infinitive in each case.

Answers

1 to buy (infinitive to explain why somebody does something)
2 seeing (gerund after prepositions)
3 Smoking (gerund as the subject of a sentence)
4 fishing (gerund with *go* to talk about physical activities)
5 cycling (gerund after verbs of liking and disliking)
6 to listen (infinitive after certain verbs like *want*)
7 opening (gerund after prepositions)
8 to help (infinitive immediately after adjectives)

Vocabulary revision p107

FRIENDSHIPS

1 Students match the words from each column to make expressions about friendships.

Answers

1 d   2 e   3 a   4 b   5 c   6 g   7 f

FEELINGS

2 Students write the nouns for the adjectives and decide if the feeling is positive (+), negative (–) or it depends (=).

Answers

1 sadness (–)   2 fear (–)   3 loneliness (–)   4 boredom (–)
5 anger (–)   6 excitement (+)   7 happiness (+)

NOUN SUFFIXES -NESS, -SHIP, -DOM

3 Students read the definitions and write the words ending with -ness, -ship or -dom.

Answers

1 weakness   2 loneliness   3 madness   4 relationship
5 illness   6 freedom   7 leadership

HOMEWORK

Assign students page 73 in their Workbook or the relevant sections of the Online Workbook.

Reading p108

> ➤ **TIP FOR READING EXAMS**
>
> Ask students to read the tip and to look at Exam Success on page 145 for more ideas.

1 Students match the words and pictures.

Answers

a grapes **b** factory **c** jam **d** recipe

2 Students read the text and find out how Fraser Doherty has become a millionaire.

Answer

Fraser Doherty has become a millionaire by inventing and selling his own unusual jams.

3 Students read the text again and decide if the statements are true or false. Tell them to write down the number(s) of the line(s) where they found the answer.

Answers

1 T, lines 4–6 **2** F, lines 8–9 **3** T, lines 7–8
4 F, lines 11–12 **5** F, lines 21–23 **6** T, lines 23–27
7 T, lines 34–36 **8** T, lines 15–17

Writing p108

> ➤ **TIP FOR WRITING EXAMS**
>
> Ask students to read the tip and to look at Exam Success on page 146 for more ideas.

Model letter

14 Southbrae St
Edinburgh
EH12 1DN

14th June 2015

Dear Mr Doherty,

I am writing in response to your advertisement in *The Standard* yesterday. I would like to apply for the job you advertised in the newspaper on 12th June. I enclose a CV with information about myself.

I am very sociable and outgoing and I am good at working in a team in a busy environment. I am very responsible, good at handling kitchen equipment and I know a lot about health and safety in the workplace. I think I have the relevant skills needed to work in your jam factory.

As you can see, I have worked for two summers as a kitchen assistant in a local café in Glasgow and I have always been interested in cooking. I think I would be a valuable team member at the jam factory.

I look forward to hearing from you.

Yours sincerely,

James McClear

4 Ask students to work with a partner and look at the advice for applying for a job. Ask them to add extra ideas.

Suggested answers

include your experience, use *Yours sincerely* if you know the person's name

5 Ask students to read the task carefully and write a formal letter of application including all the information. Remind them to invent any details they do not know. For students who are less confident, photocopy the model letter for extra support during the writing task.

Listening p109

> ➤ **TIP FOR LISTENING EXAMS**
>
> Ask students to read the tip and to look at Exam Success on page 145 for more ideas.

6 **LISTENING** ▶ 55 Play the track for students to listen to two teenagers talking about working in the summer and answer the questions. See pp158–159 for the audioscript for this exercise.

Answer

A job working as an au pair in New York

7 ▶ 55 Play the track again and ask students to choose the correct alternatives.

Answers

1 c **2** a **3** a **4** a **5** c

8 **What about *you*?** Ask students to think of their own answers to the questions. Then nominate different students to share their thoughts with the class.

Speaking p109

> ➤ **TIP FOR SPEAKING EXAMS**
>
> Ask students to read the tip and look at Exam Success on page 146 for more ideas.

9 Students look at the exam task and make notes before they complete the task. Remind them they only have a few minutes to do so and not to write full sentences.

10 **SPEAKING** In pairs, students take it turns to ask and answer questions about a time when they made a new friend.

HOMEWORK

Assign students pages 74–75 in their Workbook or the relevant sections of the Online Workbook.

'CAN DO' PROGRESS CHECK p109

1 Ask students to mark from 1–4 how well they can do the things in English.

2 Ask students to look at their marks and decide what they need to do to improve. Elicit other suggestions.

9 Bestsellers

Students will be able to:

- understand texts about authors
- talk about books and authors using reported speech
- discuss books and films
- give a presentation about a favourite book
- write a story

UNIT OVERVIEW

Vocabulary	Fiction Non-fiction PRONUNCIATION Word stress
Reading	The life of a top children's author CRITICAL THINKING Discussing how important it is for children to read
Grammar in context	Reported speech – statements
Developing vocabulary	Phrasal verbs connected with reading and writing
Life skills	Art and culture: Enjoying fiction
Listening	Book vs film
Grammar in context	Reported speech – questions
Developing speaking	A presentation
Developing writing	A story
✓ **Exam success**	Reading: Missing sentences activities Listening: Completing notes

DIGITAL OVERVIEW

Presentation Kit

- ▶ **Flipped classroom video Unit 9:** Reported speech – statements
- ▶ **Life skills video Unit 9:** Book review
- ▶ ⓥ **Vocabulary tool:** Fiction, Non-fiction
- ▶ **Interactive versions of Student's Book activities**
- ▶ **Integrated audio and answer key for all activities**
- ▶ **Workbook pages with answer key**

Teacher's Resource Centre
 TRC

- ▶ **Flipped classroom video Unit 9:** Reported speech – statements
- ▶ **Life skills video Unit 9:** Book review
- ▶ **Grammar communication activity Unit 9:** He said, she said
- ▶ **Worksheets for this unit, including:**
  - Grammar practice worksheet Unit 9
  - Flipped classroom video worksheet Unit 9: Reported speech – statements
  - Literature worksheet Units 9 and 10
  - Culture worksheet Unit 9
  - Life skills video worksheet Unit 9
  - Everyday English worksheet Unit 9

Student's App

Gateway 2nd Edition wordlist for the award-winning Sounds App (available for download)

✓ TESTING AND ASSESSMENT

Resources for exam preparation and measuring student progress

- ▶ Test Generator Units 1–9
- ▶ Printable tests Unit 9 and Review (Units 7–9)
- ▶ Gateway to exams Units 9 and 10 (end of Unit 10)

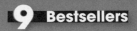

Vocabulary p110

Talking about fiction and non-fiction

>>> **FAST TRACK**

You could ask students to do exercise 4 at home before the class and check their answers at the start of the lesson.

WARMER

In pairs, students discuss the meaning of the unit title *Bestsellers* and what they think the unit is going to be about. Elicit the difference between fiction and non-fiction and ask students for examples of both. Ask students to tell their partner the names of their favourite books.

Suggested answers

Bestsellers are books which sell a lot of copies and are popular. They are usually fiction, but can be non-fiction, too.
Fiction books and stories are about imaginary events and people.
Non-fiction is about real people and events.

Fiction

1 Students look at the covers and ask if they've read any of the books. In pairs, ask students to match the words with the book covers. Nominate students to give their answers.

Answers

a play **b** romance **c** crime novel **d** fantasy
e science fiction **f** historical fiction

2 ▶ 56 Play the track for students to listen and repeat. See p159 for the audioscript for this exercise.

EXTRA ACTIVITY

Students tell you what they know about each genre in exercise 1 (vocabulary they associate with them, types of books, etc.). Build up a definition of each word on the board.

Suggested answers

comic/graphic novel: the story is told in comic form, combining writing and art; *crime novel*: fiction about crimes, spies, murders and assassinations; *fairy tale*: traditional children's story in which magic things happen, usually about princes, princesses, castles, dragons and witches; *fantasy*: with supernatural events, magic and make-believe; *historical fiction*: a story set at a particular moment in the past; *horror*: a frightening story intended to scare its readers, often with monsters, vampires or other evil creatures; *play*: performed by actors in a theatre or on television or the radio; *romance*: about people who fall in love; *science fiction*: about imaginary future events that often include space travel and creatures from other planets; *thriller*: an exciting story

3 **SPEAKING** In pairs, students take it in turns to ask and answer the questions. Finish with a short class discussion. Elicit which types of fiction students enjoy reading most or least and ask them to give reasons why.

Non-fiction

4 Students match the words in the box to the book titles. Allow students to compare in pairs before you elicit answers from the class. If necessary, remind students of the difference between a *biography* (written about someone's life by someone else) and *autobiography* (about someone's life and written by the person whose life it is).

Answers

2 manual **3** autobiography **4** biography
5 cookbook **6** atlas **7** newspaper **8** textbook
9 magazine **10** Encyclopaedia

>>> **FAST FINISHERS**

Ask students to think of or invent more book titles for each type of non-fiction. They read the titles for a partner to say the correct type of non-fiction.

5a **PRONUNCIATION** Students practise saying the words in exercise 4 and put them in the correct column, according to their stress.

Answers

1	Oo	atlas, cookbook, guidebook, manual, textbook
2	Ooo	newspaper
3	ooO	magazine
4	oOoo	biography
5	oooOoo	autobiography, encyclopaedia

5b ▶ 57 Play the track for students to listen, check and repeat the words. See p159 for the audioscript for this exercise.

5c Students say the words in exercise 1 aloud and see if they match any of the word stress patterns in the table.

Answers

1 horror, science, fiction, thriller, comic, graphic, novel
2 fairy tale, fantasy
3 –
4 historical

Sentence stress

One key area of pronunciation that is worth focusing on is the stress-timed quality of English. The amount of time it takes to say a sentence depends on the number of syllables that receive stress in the sentence, not the total number of syllables.

Giving equal weight to each syllable can make students sound unnatural and could even stop them from being understood. Focusing students' attention on the stress-timed factor of English may assist them in sounding more natural and fluid in their speech. Where possible, ask students to read full sentences when giving their answers or speaking in class rather than just giving single words so they get used to the rhythm of English.

6 **LISTENING** ▶ **58** Play the track for students to listen to the conversations and decide what types of book or publication the people are talking about. Remind students that they can be fiction or non-fiction. Elicit answers and ask students to justify their answers by referring to key words they heard in the listening (see underlined words in the audioscript). See p159 for the audioscript for this exercise.

Answers

1 crime novel **2** guidebook **3** comic/graphic novel
4 encyclopaedia **5** biography

7 **SPEAKING** In pairs, students compare how often and in what situations they read non-fiction. Ask a more confident pair of students to read out the model dialogue before they begin. Draw attention to the adverbs of frequency. Elicit other adverbs and write them on the board as prompts.

Suggested answers

I read biographies and autobiographies to find out about famous people's lives.

I sometimes read the newspaper to find out what is happening in the world. I don't read my encyclopaedia very often, but it's useful when I need information about something. I sometimes look at my atlas to find out facts and statistics about the world we live in. I read guidebooks when I go away on holiday to find out about the places we visit.

I only read manuals when I don't know how to do something. I read textbooks every day to learn about different subjects.

I often use the dictionary to look up meanings of words.

✚ EXTRA ACTIVITY

Write these questions on the board: *Which book had the biggest impact on you? What would life be like if we couldn't read? Have you ever read a book in English? Do we read enough? Do you think children in the future will read less or more than children now? Do you think that books are going to be replaced by something else in the future?*

Ask students to discuss in pairs or small groups before you develop a class discussion.

HOMEWORK

Students write a short text about whether they prefer reading non-fiction or fiction and why.

Assign students page 76 in their Workbook or the relevant sections of the Online Workbook.

Reading p111

Skimming and scanning for global and specific information

⟩⟩⟩ FAST TRACK

You could ask students to do exercise 5 at home so that less confident students can take the necessary time to look up the vocabulary in the Macmillan Online Dictionary.

WARMER

Write *Hans Christian Andersen, J.R.R. Tolkien, Ian Fleming, Agatha Christie, William Shakespeare, Mary Shelley* on the board. In pairs, students try to come up with the book title(s) and genres each author is famous for. Set a time limit of three minutes before you ask each pair to feed back to the class. Ask students if they think these are the most famous authors of the genre.

Answers

Hans Christian Andersen: fairy tales (*The Little Mermaid, The Emperor's New Clothes, The Princess and the Pea, Thumbelina, The Ugly Duckling*)

J.R.R Tolkien: fantasy (*Lord of the Rings, The Hobbit*)

Ian Fleming: thrillers (*James Bond*)

Agatha Christie: crime novels (*Poirot, Miss Marple, Murder on the Orient Express*)

William Shakespeare: plays (*Hamlet, Romeo and Juliet, Macbeth*)

Mary Shelley: horror (*Frankenstein*)

1 Students look at the photos and ask them what the person in the picture does for a job. Then ask students to read the text and put the photos in the order that they appear in the text. Tell them to scan for the information they need to complete the task. Set a strict time limit of two minutes to focus students on the task in hand. Elicit answers from the class.

Answers

1 c **2** d **3** a **4** b

ℹ CULTURAL INFORMATION

David Walliams is a British comedian, actor, television personality and writer. In Britain, he is best known for his comedy series *Little Britain* which first aired in 2003 and featured a number of caricatures of British life. Since *Little Britain*, he has co-written another comedy series called *Come Fly with Me* based in an airport and has been a judge on the talent show *Britain's Got Talent*.

He has also written a number of children's books, some of which have been made into short films by the BBC. He has received a number of awards for his work for charity, including the *Pride of Britain Award* for 'The Most Influential Public Figure' which he won in 2006 when he raised over £1 million for charity by swimming the English Channel.

✔ EXAM SUCCESS
Students read the information and decide how they can check their answers when they finish a missing sentences activity. Ask them to turn to page 146 (Reading: Missing sentences activities) to compare their answers.

2 Students read the article again and match sentences a–h to gaps 1–8 in the text. Ask students to check with a partner before eliciting answers from the class.

Answers
1 f **2** b **3** e **4** a **5** h **6** c **7** d **8** g

TEACHER DEVELOPMENT: STUDENT TRAINING

Missing sentences activities

This activity is often used in reading exams to test comprehension. The rationale behind this type of activity is to make students aware of how sentences work together to produce a logical, coherent set of ideas. In order to work out which sentence goes in which paragraph, students must focus on the main content of each paragraph and employ different strategies such as skimming for gist, scanning for detail and a careful analysis of lexis and grammar. Inserting missing information into a text raises awareness of how a text works as a whole and helps improve both reading and writing skills.

3 Students look at the photos again and explain why each one is significant for David Walliams. Students compare in pairs before you elicit answers from the class.

Suggested answers
a Walliams swam 225 kilometres of the River Thames for charity.
b 30,000 copies of one of his new books fell in the sea near China.
c He was a judge on the reality show *Britain's Got Talent*.
d He won an award for his 2nd book.

⟫⟫ FAST FINISHERS

Ask students to write a comprehension question on the text, e.g. *Who was his partner in creating* Little Britain? *What age group is* Demon Dentist *for?* They then ask their questions to the class.

4 ⚙ **CRITICAL THINKING** Students consider the questions then share their answers with the rest of the class.

Example answers

It's very important for children to read as it can improve their vocabulary and their reading skills. Also it's important to develop children's imagination, and reading is a lot of fun!

5 Students look at the underlined words in the text and guess what they mean. Allow them to check in their dictionaries.

Answers

youth = a young person, usually teenager
judge = someone who decides on the winner in a competition
award = a prize or reward for achieving something
on sale = available to buy
chills = feeling of fear or excitement
raising = to collect money for a cause
publisher = person who manages the writing and production of books

6 **SPEAKING** What about *you*? Students discuss the questions in pairs and give reasons for their answers. Ask different students to tell the class about their partner, e.g. *Sara's favourite author is Stephenie Meyer because she loves stories about vampires. She wouldn't like to read a book by Anthony Horowitz because she doesn't like James Bond and Alex Rider is like a young James Bond.*

✦ EXTRA ACTIVITY

Ask students to make a mind map for the unit theme of reading, including words from the earlier Vocabulary lesson and new words from this lesson, e.g. *author, stories, series, best-selling.* You could ask them to use their dictionaries to find other words related to books and reading, e.g. *front cover, back cover, index, spine, title, contents, hardback, paperback, e-book.*

HOMEWORK

Assign students page 77 in their Workbook or the relevant sections of the Online Workbook.

Grammar in context pp112–113

Using reported speech – statements

>>> FAST TRACK
You could ask students to do exercise 4 at home and check their answers at the next lesson.

Test before you teach: Flipped classroom
Set the Flipped classroom video and tasks for homework <u>before the lesson</u>. This will allow you to assess the needs of the students before the class. Students can then move on to the relevant grammar practice activities.

1a Students look at the things David Walliams said to a journalist (1–4) and compare them to how the journalist reported them later in a newspaper (a–d).

1b Students look at the direct and reported speech in exercise 1a and answer the questions.

Answers
1 The tense of the verbs changes when they go into reported speech; they usually go one tense 'back'.
2 In reported speech, pronouns and possessive adjectives often have to change because the person who said it is different to the person who is reporting it.
3 *Tell* is always followed by a personal object, whereas *say* does not need one.
4 We do not need to use *that* after *say* and *tell*.

✚ EXTRA ACTIVITY

Say some simple sentences in direct speech, e.g. *I like English. He's going to the bank.* Ask students to report them back to you, changing the tense, pronouns and possessive adjectives, e.g. *She said she liked English. She said he was going to the bank.*

TEACHER DEVELOPMENT: LANGUAGE

Say vs tell
The most common verbs used to report statements are *say* and *tell*. When *tell* is used in reported speech, it is always followed by a noun or a pronoun indicating the person spoken to, whereas *say* is not, e.g. *Jane said (that) we were going to the cinema on Saturday. Jane told us (that) we were going to the cinema on Saturday.* Other commonly used verbs with reported speech are: *add, admit, claim, declare, explain, indicate, mention, observe, state, reply, point out,* etc.

2 Students match the sentences in direct and reported speech. Remind them that one of the reported speech sentences can go with more than one of the sentences in direct speech. Ask students what the *'d* stands for in sentence a (*would*). Nominate students to give their answers.

Answers
2 b **3** c **4** c **5** d **6** a **7** e **8** g

3 Students look at the examples in exercise 2 and put the tenses and the verbs in the correct places in the table.

Answers
2 past continuous **3** past perfect **4** past perfect
5 *would* **6** *could* **7** *might* **8** *had to*

4 Students complete the sentences with *said* or *told*, then say which fictional character he is.

Answers
1 said **2** told **3** told **4** said **5** said **6** said
(Superman)

5 Students rewrite the sentences in exercise 4 as direct speech. Draw attention to the example. Nominate students to give their answers.

Answers
2 'I came to Earth from a different planet.' **3** 'I can fly.' **4** 'I am working as a journalist.' **5** 'I don't like kryptonite.' **6** 'I've got an 'S' on the front of my costume.'

6 Tell students that other words often change when we put statements into reported speech. Draw attention to the example and elicit that *this* changes to *that*. Ask students to use the words to complete the table. Nominate students to give answers.

Answers
2 here **3** today **4** yesterday **5** tomorrow
6 tonight **7** next (week/month/year)
8 last (week/month/year) **9** a (week/month/year) ago

7 Students report what the writer said in an interview, using *say* and *tell* as in the example sentence. Remind students to refer back to exercise 6 to see what other words often change. Ask different students to give their answers.

Answers
2 She said (that) she was 17 years old.
3 She said (that) she had already written two novels.
4 She said (that) she'd started writing when she was 14.
5 She said (that) she lives in California but she was born in Hong Kong.
6 She said (that) the first language she spoke was Japanese.
7 She said (that) apart from writing, she was a regular teenage girl.
8 She said (that) her next novel will be out that summer.

TEACHER DEVELOPMENT: LANGUAGE

Reported speech

When we use reported speech, we have to take into account how circumstances have changed since the speaker originally spoke the words. For instance, we may now be reporting what was said from a different time or place, and a different point of view. The person reporting the speech may also be different to the original speaker. This will affect our choice of pronouns or adverbials of time and place.

8a Students write a true sentence about themselves and the summer. Remind them it can be last summer, next summer or the summer in general. Draw attention to the examples and to the photo.

8b Students read out their sentences as an open-class activity or in large groups.

8c When everyone has read out their sentence, students try to remember what other students said and write the sentences down using reported speech. Draw attention to the examples.

8d SPEAKING Students work in pairs or small groups to compare answers. If they have different answers ask them to find the right answer by asking the person in question. Elicit reported speech sentences from the class.

✚ EXTRA ACTIVITY

Ask students to write three true and two false personal statements to tell their partner, e.g. *I went to Italy last year. I have two brothers. My dog's name is Patch. I speak four languages. I can ski.*

Then ask students to read their statements to their partner. Students say the sentences back to their partner using reported speech and tell him/her which statements they think are false.

Refer students to the Grammar reference on page 120 if necessary.

HOMEWORK

Assign students page 78 in their Workbook or the relevant sections of the Online Workbook.

Developing vocabulary p113

Using phrasal verbs connected with reading and writing

⟩⟩⟩ FAST TRACK

You could ask students to do exercise 1 at home and check their answers at the next lesson. Ask which answers they were able to guess, and which they had to look up.

1 Students read the sentences and guess the meanings of the words in italics. Elicit ideas from different students.

2 Now ask students to match the phrasal verbs in exercise 1 to the definitions.

Answers

1 e 2 a 3 d 4 f 5 c 6 g 7 b

TEACHER DEVELOPMENT: STUDENT TRAINING

Learning phrasal verbs

Point out to students that most dictionaries tell them when phrasal verbs are separable. If a dictionary says, e.g. *look* (something) *up*, students know that the phrasal verb *look up* is separable.

Remind them that it is a good idea to include the word *something* or *somebody* when they write a new phrasal verb in their notebooks to remind them if the verb needs a direct object and where to put it. They should also write an example sentence to show how the phrasal verb is used in context.

3 Students complete the text with the words in the box. Nominate students to give their answers.

Answers

a flick **b** on **c** look **d** over **e** out **f** cross

✚ EXTRA ACTIVITY

Ask students to write a short text about learning English in the classroom, using as many of the phrasal verbs from exercise 1 as they can.

HOMEWORK

Assign students page 79 in their Workbook or the relevant sections of the Online Workbook.

Gateway to life skills pp114–115

Enjoying fiction

To read and think about the start of a novel, to hear people recommending books to read and to read a book and discuss it in a 'book club'.

⟩⟩⟩ FAST TRACK

You could ask students to do exercise 1 at home before the class and compare their answers in pairs at the beginning of the lesson.

ⓘ BACKGROUND INFORMATION

Reading fiction provides numerous benefits for young people. Firstly, it improves literacy and expands vocabulary, and therefore encourages the reader to be more articulate and well-spoken. Secondly, it increases the reader's knowledge on anything from history to geography and from psychology to relationships. Thirdly, it can provide escapism and a way to relax away from TV and computer screens. Finally (though there are many other benefits) it can be an engaging way of exposing learners to the English language in a variety of styles, registers and contexts.

Reading doesn't necessarily need to be an anti-social pursuit either – forming book clubs or discussing books on Internet forums is a great way for teenagers to engage with their peers.

Write these questions on the board: *How do you choose what you want to read? Do you judge a book by its cover?* Ask students to discuss the questions in pairs and then with the class.

Write the choices *1) back cover blurb, 2) online review, 3) friend's recommendation* on the board and ask students which would influence their decision most in choosing a book, giving their reasons.

Ask students to read through the Key concepts before you start the lesson.

1 Students look at the cover of the novel *Maximum Ride* and answer the questions. Nominate students to give their answers.

Suggested answers

1 A teenage girl with wings, a city that looks like New York, an electric storm   **2** Fantasy or perhaps science fiction   **3** I think it might be about angels.

2 READING Students read the prologue to the novel and answer the questions. Check answers and ask students if it's the type of book they usually read.

Answers

1 Fantasy/science fiction/thriller
2 It tells you that the writer was created as part of an experiment where you only end up 98% human.

3 Students read the text again and make notes about the characters. Ask students to compare their notes with a partner.

Answers

1 lives with his family (five other kids), he's special, he is 98% human and 2% other, he grew up in a science lab/school, he has special abilities
2 there are five other people, Fang, Iggy, Nudge, the Gasman and Angel, they're not related by blood, they're all cool and smart, all part of the experiment
3 also part of an experiment, tough and smart, part human part wolf, they are guards for the school, they want to kill the other part of the experiment

4 Tell students that the author, James Patterson, is an expert at making people want to read on. Go through the techniques together as a class and draw attention to the example. Then ask students to find a sentence from the text for each technique. Nominate students to give their answers.

Answers

2 They want to kill us.   **3** Keep reading – don't let anyone stop you.   **4** Welcome to our nightmare.
5 The six of us – me, Fang, Iggy, Nudge, the Gasman and Angel – were made by the worst, most horrible 'scientists' you could possibly imagine.   **6** We're – well, we're kind of amazing.   **7** I'm risking everything that matters by telling you – but you need to know.

5 Ask students if they would like to continue reading the book. Have a show of hands and then discuss why/why not.

6a Students work in pairs, look at the three books and discuss what they know about them.

6b LISTENING ▶ 59 Tell students they are going to watch or listen to three students reading out a section of a book they have just read and giving their opinions. Play the video or track. Students listen and match each speaker to a book. See p159 for the videoscript/audioscript for this exercise.

Answers

Speaker 1: Romeo and Juliet
Speaker 2: White Fang
Speaker 3: Frankenstein

6c ▶ 59 Students listen and watch again, and write the number of the speaker next to each item.

Answers

Romance, 1; A serious message, 1; Simple sentences, 2; Interesting relationships, 3; Fascinating characters, 2; An unexpected story, 3

7 Students tell a partner which of the three books they would most like to read and why.

LIFE TASK

Tell students they are going to organise a book club.

- ***Step 1***
  Ask students if they've ever been in a book club and if they think it's a good idea. Divide the class into groups of three or four and ask students to read the instructions. Students start by choosing a book to read. Encourage them to browse local bookshops, look in the local or school library, ask family and friends for recommendations and search the Internet.

- ***Step 2***
  Once they have chosen their book, make sure they set a time to finish reading it (1–2 weeks).

- ***Step 3***
  When students have finished reading, organise them into small groups and ask them to discuss their book using the questions in the Student's Book. You could help students by giving them the following vocabulary and phrases to use in their discussion: *a simple/complex/gripping plot* (the story of the book); *an interesting protagonist* (main character); *a predictable/unpredictable ending; a good twist* (unexpected part of the story, usually at the end).

Listening p116

Listening for general and specific information

1 **SPEAKING** Students work in pairs to answer the questions. Elicit ideas from different pairs and hold a short discussion.

Suggested answers

1 *The Da Vinci Code* by Dan Brown, *Memoirs of a Geisha* by Arthur Golden, *Pride and Prejudice* by Jane Austen, *Eragon* by Christopher Paolini, the *Harry Potter* series by J.K. Rowling

2 You can read books when and where you want, you can imagine how the characters speak, what they look like and what their surroundings are like.
You can see and hear the characters and the action, films can be more exciting, it only takes a couple of hours to get through a whole story.

✓ EXAM SUCCESS Students read the information and discuss how they can predict the type of words that are missing from a text. Ask them to turn to page 146 (Listening: Completing notes) to compare their answers.

2 **LISTENING** ▶ 60 Students read the notes and try to predict the missing words. Play the track for students to listen to the woman and complete the notes using one or two words for each space. You may also like to pre-teach these words: *culture vulture* – a person who is very interested in the arts; *survey* – a set of questions you ask to find out people's opinions. See pp159–160 for the audioscript for this exercise.

Answers

a week **b** science fiction **c** year **d** Occasionally **e** are thinking **f** friends **g** look different

TEACHER DEVELOPMENT: STUDENT TRAINING

Predicting missing words

It is a good idea for students to look at the task before listening and predict the missing words. By doing this, they are activating a set of expectations which helps them interpret what they hear. They can use background knowledge, their general knowledge of the world and specific cultural knowledge, as well extra-linguistic clues, e.g. visual information. Students can also use their linguistic knowledge to decide whether the missing items are nouns, verbs, adjectives, adverbs, prepositions or key words related to the topic, so they know what type of word they are listening for.

3 ▶ 60 Students decide if the statements are true or false. Play the track again if necessary. Give students time to compare answers and then nominate students to give their answers.

Answers

1 F **2** F **3** T **4** T **5** F **6** F

✦✦ EXTRA ACTIVITY

Students correct the false statements in exercise 3.
Suggested answers

1 The interviewer asked her how often she read books.

2 He wanted to know what the last book she had read was.

5 He asked her if she liked going to see film adaptations of books.

6 He asked her whether she preferred reading the book or watching the film of the book.

HOMEWORK

Assign students page 79 in their Workbook or the relevant sections of the Online Workbook.

Grammar in context pp116–117

Using reported speech – questions

>>> FAST TRACK

You could ask students to do exercise 4 at home and check their answers at the next lesson.

Test before you teach

Write these sentences on the board: *He asked, 'Where do they live?' He asked, 'Do they live in Prague?'* Ask students to rewrite them using reported speech. Monitor to see if students are comfortable with reported questions.

Answers

He asked where they lived.
He asked if/whether they lived in Prague.

1a Students look at the questions and statements and decide which are direct questions (DQ) and which are reported questions (RQ). Elicit answers from the class.

Answers

1 RQ **2** RQ **3** DQ **4** DQ **5** RQ **6** DQ **7** DQ **8** RQ

>>> FAST FINISHERS

Ask students to match the direct questions to their reported speech equivalents in exercise 1a.
Answers

1 – 6, 2 – 4, 5 – 3, 8 – 7

Reported speech – questions

Yes/No questions in reported speech always begin with the word *if* or *whether*, e.g. *I asked her if/whether she wanted to go to the cinema.*

Wh- questions in reported speech always begin with the question word and change from question word order to statement word order, e.g. *She asked me who was sitting next to me in class today.* Point out to students that reported questions are not real interrogative questions and, therefore, they do not need question marks.

1b Students choose the correct alternatives. Nominate students to give their answers to the class.

Answers

1 change   **2** don't use   **3** don't use   **4** don't put
5 use

2 Students complete the sentences with a question word or *if/whether*.

Answers

1 who   **2** what   **3** if/whether   **4** if/whether
5 if/whether   **6** why   **7** if/whether

3 Students write what the people actually said in each situation. You could do the first one together as an example.

Answers

1 Journalist: Are you making a film at the moment?
Film director: No, I'm not, but I'm going to start a new one soon.
2 Writer: Did you enjoy my book?
Man: I think it is the most beautiful thing I've ever read.
3 Reporter: Why won't you answer any of my questions?
Singer: I only want to talk about my new album and I'm not going to talk about anything else.
4 Teacher: Can you write an essay for tomorrow?
Students: We can't because we have to study for an exam and we won't have enough time.
5 Julie: How many times have you read your comic?
Me: I've read it three times.

4 Ask two students to read out the conversation. Then ask them to rewrite it in reported speech. Nominate two students to read out the conversation.

Suggested answers

Keira asked Matt what he had done the night before. He said he hadn't done much and had just watched TV with his parents.
She asked him if/whether he had studied for the literature exam and he asked her when they had the exam. Keira replied that they were doing it that day. Matt asked her why she hadn't reminded him and she said she had told him but he hadn't been listening. She asked him why he never paid attention to her.

5a Students look at the photo and ask what event the room is prepared for (an interview). Tell students to decide as a class on a famous person they would like to interview.

5b In pairs, students prepare five questions to ask him/her. You could give students different categories to prepare questions about (e.g. their family, their childhood, their inspiration, coping with fame, etc.).

5c SPEAKING Choose a student, or ask for a volunteer to be the famous person. Ask other students to interview them and make notes of their answers.

5d SPEAKING Students work in their original pairs and report the interview back to their partner. Draw attention to the model sentences.

Refer students to the Grammar reference on page 120 if necessary.

HOMEWORK

Assign students page 80 in their Workbook or the relevant sections of the Online Workbook.

Developing speaking p118

Giving a presentation

>>> FAST TRACK

You could ask students to prepare exercise 5a at home. They could present it to the class at the next lesson.

1 Students look at the question and make notes in the You column.

2 LISTENING ▶ 61 Play the track for students to listen to a student giving a presentation about his favourite book. Ask them to complete the other column of the table with notes. See p160 for the audioscript for this exercise.

Answers

Holes, Louis Sachar, crime novel
1 It's clever.   **2** The descriptions are very/so realistic.
3 The characters are likeable.   **4** There are lots of dialogues.   **5** It's easy and fast to read.   **6** It's funny.
7 It has a happy ending.

3 ▶ 61 Students look at the Speaking bank and to complete the expressions. Play the track again if necessary.

Answers

like ... begin, of all, more, true, but not least, up

4 Students join the sentence halves with advice about giving a presentation. Elicit answers from students. Ask students if they can think of any more advice to add.

Answers

1 e   **2** d   **3** c   **4** f   **5** b   **6** a

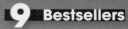

PRACTICE MAKES PERFECT

5a Students prepare a presentation about the best book that they have ever read. Remind them to use their notes in exercise 1 and the expressions in the Speaking bank. Tell them not to write a complete text, but just to write notes with the main ideas.

5b SPEAKING Students give their presentation to the class or to groups. For less confident students allow them to practise their presentation to a partner before doing it in front of a larger group. Ask other students to give constructive feedback to the speaker.

Model text

I'm going to talk about a book called *The Fault in Our Stars* by an American writer called John Green. I'd like to begin by saying that I've read this book three or four times, so it really is my favourite book. *The Fault in Our Stars* is a romance novel, but it's actually much more than that. Let me tell you why I like it so much.

Firstly, the story is very funny. The topic is very sad but all the characters are very witty and intelligent. Their dialogue is so clever that you can read it again and again and you each time you discover something that you didn't see before. What's more, the descriptions of the characters are very realistic. The two main characters are Hazel and Augustus and they are both absolutely believable. By the end of the book, you really care about what happens to them and you just want to read on to find out what happens. Another thing is that I really enjoyed the descriptions of their trip to Amsterdam to meet their favourite author. I have always wanted to visit Amsterdam and when I read the book I actually think I'm there! That shows you that the descriptions are great. Last but not least, the ending is just so sad and moving. Every time I read it I think about it for many days afterwards.

To sum up, I think *The Fault in Our Stars* is the best book I've ever read because it's a beautiful love story but it's also funny and interesting with a heart-breaking ending, too. They made a film of the book but I think the book is much better.

HOMEWORK

Assign students page 81 in their Workbook or the relevant sections of the Online Workbook.

Developing writing p119

Writing a story

⟫⟫ FAST TRACK

You could ask students to prepare their story for exercise 6 at home. They can present their story to the class at the beginning of the next lesson.

WARMER

Ask students to think of their favourite stories. In pairs ask them to write a list of what they think makes a good story. Elicit answers from different pairs, e.g. *a good ending, a strong character, a funny moment*, etc.

1 SPEAKING Students work with a partner and put the pictures in order to tell the story. Nominate a pair to give their answer.

Suggested answers

e, c, f, i, a, g, h, d, b

2 Focus students' attention on the sentence, Ask them to look at picture e and expand the sentence by adding words to describe the scene in more detail. Ask them to think particularly about adjectives and adverbs as well as the setting. Nominate different students to read their new sentences.

3 Students look at the longer sentence and identify the types of words that have been added. Ask students if they think the sentence is more interesting than the one in exercise 2 and why.

Suggested answers

adverbs and adjectives; yes, as there is more detail

4 Students read the sentences and match each one to a picture from the story. Elicit answers from different students.

Answers

1 h **2** i **3** f

5 Students look at the advice in the Writing bank. Ask students to look again at the sentences in exercise 4 to find examples of the advice.

Answers

Use adjectives and adverbs to make your writing more descriptive – *falling softly and slowly from the trees*
Use a variety of past tenses – *It was autumn and the golden leaves were falling*
Use words and expressions of time and sequence – *It was autumn, Soon after, When*

6 PRACTICE MAKES PERFECT
Students write the story in exercise 1 using the sentences on the page and the advice in the Writing bank to help. For less confident students, give them 5–10 minutes to brainstorm their ideas first.

Model text

It was a cold winter day and it was snowing outside while the young ambitious woman was busy writing her book. When she had finished her book, she took it immediately to a famous publishing company. Thousands of copies of the book were printed with a beautiful red cover. In summer, it was bought by a young man who sat reading it on a park bench on a lovely sunny day. He kept the book through autumn, but by winter it was time for him to leave his house. While he wasn't looking, two homeless men took the book and used it on their fire to keep warm while the snow was falling.

➕ EXTRA ACTIVITY

Ask for volunteers to read their stories, then ask other students to say which they found most interesting and why.

HOMEWORK

Assign students page 82 in their Workbook or the relevant sections of the Online Workbook.

Language checkpoint: Unit 9

⟫⟫ FAST TRACK

The extra support provided on the Grammar and Vocabulary reference sections makes the Grammar and Vocabulary revision section ideal for setting as homework. You could get students to complete the whole revision page or just certain exercises for homework.

Grammar revision p121

Reported speech – statements

1   Students write the sentences in reported speech.

Answers

1 My sister said she was going to a concert the following week.   2 Daniel told the teacher that he would be late the following day.   3 Holly said it was her dictionary.   4 Sylvia said she had always wanted to write stories.   5 They told us there was going to be a concert in that room.   6 They said the play would start at 7 pm the following day.   7 The students told the writer that they hadn't read any of his/her books.   8 The journalist said he/she had written the article the previous day.

Reported speech – questions

2   Students write the questions in reported speech.

Answers

1 She asked if I was from Mexico.
2 Jo asked Paul what time he was going to leave.
3 I asked Katie why she was crying.
4 The teacher asked me whether I had ever read that book.
5 Tom asked her if she would help him the following day.
6 Abigail asked her dad if the doctor had seen Sam the previous day.
7 Our teacher asked us if we knew the answer to that question.
8 I asked Jo how many pages it had.

Vocabulary revision p121

FICTION

1   Students complete the sentences with the correct words.

Answers

1 fantasy   2 thriller   3 play   4 romance   5 fairy tale   6 historical   7 graphic novel   8 horror

NON-FICTION

2   Students write which type of book or publication is best in each situation.

Answers

1 atlas   2 autobiography   3 cookbook   4 manual   5 guidebook   6 newspaper   7 textbook   8 encyclopaedia   9 magazine

PHRASAL VERBS CONNECTED WITH READING AND WRITING

3   Students match the sentence halves.

Answers

1 g   2 c   3 f   4 e   5 b   6 d   7 a

HOMEWORK

Assign students page 83 in their Workbook or the relevant sections of the Online Workbook.

10 Log on

KEY LEARNING OUTCOMES

CEF

Students will be able to:

- understand a text about the history of computing
- talk about ICT, computers and the Internet using the passive
- talk about the importance of the Internet
- compare and contrast photos
- write text messages

UNIT OVERVIEW

Vocabulary
Using a computer
The Internet
PRONUNCIATION Word stress in verbs and nouns

Reading
The computer that began it all
CRITICAL THINKING Evaluating the importance of the Internet in today's world

Grammar in context
The passive – present simple

Developing vocabulary
Collocations with *email*

Life skills
ICT: Protecting yourself on the Internet

Listening
Wikipedia

Grammar in context
The passive – other tenses
have something done

Developing speaking
Comparing and contrasting photos

Developing writing
Text messages

Exam success
Use of English: Cloze activities
Speaking: Speculating about photos

DIGITAL OVERVIEW

Presentation Kit

- ▶ **Flipped classroom video Unit 10:** The passive – present simple
- ▶ **Life skills video Unit 10:** Social networks
- ▶ V **Vocabulary tool:** Using a computer
- ▶ **Interactive versions of Student's Book activities**
- ▶ **Integrated audio and answer key for all activities**
- ▶ **Workbook pages with answer key**

Teacher's Resource Centre TRC

- ▶ **Flipped classroom video Unit 10:** The passive – present simple
- ▶ **Life skills video Unit 10:** Social networks
- ▶ **Grammar communication activity Unit 10:** Quite interesting
- ▶ **Worksheets for this unit, including:**
  - – Grammar practice worksheet Unit 10
  - – Flipped classroom video worksheet Unit 10: The passive – present simple
  - – Literature worksheet Units 9 and 10
  - – Culture worksheet Unit 10
  - – Life skills video worksheet Unit 10
  - – Everyday English worksheet Unit 10

Student's App

Gateway 2nd Edition wordlist for the award-winning Sounds App (available for download)

✓ TESTING AND ASSESSMENT

Resources for exam preparation and measuring student progress

- ▶ Test Generator Units 1–10
- ▶ Printable tests Unit 10 and End-of-year
- ▶ Gateway to exams Units 9 and 10 (end of Unit 10)

Vocabulary p122

Talking about using a computer and the Internet

>>> **FAST TRACK**

You could ask students to do exercise 4 at home before the class and check their answers at the beginning of the lesson. Ask which answers they were able to guess, and which they had to look up.

WARMER

In pairs, students make a list of all the activities they use a computer for in a typical week, e.g. *writing essays, sending emails, watching movies, downloading music, chatting online, reading the news, playing games,* etc. Ask students to estimate how many hours a week they spend on a computer.

Ⓥ Using a computer

1 In pairs, students match the words to the technology in the picture.

2 ▶ 62 Play the track for students to listen, check and repeat. Draw attention to the schwa sound at the end of *monitor, speaker, printer* and *scanner.* See p160 for the audioscript for this exercise.

Answers

a printer **b** headset (headphones/microphone)
c webcam **d** monitor/screen **e** speaker
f hard drive **g** USB port **h** USB cable **i** tablet
j scanner **k** keyboard **l** mouse
m flashdrive/pendrive **n** mouse mat

⁺⁺ EXTRA ACTIVITY

Ask students to mark the stress in each word in exercise 1.

3 Ask students to match the sentence halves. Nominate students to give their answers.

Answers

1 d **2** a **3** c **4** e **5** f **6** b

The Internet

4 **LISTENING** ▶ 63 Play the track. Students read and listen to the description of how a teenager uses the Internet. Ask students to check they understand the words in red. See p160 for the audioscript for this exercise.

Answers

broadband = a type of connection between a computer and the Internet that allows you to send or receive a large amount of information in a short time
online = connected to the Internet
surf the Net = to go on the Internet and look at different websites
websites = a set of pages on the same domain
homepage = the main page of a website
search engine = a computer program that is used for searching for information on the Internet

---

download (v) = to move information to your computer system from another computer or from the Internet
blog = a discussion site usually written in posts that people can comment on
chat online = to talk online to someone using an instant messaging system
social networking = sites such as Facebook where you can have a profile, share photos and connect with friends

⁺⁺ EXTRA ACTIVITY

Ask students to choose five of the words in red in exercise 4 and write new sentences for them.

>>> **FAST FINISHERS**

Students think of more words connected to the unit theme and look them up in their dictionaries, e.g. *podcast, virus, scanner, digital camera, software, screensaver, menu, network,* etc. They should write a definition in English for each word.

5a **PRONUNCIATION** Students decide if *download* is a verb or a noun in each sentence.

Answers

1 verb **2** noun

5b ▶ 64 Play the track for students to listen for the pronunciation of *download* in each sentence. Elicit what is different about the pronunciation for the verb and the noun. See p160 for the audioscript for this exercise.

Answer

No.
1 I want to down<u>load</u> this song.
2 The <u>down</u>load didn't work.

5c ▶ 64 Play the track again for students to listen to the sentences and choose the correct alternatives. Nominate students to give their answers.

Answers

1 second **2** first

TEACHER DEVELOPMENT: PRONUNCIATION

Word stress in nouns and verbs

Point out that there are many two-syllable words in English whose meaning and class change depending on the stressed syllable, e.g. re<u>cord</u> (v)/<u>re</u>cord (n); ob<u>ject</u> (v)/<u>ob</u>ject (n); pre<u>sent</u> (v)/<u>pre</u>sent (n). A word can only have one stress and we only stress vowels, not consonants.

⁺⁺ EXTRA ACTIVITY

Write these words on the board: *accent, combat, contract, decrease, desert, increase, present, produce, progress, project, record.* Ask students to write two column headings in their notebooks: *Verbs* and *Nouns.* Students write all the words in both columns and underline the stressed syllable in each word, depending on its class. They then practise saying the words in pairs.

Answer

As before, all verbs have the stress on the second syllable and all nouns have the stress on the first syllable.

6a SPEAKING Students decide how often they do each thing on a computer (*never, sometimes, often, very often*). Elicit answers from different students.

6b SPEAKING In pairs, students ask and answer to find out how often their partner does each thing in exercise 6a, e.g. A: *How often do you chat online?* B: *I sometimes chat online.*

✚ EXTRA ACTIVITY

Conduct a class survey of students' answers in exercise 6. Ask each question and get students to raise their hands for each answer: *never, sometimes, often, very often*. Record the results on the board (or ask a volunteer to do this for you). Use these numbers to work out some statistics, e.g. *Seventy percent of the class chat online. Twenty percent sometimes use a webcam.* Students write a short report based on the statistics in class or for homework.

HOMEWORK

Assign students page 84 in their Workbook or the relevant sections of the Online Workbook.

Reading p123

Skimming and scanning for global and specific information

⟩⟩⟩ FAST TRACK

You could ask students to do exercise 5 at home so that less confident students can take the necessary time to look up the vocabulary in the Macmillan Online Dictionary.

WARMER

Ask students to think of all the ways they have used the Internet in the last two days and write their suggestions on the board. Ask them to think if these things were impossible before the Internet or if there were/are alternative ways of doing these things. Tell students they are going to read about the World Wide Web (the system of sites accessed via the Internet, though in everyday speech *Internet* and *World Wide Web* are often interchangeable).

1 In pairs, ask students to answer the quiz questions. Encourage them to guess if they're not sure. Elicit answers from different pairs, but don't confirm them at this point.

2 Students read the text and find the answers to the quiz in exercise 1. Elicit answers from students. Did any of them guess correctly?

Answers

1 Sir Tim Berners-Lee **2** 1989 **3** more than 600 million
4 1993

ⓘ CULTURAL INFORMATION

Tim Berners-Lee invented the World Wide Web in 1989, 20 years after the first connection was made over what is now the Internet. In 1989, Berners-Lee was a software engineer at CERN. Many scientists wanted to exchange data and results, but found it difficult from different parts of the world. Berners-Lee understood this need, and submitted a proposal to his management at CERN, in late 1989, which was initially rejected. However, Tim persevered, and since 1990 the Web has changed the world. Twenty-five percent of the people on the planet are currently using the Web, changing the way we communicate, learn, find information, share, collaborate and socialise.

3 Students read the text again in more detail and choose the best answers. Allow them to compare in pairs before you elicit answers from the class. Ask students to say which part of the text helped them choose their answer.

Answers

1 c **2** a **3** a **4** c **5** c

4 CRITICAL THINKING Ask students to read the question and think of their own answer. Tell students to compare in pairs before you elicit answers from the class.

Example answer

The Internet is really important in today's world. You can use it for lots of things – for finding information, watching films and talking with friends. If we didn't have Internet, life would be very different and a lot slower.

5 Students look at the underlined words in the text and guess their meaning. Then they use their dictionaries to check their answers.

Answers

old-fashioned = not modern, from the past
graduate = a person who has just completed a degree at university
browser = something you use to access information on the Web, e.g. Internet Explorer or Firefox
mine = an underground place with materials; if somewhere is 'a mine of information', it is a place that can provide you with a lot of information
principles = ideas and beliefs, things you feel strongly about
server = a system which delivers web pages

⟩⟩⟩ FAST FINISHERS

Ask students to find other new words in the text and use their dictionary to write the real definition of the word and then create two false ones. Ask them to read their stories out to the class for them to guess the real definition.

Guessing words from context

The meaning of many words can often be ascertained from the context and without the use of a dictionary. Students need to be able to do this in exams and to ensure they are not constantly referring to a dictionary. The following ideas will help students to develop the skill of contextual understanding:

- Work out which part of speech the unknown word is, e.g. a verb, noun, preposition, adjective, time expression, etc.
- Try to deduce the meaning from the other words surrounding it.
- Look at how the word fits into the organisation of the ideas in the text.
- Check to see if the word is later defined in the text.

6 SPEAKING **What about *you*?** Students think about the questions and then discuss with a partner. Then nominate students to give their answers. Ask students if they think they could live without the Internet for a week.

Grammar in context pp124–125

Using the passive – present simple

>>> **FAST TRACK**

You could ask students to do exercise 3 at home and check their answers at the next lesson.

 Test before you teach: Flipped classroom
Set the Flipped classroom video and tasks for homework <u>before the lesson</u>. This will allow you to assess the needs of the students before the class. Students can then move on to the relevant grammar practice activities.

1a Students look at the sentences and decide which are active and which are passive. Nominate students to give their answers.

Answers
Passive: 1, 4   Active: 2, 3

1b Students decide if the statements are true or false.

Answers
1 T **2** T **3** T

1c Students complete the rules. Elicit answers from the class.

Answers
1 *be* **2** *by*

Active to passive

Go through the steps students must take to form a passive sentence from an active sentence: *The boys always eat the pizza* to the passive: *The pizza is always eaten (by the boys)*.

- Move the receiver of the action from the direct object position of the sentence to the subject position.
- Insert the correct form of the verb *be* for the new subject.
- Change the main verb to its past participle form.
- Place the 'doer' of the verb in the object position after the preposition *by* (optional).

2 Students complete the sentences with the correct form of the present simple passive.

Answers
1 is found **2** is refined **3** is heated, (is) made
4 are cut **5** are added **6** are put **7** are worn
8 are sent

3 Ask students if the sentences are grammatically correct. Check that they have identified the incorrect ones and then ask students to correct them. Elicit answers from different students.

Answers
1 More than 204 million emails are sent. **2** Around 20 million photos are seen. **3** More than 1.3 million videos are watched. **4** Correct **5** Music is played by hundreds of thousands of people. **6** More than $83,000 is spent in just one big Internet store.
7 Correct

++ EXTRA ACTIVITY

Students draw five or six pictures showing a process they are familiar with, e.g. *milk processing, coal mining, steel production, making a cake or a particular dish*, etc. They describe what happens at each stage of the process using sentences in the present simple passive.

4 Students change the sentences from active to passive or from passive to active. Remind them to include *by* plus the agent only when necessary. Do the first one together as an example.

Answers
1 A lot of silicon chips are made in India. **2** Many people are employed in the computer industry.
3 Amazing new technology is invented every day.
4 Sony, Nintendo and Microsoft create most new games consoles. **5** Computer games are played by millions of kids every day. **6** The use of the Internet is controlled by some governments. **7** A password is not needed to enter this site.

5a SPEAKING In pairs, students look at the map and answer the questions.

Answers

1 Pizza, olive oil, cars and planes are made. **2** Lemons, oranges and tomatoes are grown. **3** Tropical fruits are not grown in Italy. **4** Pizza is eaten in Italy. **5** Rugby and ice hockey are played in Italy. **6** Cars, food and planes are exported from Italy. **7** Cricket is not played in Italy.

5b SPEAKING In pairs, students use the questions to talk about their own country. If possible, give them some time to research their answers in the library on the Internet and encourage them to include more information that they think will be interesting.

Refer students to the Grammar reference on page 132 if necessary.

HOMEWORK

Assign students page 86 in their Workbook or the relevant sections of the Online Workbook.

Developing vocabulary p125

Using collocations with email

▶▶▶ FAST TRACK

You could do exercise 2 as a class activity by inviting individual students to give the answers and asking the rest of the class if they agree.

1   Students read the text and match three of the words in red italics to the icons.

Answers

1 h **2** f **3** e

2   Now ask students to match the definitions to the correct words in exercise 1.

Answers

2 bounced back **3** address **4** check(ing) **5** forward

3   SPEAKING In pairs, ask students to ask and answer the questions. Explain that spam is emails that are sent to large numbers of people on the Internet and are not usually wanted. Nominate students to share their partner's answers.

✛ EXTRA ACTIVITY

Students write about their conversation with their partner in exercise 3 using reported statements and questions.

HOMEWORK

Assign students page 87 in their Workbook or the relevant sections of the Online Workbook.

Gateway to life skills pp126–127

Protecting yourself on the Internet

To think about social media profiles, to think about good advice for safe social networking and to give advice to others about how to protect yourself online.

▶▶▶ FAST TRACK

You could ask students to do exercise 4 at home in pairs before the class and compare their answers with the whole class at the beginning of the lesson.

ⓘ BACKGROUND INFORMATION

A recent poll has shown that teenagers spend 31 hours a week on average on the Internet. The benefits of being online are numerous: they can read the news, share photos, communicate with friends and research topics for homework. However there are precautions that anyone using the Internet should take. One in four of the teenagers in the same poll admitted to talking to strangers regularly online. Though these communications are largely innocent and can be a good way to 'meet' new people and learn new ideas, there are clear dangers to forming relationships with strangers. Other Internet hazards can include identity fraud, exploitation, intrusion of privacy and data theft. This lesson focuses students on ways they can protect themselves when going online.

WARMER

Teach or elicit the term *privacy settings.* **Then ask students how many social networking sites they are on and if they know, without checking, what their security and privacy settings are (i.e. could anyone see their profile picture, their photos or their status updates). Ask students to read through the Key concepts. Then ask them to work in pairs and write new sentences using the vocabulary to check understanding.**

1a Students work with a partner and say what they do on social networking sites. Draw attention to the example. Elicit answers from the class.

Suggested answers

You can upload photos. You can send messages. You can post information about yourself. You can write a blog.

1b SPEAKING Ask students what they think the good and bad things are about using social networking sites. You could write answers up on the board in two columns and see which side is longer. Revisit the lists throughout the lesson to see if students have anything extra to add.

2   READING Students read the text and answer the questions. Elicit answers from the class.

Answers

1 How social networking can affect getting a job in the future.

2 Sometimes good and sometimes bad. You have to be careful what you put: some things can help getting a job but some things make getting a job more difficult.

3 Students read the text again and answer the questions. Allow students to check answers in pairs before nominating students to give answers to the class.

Answers

1 43 percent **2** It usually has a negative effect. **3** The candidate posted inappropriate photos or information. **4** If the qualifications are real. **5** It can make you look professional, show your personality and interests, it can show if you are creative and have good communication skills. It can also show what people think of you. **6** They want to get an idea of a candidate's behaviour and personality outside the interview. **7** Think carefully before you post anything online so your social media profile sends out the correct message.

4 Students look at the words and expressions. Tell students they are titles from a video giving advice about using social networking sensibly. In pairs, ask students to predict what the advice will be. Elicit answers from students.

Suggested answers

a Choose a good password, one that's difficult to guess. **b** Don't share private information. **c** Think carefully before posting things. **d** Don't use social networking sites with an older age limit. **e** Don't post nasty comments about people.

5 **LISTENING** ▶ 65 Students watch the video or listen to the track and to put the titles from exercise 4 in the order they hear them. Nominate students to give their answers. See p160 for the videoscript/audioscript for this exercise.

Answers

1 d **2** c **3** e **4** b **5** a

6 ▶ 65 Students watch or listen again and listen for the advice the speakers give about aspects of online safety.

Answers

1 You should be honest about your age. If you're too young for a site, don't use it. **2** You should think carefully before you post them. **3** A phone number is private information so you shouldn't put it online. **4** A good password has a combination of letters, words and symbols. **5** Don't be unfriendly or cruel. If you haven't got anything nice to say, don't say it.

7 In pairs, ask students to discuss the advice in exercise 6. Ask the class if anyone strongly disagrees with the advice and why.

LIFE TASK

Tell students they are going to give a presentation about protecting themselves on the Internet.

- **Step 1**
  Divide the class into groups of three or four and ask students to read the instructions. Students start discussing advice they could give others about keeping themselves safe on social networking websites. If students have access to the Internet, they can search for other ideas, either in class or at home.

- **Step 2**
  Remind students of the importance of organising their presentations logically and clearly. Students decide what they are going to say for each point they want to make. Circulate and monitor to ensure that all students are getting the chance to contribute.

- **Step 3**
  Students think about and create the visuals for their presentation. Encourage them to think about what type of visuals would be most eye-catching and effective in getting their points across, whether it's graphics, illustrations or other images.

- **Step 4**
  Students give their presentations to the class. Ask other students in the class to make notes during the talks in preparation for giving feedback. When students have done their presentations, have students give their feedback, but ensure that it is positive or constructive criticism. Ask students to think of one thing they did well and one thing they can work on next time.

TEACHER DEVELOPMENT: STUDENT TRAINING

Giving a presentation

Review the structure of a typical presentation with students and give some example discourse for students to use:

1 Introduction: *I would like to start by …; I shall begin by …; First, I will talk about …; Then …; Next …; After that, …; And finally, …*

2 Main section: *So, let us begin with …; Now let's move on to …; Our next point is about …; And last, but not least, …*

3 Summing up: *To sum up, …; In conclusion, you can see that …*

4 Ending the presentation: *Thank you for listening. Does anyone have any questions?*

Encourage students to practise first before giving their presentation to the class. You may wish to record the presentations and include them in their Language Portfolios.

Listening p128

Listening for general and specific information

WARMER

Ask students to try to guess the top ten most visited websites in the world. Give them two minutes to create their list in pairs, then elicit ideas from the class.

Answers
These will vary.

Some of the most popular websites today are: Google, Facebook, YouTube, Yahoo, Baidu, Wikipedia, Tencent QQ, TaoBao, Twitter, Windows Live

1 SPEAKING In pairs, students discuss what they know about Wikipedia.

2 ▶ 66 Play the track for students to listen to a radio programme about Wikipedia and check their answers in exercise 1. Give students time to compare in pairs before you elicit answers from the class.
See pp160–161 for the audioscript for this exercise.

Suggested answers
Wikipedia is an online encyclopaedia, which is written by the public. It's written in many different languages.

3 ▶ 66 Students read the text about Wikipedia. Ask students to find and correct the seven mistakes. Then play the track for students to check their answers.

Answers
Wikipedia is the <u>fifth</u> most popular website in the world. It has about 365 million readers. It was started in 2001 by two <u>Americans</u> but it isn't written by them. Their original website became a 'wiki', a website that visitors can change and add information to. In 2007, approximately <u>1,700</u> articles were being added every day. 'Wiki Wiki' is <u>a Hawaiian</u> expression which means 'quick'. Wikipedia articles can change quickly when things change in the world. Some people think this is a problem, because articles aren't always correct. <u>Culture and Arts</u> are the most popular topic. <u>14%</u> of articles on Wikipedia are about geography and places. There are more than 280 different language versions of Wikipedia. The <u>English</u> version has a total of over four million articles.

4 What about *you*? In pairs, students discuss the questions. With a less confident class, ask students to make notes first before the speaking activity.

ⓘ CULTURAL INFORMATION

Wikipedia has a pages patrol division where people check new articles. Articles that are not important enough or do not cite reliable published sources are likely to be deleted. A university teacher encouraged her students to write Wikipedia pages instead of writing assignments and found that their work was of a superior quality. The important lesson for teachers may be that students invest more in their work if there is a broad audience and sense of ownership.

✚ EXTRA ACTIVITY

If students have Internet access, ask them to either research one of the top ten most visited websites in the world that they suggested for the Warmer, or a topic of their own choice, and write an article for Wikipedia.

HOMEWORK

Assign students page 87 in their Workbook or the relevant sections of the Online Workbook.

Grammar in context pp128–129

Using passive – other tenses and have something done

⟩⟩⟩ FAST TRACK

You could ask students to do exercise 4 at home and check their answers at the next lesson.

Test before you teach
Write these sentences on the board and ask students to fill each gap with a suitable word.
The World Wide Web _____ invented in 1989.
In 1990, the World Wide Web _____ being used by scientists at CERN.
Millions of apps have _____ downloaded this year.
New technology is _____ invented right now.
If students are confident with the basic forms you could quickly move through the initial exercises, eliciting answers from students in open class.

Answers
was, was, been, being

The passive – other tenses

1a Students look at the passive sentences and say which tense each of them is in. Elicit answers from different students.

Answers
1 past simple   **2** past continuous   **3** present perfect
4 present continuous

1b Students answer the question.

Answer
the verb *to be*

2 Students change the sentences from active to passive. You could do the first one together as an example.

Answers

1 Traditional encyclopaedias have been transformed by Wikipedia.
2 Wikipedia wasn't started by Sir Tim Berners-Lee.
3 Wikipedia articles are being changed at this moment.
4 Most of the articles for Wikipedia have been written by ordinary people.
5 Some Wikipedia articles have been ruined by 'vandals'.
6 A Wikipedia for children was being created.
7 The article has been copied from Wikipedia.
8 A Wikipedia article was written by a famous scientist last year.

TEACHER DEVELOPMENT: LANGUAGE

Passive questions

Point out to students that to make object questions in the passive, we put the first auxiliary verb before the subject, e.g. *Wikipedia has been used by millions of people. How many people has Wikipedia been used by?*

✓ EXAM SUCCESS Students read the information and discuss how they decide which word is missing in a cloze activity. Tell them to compare their answers with the information on page 146 (Use of English: Cloze activities).

TEACHER DEVELOPMENT: STUDENT TRAINING

Cloze activities

Cloze activities may omit any kind of word so students have to decide what type of word it might be. Often they are articles, prepositions, linking words, auxiliaries, *wh-* words, quantifiers, modals and pronouns. To decide on the type of word, students should look at its position in the sentence. Encourage students always to read the sentences before and after the gap as they may help them to identify the missing word. Remind them that if they don't know the word in an exam, they should never write two words and leave the examiner to choose because their answer will be marked wrong.

3 Students complete the text by filling in each space with one word. Give students time to compare in pairs before you elicit answers from the class.

Answers

a were **b** which **c** by **d** have/had **e** been **f** of
g can **h** in **i** there **j** being

4a SPEAKING Students work with a partner and look at the trivia questions. Elicit answers.

Answers

1 3 **2** Brazil **3** Katy Perry **4** Microsoft **5** 1st century

4b Students work with a partner and write five trivia questions in the passive. Remind them that they must know the answers to their own questions.

4c Ask each pair to join another pair and ask them their questions.

---

have something done

Test before you teach
Write these gapped sentences on the board:
Every six weeks I _____ my hair cut.
I _____ my car fixed by a mechanic yesterday. Ask students to complete the sentences. Ask students if the person speaking did the action or someone else.

Answers

have/get, had/got

5 Students look at the sentences and choose the correct alternatives in a–e. Nominate students to give their answers.

Answers

a somebody does an action for us
b past participle **c** are **d** *by* **e** can

6 Students look at the pictures and the verb given. Draw attention to the example sentence and ask students to write sentences for the other pictures. Remind students to use the past tense. Elicit answers from different students.

Answers

2 She had her hair cut. **3** He had his eyes tested.
4 She had a dress made.

⟩⟩⟩ FAST FINISHERS

Ask students to think of three of their own examples to add to exercise 6.

7a Remind students of the word order in questions. Ask students to look at the questions and decide if they are correct or not. Then rewrite the incorrect ones. For less confident students, do the first stage as a class and identify the incorrect sentences together before students correct them individually.

Answers

1 Correct **2** Have you ever had your computer fixed?
3 Correct **4** When was the last time you had your eyes tested?

7b Students work with a partner and ask and answer the correct sentences. Circulate to check that students are using the target language accurately.

Refer students to the Grammar reference on page 132 if necessary.

HOMEWORK

Assign students page 88 in their Workbook or the relevant sections of the Online Workbook.

Developing speaking p130

Comparing and contrasting photos

>>> **FAST TRACK**

You could ask students to do exercise 4 at home in pairs and compare their answers at the next class.

WARMER

Ask students to brainstorm things they can say when they are talking about a photo. Remind them to think about each different area of the photo and to ask themselves the key questions (see Unit 1 Teacher development box, Describing a photo, page 34).

1 **SPEAKING** Students work in pairs to find similarities and differences between photos a and b. Nominate students to give their answers.

Suggested answers

Similarities: There are people using the computers together in each picture. There are two girls in each picture.

Differences: In one picture they're at school/college/ university, the other is probably an Internet café. At school they're using the computer for study whereas in the other picture it's for personal reasons. There's a teacher in the first picture, but not in the second.

2 **LISTENING** ▶ 67 Play the track for students to listen to a student talking about the photos in an exam. Tell students to listen for any of their ideas from exercise 1. Ask if they thought the student did the exam well and explain why or why not. See p161 for the audioscript for this exercise.

3 ▶ 67 Students look at the expressions and put them in the correct section of the Speaking bank. Ask students if they can remember which expressions the student used. Play the track again if necessary. Chorally drill the expressions.

Answers

Comparing: Both of the photos show …

Contrasting: In this photo … but/whereas in the other photo …

She uses all the expressions except *Another thing they have in common* …

4 Students complete the sentences with words from the Speaking bank. Elicit answers from different students.

Answers

1 similarity **2** Both (of the) **3** whereas **4** However
5 common **6** contrast

TEACHER DEVELOPMENT: PLANNING

Assessment guidelines

It is a good idea to make students aware of the different areas they will be assessed on in an oral exam. Brainstorm the different categories for assessment, e.g. their pronunciation, how well they answer the task, fluency, accuracy, range of vocabulary and grammar, how long they speak for, communication between students, etc. Give students a copy of the assessment grid to assess each other when they do this kind of activity.

✓ **EXAM SUCCESS** Students discuss in pairs what they can do if they aren't 100% sure of what they can see in the photos. Ask them to compare their answers with the information on page 146 (Speaking: Comparing and contrasting photos).

PRACTICE MAKES PERFECT

5a Students work with a partner. Ask one of them to be Student A and look at the two photos at the bottom of page 148 and the other to be Student B and look at the two photos at the top of page 148. Ask students to make notes about the similarities and differences between the photos. Set a time limit of two minutes for this.

5b **SPEAKING** Students take it in turns to talk for about a minute about the two photos, saying which photo they prefer and why. Ask students to give constructive feedback to their partner. For less confident students, photocopy the model dialogue below and ask them to read it aloud in pairs. Ask them which photo the dialogue is about (the one on the left). Then ask them to talk about the photo on the right.

✂

Model dialogue

A: What can you see in the picture?

B: I can see a young woman. It looks like she's about 20. I'm not sure, but I think she's in the living room or maybe the bedroom in her house.

A: What do you think she's doing?

B: I think she's buying something online with a credit card. Maybe she's going to the cinema or the theatre, or buying train or plane tickets.

A: How do you think she feels?

B: It looks as if she's smiling. I imagine that she's happy about the thing she's buying. Perhaps she is buying tickets to go and visit a friend she hasn't seen for a long time.

A: Do you buy things on the Internet?

B: Yes, I do. I have bought tickets for concerts on the Internet and I have also bought books and DVDs. It's so much better than going to the shops. I hate going to the shopping centre because it's always so busy. I much prefer doing my shopping at home while I sit on the sofa! The only thing I don't buy online is clothes because you really need to try things on.

HOMEWORK

Assign students page 89 in their Workbook or the relevant sections of the Online Workbook.

Developing writing p131

Writing text messages

>>> **FAST TRACK**

You could ask students to prepare their text messages for exercises 6a and 6b at home with a partner. They can present their texts to the class at the next lesson. Find out which pair used the fewest texts.

WARMER

Ask students to look at the photos of mobile phones on page 131 of the Student's Book and discuss which one they like the best and why. Elicit what different features students look for in a mobile phone, e.g. text messaging, camera, video, Internet access, MP3 player, etc.

1 Students match the words and the abbreviations used in text messages.

Answers

1 j **2** e **3** k **4** l **5** d **6** g **7** f **8** b **9** a
10 i **11** h **12** c

2 Students read the text messages and put them in the order they were sent. Students compare in pairs before you elicit answers from the class.

Answers

2 e **3** c **4** d **5** a

3 Students write out the text messages in exercise 2 as full sentences using the information in exercise 1 to help them. Draw students' attention to the example. Nominate a pair to read the text conversation out.

Answers

2 OK. Sarah and Matt are coming, too.
3 Great. What time?
4 We can't come before eight.
5 OK. See you at eight. Please bring your laptop. See you later.

4 Students read the information in the Writing bank and discuss what they think the complete words are in the common examples of abbreviations.

Answers

be, because, homework, late, message, speak, thanks, today, tomorrow, weekend, excellent

5 Students use the abbreviations from exercise 1 and the Writing bank to help them make the text messages shorter.

Answers

2 THX 4 helping me with my HMWK.
3 Can U come 2MORO 2 fix my computer?
4 U should B happy BCZ YR exam results R XLNT.
5 Don't forget 2 send me a MSG L8R 2nite.
6 I want 2 C U n Jo B4 I SPK 2 the teacher 2MORO.

PRACTICE MAKES PERFECT

6a Students look at the task and write a message on a separate piece of paper or in their notebooks following the advice in the Writing bank and using the abbreviations.

6b Students give their message to their partner and write a reply to the message. Ask them to keep sending messages to each other until they know the details of their meeting. Nominate a few pairs to give their plans.

Model text

Can I come 2 YRS 2MORO 2 do HMWK BCZ Internet not working? ☹
OK. WOT time?
THX! I'll B there @ 11. Do U want 2 go 2 the cinema after?
OK. XLNT. C U 2MORO.

Refer students to the Writing bank on page 151 if necessary.

HOMEWORK

Assign students page 90 in their Workbook or the relevant sections of the Online Workbook.

Language checkpoint: Unit 10

>>> **FAST TRACK**

The extra support provided on the Grammar and Vocabulary reference sections makes the Grammar and Vocabulary revision section ideal for setting as homework. You could get students to complete the whole revision page or just certain exercises for homework.

Grammar revision p133

The passive – present simple

1 Students write the sentences in the present simple passive.

Answers

1 Computers are used everywhere.
2 A lot of chocolate is eaten in the UK.
3 Shoes aren't worn in mosques.
4 Portuguese is spoken in Brazil.
5 Fish isn't sold at the butcher's.
6 Cars are made by robots in this factory.
7 This programme is watched by thousands of people.
8 The New Year is celebrated in many countries.

The passive – other tenses

2 Students correct the mistake in each sentence and rewrite the sentence correctly.

Answers

1 was sung   **2** was won   **3** visited by
4 was invented   **5** are made   **6** was seen
7 has been stolen   **8** was hit

have something done

3 Students write sentences with *have/get something done*.

Answers

1 They had/got it painted.
2 He has/gets it repaired.
3 We had/got it built.
4 I had/got it corrected.
5 She has/gets it done.

Vocabulary revision p133

USING A COMPUTER

1 Students match to make words or phrases.

Answers

1 f   **2** b   **3** a   **4** c   **5** e   **6** d   **7** g

THE INTERNET

2 Students write the correct words for the definitions.

Answers

1 surf   **2** search engine   **3** blog   **4** online
5 download   **6** homepage

COLLOCATIONS WITH *EMAIL*

3 Students complete the sentences with six of the words.

Answers

1 reply   **2** forward   **3** delete   **4** bounce   **5** address
6 check

HOMEWORK

Assign students page 91 in their Workbook or the relevant sections of the Online Workbook.

Reading p134

> **TIP FOR READING EXAMS**
>
> Ask students to read the tip about completing texts with missing sentences and look at Exam Success on page 146 for more ideas.

1 Students read the text quickly and find out the connection between studying and the Internet. Set a strict time limit of one minute before asking students for their answers.

Answer

The text is about students 'buying' essays online.

2 Students put the sentences in the correct place in the text. Remind them that there is one extra sentence that they do not need.

Answers

1 C **2** A **3** E **4** D

3 Students read the text again and choose the best answers.

Answers

1 c **2** a **3** b **4** c **5** b

4 SPEAKING **What about you?** In pairs or small groups, students discuss their thoughts on buying online essays. Ask students to share their opinions with the class.

Use of English p135

> **TIP FOR USE OF ENGLISH**
>
> Ask students to read the tip about gap-fill activities and to look at Exam Success on page 146 for more ideas.

5 Students complete each gap with one word.

Answers

1 in **2** by **3** on **4** written **5** who **6** the **7** been
8 through **9** look

Speaking p135

> **TIP FOR SPEAKING EXAMS**
>
> Ask students to read the tip and look at Exam Success on page 146 for more ideas.

6a Students look at the photos on page 148 and make notes about things they can say about it. Remind students not to write full sentences. You could set a time limit of three minutes.

6b SPEAKING In pairs, students compare and contrast the photos. Ask them to say which they prefer and why.

Listening p135

> **TIP FOR LISTENING EXAMS**
>
> Ask students to read the tip and look at Exam Success on page 146 for more ideas.

7 LISTENING ▶ 68 Play the track for students to listen to a programme with information about the history of SMS text messages and complete the notes. See p161 for the audioscript for this exercise.

Answers

1 1992
2 Short Message Service
3 160
4 Merry Christmas
5 different phone company
6 1999
7 Teenagers
8 cheaper

HOMEWORK

Assign students pages 92–93 in their Workbook or the relevant sections of the Online Workbook.

'CAN DO' PROGRESS CHECK p135

1 Ask students to look at statements a–j and give themselves a mark from 1 to 4.

2 Ask students to look at the ideas for improvement and decide what they need to do. Ask students if there's anything they can add to the list in the 'Other' category.

Class audioscript

Unit 1

Vocabulary p6

3 ▶ 01

birth
childhood
adolescence

middle age
old age
death

8 ▶ 02

1 Joshua: My name's Joshua. I'm ten years old. I've got three brothers and three sisters. One of my sisters is very special to me. I think that's because she's almost the same age as me. She's 11.

2 Olivia: Hi, I'm Olivia and I'm 15. I'm an only child. My parents are divorced and I live with my father. I've got one cousin. Her name is Olivia, too! We spend a lot of time together.

3 Jessica: My name's Jessica and I'm 78 years old. I've got four children, six grandsons and six granddaughters. I love being with them all; it's great having a big family. And even after all this time, my husband is so important to me. We got married 55 years ago. Can you believe it? … 55 years, but it feels like it was yesterday!

Gateway to life skills pp10–11

4 and **5** 🎬 ▶ 03

Grace: I have a younger brother. I pick him up from school and look after him until my mum comes home. She has a new timetable and works until about half past six some days. I enjoy being with my brother, it's just for two or three hours, I make him some food and I help him with his homework. And now mum sees that I can be responsible and she gives me more freedom to do other things. It *is* hard work sometimes. And I need to find time to do homework. Now I realise how hard my mum works. She does a lot for us, and I want to do what I can to help her.

Louis: As you can see, we have a dog and it needs lots of exercise. I take him for walks every evening. When my dad gets in, he's usually quite tired from work. And my mum's usually busy doing work or doing other things. I'm an only child, so the dog is my responsibility. I see now that a dog is a big responsibility. It's not nice when it's cold or wet but you still have to walk him.

It was my idea to get a dog, so I take responsibility for it. You can't just enjoy the good things and leave the bad things for other people! And now my mum and dad see that I help out more at home and they have more confidence in me. They said I can have a pet snake if I want!

Jessica: I visit my grandmother every day. Just to say hello and to take her bread and milk. My grandmother lives very near to us and I'm her only grandchild. Usually my mum visits her in the afternoon for ten to fifteen minutes, but she's doing this course at the moment and she's at the university most afternoons. It's made a difference to how I spend my free time because it means that sometimes after school I can't hang out with my friends. But I enjoy it. My grandmother tells me funny stories, especially about my mum when she was a girl. And she also makes great cakes!

Listening p12

2 and **3** ▶ 04

Presenter: And today on the programme we're talking about family dinners. Do families eat together these days or is the family dinner just a thing of the past? We wanted to find out what you think so we asked you to contact us. Here are some of the things you said.

Speaker 1: Hi, er, my name's Mike. I think family dinners are a really great idea, but I'm a computer technician and I can work 70 hours a week. I travel all over the country and when I finally get home at night, my two kids are often already in bed. Sometimes my wife has gone to bed too and is fast asleep! It's fine for the government to talk about how important family dinners are, but how can you have a family dinner when you get home late from work every day?

Speaker 2: Yeah hi, I'm Chris. Both my parents work so they're never there when I come back from school. We never sit down and have a meal together. To tell you the truth, I don't really have a proper dinner. I just go to the fridge, see what's there and that's it. I have a sandwich, a pizza or something like that. I just take whatever's there and eat it on my own. I don't mind.

Speaker 3: Hi there, my name's Sally. Both my parents work and they usually get home quite late, but my sister and I always wait for them and then we all eat together. I think family dinners are really important. It's a time when we all get together at the table and talk and find out what's going on with each other. It's so important for a family to talk, I think.

Speaker 4: Hello there. My name's Alice and I'd just like to make a comment about family dinners. I've got two children and three grandchildren and we *always* eat together at the weekend, either on Saturday or Sunday. Everyone's too busy to eat in the week, unfortunately, but we *always* make an effort at the weekend. We *love* eating together, even if it's just once a week.

Speaker 5: Hi. I'm Jennifer. My family loves eating together and we try to do it nearly every day. And … well … actually, that's why I'm calling. My parents have a meeting at school tonight so I made my own dinner and I'm eating it here now, on my own! You know it makes me realise how lucky I am. It's just not the same if you're on your own.

Speaker 6: Hello, Daniel here. I want to ask 'What *is* a family dinner?' In my family we always eat together, and it's either my mum or my dad who does the cooking. But the thing is, nobody says anything at dinnertime. You know why? Because the TV's always on and we all just sit and watch it! So my question is: is it a family dinner if nobody in the family says anything?!

Grammar in context p12

2a and **2b** ▶ 05

List A	List B
the problem	the end
the dinner	the important thing
the government	the evening
the weekend	the afternoon

Developing speaking p14

3 ▶ 06

Emma: Have you got any brothers or sisters?
Liam: Yes, I've got one brother.
Emma: Me too. How old is he?
Liam: He's 22.
Emma: Does he live at home?
Liam: No, he doesn't. He's at university in Manchester.
Emma: How often do you see him?
Liam: About once a month, when he comes home for the weekend.
Emma: That's good! I see my brother every day because he's only 14. What do you usually do at the weekend?
Liam: I usually go out with my friends on Saturdays and we sometimes play football on Sundays. What about you?

Emma: My brother and I often go to the cinema on Saturdays. But I never play football because I don't like sport.

5a and 5b ▶ 07
Have you got any brothers or sisters?
How old is he?
Does he live at home?
How often do you see him?
What do you usually do at the weekend?
What about you?

Unit 2

Vocabulary p18

3 ▶ 08
1 burglar
2 mugger
3 fraudster
4 pirate
5 robber
6 shoplifter
7 thief
8 vandal

4 ▶ 09
1 Three men entered the National Bank in Bristol last night and took over a million pounds. Police do not know how the criminals entered the bank, but they are looking to trace a white van which was parked outside the bank yesterday afternoon.
2 Police arrested six young men in Brighton city centre yesterday. The men broke the windows of several shops and damaged a number of cars parked there.
3 In entertainment news, pop star Pink has a new album out this week, but the artist is unhappy because there are already thousands of illegal copies on sale. The singer is asking her fans not to buy these illegal copies.
4 Supermarket chain Bestco said yesterday that they are very worried about the number of thefts in their supermarkets. Bestco lose millions of pounds each year because of the theft of all kinds of products, from milk to perfume.

Grammar in context p20

2b ▶ 10

List A:	finished	watched
	liked	passed
List B:	wanted	needed
	painted	started
List C:	stayed	arrived
	discovered	planned

Gateway to life skills pp22–23

4 and 5 🎬 ▶ 11
James: Well, what happened was this. I had some people round at my house. About ten or twelve people turned up in total. Anyway, we were having a good time, listening to music and stuff. Then we started playing with a ball, a football, in the living room. It was a stupid idea, but we were all part of the football team. Anyway, I was passing the ball to my friend, Oliver. But I kicked it really hard. I broke a clock. It was an old clock that my mum really loved. Anyway, afterwards, when my parents came home, they found the broken clock straight away. And, I don't know why, but I told my mum that Oliver did it. I didn't want her to be angry with me. But I felt really terrible after, because Oliver didn't do anything. But the other thing is my mum is friends with Oliver's mum, and I don't know if one day when she sees her, she may say something to her, because, well, my mum is still angry about it. What do I do?

Jessica: Last week we had a history exam. I studied really hard for it and I didn't go out at the weekend. One of my best friends, Kayla, didn't study at all. And I know she went out on Saturday *and* Sunday. Anyway, on the day of the exam, Kayla sat next to me. All through the exam she was trying to read my answers. But I didn't want her to copy. I didn't think it was fair, that I studied all weekend, but she went out. And I also knew that the teacher could look into it and think that I copied from her. But after the exam, Kayla was really angry with me. She said she doesn't want to be my friend now because I didn't help her. She's telling people to keep away from me and I think some people who were her friends and my friends are starting to side with her, and not me. I don't know what to do.

Listening p24

2 and 3 ▶ 12
Daniel: Hi Jim.
Jim: Hi Daniel.
Daniel: Jim, did you watch that new detective film on TV last night?
Jim: What? That American film that was on in all the cinemas last year?
Daniel: No, no, this was a documentary film. It was explaining how modern detectives work and how they investigate cases.
Jim: No, no, I didn't. I studied in my room for an hour or two, then had dinner and read for a while.
Daniel: Well, I watched it, but I had a really unusual evening in the end.
Jim: Why? Wasn't it interesting?
Daniel: Oh, no, it was great. It had lots of really interesting facts …
Jim: So, what was the problem?
Daniel: Well, my parents weren't watching the programme with me. They were doing something on the computer together in another room. I think my dad was teaching my mum to do something.
Jim: And?
Daniel: Yeah, so while I was watching the programme, I suddenly heard a really loud noise, like a big crash. I didn't know what it was.
Jim: So what did you do?

Daniel: The first thing I did was call my mum and dad, but they were in the other room and they probably had music on so they couldn't hear me.
Jim: Weren't you scared?
Daniel: Yeah, but because of the detective programme I thought I should go and investigate, you know. So I went towards the kitchen, which is where I thought the noise came from.
Jim: Could you hear anything now?
Daniel: Yes, somebody was crying. Well, that's what I thought at first. I was quite frightened to be honest. But I decided to be brave and go inside. I opened the door slowly and straight away I saw broken plates and glasses and dishes all over the floor.
Jim: What! Who did that?
Daniel: You'll never guess … Our new cat! I don't know what he was doing in the kitchen because we never let him in there. But he got in, and jumped onto the table, maybe to get some food or something. He obviously knocked over all the plates and dishes that were there after dinner.
Jim: And the crying?
Daniel: It wasn't a person crying. It was the cat. He was making a terrible noise because I think when everything fell off the table; a big empty box fell on him. He was frightened because suddenly he couldn't see anything or move!
Jim: Good detective work!
Daniel: Hmm, yeah, I suppose so. But I decided last night that I don't enjoy surprises like that, so I don't want to be a detective! Tonight there's a documentary about animals. Maybe I need to watch that so I can teach my cat to behave!

Developing speaking p26

3 and 4 ▶ 13
1
Girl: Hey, where's my water? I left a bottle here on my desk just a moment ago.
Boy: Oh no. I'm sorry. Was it yours?
Girl: Yes. Did you take it?
Boy: Yes. I'm so sorry. I was really thirsty and I just saw it there.
Girl: Oh well. It doesn't matter. It's only water.
Boy: Let me get you a new bottle in the break.
Girl: Don't worry about it.
2
Boy 1: Hi Dylan. Did you bring my book?
Boy 2: Which book?
Boy 1: The book we have to read for English. The one I lent you yesterday.
Boy 2: Oh no! I left it at home. Sorry!
Boy 1: But I need it for my class now. The teacher's going to be really angry!
Boy 2: I'll make it up to you.

Boy 1: How?

Boy 2: Erm …

Boy 1: Dylan, that's the last time I lend you anything.

Boy 2: I'm really, really sorry. I feel terrible.

Gateway to exams: Units 1–2

Listening p31

5 and 6 ▶ 14

The correct name for the British Secret Service is the SIS or Secret Intelligence Service, but most people call it MI6. MI6 stands for Military Intelligence Section 6. This department generally works abroad, outside Britain.

Of course, when people hear the name MI6, they often think of James Bond. Bond's adventures are obviously not true, but some things are similar to the real SIS. For example, Bond's boss doesn't have a name. She's just called 'M'. In real life, the director of the SIS is called 'C'. The reason for this is because the first director of the Intelligence Service was Sir Captain George Mansfield Smith-Cumming. He wrote the letter 'C' in green ink at the bottom of official papers and letters. 'C' then became the code name for the director of the SIS.

Another popular character in the James Bond films is 'Q'. 'Q' is the inventor of the gadgets and equipment that Bond uses on his adventures. In fact, the SIS really does have a similar person, the director of their new technology department. This director of technology works in the new headquarters of the SIS in London. This central headquarters is next to the River Thames. The outside of the building appears in three or four Bond films. Rather surprisingly the inside of the building also appears in one of the Bond films. Not very secret for a secret service, perhaps! One thing that is more or less secret though is a possible tunnel that begins inside the headquarters and then goes right under the River Thames. Many people think this tunnel exists, but nobody knows the details … or, at least, nobody is talking.

Unit 3

Vocabulary p32

3 and 4b ▶ 15 and 16

1 Arge**ntin**a	Arge**ntin**ian	**Spa**nish
2 **Aus**tria	**Aus**trian	**Ger**man
3 Bra**zil**	Bra**zil**ian	Portu**guese**
4 Bul**gar**ia	Bul**gar**ian	Bul**gar**ian
5 **E**gypt	E**gyp**tian	**A**rabic
6 Ja**pan**	Japa**nese**	Japa**nese**
7 **Mex**ico	**Mex**ican	**Spa**nish
8 **Po**land	**Po**lish	**Po**lish
9 **Russ**ia	**Russ**ian	**Russ**ian
10 **Swit**zerland	**Swiss**	Roma**nsh**/ I**tal**ian/ **Ger**man/ **Fre**nch
11 **Thai**land	**Thai**	**Thai**
12 **Tur**key	**Tur**kish	**Tur**kish

Developing vocabulary p35

3a and 3b ▶ 17

il**le**gal	in**vi**sible
im**pos**sible	ir**re**gular
inco**rrect**	un**hap**py
in**for**mal	u**nu**sual

Gateway to life skills pp36–37

5 and 6 🎬 ▶ 18

Amy: We all have to speak in public sometimes. Maybe we need to give our ideas or answers to the rest of the class.

Marcus: At university, students often have to give presentations to show they understand something.

Amy: At work, you may need to explain something to a group of colleagues or your bosses.

Marcus: Here are some of our ideas to help you give a good impression in these situations.

Amy: First of all, stand up straight. When you stand up straight, you look confident and secure.

Marcus: Use hand gestures. But not too much otherwise they won't be listening to what you're saying, they'll be looking at your hands!

Amy: Look up and at the people you're speaking to. This can help you keep their attention. It can also help you to see if they're interested and understand.

Marcus: Speak at the right volume. Not too loud or they might be uncomfortable. But not too quietly either, otherwise they won't understand what you're saying.

Amy: Speak fluently. This means don't stop all the time. If you speak too slowly, people may lose interest. But speaking fluently doesn't mean speaking fast. If you speak too fast, it can be difficult for people to understand you. If you speak too fast, it can be difficult for people to understand you.

Marcus: Use intonation and stress to make yourself sound more interesting. If you speak like this, with no ups and downs, you can be seen as uninterested or uninteresting. By giving stress and emphasis on important words, you may get your message across easier.

Amy: Of course, these are all things you need to remember in the middle of giving your talk. But remember – always prepare carefully what you're going to say *before* your talk!

Listening p38

2 and 3 ▶ 19

Speaker 1: I love languages. The first foreign language I studied was French, at school. Then I learned Spanish. I also did a bit of Japanese because I had a Japanese friend. But now I'm learning an artificial language … No, it isn't Klingon or anything like that. I'm learning Esperanto. A Polish man called Zamenhof was the man who created Esperanto. He thought that a new, universal language could stop war and bring peace. You know, I actually really like that idea. That's why I started learning it. It isn't a very difficult language, and they say that there are more than a million people who speak it!

Speaker 2: French was the first foreign language that I studied at school. But I was never very good at it to be honest. I think that's because I never thought it was very useful. I had no intention of ever going to France or Switzerland. But now I work for a big multinational company and I travel a lot. Mexico and Argentina are two countries where I do a lot of business. So, I'm learning Spanish. It helps me to communicate when I work there, and it means I can chat to people there and make friends. Apart from that, did you know that over 400 million people speak Spanish? That's another good reason to learn it. And I'm really enjoying it, too!

Speaker 3: Well, I love comics and fantasy and science fiction. I always loved the Star Trek films, for example, and I wanted to learn Klingon for a while. But then I started getting interested in manga. You know, they're comics that come from Japan. That was when I decided to start learning Japanese. I wanted to be able to read the comics and also to understand more about the culture of the country. I think learning a language is more than just grammar and vocabulary. It's getting an idea about how people think. That's especially interesting with Japanese because I think the culture is totally different from British culture.

Speaker 4: Klingon is an incredibly difficult language to learn! It was a TV series called *The Big Bang Theory* which made me want to learn it. There's a character in the series called Sheldon. He's the character that I like the most, and he can speak Klingon. I know that it came from the Star Trek TV series but I don't know whose idea it was to create the language … It's true that it isn't very useful but people are always interested when I tell them that I'm learning it. They can't believe it when I tell them that over 300,000 people bought the English-Klingon dictionary, or that somebody translated Shakespeare into Klingon!

Developing speaking p40

2 ▶ 20

Receptionist: Good morning. This is the Cardiff English Centre. How can I help you?

Student: Good morning. I'd like some information about your summer courses.

Receptionist: Yes, of course. We have a course for students aged between 14 and 17. It begins on the 10th of July.

Student: Sorry, did you say the 10th of July?

Receptionist: Yes, that's right. The course lasts two weeks.

Student: Do you organise accommodation?

Receptionist: Yes, we do.

Student: How much is the course?

Receptionist: The price of a two-week course is £815.

Student: Could you repeat that?

Receptionist: Yes, I said the price is £815.

Student: Does the price include other activities?

Receptionist: Yes, it does.

Student: What other activities are there?

Receptionist: There are excursions, discos and sports activities, including sailing.

Student: Oh, that sounds interesting. Can you send me a registration form?

Receptionist: Yes, of course. Can you give me your name and address?

Student: Yes, it's …

Unit 4

Vocabulary p44

2 ▶ 21

1 forehead	9 shoulder
2 cheek	10 chest
3 chin	11 elbow
4 throat	12 hip
5 back	13 thigh
6 wrist	14 knee
7 thumb	15 heel
8 neck	16 ankle

5 ▶ 22

Speaker 1

Woman: What's the matter?

Man: It's my stomach.

Woman: Did you eat something bad?

Man: I don't think so. I know five or six people at work who've got the same thing at the moment.

Woman: Yes, there are a few people in our office who are ill with it, too. Go home and stay in bed. And don't forget to drink lots of liquids.

Speaker 2

Man: Are you OK?

Woman: No, not really. I've got …

Man: Wait, I'll get you some water.

Speaker 3

Girl: What's the matter?

Boy: I can't think, I can't concentrate. It really hurts!

Woman: Take an aspirin.

Boy: I took one an hour ago, but it still hurts.

Girl: Well, stop doing your homework, lie down and close your eyes. That might help.

Speaker 4

Ow, that hurts! Oh, I can't eat anything at the moment. Whenever I eat something cold like ice cream, this tooth starts to hurt … Ow!

Developing vocabulary p47

2 ▶ 23

1 painkiller
2 heart attack
3 health centre
4 waiting room
5 food poisoning
6 first aid

3a ▶ 24

1 <u>pain</u>killer
2 <u>heart</u> attack
3 <u>health</u> centre
4 <u>wait</u>ing room
5 <u>food</u> poisoning
6 first <u>aid</u>

Gateway to life skills pp48–49

7 ▶ 25

The recovery position is useful when an adult or child is unconscious but breathing. It can help them to continue breathing. One thing – DO NOT move a patient who has had a bad fall or a serious back injury!
First, kneel on the floor on one side of the person. Check the person is breathing and open the airway. To do this, place your hand on the person's forehead and gently move the head backwards a little. Then, place two fingers on the tip of the casualty's chin and lift the chin. Look and listen carefully for ten seconds to check if they are breathing or not and make sure the chest is moving up and down.
Then, place the arm near you at a right angle.
Move the other arm, with the back of their hand against their cheek.
Take the knee furthest from you and pull it up until the foot is flat on the floor.
Pull the knee towards you, keeping the person's hand pressed against their cheek,

and position the leg at a right angle. Make sure the airway remains open by gently moving the head back and lifting the chin.
Remember that we only put the person in the recovery position after opening their airway, to ensure that they are breathing.

Listening p50

2 and **3** ▶ 26

Presenter: Now, of course, what a lot of people don't realise is that acting can be quite dangerous, can't it?

Expert: Yes, it can. We watch a film now and think it's all computers and special effects. Of course, computers and special effects help to create the action. But the actors, and their doubles, do a lot of the things that you see, too.

Presenter: The 'doubles'? Those are people who look like the real actor and do all the dangerous scenes?

Expert: That's right. All actors have a double for some scenes. But there ARE *some* famous actors who do the dangerous action scenes themselves. Jackie Chan is a famous example.

Presenter: Jackie Chan? The famous actor from Hong Kong? Has he had any accidents?

Expert: Are you joking? He's already had lots and lots of serious accidents!

Presenter: Oh, really?

Expert: Yes, he's just made a new film and he's done something interesting to promote it. He's made a poster with a list of all his injuries. Let's see. It says here that he's broken his nose, not once, not twice, but at least three times!

Presenter: Ouch!

Expert: He's broken his ankle twice and he's lost a tooth.

Presenter: Has he ever had a *really* serious accident?

Expert: Yes, he has.

Presenter: What happened?

Expert: It was in 1986. He jumped down from a wall to a tree. He didn't catch the tree, he fell several metres and hit his head on a rock. He nearly died.

Presenter: That's terrible! It's amazing that he hasn't stopped making films yet!

Expert: I don't think he'll ever stop! He's often had serious accidents and continued to work the next day.

Presenter: Really?

Expert: Yes, even with a broken ankle!

Presenter: How can he do that?

Expert: Maybe actors start believing that they're somebody else, that they're superhuman and that nothing can hurt them. Especially when they play action heroes.

Presenter: What about the most famous action hero, James Bond? Has Daniel Craig ever hurt himself making the Bond movies?

Expert: Yes! He doesn't do *all* the action scenes himself. But he has cut his finger and his face, he's also broken a finger and he's hurt his arm. Actors like Daniel Craig and Jackie Chan want to make the action look real. So there are always scenes where you can see that it's them doing the action.

Presenter: Well, it all looks very exciting in the cinema. But in real life, you need to remember that you can get a serious injury doing these things. Just look at Jackie Chan and Daniel Craig!

Developing speaking p52

2a, 2b and 4 ▶ 27

Well, er, let's see, there, there are two people in the picture and, er, I think they're in a hospital, yeah a hospital, or maybe, maybe in a school hall, yes, probably in a school hall because the man looks like a teacher I think. And there is a girl, I think she's a student, maybe she's about 15 or 16. There's a body on the floor, but it's, erm, I don't know the word, but it isn't a real person. It's, erm, it looks like the teacher is explaining parts of the body, or maybe he's explaining what to do if somebody is ill. Maybe he's also a doctor or a nurse, I'm not really sure because he's not wearing a uniform, just jeans and a T-shirt. I think it's a first aid class and the teacher has shown the girl how to help someone in an emergency, er, and the girl is now practising. I'm not totally sure what the emergency is, I imagine that the person's heart has stopped working. The thing is I've never done first aid, but I think it's useful, yeah, it can be very useful … in some situations.

Unit 5

Vocabulary p58

3b ▶ 28

advert	film
cartoon	game show
chat show	reality show
comedy	soap
cookery programme	sports programme
documentary	the news
drama	

7 ▶ 29

1 Oh, I *love* watching this programme. You learn so much about nature, about animals and plants and everything. It's *so* informative.

2 Did you see last night's episode? It really made me laugh. You know, when you suddenly remember that the characters aren't real, they're just drawings, it's incredible that they can be so realistic and so funny.

3 Wow! Come and watch! It's really exciting. It's 2-2 and there's only two minutes of extra time left. Who do you think is going to win?

4 Tonight the presenter is interviewing Angelina Jolie. I want to watch because she's always got a lot of interesting things to say. And that presenter doesn't just ask the typical boring questions that other people ask.

5 Did you watch it last night? The prize was £10,000. The contestant just had one more question to answer. It was really easy, even *I* knew the answer. But you know what? She got it completely wrong and lost everything!

Grammar in context p60

2a and 2b ▶ 30

a Films are longer than game shows.
b Books are more interesting than films.
c This programme was better than that one.
d Soaps are more popular than reading.

Gateway to life skills pp62–63

5 and 6a 🎬 ▶ 31

Molly: Yeah, I'd quite like to be famous. I love music and singing and I spend a long time practising after school. I think one day I'd like to be a professional singer and song writer. Making a real CD would be amazing. But I wouldn't want to be REALLY famous like Adele or Beyoncé or somebody. I wouldn't want people to stop me in the streets and things like that. I'd like my music to be famous, not me.

Kieran: Would I like to be famous? Yes, I would! But I'm not really very good at anything. Maybe I could be an actor. You don't need to do anything special, do you? You just stand there and say what they tell you. Yeah, I think I could do that. And it's a great life, isn't it? Living in Hollywood and being on holiday. And you have lots of famous friends, too.

George: Being famous isn't a realistic ambition, is it? Only a few people can be famous. Anyway when you see a famous person on TV it's all about appearance and money. That stuff doesn't interest me. I want to do something useful with my life. I don't want to be on TV or in the newspapers for no reason. My dream is to study medicine. Doctors don't become famous; they're too busy doing useful things and actually help people!

Amelia: I want to be a writer, and I don't think writers are very famous usually, apart from one or two. I mean writers don't usually appear on TV or do things like that. But that's fine by me. Fame doesn't really interest me. What's most important to me is that people

read what I write, and I make money to continue writing. I think writers write because they need to, not because they want to be famous.

Listening p64

2 and 3 ▶ 32

Presenter: Good morning everybody. This is Anne Davis and you're listening to Radio West. Now, last night was the start of a new series of *Downton Abbey*. Some people are saying that TV in the UK at the moment is better than ever, but others say the programmes just aren't good enough. So for our radio phone-in today, I want you to tell me what *you* watch and what you think of today's TV in the UK. Our phone lines are now open, and yes, I think we have our first caller. Hi there. What's your name and where are you calling from?

Tyler: Hi Anne, I'm Tyler and I'm calling from Bristol.

Presenter: Hi Tyler. So, what do you think of TV at the moment, and what do you usually watch?

Tyler: Well, you talked about *Downton Abbey*. I never watch British drama series like that. They're too slow and boring. In my opinion, British drama isn't as good as American drama. In fact, really the only thing I like watching on British TV are the comedy series. Most programmes are too serious for me – you know, the news, all those long documentaries … I'm tired at the end of the day. All I want to do is relax and have a laugh.

Presenter: Okay. Thanks Tyler. Our next caller is …

Olivia: … Oh, is it me? I'm Olivia. Morning, Anne.

Presenter: Morning to you, Olivia and where are you calling from?

Olivia: Blackpool.

Presenter: Okay, what do you usually watch and what do you think about the state of TV here in general?

Olivia: I really love doing sport in my free time and NOT watching TV. The thing is, I think that people in this country watch too much television. People are too lazy to switch the TV off and get up off the sofa. Then, when I go to school, everybody's talking about a new reality show or a chat show. It's like they're talking a different language! People say they haven't got enough free time. But the only thing people do in their free time is watch TV!

Presenter: Hmm. Okay. Thanks Olivia. And who's our next caller?

Harry: Harry … From Oxford.

Presenter: Thanks for calling, Harry. What would you like to say?

Harry: Well, I don't agree with the first caller. I think our TV is as good as TV in the US for example. It's true, they have hundreds of channels. But there's nothing good on them! Their programmes are less informative than ours. I mean, personally, I love documentaries. And I think our documentaries are probably the best in the world!

Presenter: Thanks, Harry. One last caller before we listen to the new single from Rihanna. Hello? Who's calling?

Lily: Hello there, Anne. I'm Lily, calling from Cardiff. I'm happy enough with TV today. I mean, it's as good, or as bad, as it's always been. There are some great programmes and some awful ones. You can learn a lot from watching the TV if you choose the right programmes. Me, I always watch game shows and quiz programmes. They can be good fun. But you can also get a lot of information – some of it's useful, some of it isn't, but it's always interesting. Of course, it's also very important to switch off the TV when there isn't anything good on.

Presenter: Lily, thanks very much for that. Definitely agree with your last point. Anyway, we'll be taking more of your calls in a moment, after this song by …

Developing speaking p66

2a and **3** ▶ 33

Girl 1: Shall we go out tonight?

Girl 2: No, I'm a bit tired. Why don't we stay in and watch TV?

Girl 1: OK. Do you know what's on?

Girl 2: Let's have a look at the TV guide. Hmmm. At nine o'clock there's that new drama series set in the future, *Space 2112*.

Girl 1: I don't really like drama series, especially not science fiction.

Girl 2: OK then, what about this? At 9 pm on the other channel there's a documentary about how the world will end. It's called *Catastrophes*.

Girl 1: That sounds a bit too serious and scary for me. What do you think? Isn't there anything more relaxing?

Girl 2: Well, on BBC2 there's a documentary about crime in the UK.

Girl 1: *That's* not very relaxing!

Girl 2: Well, all right then, there's a cookery programme on ITV. Mmm … I find food shows can be a bit boring.

Girl 1: I know what you mean, but I think it's better than the usual cookery programmes because it's a cookery competition for famous people.

Girl 2: Okay. You're probably right. Let's watch the cookery programme then.

Girl 1: Fine!

Unit 6

Vocabulary p70

2 ▶ 34

beach	jungle	ocean
desert	rainforest	sea
forest	lake	river
ice cap	mountain	valley
island	mountain range	

6 ▶ 35
1

Girl: Isn't it terrible what's happening in the village?

Boy: I know, it started raining on Sunday and it just hasn't stopped for days.

Girl: Yeah, and with all that water, lots of people are leaving their homes. It's just too dangerous to stay there.

Boy: Yeah, and have you seen how the water just carries away all the cars? Scary! Really scary.

2

Teacher: OK and what's this? Well, it's a region of the upper atmosphere, between about 15 and 30 kilometres in altitude. It has quite a lot of ozone and the ozone absorbs the sun's ultraviolet radiation. But the big problem is the hole right here, over the Antarctic and the Arctic. This hole is caused by CFC gases and other gases.

3

Man: Well, it's stupid, isn't it?

Woman: I know, they always tell us to sort our rubbish and to recycle it, but then they don't give us anywhere to put bottles and glass.

Man: That's right. And in the end there's no alternative. You have to put all the rubbish in the same bin.

4

Woman: It's so hot today, though, isn't it?

Man: Certainly is. They say it's the hottest day of the year. Well, no, not of the year, the hottest day in the last ten years.

Woman: And they say it's going to get hotter.

Man: One day this is all just going to be desert, believe me.

Grammar in context p72

2b and **2c** ▶ 36

1 The situation is going to get worse.
2 Temperatures are going to go up.
3 It's going to be a hot summer.
4 We're all going to have problems.
5 I'm going to do something to help.

Gateway to life skills pp74–75

5 and **6** 🎬 ▶ 37

Marcus: Well, in school we use a lot of paper and sometimes people put paper in the bin, and they've only used one side. That's just a waste. So we decided to have two boxes: one for reusing and one for recycling. Reusing and recycling saves water, money and trees. Did you know it takes 11 litres of water to make ONE sheet of paper?

Amy: We decided that recycling paper wasn't enough. Every day at school people throw away cans with their soft drinks, and plastic bottles for juice and water. So, we made bins for cans only and some for plastic. We can recycle easily now. And it's funny, because the school's a lot cleaner, too. Maybe that's because we asked students to bring in bottles and containers that could be used again and again. This stops all the plastic that people use. And it's healthier to bring in fruit and other natural products. Before, people were bringing foods with a lot of plastic packaging.

Marcus: We put posters and signs up in the washrooms. Sometimes people would forget to turn the tap off when they were finished washing their hands. That's a real waste of water. Especially after break, if no-one goes in there until the next break. Also, paper towels; people would just have a lot of paper towels and then just not use them all and then throw them on the floor. We put posters up and most people stopped doing this. Every little thing helps! That's what we said on the posters.

Amy: This sounds simple and not very important. But at the end of the day there is always a classroom with all the lights switched on and everyone's gone home. The room's empty but the lights are still switched on. It's actually a school rule, that the last person to leave the room switches the light off. But we always forgot or left it for somebody else. So we made signs and posters and put them on the doors, to remind us to do it, and to remind us *why* it's important to do it. It can help save a lot of electricity. Did you know that it takes over 10,000 litres of water to power an average light bulb for twelve hours?

Listening p76

2 and 3 ▶ 38

Richard: Our next story on *Green World* is about a school in England. This school has had a great idea for creating green, sustainable energy. Here to tell us about it is Cathy Smith. Cathy, what is this idea?

Cathy: Hi Richard. Well, in most schools, if you run in the corridors, you get into trouble. But at Simon Langton Grammar School if you run in the corridors, the teachers will probably be really happy.

Richard: Why is that?

Cathy: Because if you run, you help to produce electricity for the school. And it's all thanks to an old student from the school, Laurence Kemball-Cook.

Richard: That sounds amazing. How does it work?

Cathy: Well, one of the corridors has a special floor. It has 12 metres of special squares or tiles. When you walk on them you produce electricity. Just one step produces about four watts of power. And you produce more energy if you walk fast. Laurence says the squares will produce 100 watts when the corridor is busy. And he also calculates that if the students walk on the squares for one year they'll produce enough electricity to charge 853 mobile phones, or one mobile phone for two and a half years, and keep one light working for more than two months!

Richard: So if they produce extra electricity, the school will save money.

Cathy: That's right. And of course they don't create any pollution because this is green energy. It's interesting because the special corridor goes to the technology classrooms. So when students walk to class they can see a practical example of how clever and important technology can be.

Richard: It's a brilliant idea, isn't it? How did Laurence think of it?

Cathy: He first had the idea when he was at Victoria Station in London. It was the busiest time of the day. He just thought – look at all this energy! How can we use it? The amazing thing is that he was still at university at this time.

Richard: Is his school the only place where he's used this technology?

Cathy: No, he started by putting a special floor in an underground station in London during the Olympic Games. They produced enough electricity to light the station at night! He also did something similar at the Paris marathon. Imagine how much energy you can get from all those people running!

Richard: It's such a simple idea, turning energy from walking and running into electricity.

Cathy: Yes. If they do this in every school in the country, we'll save a lot of money and help the environment, too. You know, another one of Laurence's ideas was to use it on a dance floor at music festivals. When you dance on the special floor you can use the energy to charge your mobile phone!

Richard: Wow! Maybe if the teachers let them, students won't run in the corridors – they'll start dancing!

Developing speaking p78

2, 3 and 5a ▶ 39

Jamie: Listen. Are you up to anything this weekend?

Danny: Not really. What about you?

Jamie: If the weather's good, Alex and I are going to go to the beach. Do you fancy coming?

Danny: Sure. What time shall we meet?

Jamie: How about 11 o'clock?

Danny: OK. Why don't we meet at the station?

Jamie: Fine. I'll bring some sandwiches and we can have lunch on the beach.

Danny: What will we do if it rains?

Jamie: I'll give you a ring on your mobile and we'll go somewhere else.

Danny: OK. Listen. I'll ring Liz too and ask her to come.

Jamie: Good idea. See you tomorrow at 11.

Gateway to exams: Units 5–6

Listening p82

2 and 3 ▶ 40

Presenter: Good morning! I'm Scott Wilson and the topic of our phone-in today is how do you like to find out the news? Do you prefer to watch it on TV or maybe you 'read all about it' in a newspaper? Perhaps you read news magazines or are you the kind of person who catches up with all the latest news on the Internet? Maybe, just maybe, you listen to your friendly, local radio station … ? Whatever the answer, our phone lines are now open, and … yes, I think we have our first caller. Hi there. What's your name and where are you calling from?

Amanda: Hi, Scott. I'm Amanda and I'm calling from Cambridge.

Presenter: Hi, Amanda. So, how do you keep up with the news?

Amanda: I prefer the TV really. I mean, I know I shouldn't say this because we're on the radio, but, er, I just think the news on the radio isn't as interesting as

on the TV. Just because, well, you know, you can't see what's happening. It's less dramatic on the radio, I think. A picture tells a thousand words, don't they say?

Presenter: OK. Thanks, Amanda! Our next caller is …

Jerry: Oh, is it me? Sorry. I'm Jerry. Morning, Scott.

Presenter: And a very good morning to you, Jerry. Where are you calling from?

Jerry: Sunny Stockport.

Presenter: OK, and how do you find out what's going on in the world, Jerry?

Jerry: Well, maybe I'm old-fashioned, but I really like the radio, and I'm not just saying that, honestly! The thing is, on TV they're too interested in sensationalism these days. TV news isn't serious enough for me. It's like watching a soap or a show or something. They show you all these spectacular images, but they don't really inform you properly.

Presenter: Thanks for that, Jerry. Good point. And who's our next caller?

Sarah: Sarah … from Leeds.

Presenter: Thanks for calling, Sarah. What would you like to say?

Sarah: Just following on from the last caller, I think the news on the radio is just as good as the news on TV, but, to be honest, there's no comparison with the Internet. I work at my computer all day and I can find out what's going on anywhere in the world as it's happening. The radio and TV, and especially newspapers, they're just, I dunno, they're just too slow.

Presenter: Cheers, Sarah. Appreciate the call. One last caller before we listen to the new single from Kanye West. Hello? Who's calling?

Dan: Hello there, Scott. I'm Dan, calling from London. I, like … , I agree with the last speaker, because, you know, the Internet has changed everything. But I just think that although newspapers aren't as up-to-the-minute as the Net, they're much more informative. They tell you the full story about what's going on. What could be better than reading the paper when you're having your tea and toast in the morning, or at the weekend? I'm tired of looking at the computer all day. I spend enough time in front of a computer at work thank you very much!

Presenter: Dan, thanks very much for that. Definitely agree with you about the tea and toast. Anyway, we'll be taking more of your calls in a moment, after this song by …

Unit 7

Vocabulary p84

2 ▶ 41

builder	nurse
fashion designer	plumber
firefighter	police officer
journalist	receptionist
librarian	shop assistant
mechanic	vet

6 ▶ 42

Speaker 1: In my job, I work both outside and inside. I get my hands dirty a lot of the time! I need to be very fit and strong because I'm sometimes carrying heavy objects – mainly bricks! I have to be hard-working and reliable because my clients want me to get the job done on time.

Speaker 2: I need to be very creative in my job. I'm always thinking of new materials, new combinations of colours, new styles. I can never repeat myself. People want their clothes to be original, different. It's my job to create those clothes.

Speaker 3: Well, I think I'm well-organised. It's essential in my job. There are the phone calls, emails, customers coming and wanting information, the people in the office asking me for things. I'm always giving people messages and all day people are going past the desk and stopping to chat.

Speaker 4: The best thing and the worst thing about my job are the customers. I love meeting people and helping them to choose what they want to buy, but some customers are so difficult, they're just impossible to keep happy. And then they say, 'Ooh, your clothes are really expensive, aren't they?' I just want to tell them 'I don't decide the prices, do I? I just work here.'

Grammar in context p86

2b ▶ 43

1 Firefighters should be calm.
2 You mustn't talk to the bus driver.
3 Discipline can be important.
4 My science teacher comes to school at half past eight.
5 Fashion designers shouldn't copy other people's designs.
6 He works as a guide at the castle on the island.

Developing vocabulary p87

2 and 3a ▶ 44

1 part-<u>time</u>
2 easy-<u>going</u>
3 badly-<u>paid</u>
4 full-<u>time</u>
5 well-<u>paid</u>
6 blue-<u>eyed</u>, brown-<u>eyed</u>, green-<u>eyed</u>
7 right-<u>handed</u>, left-<u>handed</u>
8 good-<u>looking</u>
9 well-<u>known</u>
10 well-<u>off</u>

Gateway to life skills pp88–89

5a and 5b 🎬 ▶ 45

Amelia: I love basketball. I've always played on the school team. This year they asked me to help train our youngest team. The girls are only eleven. We only had seven girls on the team when I first started training them. Now we have a full team of twelve. That's because the girls have told their friends, they enjoy training and playing more this year. I enjoy being with the girls and I think I've got a good relationship with them. Last year, their coach shouted at them and was always angry. But I'm not like that. I want to know how they feel and try to motivate them. Also last year they never knew when they were going to train. But I've made a timetable so they know what day and what time we have training sessions and matches.

Kieran: Everybody in my class knows I love computers and that I'm a bit of an expert. So every time they have a problem, they ask me for help. That's fine, I enjoy it. It's interesting because I usually know exactly what to do. But it's useful for me to teach it to others and to learn to express myself clearly. I want people to understand what I'm telling them. I'm getting better at finding the exact words to help them. I mean, it's true; some people take a long time to understand different programs or software. I'm quite good at staying calm and explaining myself as many times as necessary until people understand me. People like the fact that I never get impatient.

Molly: In our school, we have an end of year trip. Last year we went to Italy. I had an idea to get some money for the trip, and the school liked it. We had a raffle, like a mini-lottery. We sold tickets for the lottery to parents, relatives, neighbours, anybody we could. I sold lots and lots of tickets and got the most money in the end. It was quite a lot, so I had to keep it safe. Because it was the first time we did it, there were a few problems.

It was my idea so I felt it was my responsibility to help to find solutions. The school liked the idea so much that they're going to do the same again this year. I think I'll help them. I really like working with others.

Listening p90

2 and 3 ▶ 46

Sarah: Hey, Evan. How you doing?

Evan: Hi, Sarah. I'm fine. What's up with you? You look a bit worried.

Sarah: No, it's just … I don't know what to do this weekend.

Evan: Why? What's happening?

Sarah: Well, have you heard that they're making a film near here this weekend? They're looking for extras, you know, people to stand around and make the scenes look real. My mum knows the director and they've offered me a job. I'm just not sure if I want to do it.

Evan: Don't you have to be a professional actor?

Sarah: No, not necessarily. Extras are usually just normal people. But it's true that if I went I'd probably meet some famous actors.

Evan: Wow! Can you imagine? If you met somebody like Lily Collins you'd be able to get their autograph.

Sarah: No, because they tell you that you can say a quick hello to famous actors but you mustn't ask them for autographs or have conversations with them.

Evan: Why not?

Sarah: If everybody asked for an autograph, they'd never finish. They just want to do their job in peace.

Evan: Okay, but, still, it'd be brilliant if you appeared in the film.

Sarah: Yeah, I suppose so. But to be honest being an extra isn't so exciting. You have to be patient because you wait around for hours and hours. Finally they call you, you do the scene in five minutes and then you have to wait another few hours for the next scene. And sometimes you do the same scene again and again.

Evan: How do you know all this?

Sarah: My cousin was an extra once and he didn't really enjoy it. And I think this film is historical fiction. I love historical fiction. But it'll probably take ages to prepare for it. You have to get dressed up and wear lots of make-up.

Evan: Well, don't do it then!

Sarah: Yeah, well, the thing is, I want to get a tablet and I haven't got much money. I think that I'd probably earn one or two hundred pounds if I worked all weekend.

Evan: Wow! Let me do it!

Sarah: No, they're looking for a girl.

Evan: Listen, if I were you, I'd do it. We've got a history exam next week. Take your history book and study in all those long, boring moments. That way you can prepare for the exam, make some money … <u>and</u> you can appear in a film!

Sarah: Hmm, THAT's a good idea. I'll do that!

Evan: And perhaps in the end the director will see you and offer you an acting job in Hollywood!

Sarah: Okay! This could be my first step to winning an Oscar!

Developing speaking p92

2 and 3 ▶ 47

Simon: Good afternoon?

Girl: Good afternoon. I'm calling about a job that was in the newspaper yesterday.

Simon: Ah, yes. So, are you interested in applying for the job then?

Girl: Well, er, could I ask for some information first?

Simon: Certainly.

Girl: Thanks. Could you tell me if the job is full-time or part-time?

Simon: Well, we have both full-time and part-time jobs.

Girl: Oh, I see. Could you tell me how many hours a part-time job is?

Simon: Yes, normally a part-time job is 24 hours a week.

Girl: Aha. Do you have to work at the weekend?

Simon: Well, on Saturdays of course! That's when most people go shopping.

Girl: Oh, yes. Sorry. That was a silly question. Erm. Do you need any experience of working in a clothes shop?

Simon: No, no experience is necessary. You'll learn the job in no time.

Girl: Great. And is the job for the whole of the summer, from July to September?

Simon: No, we only need extra shop assistants in July and August, not September.

Girl: Oh, that's perfect. What sort of person are you looking for?

Simon: Someone interested in fashion, who is very sociable and friendly, who can talk to customers easily. But it's also very important that you are reliable and hard-working.

Girl: Okay. Can you tell me what the wages are?

Simon: Ah! I thought you'd never ask. For part-time posts, the wages are 140 pounds a week.

Girl: 140 pounds. I see. Could you tell me how to apply?

Simon: Easy. Just send a letter and CV to me. That's Simon Kent, at PO Box 908, Nottingham.

Girl: Would you mind repeating that?

Simon: Certainly. Simon Kent, PO Box 908, Nottingham.

Girl: Thank you so much.

Simon: Not at all. Look forward to getting your application. Bye.

Girl: Bye.

Unit 8

Vocabulary p96

6 ▶ 48

Adjectives	Nouns
afraid	fear
angry	anger
bored	boredom
excited	excitement
happy	happiness
lonely	loneliness
sad	sadness

7 ▶ 49

Speaker 1: What is it? It's so dark. I can hardly see. Oh no! It's coming this way! You don't think that it's a … no, it can't be … no, no, watch out! Aargh!

Speaker 2: Yeah. Well, this isn't exactly a great film, is it? What time does it finish again? It's already been on two hours. Hmmm. Oh dear. Nothing's happening, is it? When, oh when, is something interesting going to happen in this stupid film?

Speaker 3: Come on, come on, you can do it! Oh no! Just missed! I know we can win this match. We're going to get a goal any second. Watch! Watch! Yes, he's going to score, come on, come on. Aw!

Speaker 4: Who did this? Who broke the window? Come on! Own up. I know it was one of you. Who did it? I told you last week to be more careful with that football. And now look what you've done. I've had enough. Next time I'm calling the police. Do you hear me?

Speaker 5: Oh yes. I love it! What a beautiful present! Thank you so much. That is so nice of you, and I'm so glad you came yourself to give it to me. Wait 'til I tell all my friends. I'm having such a fantastic day!

Grammar in context p98

2b and 2c ▶ 50

1 He**'d** known him since he was five.
2 They went to live in another town.
3 She**'d** gone to the shops.
4 We**'d** seen him that morning.
5 She took her phone with her.
6 I**'d** given him my pen.

Developing vocabulary p99

2 ▶ 51

bored – boredom	leader – leadership
free – freedom	lonely – loneliness
friend – friendship	mad – madness
happy – happiness	relation – relationship
ill – illness	sad – sadness
king – kingdom	weak – weakness

Gateway to life skills pp100–101

5b, 5c and 6 🎬 ▶ 52

Presenter: The first few weeks in a new environment can be difficult. You have to learn where everything is, start a new routine, and you have to make new friends. University is a good example. Many students are starting a new life away from home. It can be difficult. But don't worry. In the end, everyone finds a friend. We spoke to different students and asked them how they did it, and what advice they would give to new students.

Speaker 1: Well, I think the best advice is: keep your door open. It's easy to just sit there and hide in your room. But you'll never make friends that way. I was in a student residence and what I did was keep my door open. People used to come by, say hello, started a conversation. I used to invite them in for tea and coffee. And before you know it there's this big group of people in my room. My room was like a meeting room!

Speaker 2: I made friends easily. How? We have a kitchen that all six of us use and I like cooking. I must admit my chocolate brownies are brilliant! And I can tell you, I became popular very quickly because of them. People used to come out of their room just with the smell. When I was feeling lonely, I made something to eat and suddenly people appeared out of nowhere. Then we used to sit around and have a chat and a cup of tea. Also they offered to cook me something for the next time. Suddenly I had a circle of friends!

Speaker 3: I'm not mad about sports. I mean, I've never been in a team or anything. But I like getting outside. So when I went to university I took a football and a Frisbee. When the weather was good, I went knocking on doors and asking if anybody wanted to do some sport for a while. People are usually studying hard, so they need a break. They really liked my idea! In the end, we didn't really play much football or anything. But it was a great excuse to go out, chat, laugh and make friends.

Speaker 4: I find it really difficult to introduce myself to people and make friends quickly. Whenever I first meet someone I find it really hard to talk about myself. If you're anything like me, the best thing to do is to join a club or a society. Find a club about something that you're interested in. In my case, I like photography so I joined the Photography Society. The best thing about societies and clubs is that you meet up regularly. It's true, in the first and second week I didn't really make any friends. But after a month or so I was really happy and comfortable talking to people. That's how I met my best friend and we're really close now. To think it all started at the Photography Society!

Listening p102

3 and 4 ▶ 53

Jack: Hi, Jessica. Woah, what's the matter with you? You look angry.

Jessica: I am, Jack. It's this stupid magazine.

Jack: Why? What's the matter with it?

Jessica: There's this questionnaire, one of those personality questionnaires. I've just done it now and it says that I'm bossy, that I like being in control all the time.

Jack: Well …

Jessica: Do you think I'm bossy?

Jack: Well, look, you ticked the statements, didn't you? 'In a group, I'm the one who makes decisions'. That's true, isn't it? Remember last week? When we all went to the cinema? You decided what film we all saw!

Jessica: Yeah, because nobody else said anything. Nobody wanted to take the decision, so I did.

Jack: Mm, but that's what it says in the next statement: 'I hate being with people who can't make decisions'. Well, that's true, isn't it? You get angry when people take a minute to decide anything. You're not very patient, are you? You hate waiting.

Jessica: What about you?! You were angry with me last week when we went out because you had to wait five minutes while I was talking to my friend.

Jack: Five minutes?! It was half an hour!

Jessica: No, it wasn't.

Jack: Yes, it was.

Jessica: Wasn't.

Jack: Was. Look. That's it. The next statement: 'I love having a good argument'. You do, don't you?

Jessica: No, I don't!

Jack: Yes, you do.

Jessica: It's just that I'm not afraid of telling people what I think.

Jack: Exactly. That's the next one. Don't you remember last night when you told the waiter precisely what you thought of the meal?

Jessica: But it was horrible. The burger was frozen in the middle!

Jack: But you didn't have to tell everybody in the restaurant. You called it an ice burger. I felt terrible.

Jessica: Oh. I'm sorry. Sometimes I don't think.

Jack: What did you say?

Jessica: I said I'm sorry.

Jack: Well, Jessica, that's the first time I've ever heard you say sorry. That's something, at least.

Developing speaking p104

2 ▶ 54

Cathy: Hi, Lee. How are things? Did you have a good weekend?

Lee: Yeah. Brilliant, thanks, Cathy.

Cathy: What did you do?

Lee: Oh, I went to a great barbecue on Saturday.

Cathy: Whose barbecue was it?

Lee: It was Joe's. Do you know Joe, Mike's brother?

Cathy: Yeah, I know him. Why did he have a barbecue? Was it to celebrate anything special?

Lee: Yeah. He'd passed his driving test on Thursday so he decided to have a barbecue.

Cathy: Where was it? At his house?

Lee: No. His parents have got a holiday home in the country. We went out there. We used to go there a lot when we were smaller. It's a beautiful place. And it was a good idea because there were no problems with the music or noise because there aren't any neighbours close by.

Cathy: What was the music like?

Lee: That was one of the best things about the party. One of Mike's friends is a really good DJ, he brought some cool music.

Cathy: That's good. Were there a lot of people there?

Lee: Yeah. There were about 50, I reckon, more or less. There were all of Joe's friends and some of Mike's, too. I knew most of the people there.

Cathy: Was the food good?

Lee: Yes, it was really good. Joe's parents had made lots of food. Burgers, chicken, salads, you know, the usual. And there was an amazing cake … Oh, do you know what? When I was getting something to eat I met Oliver. Do you remember Oliver? I hadn't seen him for ages!

Cathy: Yeah, of course I remember him. How is he? How's his new school?

Lee: Great. We're going to meet up again next weekend. You should come with us!

Cathy: Cool! I'd love to!

Gateway to exams: Units 7–8

Listening p109

6 and 7 ▶ 55

Sarah: Hey, Jim. How you doing?

Jim: Hi, Sarah. I'm fine. What's up with you? You look worried or something.

Sarah: Well, I'm not worried exactly. It's just that I'm thinking about what to do this summer and I've got a bit of a problem.

Jim: What's up?

Sarah: Well, my uncle has found me a job … in New York, which is great. I really want to go, but I'm just not sure about the job.

Jim: Why? What is it?

Sarah: It's working as an au pair, looking after three children. If I liked working with kids, I'd say yes straight away. But I don't think I'm patient enough to spend the summer looking after three little ones. I've never done it before, so I just don't know. Have you ever worked with kids?

Jim: Yeah, I worked on a summer camp once in Spain. It was great. The kids were good fun. To be honest, the time went quickly, you know, swimming, doing sport, going out on excursions. It was really tiring because I didn't have much time for myself. I was always busy, but I had a good time. If you took the job, what would the conditions be?

Sarah: Well, they said they'd pay for both my flights, there and back, and they'd give me $150 a week pocket money. And then if I stayed there, I wouldn't have to pay for food or accommodation.

Jim: Hmmm, that's not bad. In fact, it's quite good really.

Sarah: The thing is, what would I do if I went and then found that I didn't like it? Then they wouldn't pay for my flight back and I wouldn't have enough money to pay for the flight myself.

Jim: But is the job for the whole summer?

Sarah: No, just August.

Jim: Look, if I were you, I'd take the job. It's only a month. If you found that you didn't like working with kids, then you'd know not to do it again. But you'll probably find that you love it. And think – you might not get another opportunity to live for a month in New York again. I'd definitely go for it.

Sarah: Yeah, you're probably right. I'm going to think about it a bit more, but I think I'll probably do it, just for the experience.

Unit 9

Vocabulary p110

2 ▶ 56

comic	horror
crime novel	play
fairy tale	romance
fantasy	science fiction
graphic novel	thriller
historical fiction	

5b ▶ 57

First column: atlas, cookbook, guidebook, textbook
Second column: manual, newspaper
Third column: magazine
Fourth column: biography
Fifth column: autobiography, encyclopaedia

6 ▶ 58

1

Boy: So, do you know who did it yet?

Girl: Well, I'm not sure, but I think it might be the caretaker.

Boy: Oh yes? And why's that then?

Girl: Because he was angry with Harper because Harper had stolen some money from his room, so he definitely had a reason for killing him.

Boy: OK, but how did he get the poison to do it?

Girl: That I don't know … I'm just going to have to carry on reading until I find out.

2

Girl: Where do we go now?

Boy: Look. The map says it's this way. First right and then second left.

Girl: And when we get there?

Boy: Well, the museum should be on one side and the palace on the other.

Girl: Which shall we visit first?

Boy: Well, the book says that the museum is pretty spectacular. Let's start with that.

3

Girl: Oh, don't tell me that you like reading that stuff!

Boy: Yes, I do actually. So what?

Girl: Nothing. It's just that … I don't know. Isn't it a bit childish, you know, reading stories about people with super powers, wearing tights and strange costumes?

Boy: Well, all kinds of people read stories about Hercules or heroes like that. And anyway it's not just the story. I love the art, too. A lot of artistic skill goes into these books, you know.

4

Boy: Pass me that book, will you?

Girl: Which one? This one? Ooof, it's heavy. Why do you want it?

Boy: I just need to find some information about Chile for a project I'm doing at school.

Girl: What do you need to know?

Boy: Let's see … I need to know about the history of Chile from 1900 to the present day. Let's have a look. Chihuahua, Chilblain, Child, here we are, Chile. 'Chile: Country on the west coast of South America between the Andes and the Pacific Ocean, official language Spanish …'

5

Girl: I'm reading this really interesting book at the moment.

Boy: What's it about?

Girl: It's David Beckham's life. I didn't know he'd done so much work to help children.

Boy: Well, I didn't know he'd written a book about himself!

Girl: I don't think he has. The book that I'm reading is by his dad. It's good because he talks a lot about when David was young.

Gateway to life skills pp114–115

6b and **6c** 🎬 ▶ 59

Speaker 1:

Juliet: 'It is only your name that is my enemy. If you had another name you would still be the same person. A rose would still smell as sweet if it were called something different. And Romeo would still be as perfect even if he were not called Romeo. Give up your name, Romeo – it is not part of you, anyway – and take me instead.'
Romeo: 'Just call me 'love' and I shall never be Romeo again.'
This is one of Shakespeare's most famous plays. That's why I decided to read it. Of course, it's a very romantic story, and I like romances. But it also has a very serious message that's important today. Romeo and Juliet love each other but their families won't let them. There are things in society that separate people from loving each other. But in the end love always wins. The end is very sad though.

Speaker 2:

The cub had many things to learn. The world was full of surprises for him. He was very much alive, very happy, and very proud of himself.
One day, however, life suddenly changed. The cub ran down the river to drink early one morning. Suddenly, he saw and smelled something strange. Five strange animals were sitting in front of him. The cub had never seen men before, and suddenly he felt very small.
I really enjoyed reading this book. The sentences were short and direct and it was easy to understand. And the writer introduced characters really clearly, like White Fang. It was interesting to see how White Fang changed throughout the novel. At first his old masters treated him really badly and were aggressive towards him, so he was aggressive in return. And then, in the end, his new masters treated him with love so he changed.

Speaker 3:

'Do not kill me yet,' the Monster cried. 'Listen to what I have to say.'
'What can you say to me?' I replied. 'You have destroyed everything I loved. You are a thing of evil, a wicked creature.'
'You made me,' the Monster replied. 'I did not wish to be evil. I wanted to be your friend. But you made me ugly and ran away from me. I asked you to create a friend for me but you destroyed her. I had no family to love, so I destroyed yours. It is your fault.'
This is from the end of the book. At first I didn't want to read this book because I thought it was just a simple horror story. But it's actually more than that. The relationship between the doctor and the monster is really interesting. In fact, the monster isn't really the monster, like it says here. In some ways the doctor is the monster. So, it's a book that makes you think, and that's what I like.

Listening p116

2 and **3** ▶ 60

Interviewer: Hello. I'm from Culture Vulture magazine and we're doing a survey about books and films. Can I just ask you a few questions? It won't take long.

Girl: Uhm, right, OK. Go on then.

Interviewer: Right, thanks. How often do you read books? Very frequently, sometimes, not very frequently or never?

Girl: Very frequently. I think I read one or two books a week. I love a good book.

Interviewer: And what was the last book you read?

Girl: *Mockingjay*. It's the last book in *The Hunger Games* trilogy. I've read the whole trilogy before. So I think that was the third time I read *Mockingjay*.

Interviewer: Really? OK then, and what are you reading at the moment?

Girl: Ermm. Let me think. Oh yeah. A book called *Across the Universe* by Beth Revis. It's basically a science fiction story; they're travelling to a different planet in the future.

Interviewer: Oh, sounds interesting! Now, the next question is about the cinema. How often do you go to the cinema?

Girl: Erm. Not very often. I suppose about two or three times a year.

Interviewer: Right, two or three times a year. OK. Now, let's see. Do you like going to see film adaptations of books?

Girl: Mmm. I've never thought about that really. Erm. For example, I did go to see *The Hunger Games* films when they came out. I occasionally go to see film adaptations of books, I suppose. Some are alright.

Interviewer: And in general which do you prefer, reading the book or watching the film of the book?

Girl: Oh, reading the book, definitely.

Interviewer: OK. Do you know why? What is it that you prefer about books?

Girl: Hum. I think it's because … er … with a book you know exactly what the characters are thinking. I dunno. It's like, it's like you get to know the characters much better. Often when I read a book, you know, the characters become friends almost. And I think with books I have a clear picture in my head of what the characters look like, and sometimes when you see a film they look totally different to the way I'd imagined. It can be a real shock sometimes.

Interviewer: Well, that's great. Thanks. Can I just finish by asking you some personal details? Let's see …

Developing speaking p118

2 and 3 ▶ 61

I'm going to talk about a book called *Holes* by an American writer called Louis Sachar, that's S-A-C-H-A-R. I'd like to begin by saying that I've read this book about six or seven times, so it really is my favourite book. *Holes* is a crime novel, but it's actually much more than that. Let me tell you why I like it so much.
First of all, the story is very clever. Nothing happens in the story without a good reason. And the story is so clever that you can read it again and again and each time you discover something that you didn't see before. What's more, the descriptions are very realistic. A lot of the action happens in a hot desert. And it's funny because when I read the book, it actually makes me feel thirsty! That shows you that the descriptions are great. It's also true that I like the book because of the characters. The two main characters are Stanley and Zero. One of the most important parts of the book is the story of their friendship. It's easy to like Stanley and Zero, and I prefer books where you really care about the characters.
Last but not least, there are a lot of dialogues in the story. So it's easy and fast to read, and the dialogues are realistic and funny.
To sum up, I think *Holes* is the best book I've ever read because it's a great story, it's funny, it's interesting and it has a happy ending, too. They made a film of the book but I think the book is much better.

Unit 10

Vocabulary p122

2 ▶ 62

a	e	j
printer	speaker	scanner
b	**f**	**k**
headset	hard drive	keyboard
headphones	**g**	**l**
microphone	USB port	mouse
c	**h**	**m**
webcam	USB cable	flashdrive
d	**i**	pendrive
monitor	tablet	**n**
screen		mouse mat

4 ▶ 63

I've got broadband so my connection to the Net is quite fast. I usually go online in the evenings, after I've finished my homework, but sometimes I use the Net for schoolwork too. I surf the Net and look at my favourite websites (my homepage is a website about fashion). My favourite search engine is Google. I sometimes download music and films, but not often. I haven't got a blog but I chat online with my friends using a social networking website.

5b and 5c ▶ 64

1 I want to down**load** this song.
2 The **down**load didn't work.

Gateway to life skills pp126–127

5 and 6 🎬 ▶ 65

Girl 1: Most social networking websites have age limits. I think the most important thing is to be honest about your age. If you're too young for a website, don't use it. You can stop a lot of possible problems by simply not lying about your age.

Boy 1: I agree. People forget that the age limit is there to protect you and you can get into big trouble if you don't follow them.

Boy 2: I also think that you can get into big trouble just because everything is so fast. People suddenly get an idea or they take a photo or make a video. And in the next second they put it online. That can be good. But often people are excited or angry.

Girl 2: They aren't thinking. They post something then they realise it's a bad idea.

Boy 2: But by then it's too late.

Girl 1: And other people have shared it and you can't stop other people sharing it, too.

Boy 2: Exactly. So my advice would be: stop and think really hard before you post comments or photos.

Girl 2: Now that we're talking about it, someone actually gave me a really good piece of advice one time. Don't attack anyone on social networking sites. It's unfriendly and it's cruel. When you're sitting at home behind a computer it's easy to think that you can say anything that you like. But, you know what they say. If you haven't got anything nice to say, don't say anything at all.

Boy 2: Hmm. Yeah. After all, you wouldn't like it if somebody attacked you. So, yeah, it doesn't cost anything to be kind to others.

Boy 1: Good point. Also I think there's one word that we haven't mentioned, and that I think is important: privacy. Keep things private. Don't make private information public. Don't give information about where you're from, what school you go to, your phone number and your family …

Girl 2: That's right. You have to remember that on social networking sites you're just giving information out to strangers. You don't know who they are; you have to be very, very careful with information like that.

Boy 2: And keep your password private, too! It's like the key to your house. You wouldn't give your key to just anybody, so don't do the same with your password.

Girl 2: That's true. People forget the importance of passwords. Not just 'Password' or '1234'. A good password is a combination of letters and words and symbols. Don't use your name or the name of your favourite singer or team.

Boy 2: Good point …

Listening p128

2 and 3 ▶ 66

Female presenter:
When you look for information about almost any subject on the Internet, one of the most common places you'll find it is in Wikipedia. Wikipedia is the biggest encyclopaedia in the world and the fifth most popular website in the world. It's the most popular reference work on the Net, with approximately 365 million readers worldwide.

Male presenter:
It was started in 2001 by two Americans, Jimmy Wales and Larry Sanger. However, the encyclopaedia isn't written by them. It's written by thousands of ordinary people around the world. Wales and Sanger's original idea was to create an encyclopaedia in the traditional way by asking experts to write articles. But after one year, they only had 22 articles. They realised that a small group of experts couldn't write all the articles themselves. It would take forever. They needed to have the articles written by other people. Then they came across 'wikis'.

Female presenter:
'Wikis' are websites that allow visitors to add, take away or change the content. This idea of normal people sharing information is a central philosophy of the web and now also of Wikipedia. The idea became the creation of the first *people's* encyclopaedia, written *by* normal people *for* normal people. Anybody can write an article. But writers get their work checked and edited by other readers.

Male presenter:

After just two weeks with this new philosophy they had more articles than in the first year! In 2007, 1,700 articles were being added every day. So far over 24 million articles have been written. Somebody has calculated that you would need nearly 17 years to read the complete English Wikipedia.

Female presenter:

The word 'Wiki' comes from an expression, 'Wiki Wiki', which comes from Hawaii. It means 'quick'. One of the most important things about Wikipedia is that it can change very quickly if necessary. When important events happen in the world, Wikipedia articles change sometimes from one second to the next. Some people say that this is the problem with Wikipedia. They say that you can't always believe everything you read there because the articles are written quickly. And sometimes incorrect information is being added by people who aren't experts in the subject of the article.

Male presenter:

Meanwhile, what _is_ true is that Wikipedia articles talk about all kinds of subjects. The most popular topic, with 30% of all Wikipedia articles, is Culture and Arts. 15% of articles are biographies or information about people. 14% are about geography and places.

Female presenter:

There are over 280 different language versions of Wikipedia. The top three versions are English, German and then French. The biggest, in English, has over four million articles. The smallest is in Herero, an African language. It only has 118 articles. But it's important to say that all these statistics are changing very, very quickly. After all, remember that that's what the 'Wiki' in Wikipedia means!

Developing speaking p130

2 and 3 ▶ 67

OK, so, both of the photos show people using computers, of course. But in the first photo, they're using computers for work, I think, for school work, whereas in the second photo I think they're using the computer more for fun. In the first photo, the man looks like a teacher, and the girls look about 18 or 20, so maybe they are university students. I'm not sure but I think they're probably in a computer class at university. However, in the second photo the people are having a coffee and laughing. They're probably in a café or somewhere like that. I suppose one similarity between the photos is that they both show public places. You know, they aren't just using computers on their own at home. But another important difference between the photos is that maybe the people in the second photo are using their own laptop but they have to pay to be in that place. I mean, they have to pay because they have to buy a cup of coffee or something, and sometimes that is expensive. In contrast, in the first photo, they don't have to pay

to use the computers in their class. Erm, personally I never go to places like the one in the second photo because I prefer to have a coffee and use my computer at home. I use my computer for school work and to play and surf the Net. I spend quite a lot of time online. My mum says too much time!

Gateway to exams: Units 9–10

Listening p135

7 ▶ 68

Presenter: Well, believe it or not, today is the anniversary of an invention that is such an important part of our lives, it seems like it's been here forever. Yes, on this day in 1992, the first SMS text was sent. Here is Katie Dunne to tell us a bit more. Katie, first of all, what do the letters SMS stand for?

Katie: SMS means Short Message Service. Of course, it's called _short_ message service because SMS texts can usually only have 160 characters of the Latin alphabet.

Presenter: 160, that's not a lot is it?

Katie: No, that's why, you know, people have invented all these abbreviations, like the letter 'U' instead of writing Y-O-U. So they can write a complete message but with only a few characters.

Presenter: Right. Anyway, we said the first SMS text message was in 1992. Who was it sent by?

Katie: Well, in fact, it was sent by a man who was working for the Vodafone company in Britain. He sent the message to someone he was working with at Vodafone.

Presenter: So, go on, what did the message say?

Katie: Well, it wasn't very original. It was just 'Merry Christmas'.

Presenter: Oh, right, that _isn't_ very original, is it? And was sending text messages popular right from the start?

Katie: No, not really. One problem was that you couldn't send messages to someone who was with a different phone company. When that stopped in 1999, SMS texts became much more popular.

Presenter: Whenever I think of text messages, I think of teenagers. My teenage son is always sending and receiving them. Were teenagers responsible for making it popular?

Katie: Well, yes, they were, really. The telephone companies weren't very interested in SMS messages initially, but teenagers saw that it was cheaper to send a message than to make a call, so they sent lots of messages.

Presenter: Hmmm. Maybe I should send a message to my son right now to see if he's doing his homework. Katie, thanks for coming in.

Workbook answer key

Unit 1

Vocabulary p4

1
1 senior citizen 2 middle 3 aged
4 adolescence 5 baby 6 old age
7 death 8 birth 9 teenager

2
1 birth 2 death 3 Adolescence
4 senior citizen 5 old age

3
2 wife 3 cousin 4 mother-in-law
5 brother-in-law 6 uncle 7 niece
8 nephew 9 granddaughter
10 husband

4
1 d 2 g 3 e 4 a 5 c 6 b 7 f

VOCABULARY EXTENSION p4

5
1 twin 2 orphan 3 graduate
4 pensioner 5 toddler 6 infant
7 tween

Reading p5

1
c

2
1 a 2 b 3 a 4 b 5 c

3
Good: 4 6 7
Bad: 1 2 3 5

4
1 gets me down 2 furious 3 absolute
nightmare 4 borrows 5 repairs

5
1 gets me down 2 absolute nightmare
3 furious 4 repair 5 borrow

Grammar in context p6

1
a C b S c S d S

2
1 a 2 b 3 b 4 c 5 a 6 d 7 d
8 b

3
1 wants, knows 2 are, studying 3 read,
write 4 's singing 5 don't speak
6 's cooking 7 finishes 8 's speaking

4
2 Where does your mother work?
3 Do you have a best friend at the
moment? 4 Does your friend speak
English well? 5 Are you doing your
homework at the moment? 6 What
sports do you do? 7 What is your friend
reading at the moment? 8 Who do you
usually sit next to in English lessons?

GRAMMAR CHALLENGE p6

5
1 writing 2 Does she have 3 Are you
studying 4 correct 5 Does your brother
play 6 correct 7 have 8 are you
doing, I'm listening 9 Do your parents
work 10 I love

Developing vocabulary and listening p7

1
1 concentration 2 description
3 argument 4 independence
5 discussion 6 improvement
7 retirement 8 movement
9 adolescence 10 information
11 difference 12 confidence

2
1 information 2 improve 3 difference
4 argument 5 discuss 6 adolescent

3
b

4
1 b, c 2 a, f 3 h, e 4 d, g

VOCABULARY EXTENSION p7

5
2 singer 3 driver 4 inventor
5 scientist 6 economist 7 teacher
8 player 9 photographer 10 director
11 writer 12 builder

6
1 player 2 director 3 scientist
4 driver 5 singer 6 economist
7 inventor 8 teacher 9 photographer
10 writer 11 artist 12 builder

Grammar in context p8

1
1 a 2 0 3 a 4 The 5 the

2
a 2 b 4 c 1 d 5 e 3

3
1 The 2 a 3 the 4 an 5 The
6 the 7 a 8 an 9 the 10 a
11 the 12 an 13 a 14 The

4
1 a 2 The, the 3 0 4 the
5 0, 0 6 the, a 7 The 8 0

GRAMMAR CHALLENGE p8

5
1 the 2 am 3 are 4 the 5 is 6 is
7 do 8 The 9 not

Developing speaking p9

1
1 ✓ 2 ✗ 3 ✓ 4 ✓ 5 ✓ 6 ✗

2
1 What's your name? 2 How often do
you see them? 3 Do you like computer
games? 4 Have you got any brothers or
sisters? 5 Do they go to your school?
6 What do you do in the evenings?

3
1 4 5 2 6 3

4
1 b 2 g 3 e 4 a 5 d 6 f 7 c

PRONUNCIATION p9

5
1 <u>What</u> do you <u>do</u>?
2 <u>Where</u> do you <u>live</u>?
3 What <u>sports</u> do you <u>like</u>?
4 <u>Where</u> does your <u>dad</u> work?
5 <u>How</u> do you <u>travel</u> to <u>school</u>?

DESCRIBING PICTURES p9

6
Students' own answers

7
1 a mum and a dad, two young children
and their grandmother and an uncle
2 at the parents' home
3 having a meal together, dinner or lunch
4 I think they're enjoying the meal because
they're smiling. I imagine they're happy
because they're spending time together.

8
Students' own answers

Developing writing p10

1
Paragraph 2: B
Paragraph 3: A
Paragraph 4: E
Paragraph 5: C

2
1 Best wishes 2 ☺ 3 Anyway 4 I'm
5 Hi

3
Students' own answers

Revision: Unit 1

Grammar p11

1
1 watches 2 don't read 3 makes
4 Does, rain, does 5 studies 6 Do, see
7 don't think 8 do, visit

2

a are, putting **b** is beginning **c** 'm not staying **d** 's coming **e** 's carrying

3

a a **b** 0 **c** an **d** a **e** The **f** the **g** a **h** a **i** a **j** the

Vocabulary p11

1

1 uncle **2** brother-in-law **3** stepmother **4** niece **5** husband **6** grandfather **7** cousin **8** only child

2

1 birth **2** adolescence **3** death **4** childhood **5** old age

3

1 b **2** e **3** a **4** c **5** d

4

1 discussion **2** difference **3** improvement **4** argument **5** information **6** description **7** concentration **8** confidence

Unit 2

Vocabulary p12

1a

burglary fraud mugging piracy robbery shoplifting theft vandalism

1b

2 fraud **3** mugging **4** piracy **5** robbery **6** shoplifting **7** theft **8** vandalism

2

1 burglar **2** fraudster **3** mugger **4** pirate **5** robber **6** shoplifter **7** thief **8** vandal

3

1 burglar/thief **2** vandals **3** mugger **4** shoplifters **5** Pirates **6** thief **7** robberies

4

1 investigating **2** analysing **3** arrested, questioned **4** charge, prove **5** accusing

5

1 proof, suspect **2** analysis, investigation **3** charge, accusation **4** collection, arrest

VOCABULARY EXTENSION p12

6

2 mug **3** commit fraud **4** pirate **5** rob **6** shoplift **7** steal **8** vandalise

Reading p13

1

Poirot = 1920s, Inspector Morse = 1970s

2

1 c **2** b **3** b **4** a **5** b **6** b

3

2 3 5

4

1 original **2** memorable **3** vain **4** instinct **5** method

Grammar in context p14

1

1 appeared **2** didn't **3** Did **4** was **5** weren't

2

-aught	-ang	-ank
caught	sang	drank
taught		sank
-ew	-oke	-old
drew	broke	sold
threw	spoke	told
-ook	-ought	-ut
took	bought	cut
	brought	put
	thought	shut

3

a became **b** stole **c** didn't have **d** caught **e** went **f** escaped **g** changed **h** left **i** worked **j** recognised **k** flew **l** lived **m** came **n** became **o** allowed **p** died

4

2 What crime did he commit?
3 How much did he steal?
4 Did the police catch him?
5 Why did he fly to Brazil?

5

2 Ronnie Biggs didn't commit fraud. He committed a train robbery.
3 Biggs didn't steal 2.6 million dollars. He stole 2.6 million pounds.
4 He didn't run away to Madrid. He ran away to Paris.
5 A police officer didn't recognise him in Australia. A reporter recognised him.

GRAMMAR CHALLENGE p14

6

When I was very young some of my friends ~~taked~~ **took** me to a shop to get ~~the~~ sweets. They ~~hadn't~~ **didn't** have any money so one of them ~~putted~~ **put** some sweets in his pockets, but he ~~didn't paid~~ **didn't pay** for them. I liked chocolate bars (and I ~~am still liking~~ **still like** them now) so I put ~~an~~ a bar in my pocket. But the assistant ~~seed~~

saw me. He ~~callt~~ **called** the manager of the shop and he phoned my parents. I ~~did feel~~ **felt** terrible. I ~~were~~ was only five years old, but I ~~am~~ remember it now and feel very embarrassed.

Developing vocabulary and listening p15

1

1 find **2** look **3** look **4** turn **5** come **6** work

2

1 looked for **2** worked out **3** turn up **4** came across **5** found out **6** look into

3

Edinburgh

4

1 F **2** T **3** NM **4** F **5** F **6** F **7** NM **8** T

5

1 working out **2** find out **3** looks into **4** comes across, looking for **5** turns up

VOCABULARY EXTENSION p15

6

1 f **2** a **3** e **4** b **5** d **6** c

7

1 round **2** forward **3** ahead **4** after **5** back **6** out

Grammar in context p16

1

past, present

2

1 d **2** c **3** a **4** e **5** b

3

a were, doing **b** were visiting **c** wasn't feeling **d** was, doing **e** was sitting **f** were having **g** were talking **h** was feeling

4

a were playing **b** were losing **c** recognised **d** was playing **e** knew **f** were looking **g** stopped **h** arrested **i** started **j** won **k** went

5

2 What was your family doing at 7 pm?
3 What did you do after the film?
4 Were you sleeping at 9 pm?
5 What were you doing at 11 pm?
6 When/What time did you go to sleep?

GRAMMAR CHALLENGE p16

6

Last night we were watching a film on TV when suddenly we ~~did~~ heard a sound like an explosion. At first we thought that it ~~was~~ came from the TV, but then we realised the noise came from the kitchen.

My dad ~~he~~ thought it was a burglar and so went to the kitchen to ~~be~~ see if he was right. He was opening the door when ~~that~~ something flew out really fast! Then there ~~did~~ was another sound. We went back to the living room. The lamp was on the floor. In the corner there was a parrot. My family and I ~~we~~ recognised it – it was my neighbour's parrot. The parrot was knocking things onto the floor while it ~~is~~ was flying through our house. We ~~did~~ rang the neighbour and he came to take his parrot back. So, we didn't see ~~of~~ what happened in the film we were watching.

Developing speaking p17

1

1 no **2** so **3** matter **4** worry **5** feel
6 mind **7** last, ask **8** really **9** that
10 Let **11** make **12** only

2

4 6 9 12

3

Making apologies: 1 2 5 8 10 11
Responding to apologies: 3 4 6 7 9 12

4

b d f e g a c

PRONUNCIATION p17

5

1 I felt <u>awful</u>.
2 I'm <u>so</u> sorry.
3 That's the <u>last time</u> I lend you anything.
4 Don't <u>worry</u> about it.
5 Oh <u>no</u>!

DESCRIBING PICTURES p17

6

Students' own answers

7

a shop **b** big **c** see **d** can
e middle-aged **f** smart **g** inside
h book **i** stealing **j** bad **k** don't

8

Students' own answers

Developing writing p18

1

b

2

a Suddenly, **b** At first, **c** Then **d** But
e Next **f** Then **g** In the end,
h The next day

3

Students' own answers

Revision: Units 1–2

Grammar p19

1

1 watched **2** wasn't **3** didn't enjoy
4 Do you like **5** were you **6** goes

2

1 was studying **2** were walking
3 was telling **4** Is, cooking
5 were watching **6** 'm doing

3

a was walking **b** saw **c** was singing
d were watching **e** didn't recognise
f arrived **g** was **h** came
i were talking

Vocabulary p19

1

1 suspect shoplifter **2** Vandals
3 evidence **4** theft **5** steals **6** prove

2

1 burglar **2** fraud **3** mugger
4 vandalism **5** piracy **6** robber

3

a looks **2** works **3** looks **4** turns

4

1 childhood **2** brother-in-law
3 old age **4** only child **5** senior citizen

Gateway to exams: Units 1–2

Reading p20

1

1 c **2** b **3** b **4** c **5** b

2

1 Because they are bored, because the work is too hard or because their classmates bully them.
2 Because some schools are so big that it is difficult to know who is playing truant.
3 It doesn't stop ringing until someone answers it.
4 100 times

Listening p20

3

1 c, f **2** e, g **3** b, h **4** d, i **5** a, j

Use of English p21

4

a went **b** on **c** the **d** were **e** a
f not **g** was **h** the **i** was **j** did
k for **l** is

Writing p21

5

Students' own answers

COMMON MISTAKES p21

6

1 a new job as an engineer **2** Do you often go **3** Write to me/Write back soon **4** we all said **5** make it up **6** got, First, next **7** burglar **8** doesn't give us homework on Mondays **9** am working **10** It doesn't matter. **11** doesn't like dogs or cats **12** were you doing

---

Unit 3

Vocabulary p22

1

a Mexico **b** Mexican **c** Spanish
d Poland **e** Polish **f** Polish **g** Japan
h Japanese **i** Japanese **j** Thailand
k Thai **l** Thai **m** Brazil **n** Brazilian
o Portuguese **p** Egypt **q** Egyptian
r Arabic

2

1 F (Russian) **2** F (Romansh, French, German, Italian) **3** F (Bulgarian) **4** F (Arabic) **5** T **6** F (Turkish) **7** F (Portuguese) **8** F (Austria)

3

1 practise **2** Translation **3** make
4 took **5** doing **6** practice **7** revise
8 memorising

4

1 took **2** make **3** doing **4** do
5 write **6** memorise **6** study

VOCABULARY EXTENSION p22

5

1 in **2** up **3** down **4** of **5** off
6 in **7** up

Reading p23

1

c

2

1 T **2** F **3** F **4** F **5** NM **6** NM
7 T **8** T **9** NM **10** F

3

a b e

4

1 c **2** d **3** e **4** b **5** f **6** a

5

1 congress **2** rare **3** items
4 nowadays **5** former **6** available

Grammar in context p24

1

Plural countable: any, many, a lot (of), a few
Uncountable: any, much, a lot (of), a little
Affirmative: a lot (of), a few, a little
Negative & questions: any, much, many, a lot (of), a few, a little
Large quantity: a lot (of), much, many
Small quantity: a few, a little

2

1 U **2** C **3** C **4** C **5** C **6** C **7** U **8** U **9** C **10** U

3

1 many **2** much **3** much **4** many **5** much **6** many **7** much

4

2 some **3** many **4** some **5** much **6** many **7** a little **8** many **9** Any

5

1 many **2** a little **3** a lot **4** much **5** a few

6

2 There are a few biscuits. **3** There are a few people/cups. **4** There's a little sugar. **5** There's a little chocolate. **6** There are a few bananas.

GRAMMAR CHALLENGE p24

7

I live in a small village called ~~the~~ Marshwood. There aren't ~~much~~ **many** people in my village. There are only a ~~little~~ **few** houses and shops. However, the shops sell a ~~lots~~ **lot** of basic things like ~~the~~ bread and ~~the~~ milk. There isn't ~~many~~ **much** public transport either. There are only ~~a little~~ **a few** buses during the week and on Sundays there aren't ~~some~~ **any**. Most of ~~a~~ **the** people travel by car to work in the city.

Developing vocabulary and listening p25

1

1 irregular **2** unhappy **3** impossible **4** incorrect **5** invisible **6** unusual **7** illegal **8** informal

2

1 invisible **2** unusual **3** impossible **4** incorrect **5** irregular **6** unhappy **7** informal **8** illegal

3

1 d **2** b **3** a

4

a 3 **b** 2 **c** 1 **d** 3 **e** 1 **f** 2

VOCABULARY EXTENSION p25

5

1 impatient **2** improbable **3** irrelevant **4** illogical **5** irresponsible **6** illegible **7** unofficial **8** impractical

6

1 irrelevant **2** illegible **3** impatient **4** irresponsible **5** illogical **6** unofficial **7** impractical **8** improbable

Grammar in context p26

1

1 who **2** which, that **3** whose **4** when **5** where

2

1 that, 0 **2** who **3** whose **4** where **5** where **6** which, that **7** when **8** where **9** whose **10** which

3

1 where **2** when **3** 0 **4** which/that **5** where **6** who **7** when **8** whose

4

1 … where you can get vegetarian food.
2 … who taught me maths last year.
3 … when we have a lot of tests.
4 … which I enjoyed reading.
5 … which is difficult to learn.

GRAMMAR CHALLENGE p26

5

1 which **2** that/who **3** when **4** that **5** which **6** who/that

6

1 summer **2** vandal **3** adolescence **4** Japan **5** exam **6** stepmother

Developing speaking p27

1

1 Pardon, sure **2** price **3** repeat **4** registration **5** Sorry **6** information **7** much **8** last

2

a 6 **b** 5 **c** 8 **d** 1 **e** 7 **f** 3 **g** 2 **h** 4

3

1 Could you repeat that?
2 Did you say on the 30th July?
3 I'm not sure I understood.

PRONUNCIATION p27

4

1 interested + in + a **2** did + you **3** Could + you **4** Can + I, help + you **5** much + is **6** price + is, pounds + a

DESCRIBING PICTURES p27

5

Students' own answers

6

1 There are some boys, girls, a teacher – the students are probably teenagers.
2 They're in a language school classroom.
3 They're talking to other students not to the teacher.
4 They're talking about something in their book, maybe grammar, or discussing questions. Because talking together helps practise spoken English. They don't worry about speaking in front of the whole class.

7

Students' own answers

Developing writing p28

1

1 D **2** B **3** A **4** E **5** C

2

1 E **2** B **3** C **4** D **5** A

3

1 C **2** D **3** B **4** E **5** A

4

Students' own answers

Revision: Units 1–3

Grammar p29

1

1 much **2** any **3** a lot of/some **4** correct **5** a few **6** some **7** correct

2

1 who **2** where **3** when **4** whose **5** that **6** that/which

3

1 who **2** where **3** whose **4** 0 **5** who **6** when **7** where **8** 0

4

a the **b** some **c** lot **d** few **e** some **f** the **g** any

Vocabulary p29

1

a Poland **b** Brazilian **c** Mexico **d** Turkey **e** Japanese **f** Thailand **g** Russian **h** Austria

2

1 made **2** doing **3** revise **4** independent **5** practise **6** burglar

3

1 impossible **2** irregular **3** illegal **4** incorrect **5** unhappy **6** invisible

4

1 revision 2 analysis 3 translation
4 retirement 5 collection 6 discussion
7 vandalism 8 investigation
9 memorisation 10 improvement

Unit 4

Vocabulary p30

1

1 ankle 2 back 3 cheek 4 chin
5 face 6 heel 7 hip 8 knee
9 shoulder 10 thigh 11 throat
12 thumb

2

1 finger 2 head 3 forehead
4 ear 5 nose 6 mouth 7 neck
8 hand 9 elbow 10 chest 11 wrist
12 stomach 13 toe 14 leg 15 foot

3

1 sore 2 headache 3 hurts 4 pain
5 broken

VOCABULARY EXTENSION p30

4

1 swollen 2 bruise 3 burned
4 sneezing 5 rash 6 dizzy

Reading p31

1

a

2

1 T 2 M 3 M 4 W 5 T 6 M
7 W 8 M 9 W 10 T

3

1 F 2 F 3 O 4 F 5 O 6 F

4

1 patients 2 brake 3 is killing me
4 crutches 5 helmet 6 operation

5

1 is killing me 2 crutches 3 operation
4 patient 5 helmet 6 brake

Grammar in context p32

1

a have, past
b ever, never

2

1 've broken 2 've been 3 has done
4 have lived 5 've bought
6 has painted 7 has had

3

1 b 2 c 3 b 4 c 5 a 6 b 7 c

4

2 Have your parents ever visited the North
Pole? No, they've never visited the
North Pole.
3 Have you ever spoken to the Queen of
England? No, I've never spoken to the
Queen of England.
4 Has he ever won an Oscar? No, he has
never won an Oscar.
5 Have you ever ridden an elephant? No,
I've never ridden an elephant.
6 Has your English teacher ever starred in
a film? No, my English teacher has never
starred in a film.
7 Have you ever sung in a concert? No,
I've never sung in a concert.

5

a for b since

6

1 never 2 since 3 ever
4 2009 5 has had 6 for 7 ever
8 never

GRAMMAR CHALLENGE p32

7

1 for a long time 2 since she was seven
3 Have you ever met 4 I've never been
5 Have you ever worn
6 since the operation 7 for ages

Developing vocabulary and listening p33

1

1 first aid 2 waiting room
3 food poisoning 4 health centre
5 heart attack 6 painkillers

2

1 waiting room 2 painkillers
3 heart attack 4 food poisoning
5 health centre 6 first aid

3

c

4

1 F 2 T 3 T 4 F 5 F 6 F

5

b

VOCABULARY EXTENSION p33

6

1 b/d 2 f 3 b/c/e 4 a/f 5 b 6 c

7

1 armchair 2 footprints 3 hairdresser
4 headband/hairband 5 toothbrush
6 handbag

Grammar in context p34

1

2 yet 3 already 4 just/already 5 yet
6 yet 7 yet 8 just/already

2

2 He has just won a prize.
3 They have just seen a horror film.
4 We have just done our homework.
5 I have just finished this exercise.

3

2 My sister has just arrived home.
3 Holly and Jack have already eaten lunch.
4 My mum has just got back from work.
5 Have you seen that film yet?
6 Have you just met the new teacher?
7 Has the bus already gone?
8 We haven't studied for the exam yet.

4

1 has been 2 have had 3 won
4 appeared 5 Have, eaten
6 have lived 7 bought 8 flew

GRAMMAR CHALLENGE p34

5

1 has lived 2 Have you ever visited
3 My parents won 4 We haven't done
5 I saw 6 I have had them
7 for half an hour 8 have never seen

Developing speaking p35

1

2 b 3 e 4 a 5 c

2

1 er 2 you know 3 I'm not really sure
4 well 5 The thing

PRONUNCIATION p35

3

'First aid' is different (the stress is equal on
both words; the stress on the other words is
on the first syllable.)

DESCRIBING PICTURES p35

4

Students' own answers

5

a in b well c perhaps d carrying
e red f injured g hurts

6

Students' own answers

Developing writing p36

1

Yes

2

1 c 2 a 3 b 4 d

3

1 for example **2** here is some extra information **3** that is, this is exactly what I mean **4** as soon as possible **5** please pay special attention/Nota bene (Pay attention) **6** and other things of the same type/etcetera

4

Joe

Great news about your team. Congratulations!

Sorry to hear about your injured knee. I came round to see you, but your mum said you were at the hospital. Call me asap. We all want to celebrate.

NB I left the signed football that you lent me in your bedroom. Make sure your brother hasn't taken it!

Sam

5

Students' own answers

Revision: Units 1–4

Grammar p37

1

1 Have you ever visited an art gallery?
2 William has never ridden a horse.
3 Joe and Ellie have just come back from their holiday.
4 I have already spoken to George.
5 Have you written your email yet?
6 We haven't bought bread yet.

2

1 for **2** since **3** since **4** for **5** for

3

1 have had **2** visited **3** has lived
4 was **5** have bought **6** forgot

4

1 'm writing **2** 've been
3 don't feel/am not feeling **4** 'm eating
5 has disappeared **6** brought **7** went
8 Have, finished **9** did **10** 've, emailed

Vocabulary p37

1

1 neck **2** toe **3** thigh **4** nose
5 elbow

2

1 sore **2** waiting room **3** broken
4 first aid **5** cough **6** virus
7 backache

3

1 d **2** i **3** e **4** h **5** f **6** c **7** g
8 b **9** a

Gateway to exams: Units 3–4

Reading p38

1

1 A **2** A **3** B **4** C **5** C **6** B **7** C
8 A **9** B

Listening p38

2

a French **b** Russian **c** nine
d mistakes (making mistakes)
e Miss Painter **f** games **g** grammar
h Russian books

Use of English p39

3

1 A **2** C **3** A **4** B **5** C **6** A **7** C
8 C **9** B **10** D

Writing p39

4

Students' own answers

COMMON MISTAKES p39

5

1 any free time **2** much money/any money **3** a lot of/lots of **4** who/that
5 Have you already studied
6 I think, has just won **7** repeat that again, please **8** where **9** have never learned **10** sounds interesting **11** went
12 Could you send

Unit 5

Vocabulary p40

1

documentary the news film advert drama game show chat show cartoon
1 film **2** documentary **3** chat show
4 game show **5** the news **6** cartoon

2

1 channels **2** switch off **3** remote
4 series **5** turn on **6** live

3

1 channels **2** series **3** off **4** turn
5 remote **6** live

4

1 scary **2** informative **3** moving
4 funny **5** boring **6** popular **7** awful
8 exciting

VOCABULARY EXTENSION p40

5

1 e **2** f **3** d **4** b **5** c **6** a

6

1 first episode **2** breaking news
3 newsreaders **4** sports commentators

Reading p41

1

b

2

1 c **2** b **3** b **4** c **5** b

3

1 O **2** F **3** F **4** O

4

1 contestant **2** interaction **3** tweet
4 in real time **5** issue **6** viewer

Grammar in context p42

1

a small, smaller, the smallest
b fit, fitter, the fittest
c easy, easier, the easiest
d boring, more boring, the most boring
e good, better, the best

2

1 cheaper **2** hotter **3** more frequent
4 further/farther **5** worst **6** most popular **7** most important **8** better

3

2 is taller than **3** is the tallest
4 is more talkative than **5** is better at sports **6** is the best at sport.

4

2 A motorbike is heavier than a bike.
3 Matthew is the oldest boy in this class.
4 Einstein was the most intelligent person in the 20th century.
5 My brother's bedroom is smaller than my bedroom.
6 I think a Ferrari is better than a Peugot 507.

GRAMMAR CHALLENGE p42

5

1 exciting than **2** more popular
3 the scariest **4** longer than
5 any good **6** the best **7** I've ever
8 for three

Developing vocabulary and listening p43

1

a is boring **b** is frightened
c is confusing **d** is relaxing
e is embarrassed **f** is interested
g is surprising **h** is tired

2

1 Sue **2** Ben **3** Sarah **4** Lily

3

1 b **2** a **3** c **4** b

VOCABULARY EXTENSION p43

4

1 c **2** b **3** a **4** e **5** f **6** d

5

1 depressed **2** disgusted **3** exhausted
4 worried **5** terrified **6** amazed

6

1 disgusting **2** exhausted
3 depressing **4** worried **5** terrifying
6 amazed

Grammar in context p44

1

1 as … as **2** not as … as, less … than
3 not as … as, less … than, more … than

2

1 Italy isn't as big as Russia./Italy is less big than Russia.
2 Hamsters are less dangerous than snakes./Hamsters aren't as dangerous as snakes.
3 The River Thames isn't as long as the Amazon./The River Thames is less long than the Amazon.
4 A kilo of gold is as heavy as a kilo of rice.
5 Chocolate isn't as expensive as caviar./Chocolate is less expensive than caviar.

3

1 too **2** enough **3** expensive
4 good **5** big

4

1 He isn't old enough to vote.
2 I'm too poor to buy that.
3 Megan is too short to close the top window.
4 Her car isn't fast enough to win the race.
5 That documentary isn't interesting enough to watch twice.

5

2 good enough **3** old enough **4** too long **5** warm enough **6** too expensive

GRAMMAR CHALLENGE p44

6

1 Children are not old enough to vote.
2 Bicycles are less expensive than motorbikes.
3 There are only a few seats left.
4 Dolphins are not as dangerous as tigers.
5 The Thames is not as long as the Nile.
6 Have you got a lot of information about the programme?
7 The actor was too ill to go on stage.
8 He's the man who we met yesterday.

Developing speaking p45

1

1 don't **2** idea **3** neither **4** Shall
5 sure **6** mean **7** about **8** what
9 let's **10** Great

2

Make a suggestion: Why don't we, Shall we go, How about, Let's
Respond – no/maybe: I'm not sure, But what about
Respond – yes: Great!, Good idea!

3

1 A: It would be nice to go out tonight.
2 B: OK. Where shall we go?
3 A: How about going to the cinema? The new Johnny Depp film is on.
4 B: I'm not sure – I don't really like Johnny Depp.
5 A: OK. How about going to the Salad Social for dinner?
6 B: Good idea, but it's closed on Sundays, remember?
7 A: You're right. Then why don't we go dancing?
8 B: But what about your ankle – you hurt it last week.
9 A: It's not hurting much now … but I don't want to make it worse. Let's go shopping then!
10 B: Great. I need to get a present for Dan!

PRONUNCIATION p45

4

/eɪ/	/æ/
sale	ankle
play	haven't
rain	at
game	shall
taking	Maddy
made	am

'air' has a different sound

DESCRIBING PICTURES p45

5

Students' own answers

6

a looking **b** sitting **c** remote control
d look **e** happening **f** carefully
g next

7

Students' own answers

Developing writing p46

1

all except d and j

2

1 Personally **2** think **3** In my opinion
4 would recommend **5** As far as

3

1 b **2** a **3** d **4** c

4

Students' own answers

Grammar p47

1

1 hotter **2** thinner **3** best **4** silliest
5 most intelligent **6** worse

2

1 is less important than love
2 isn't as easy as biology
3 too young to see that film
4 not hot enough to swim in the sea today
5 as clever as her sister
6 isn't fast enough to win the race

3

1 for **2** who **3** as **4** much **5** the
6 yet **7** any **8** too **9** never
10 think

4

1 I'm working **2** have you lived
3 a lot of/lots of **4** were you doing
5 that/which, 0

Vocabulary p47

1

1 game show **2** cartoon
3 documentary **4** advert
5 cookery programme **6** drama

2

1 funny **2** surprised **3** interesting
4 scary **5** confused **6** relaxing

3

1 cousin, nephew **2** Russian, Turkish
3 childhood, death **4** piracy, burglary
5 thumb, knee **6** virus, cold

4

1 waiting **2** aid **3** incorrect **4** aged
5 painkillers

Unit 6

Vocabulary p48

1

1 mountain range **2** valley **3** rainforest
4 river **5** forest **6** beach **7** ice cap
8 desert **9** island

2

a drought – 2
b flood – 6
c global warming – 7
d greenhouse effect – 4
e ozone layer – 5
f recycle – 1
g save water – 3
h waste water – 8

VOCABULARY EXTENSION p48

3

1 away **2** out **3** down **4** out **5** in
6 after **7** up

Reading p49

1

c

2

1 was, p4 **2** contribute, p2 **3** was, p3
4 keep getting bigger, p2 **5** will, p4
6 attracted, p1

3

c, e, f

4

1 nature **2** goes down **3** artificial
4 enormously **5** tasty

Grammar in context p50

1

1 I'll **2** 'm going to **3** will **4** will
5 's going to

2

a going to **b** will **c** will **d** going to
e will
1 e **2** d **3** c **4** b **5** a

3

1 'll **2** are going to **3** will you
4 's going to **5** 'll

4

1 c **2** e **3** c **4** c **5** c **6** b **7** d
8 a

5

1 Perhaps our team will win the
competition. = 50%
2 It probably won't be cold tonight. = 80%
3 I will definitely finish my homework soon.
= 100%
4 She definitely won't go out tomorrow. =
100%
5 They may do the exam next week. =
50%
6 My brother will probably call this
afternoon. = 80%

GRAMMAR CHALLENGE p50

6

I'm not feeling very well so I ~~won't definitely~~
definitely won't go swimming this evening.
Mum ~~is~~ has made me an appointment
and I'~~ll~~ **'m** going to see the doctor this
afternoon. He ~~will~~ **might** tell me to stay
in bed – I'm not sure. I '~~ll~~ expect Miss
Jones will give back our homework in class
tomorrow. ~~May~~ **Can/Could** you collect mine
for me please? I ~~definitely~~ **will definitely**
be at home this evening and I'll ~~probable~~
probably be in bed – so perhaps I'll
~~phoning~~ **phone** you then.

Developing vocabulary and listening p51

1

2 receive **3** arrive at **4** buy **5** buy
6 become **7** arrive **8** become
9 receive **10** obtained **11** bring

2

b

3

1 got some really interesting homework
2 getting energy
3 getting worse
4 get permission
5 gets very annoyed
6 get me some information
7 don't get a good signal
8 he gets to work

VOCABULARY EXTENSION p51

4

1 d **2** a **3** c **4** e **5** b

Grammar in context p52

1

1 something that is generally true
2 both halves

2

1 f **2** g **3** d **4** a **5** e **6** c **7** b

3

1 possible **2** the present simple

4

1 make, won't be **2** won't, don't
3 doesn't, will take **4** need, will come
5 will arrest, find **6** play, will go
7 doesn't, will lose

5

1 If he has a problem, he'll speak to the
teacher.
2 I'll go to the doctor if my hand hurts
tomorrow.
3 He won't be happy if he misses the bus.
4 If my sister goes to music lessons, my
mum will buy her a guitar.
5 If you see the film tomorrow, you'll know
how the story ends.
6 The teacher will give me a bad mark if I
don't give her my homework.
7 You won't see me if you come late.
8 If you don't switch off your mobile
phone, people will get angry.
9 The picnic will be a disaster if the
weather is bad.
10 If we don't go to the shops, we won't
have enough food.

GRAMMAR CHALLENGE p52

6

1 doesn't come, 'll go **2** 've, seen,
's going to rain **3** woke, was blowing
4 may/might go, isn't working, 'll definitely
go **5** is going to watch, will be

Developing speaking p53

1

a up **b** about **c** fancy **d** shall
e How **f** don't **g** OK, **h** Great

2

Asking about somebody's plans

a What are you up to tomorrow?
b Do fancy going to the Planet Earth
exhibition in town?
Arranging to meet
c What time shall we meet?
d How about half past ten?
e Why don't we meet at the bus stop?
Responding to plans and arrangements
f Fine.
g Good idea.
h OK.

PRONUNCIATION p53

3

In 'wh' questions 1, 2, 4, 5 and 8 the voice
goes down, in yes/no questions 3, 6 and 7
the voice goes up.

DESCRIBING PICTURES p53

4

Students' own answers

5

a cycling **b** countryside **c** background
d past **e** in **f** looks **g** on **h** fun
i healthy

6

Students' own answers

Developing writing p54

1

Sequence: Firstly, Next, Finally
Addition: Furthermore, What's more
Contrast: However, Nevertheless

2

d

3

1 Firstly, Next, Finally
2 However, What's more

4

Students' own answers

5

Students' own answers

Revision: Units 1–6

Grammar p55

1

1 may **2** probably won't
3 is going to snow **4** will definitely
5 might **6** 'll

2
1 goes 2 tell 3 will get 4 'll travel
5 is 6 will do, thinks
3
1 If Anna phones later, we can go shopping together.
2 I have never been to/visited France before.
3 We might get our results tomorrow.
4 My bag was more expensive than Jack's.
5 How much was your new laptop?
6 We moved/started living here two years ago.

Vocabulary p55

1
1 jungle 2 forest 3 desert
4 mountain range 5 island 6 beach
7 valley 8 ocean
2
1 flood 2 recycle 3 waste
4 ozone layer 5 drought 6 save
3
1 bring 2 buy 3 arrives
4
1 b 2 a 3 d 4 e 5 c

Gateway to exams: Units 5–6

Reading p56

1
1 b 2 a 3 b 4 b 5 a 6 a

Listening p56

2
1 d 2 a 3 e 4 c

Use of English p57

3
1 if I don't read 2 We might have a test
3 earn less than 4 if I come home early
5 isn't as easy as 6 isn't old enough
7 'm going to talk
8 are more expensive than

Writing p57

4
Students' own answers

5
1 as clever as 2 most difficult
3 I'll see you 4 Will you help me
5 I stay 6 It wasn't warm enough
7 Are you up to anything
8 It will definitely rain 9 very tasty
10 may go 11 fancy coming round
12 What's more

Unit 7

Vocabulary p58

1
1 receptionist 2 builder
3 shop assistant 4 mechanic
5 fashion designer 6 journalist
2
1 F 2 T 3 T 4 F 5 T 6 F 7 T
8 T
3
1 creative 2 fit 3 strong 4 clever
5 caring 6 sociable 7 reliable
8 calm 9 ambitious

VOCABULARY EXTENSION p58

4
1 ambition 2 confidence 3 reliability
4 creativity 5 strength 6 fitness
5
1 strength 2 confidence 3 ambition
4 fitness 5 creativity

Reading p59

1
c
2
1 T, line 7 2 F, line 13 3 F, line 20
4 T, line 18 5 F, line 22 6 F, line 28
7 F, line 30 8 T, line 33 9 T, line 41
3
1 F 2 O 3 F 4 O 5 F 6 O
4
1 sculpture 2 enlarge 3 carving
4 chance 5 have a go 6 option
7 calcium 8 career

Grammar in context p60

1
1 no obligation 2 obligation
3 recommendation 4 no obligation
5 obligation 6 advice 7 prohibition
2
1 Normally teachers don't have to wear a uniform.
2 Normally a firefighter has to wear a uniform.
3 I don't have to go to school on Sunday.
4 A receptionist has to know how to use a computer.
5 Builders have to wear hard hats.
3
1 You must write 2 People mustn't make
3 Students mustn't use
4 Professional musicians must practise

4
1 People shouldn't use 2 You shouldn't take 3 You should help 4 you should practise 5 People should switch off
5
1 have to 2 mustn't 3 must/have to
4 have to/must 5 mustn't 6 mustn't

GRAMMAR CHALLENGE p60

6
1 must go 2 don't have to
3 you break 4 should do
5 don't have to 6 have to do
7 mustn't 8 mustn't 9 shouldn't

Developing vocabulary and listening p61

1
1 working 2 going 3 time 4 looking
5 organised 6 handed 7 eyed
8 paid
2
b
3
1 D 2 D 3 D 4 A 5 D

VOCABULARY EXTENSION p61

4
1 self-reliant, e
2 open-minded, a
3 well-dressed, f and c
4 bad-tempered, d
5 old-fashioned, b
6 well-respected, c and f
5
1 well-dressed 2 open-minded
3 self-reliant 4 bad-tempered
5 well-respected 6 old-fashioned

Grammar in context p62

1
1 e 2 a 3 c 4 b 5 d
2
1 T 2 F 3 F 4 T 5 F
3
1 weren't 2 wouldn't 3 were
4 didn't 5 would 6 would 7 was
8 weren't 9 could 10 wouldn't
4
1 had 2 'd walk 3 wouldn't be
4 played 5 learned 6 'd play
7 didn't like 8 'd tell 9 found
10 had 11 'd ask

GRAMMAR CHALLENGE p62

5

1 You should stay home   2 don't have to give   3 We mustn't eat   4 If I were rich, I'd go   5 If I were you, I'd go   6 were you, I would buy your mum a present   7 not hot enough to go   8 are not as healthy as

Developing speaking p63

1

1 Can you tell me when the job starts?
2 Could I ask if you need any experience?
3 Could you tell me how I can apply?
4 Can you tell me what we have to do?
5 Could I ask what the basic wages are?
6 Can you tell me what your address is?

2

a 1   b 4   c 2   d 5   e 3   f 6

PRONUNCIATION p63

3

1 Can you tell me when the **job** starts?
2 Could I ask if you need any **experience**?
3 Can you tell me how I can **apply**?
4 Can you tell me what we have to **do**?
5 Could I ask what the basic **wages** are?
6 Can you tell me what your **address** is?

Can is pronounced with /ə/

DESCRIBING PICTURES p63

4

Students' own answers

5

a in   b at   c down   d because   e in
f Perhaps   g maybe   h probably   i so
j if

6

Students' own answers

Developing writing p64

1

c

2

a Dear   b in   c I would   d for
e enclose   f As   g experience   h well
i hard   j hearing   k Yours sincerely

3

1 d   2 b   3 a   4 c

4

a 1   b 3   c 2

5

Students' own answers

6

Students' own answers

Revision: Units 1–7

Grammar p65

1

1 don't have to   2 mustn't
3 don't have to   4 doesn't have to
5 mustn't   6 mustn't

2

1 have to, should   2 might, should
3 will, shouldn't   4 have to
5 has to, don't have to

3

1 comes, wake up, is   2 'll go, get
3 wouldn't work, paid   4 didn't have, 'd sit   5 have, will you help

Vocabulary p65

1

1 plumber   2 mechanic   3 builder
4 receptionist   5 shop assistant   6 vet

2

1 hard-working (P)   2 easy-going (P)
3 part-time (J)   4 right-handed (P)
5 good-looking (P)   6 well-paid (J/P)

3

1 ambitious   2 confident   3 creative
4 sensitive   5 fit   6 clever

4

1 caring   2 calm   3 sociable
4 reliable   5 disappointed   6 broken
7 sore   8 moving

Unit 8

Vocabulary p66

1a

1 fall out   3 make it up
2 see eye to eye   4 hang out

1b

1 get on well
2 have a lot in common
3 have an argument
4 circle of friends

2

1 see eye to eye   2 has had an argument
3 have a lot in common   4 made it up

3

2 boredom   3 excitement   4 fear
5 happiness   6 loneliness
sadness: negative

VOCABULARY EXTENSION p66

4

1 confusion   2 relaxation   3 stress
4 embarrassment   5 disappointment
6 depression   7 worry   8 surprise

5

1 confusion   2 disappointment
3 Relaxation   4 worry/stress   5 surprise

Reading p67

1

b

2

1 c   2 b   3 b   4 a   5 a

3

1, 5

4

1 icon   2 guilty   3 share   4 over
5 destroyed   6 nasty

Grammar in context p68

1

1 past   2 before

2

recently, while

3

1 c, we had had the argument
2 f, I had sent the nasty message
3 g, she had finished the one she was reading
4 e, They hadn't eaten anything all day
5 a, they had had their dinner
6 d, he had forgotten to bring his towel
7 b, They had won the competition
Verbs: past perfect

4

2 By 1400 they hadn't started to print books
3 By 1805 they had made the first battery.
4 By 1895 they had discovered X-rays.
5 By 1900 they hadn't flown for the first time.
6 By 1910 they hadn't discovered penicillin.
7 By 1932 they had split the atom.
8 By 1953 they had found the structure of DNA.
9 By 1960 they hadn't walked on the moon.

5

c

6

1 used   2 use   3 use

7

1 used to live   2 used to go   3 didn't use to watch   4 Did you use to walk
5 used to take   6 didn't use to have

GRAMMAR CHALLENGE p68

8

Danny is playing **plays** tennis every Saturday with his friend Jordan. One Saturday, they started playing at 12 o'clock and by 5.30, they played **had played** five whole games. After they were finished **had** finished the last game, Danny had a shower and went home. But his back and neck ~~had really hurt~~ **were really hurting**. He was a bit worried. Maybe he ~~injured~~ **had injured** his back during the tennis game. When he was younger his neck ~~wasn't hurting~~ **didn't use to hurt** after tennis. Perhaps he ~~must~~ **should** visit the doctor. Danny decided to have a long hot bath and then go to bed. Luckily, when he ~~had got up~~ **got up** the next morning, his pain ~~went~~ **had gone**. It ~~wasn't been~~ **hadn't been** anything serious after all. Next Saturday he would play six games!

Developing vocabulary and listening p69

1

-ness: illness, weakness, sadness, madness, happiness, loneliness
-ship: friendship, relationship, leadership
-dom: boredom, kingdom

2

2 relationship **3** freedom **4** happy
5 lonely **6** weak **7** friendship **8** sad
9 leadership **10** boredom **11** kingdom
12 mad

3

b

4

1 15 **2** illness **3** school
4 loneliness, boredom **5** black
6 freedom **7** biscuits **8** sad

VOCABULARY EXTENSION p69

5

1 b **2** d **3** e **4** f **5** a **6** c **7** h
8 g

Grammar in context p70

1

1 f **2** d **3** a **4** b **5** e **6** g **7** c
2

1 f **2** e **3** d **4** a **5** c **6** b
3

1 doing **2** shopping **3** Doing
4 doing **5** reading **6** to do
7 to make **8** doing
a Doing **b** to know **c** seeing
d playing, swimming **e** looking, buying
f to become, painting, drawing
g Getting, to do
h Cleaning, to do, going

4

1 c **2** e **3** d **4** a **5** b **6** f **7** g
8 h

GRAMMAR CHALLENGE p70

5

Every Saturday my friends ~~going~~ **go** into town to ~~watching~~ **watch** football. I don't enjoy ~~to watch~~ **watching** sports so I usually go to the library while they're in the stadium. Then we meet up afterwards to ~~having~~ **have** a pizza. Last Saturday they persuaded me ~~going~~ **to go** with them because it was an important match. Unfortunately, it started ~~raining~~ **to rain** and we ~~haven't~~ **hadn't** brought our umbrellas. It was terrible. Next week ~~will going~~ **I'm going to go/I'll go** to the library again – no more football for me.

Developing speaking p71

1

c

2

1 was **2** had organised **3** used to work
4 started **5** were **6** knew **7** ate
8 were having

3

Students' own answers

PRONUNCIATION p71

4

1 down **2** up **3** down **4** up
5 down **6** down

DESCRIBING PICTURES p71

5

Students' own answers

6

1 some young people/teenagers/some boys and some girls
2 on a beach
3 probably having a party/barbecue/picnic
4 relaxed and happy, enjoying the afternoon

7

Students' own answers

Developing writing p72

1

c

2

a 3 **b** 2 **c** 1

3

1 First, Firstly **2** Then, After that, So
3 Finally

4

1, 2, 4

5

Students' own answers

Grammar p73

1

1 After I had got up, I made my breakfast.
2 When he had finished his lunch, he wasn't hungry.
3 When she had swum for 20 minutes, she got out of the swimming pool.
4 After I had written the email, I sent it.
5 After I had played tennis, I had a shower.
6 After I had put on my pyjamas, I went bed.
7 After we had watched the film at the cinema, we caught the bus home.

2

1 I didn't use to enjoy **2** Did, use to live
3 used to be **4** used to be
5 didn't use to like

3

1 Doing **2** to do **3** watching
4 to watch **5** swimming **6** to swim

Vocabulary p73

1

1 circle **2** argument, made
3 eye to eye **4** get on well **5** fallen out

2

1 sadness/unhappiness **2** loneliness
3 fear **4** boredom **5** anger

3

1 excitement **2** friendship
3 relationship **4** freedom **5** weakness
6 illness **7** leadership **8** madness

4

1 step **2** sore **3** lifting **4** game
5 range **6** warming

Reading p74

1

1 T, line 21 **2** F, line 12 **3** F, line 11
4 T, line 17 **5** T, line 20 **6** F, line 34
7 T, line 38 **8** T, line 52

Listening p74

2

1 c **2** b **3** c **4** a **5** a **6** c

Use of English p75

3

1 C **2** A **3** C **4** B **5** C **6** C **7** B
8 D

Writing p75

4

Students' own answers

COMMON MISTAKES p75

5

1 I had finished **2** I didn't use to
3 Learning another language **4** Do you enjoy working **5** First of all, should go
6 Are you interested in coming **7** Dear Mr Brown, I'd like to apply for the job
8 I don't have to go **9** If I had enough money, I'd travel … **10** You shouldn't eat, It isn't **11** We used to live **12** someone had stolen

Unit 9

Vocabulary p76

1

1 play **2** comic **3** horror **4** fantasy
5 romance **6** thriller **7** fairy tale
8 crime novel **9** science fiction
10 graphic novel **11** historical fiction

2

1 fantasy/fairy tale **2** science fiction
3 comic/graphic novel **4** historical fiction
5 fairy tale **6** crime novel/thriller

3

1 c **2** f **3** b **4** g **5** a **6** e **7** d
8 h

VOCABULARY EXTENSION p76

4

1 index **2** articles **3** headline
4 contents **5** chapter **6** acts
7 scene

Reading p77

1

b

2

1 c **2** f **3** d **4** a **5** e **6** b

3

1 D **2** A **3** D **4** B

4

1 dramatic **2** reflect **3** interact
4 combination **5** generation

5

1 generation **2** reflect **3** combination
4 interact **5** dramatic

Grammar in context p78

1

1 goes one tense back **2** must, mustn't
3 change

2

1 wrote **2** was writing **3** had written
4 had written **5** had written
6 would write **7** could write
8 might write **9** had to write

3

1 no **2** told us **3** told the students
4 no **5** no **6** told her mum **7** no
8 told James

4

1 she loved **2** they were **3** was his
4 her, needed **5** was

5

1 Jamie said he was going to start playing basketball the following month.
2 Jack said his friend had got a new computer game.
3 Emily and Evie said that they had finished school the previous Friday.
4 Charlotte said that she thought that was the answer.
5 The students said that they didn't need help.

GRAMMAR CHALLENGE p78

6

1 told Oliver that he had to
2 was the restaurant where they had had
3 I shouldn't work too late at night
4 the following day she/he would

Developing vocabulary and listening p79

1a

1 c/d **2** g **3** f **4** d/c **5** b **6** a
7 e

1b

1 read on **2** turn over **3** flick through
4 read out **5** look up **6** cross out
7 fill in

2

1 in **2** out **3** look **4** over **5** flick
6 out **7** on

3

a

4

1 Speaker 2
2 Speaker 1
3 Speaker 2
4 Speaker 3
5 Speaker 2
6 Speaker 3
7 Speaker 1

5

1 F **2** T **3** F **4** T **5** F **6** T

VOCABULARY EXTENSION p79

6

1 d **2** c **3** b **4** a

7

1 note down **2** dipped into
3 read up on **4** sum up **5** note down

Grammar in context p80

1

1 F **2** T **3** F **4** T **5** T

2

1 asked the boy if he was sure about that answer
2 asked the boy why he was crying
3 asked Nathan if it was his birthday that day
4 asked Mia if she knew the time
5 asked his granddaughter where she had put his glasses
6 asked the girl how she had known his name
7 asked Tom if he had read that book
8 asked Sally if she liked crime novels
9 asked Hannah if she had to wear a uniform to school

3

1 whether she liked **2** if I was listening
3 where Daisy lived. **4** why her mobile phone wasn't working **5** that day
6 why he was **7** if/whether they had enjoyed the meal.

GRAMMAR CHALLENGE p80

4

1 Are you tired?
2 Yes, I am because I watched a late film last night. Why did you ask that?
3 You look pale. Why did you watch until so late? You shouldn't watch late films on school nights.
4 You're right, but I needed to watch this film. I had to write a review of it for my English teacher.
5 I understand, but next time you should record it. Then you can watch it earlier in the day.
6 Next time, I will record it.

Developing speaking p81

1

1 talk **2** by **3** all **4** more **5** true
6 least **7** thing **8** sum
✓: all except 'Another thing is that …'

2

1 B **2** G **3** B **4** B **5** B **6** G

PRONUNCIATION p81

3

1 I'd <u>like</u> to begin by <u>saying</u> that
2 <u>Last</u> but not <u>least</u>
3 <u>It's</u> also <u>true</u> that
4 <u>Another</u> thing is that
5 To <u>sum</u> up

DESCRIBING PICTURES p81

4
Students' own answers
5
a bookshop **b** right **c** student
d casual **e** older **f** library **g** standing
h sit **i** flicking **j** decide **k** serious
l concentrating **m** good
6
Students' own answers

Developing writing p82

1
1 B **2** D **3** C **4** A
2
B: **a** six o'clock in the evening **b** big
  c wet **d** smart
D: **a** quickly **b** hadn't noticed
  c was standing
C: **a** brightly **b** completely
A: **a** Suddenly **b** placed
3
Students' own answers

Revision: Units 1–9

Grammar p83

1
1 her **2** the previous week **3** That day
4 He'd **5** she **6** the following day
2
1 his **2** whether **3** he was
4 had ever had **5** liked **6** had seen
3
1 Nick said he had found the information
  on that website.
2 Angela asked Lynn if she was going to
  see the new film the following day.
3 The teacher asked Kerry and Liz where
  they had been.
4 Sonya asked Ryan if he had gone to
  Dave's party the previous day.
5 Alice told Mike that she hadn't finished
  reading his book yet.
4
a watching **b** have seen **c** started
d whose **e** much **f** some
g don't usually see

Vocabulary p83

1
1 autobiography **2** fairy tale
3 cookbook **4** science fiction
5 manual **6** play
2
1 cookbook **2** science fiction
3 manual **4** fairy tale **5** autobiography
6 play
3
1 on **2** out **3** flick **4** up **5** up

4
1 d **2** h **3** c **4** b **5** g **6** a **7** e
8 f

Unit 10

Vocabulary p84

1
1 keyboard **2** monitor **3** webcam
4 speaker **5** printer **6** flash drive
7 scanner **8** mouse
2
1 f **2** c **3** e **4** d **5** a **6** b **7** g
8 h
3
1 chat online **2** surfs the Net
3 (fast) broadband **4** download
5 social networking **6** blog

VOCABULARY EXTENSION p84

4
1 b **2** a **3** d **4** f **5** c **6** e **7** h
8 g

Reading p85

1
b
2
1 c **2** a **3** a **4** b **5** a
3
1 O **2** O **3** F **4** O **5** O **6** F
4
1 antivirus **2** keep(ing) in touch
3 whistling **4** convicted **5** confidential
6 controversy **7** over-reacted

Grammar in context p86

1
1 past participle **2** by **3** the action
2
1 are **2** are **3** found **4** by **5** is
6 spoken
3
1 are **2** drunk **3** spoken **4** write
5 is **6** does **7** is taught **8** is sung
9 are **10** send
4
1 are worn **2** is played **3** are written
4 is made **5** is taught **6** is checked
7 are driven
5
1 The new MINI is made by BMW.
2 Gold is sometimes found in this river.
3 Football matches aren't stopped if it
  rains.
4 A prize is given to the best actor.
5 In this hotel your bags are taken to your
  room.
6 Tea isn't grown in Scotland.
7 In Japan the classrooms are cleaned by
  students.

8 Public transport is used by a lot of
  people.

GRAMMAR CHALLENGE p86

6
1 by thousands **2** is played **3** are
made **4** are drawn **5** are seen **6** are
eaten **7** if I liked **8** that/which

Developing vocabulary and listening p87

1
reply, account, send, check, forward,
address, bounce, delete
2
1 address, send **2** delete **3** reply
4 forward **5** bounce **6** account
7 check
3
1 b **2** c **3** a
4
1 b **2** b **3** a

VOCABULARY EXTENSION p87

5
2 digital versatile disc **3** compact disc
– read-only memory **4** short message
system **5** global positioning system
6 frequently asked questions **7** personal
identification number
6
1 PIN **2** DVD **3** FAQ **4** WWW
5 CD-ROM **6** GPS **7** SMS

Grammar in context p88

1
False
2
1 was **2** are being **3** have already
been **4** was **5** have been **6** is
3
1 was created **2** has been renamed
3 was made **4** were drawn **5** is being
followed **6** were produced **7** is being
interviewed.
4
1 The novel *Animal Farm* was written by
  George Orwell in 1945.
2 The race is organised by the school each
  year.
3 Dynamite was invented by Alfred Nobel
  in the 19th century.
4 Cartoons are being watched by
  thousands of children around the world
  at the moment.
5 The FIFA World Cup has been won
  several times by Brazil since 1958.
6 The planet Uranus was found by William
  Herschel in 1781.
7 The men's 100-metre world record was
  broken by Usain Bolt in August 2009.

5
1 T **2** T **3** F **4** T
6
1 had it cut **2** have/get it checked
3 'm having it fixed
4 had my eyes tested

GRAMMAR CHALLENGE p88
7

Hi Lily,
Has your computer ~~fixed~~ **been fixed** yet? I need to get my laptop ~~repairing~~ **repaired** soon. I ~~am~~ **was** sent a strange email last week. I opened it, but it was just a lot of numbers. Anyway, after that I started to lose lots of my files. I've ~~being~~ **been** asked to give a talk at school and all my files ~~are~~ **have been** deleted by this virus. When I bought the laptop I ~~have~~ **had** antivirus software installed, but it obviously ~~isn't~~ **didn't** work. So, can you tell me where I can get my computer ~~fix~~ **fixed** and how much I will be charged? Thanks a lot. By the way – I'm using my brother's tablet to send this email so you won't get the virus, too!
Love
Kim

Developing speaking p89
1
a both **b** whereas **c** However
d Another **e** contrast **f** similarity
g common **h** second
2
1 Both of the photos show
2 Another important similarity between the photos is
3 Another thing they have in common is
4 One big difference between the photos is
5 In contrast, the other people

PRONUNCIATION p89
3
1 Another important thing is the location.
2 This weather is normal for this month.
3 These are my brother's clothes.
4 Thank you for your kind thoughts.
5 My teeth were checked on the third of June.
6 I threw away the dirty cloth yesterday.

DESCRIBING PICTURES p89
4
Students' own answers
5
1 Five people, two boys and three girls. They look like students.
2 Outside, sitting on some grass in the countryside or a park, or big garden. It might be a forest.

3 They're looking at computers and they are talking – perhaps about what they've found on the computers.
4 Relaxed and happy. They're smiling.
6
Students' own answers

Developing writing p90
1
1 4 **2** U **3** R **4** 2 **5** C **6** B
2
1 today **2** tonight **3** tomorrow
4 before **5** late **6** great **7** wait
8 later
3
1 your **2** please **3** what **4** because
5 speak **6** weekend **7** thanks
8 excellent **9** message **10** homework
4
1 Can you please come to see me later?
2 I'll see you tomorrow before school.
3 I'll wait for your next message. **4** What are you doing at the weekend? **5** Will you be at home later today? **6** Thanks for the presents. They're great. **7** I can see you at six because I haven't got any homework.
5
1 Wot R U doing 2nite?
2 Amy and I R going 2 eat out BCZ it's her birthday 2day. Do U want 2 come?
3 OK. THX. Wot time R U meeting?
4 @ 8 BCZ B4 that I have 2 study 4 an exam 2moro.
5 Wot time is YR exam?
6 @ 10. I have 2 go now. I'll speak 2 U L8R.
7 GR8!

Revision: Units 1–10

Grammar p91
1
1 are played by grandparents, too
2 were invented by Arthur Wynne in 1913
3 is opening a museum tomorrow
4 saw the concert
5 was won by Alex Smith
6 are designed in Japan
2
1 will tell, see **2** would help
3 were, would build **4** had, was playing
5 might, hasn't decided **6** Surfing
7 hadn't seen
3
a a **b** has **c** that/0 **d** much
e enough **f** send/check **g** watching
h the

Vocabulary p91
1
1 c **2** f **3** h **4** h **5** g **6** j **7** e
8 a **9** d **10** b
2
1 log **2** chat **3** forward **4** click
5 make/print
3
a address **b** send **c** receive **d** reply
e delete **f** bounces
4
1 off **2** across **3** in **4** out **5** out
6 over **7** through

Gateway to exams: Units 9–10

Reading p92
1
1 c **2** a **3** b **4** d

Listening p92
2
1 science fiction, online **2** all the information, broadband **3** teenage boy, to borrow **4** prefers, easy to

Use of English p93
3
1 Jenny where she had been
2 had my car checked by **3** told us that we did **4** bag was found
5 me if I liked my **6** is being interviewed

Writing p93
4
Students' own answers

COMMON MISTAKES p93
5
1 told me that **2** by millions
3 had a wall built **4** he would phone
5 was made **6** asked if we wanted
7 Both (of the) pictures
8 by saying **9** was arrested **10** told us what we would do **11** Last but not least
12 In the first, in the second

Workbook audioscript

Unit 1

Developing vocabulary and listening p7

3 and 4 ▶ 01

Anna:
I love my family a lot, but I recently moved into my own flat near the beach because all my friends live there. Also, it's easy to get to work because my bus stops right outside the flat! The flat's a bit small, but it's got a kitchen, one bedroom and a living room. It's enough for me. And I love the independence. I can do what I want when I want to. I don't mean stay out till late – but just cooking, watching what I like on TV, you know.

Ethan:
OK, well I now live in a flat with my cousin and it's all right, but we hate cleaning or tidying up! So I take my washing to my mum's house! She's such a great mum! I moved out really because I was having a lot of arguments with my parents. You know – about when I come home, what clothes I wear and so on – even about politics! Now, our relationship is much better. We never argue when we meet. I go round there every weekend for lunch and we have a cool time.

Alex:
The reason I moved out was the noise. I have three brothers and sisters and they are so noisy! It's not their fault. They're kids! But I'm at university and I need to study a lot so now I share a flat with another friend who is doing the same course as I am. The difference in my work is amazing. I can concentrate more and there's a big improvement in my marks! Good decision.

Grace:
I moved mainly because of work. I'm a restaurant manager and I finish late every night. When I was at home it was difficult not to wake people up when I got back. I have a very young sister and she doesn't sleep very well. She wakes up very easily. It wasn't fair for her really. Also – because I have late nights, I like to sleep late in the mornings. I get very tired! And that's hard when my sister is running around getting ready for school! So, now I'm in a flat and it's good for everyone!

Developing speaking p9

1 and 3 ▶ 02

A: Hi! My name's Pete. What's your name?
B: Hi, I'm Marie.
A: Have you got any brothers or sisters?
B: Yes, I've got a brother and a sister.
A: Do they go to your school?
B: No, they're older than me. They go to university.
A: How often do you see them?
B: My brother comes home at weekends. But my sister, Jenny, only comes home once a month.
A: What do you do in the evenings?
B: I usually go round to my friend's house and we do our homework together.

A: Do you like computer games?
B: Not really. But I watch a lot of films on my tablet. What about you?
A: I spend a lot of free time playing computer games. I love them!

PRONUNCIATION p9

5 ▶ 03

1 What do you do?
2 Where do you live?
3 What sports do you like?
4 Where does your dad work?
5 How do you travel to school?

DESCRIBING PICTURES p9

7 ▶ 04

This is a family and they are having a meal together. There's a mum and dad and two young children and I can also see an older woman and another man. Perhaps they are the grandmother and an uncle? I imagine they're at home, probably the mum and dad's home, because it looks like a modern kitchen/dining room. I think they're having dinner or maybe lunch because there's some bread on the table. I think they're enjoying their meal because they're smiling and laughing about something. I imagine they're also happy because they're spending some time together as a family.

Unit 2

Developing vocabulary and listening p15

3 and 4 ▶ 05

I love crime fiction, in books and on television. I enjoy working out puzzles and I love finding out who committed the crime, how and why! My favourite at the moment is the Inspector Rebus series. I've read all of them. The writer is Ian Rankin, a Scottish author. The stories are great. They all take place in Edinburgh and I found out a lot about the city while I was reading the series. It sounded lovely and I decided to visit the place. When you read these books you find out a lot about the popular parts of Edinburgh but also about the parts the tourists don't see, too! When I was walking round the city, I was thinking about all the different places Rankin described in the Rebus books.
Inspector John Rebus is not a traditional detective. He has a lot of bad habits and he doesn't care about his appearance. He's definitely not vain like some other detectives! But he's very clever. He looks into all sorts of crimes. And he comes across some interesting people while he's looking for robbers and thieves! One of these is the boss of a big criminal gang, called Ger Rafferty. Although they're very different, Rebus and Rafferty get to know each other very well. They even help to solve some crimes together! Rafferty turns up in lots of the books. I think he and Rebus are opposite types of people, but they understand

each other. A few years ago Rebus retired from the police because he was too old. Everyone was worried that the books would stop. Luckily, Ian Rankin is continuing to write books with Rebus. I hope he's going to solve more crimes for a long time yet.

Developing speaking p17

2 ▶ 06

A: Hi! Did you enjoy the party at Hiroko's last night?
B: Yeah. It was really good. It's a shame you couldn't go.
A: I know I felt awful. But I was feeling ill all day yesterday. I spent the evening in bed!
B: You poor thing. I hope you're better now.
A: Yes thanks. Did Hiroko like my present?
B: Oh no!
A: What?
B: I forgot to give it to her. I'm so sorry.
A: It doesn't matter. I'm seeing her later today, I'll give it to her then. You told her I was ill, didn't you?
B: I forgot that, too. There were a lot of people and she was very busy. I feel terrible.
A: So, she thinks I just didn't turn up. That's the last time I ask you to give a message to someone for me!
B: I'm really, really sorry. Let me talk to her now.
A: Next time, please remember what I ask you!
B: Of course I will. I'll make it up to you. I'll buy you a burger!

PRONUNCIATION p17

5 ▶ 07

1 I felt awful.
2 I'm so sorry.
3 That's the last time I lend you anything.
4 Don't worry about it.
5 Oh no!

DESCRIBING PICTURES p17

7 ▶ 08

I think this is in a shop – maybe a supermarket, but not a very big one. It might be one of those small shops that you see on the corner of the street. I can see a man inside the shop. He's middle-aged, maybe around 50, and he's wearing a smart suit and tie. He's putting something into his inside jacket pocket. I think it's a book and I imagine he's stealing it. I think this crime happens a lot these days. It's very bad because sometimes the owners of small shops don't earn much money.

Gateway to exams: Units 1–2

Gateway to exams p20

3 ▶ 09

Taylor:
I have a very big family. I've got two sisters and two brothers and they're all older than me. Most of the time it's great fun to be part

of a big family. It's never boring or quiet in the house! Sometimes, however, it would be nice to have some time to sit and read alone. I can't because there's always noise in the house. My family likes music so there's always a radio on or one of my brothers or sisters is playing the guitar!

Cristina:

I've got two sisters and we're good friends as well as sisters. Well, most of the time we are. But last year I started having problems with my younger sister. I found out she was taking my things without asking. When you're part of a big family, it's important not to go in their rooms when they're not there. In fact, in every family that's important, isn't it? Well, my sister regularly goes into my room and steals my clothes and my magazines. One day I was having a shower and she went into my room and took the jeans I wanted to wear! I don't know what to do!

Ella:

I'm the youngest of four children and I love it. My parents have a lot of rules for my older brothers and sisters, but I can do nearly anything I like! Also, I get a lot of things from them. Like last week – one of my brothers gave me his smartphone because he's got a new one. My sister gave me a beautiful dress because it doesn't fit her now. And my other brother gave me his guitar because he's stopped playing it. He's started sailing instead! It's cool. Of course, sometimes they annoy me, but not often. I think I'm very lucky.

Miranda:

It isn't always easy to be part of a big family but there are some big advantages. For example all my brothers and sisters like to go out a lot and they have lots of friends. Sometimes we have parties and all their friends come. It's brilliant. I meet them all and it's always good fun. Some of their friends have become my friends, too – which is cool. Another thing is that we all go to the same school at the moment. I never have any problems with classmates or anything because my older brothers and sisters (and their friends) look after me.

Mark:

Sometimes I'd really like to be an only child. I mean, I love my family but my two brothers and my sister are all really clever. They get top grades in exams and my older brother is studying medicine at university. He wants to be a top doctor. I'm not very good at school. And my parents always tell me to be like my brothers. They can't understand that I can't! My other brother is brilliant at sports and he wins tennis matches and swimming races. I'm terrible at sports, too! I feel very depressed about it.

Unit 3

Vocabulary and listening p25

3 and **4** 10

Laura:

I have a very interesting job. I work with languages which is great. I use three languages that I learned at school in my job

and I really enjoy speaking them every day. I go to international meetings where there are people from many different countries and they have to understand each other. So I, and people like me, translate for them. It's sometimes quite difficult because they speak quickly and they don't slow down for me! And I have to be careful. I can't give an incorrect translation or they might make the wrong decisions.

Rachel:

I work with children aged between 11 and 15. My languages are French and Russian. I really enjoy my classes – and I hope the children enjoy them, too! Sometimes it's hard because the students don't like learning about irregular verbs and things like that. But there's no choice when you're learning a language. In the summer I often take the classes outside where we have an informal lesson in the garden. I think it's easier to speak a language when you're relaxed. That's when you make the most progress I think.

Michael:

I studied in Paris for a year and that's where I first did some work for a film company. I wanted a part-time job which wasn't too boring while I was studying. So I applied for the job of playing the role of an English student in a French film that they were making in Paris. I loved every minute. In fact, I spent more time acting than I did studying! It was an unusual part-time job – and much better than working in a restaurant, like my friends! They paid me a lot of money, too. Now, I'm training at a drama school and I hope I'll get more jobs like that in the future.

Developing speaking p27

1 11

Receptionist: Good morning. This is the Bradford School of English. How can I help you?

Student: Good morning. I'm calling from Italy. Could you give me some information about your summer courses?

Receptionist: Yes, of course. We have a course which begins on the 13th of July.

Student: Sorry. Did you say on the 30th July?

Receptionist: No, on the 13th.

Student: Ah, I understand. How long does the course last?

Receptionist: 20 days.

Student: Do you organise accommodation?

Receptionist: Yes, we do. Students usually live with local families.

Student: Pardon? I'm not sure I understood.

Receptionist: You can stay with a family near the school.

Student: OK. Thank you. How much is the course?

Receptionist: £950.

Student: Could you repeat that?

Receptionist: Yes, I said the price is £950.

Student: Does the price include other activities?

Receptionist: Yes, it does. It includes excursions and social activities.

Student: I'm very interested in the course. Can you send me a registration form?

Receptionist: Yes, of course. Can you give me your name and address?

PRONUNCIATION p27

4 ▶ 12

1 I'm interested in a new course.
2 Sorry, did you say the 10th May?
3 Could you say that again?
4 Can I help you?
5 How much is the course?
6 The price is fifty pounds a week.

DESCRIBING PICTURES p27

6 ▶ 13

I can see some students in a classroom. There are some boys and some girls. I think they're teenagers. I imagine they're at a special language school because I think they are different nationalities and they're not all the same age. Two of them are talking to each other, not to the teacher. I imagine they're doing this to practise their speaking. They're probably talking about something in their book – like a grammar point or maybe discussing a question from the book. Talking together helps you speak a language better. You don't worry about making mistakes when you're not saying things in front of the whole class!

Unit 4

Developing vocabulary and listening p33

3 and **4** ▶ 14

Girl: Hey, how are you?

Boy: Good thanks. I've just watched an episode of series nine of Grey's Anatomy. You can borrow the DVD when I've finished with it.

Girl: Great. I love Grey's Anatomy – it's such a good series. I've watched it since it started in 2005.

Boy: Me too, and it's actually made me much better at first aid!

Girl: So, what happened?

Boy: Well – a group of new doctors has just joined the show and on their first day they already have to help lots of people in trouble. There's a lot of competition between them because they all want to do operations to learn more and make the senior doctors like them. Two of the new doctors were fighting over one patient. But they weren't paying attention to him properly and he had a heart attack and nearly died. Luckily, they managed to save the patient, but they got into a lot of trouble about that. And one of the new doctors, Jo, had to help a baby who was born too early. The baby was really small, but they found it in the rubbish outside the hospital! I couldn't believe it.

It wasn't even in the waiting room! And Derek Shepherd, you know, the doctor who helps people with injured heads, has hurt his hand badly and he needs treatment. It's a bad injury and it's difficult to operate, but Callie and Jackson have just found a way to help him. But for some reason he doesn't want their help yet! I don't know why and maybe he won't be a doctor anymore.

Girl: Well – it sounds like another interesting day at the hospital!

Boy: Yes, and the new doctor – remember I said her name was Jo, well … she likes Doctor Karev a lot … and I think he likes her too, but it's difficult because she's just started at the hospital and he's been there for a long time and she has to work for him, but I think that they …

Girl: OK, OK! Don't tell me … I haven't seen series nine yet!

Developing speaking p35

1 and 2 ▶ 15

There are four people in the picture and, … er, they're in a waiting room. It's probably a waiting room in a health centre. I imagine it's the morning or the afternoon because that's when people usually go to the doctor's. Er, three of the people are patients, they're waiting to see the doctor. The doctor is also in the room. The patients are looking at him. They look ill or, you know, have health problems. For example, I think the woman on the left has got a broken arm or maybe it's her wrist. I'm not really sure, but I think the woman in the middle has got a sore neck because she's wearing a collar round it. The room isn't very exciting. There aren't, well, any pictures on the wall. I can also see some magazines. I think they're probably giving information to the patients. I've been in a waiting room like this when I've been ill. I don't like waiting rooms because they always seem sad and grey. The thing is, the picture makes me think about times when I've been ill so I don't really like it much.

PRONUNCIATION p35

3 ▶ 16
waiting room
food poisoning
health centre
first aid
heart attack

DESCRIBING PICTURES p35

5 ▶ 17
There are four people in the photograph. They are in the countryside near the mountains. One of the people isn't very well. I imagine he has fallen over or perhaps he's got a virus. Two people are carrying him. They are probably going to hospital. In the background there's a car with red lights. I think it's a police car or a small ambulance. I think the man who is injured is feeling quite bad. Perhaps his leg hurts.

Gateway to exams: Units 3–4

Gateway to exams p38

2 ▶ 18

Hi! I'm going to talk about my language learning experiences. We've heard from some other students already about their problems learning a language. I agree – there are a lot of problems, but I've had some good experiences, too. The language that I'm best at is French, but I can also speak a little Russian. I started learning French when I was at primary school – at the age of nine, but I've only learned Russian for a year. I think it was good to start learning French when we were young. It's easier to learn to pronounce the different sounds. Also, you don't worry too much about making mistakes. That's worse when you get older, isn't it? Your first teacher is also very important. I was very lucky and I had an excellent teacher called Miss Painter. She clearly loved French and because of that we loved it, too. We had posters in French on the classroom walls and every week she brought in French sweets or French music. We realised that French wasn't just a boring subject … but it was real and there was a country with people who really spoke that way all the time! When we learned a bit more French we played games and those were fun, too. We didn't have tests or lots of homework so we enjoyed the subject a lot more I think. Now, learning Russian has been a bit different! It's more serious and because we're older it's harder to learn. We haven't done much grammar yet, but I know it's going to be difficult! The letters are completely different and I still don't write it very well. But it's interesting and I want to learn it well because I like reading Russian books. So, maybe in another five years …

Unit 5

Developing vocabulary and listening p43

2 and 3 ▶ 19

Lily:
Last night I went to a musical with my best friend. We were lucky to find tickets because it's the most popular show in London at the moment. It was definitely as good as the reviews said. The singers were brilliant – the dancers, too. But just as the girl was singing a very sad song and the audience was very quiet, my mobile started ringing! Everyone was staring at me.

Ben:
We had a dinner party at school last week to help raise money for the local community garden. We sold tickets to our friends and family and then we cooked them a three-course meal. Doing all the cooking was less tiring than I thought because we all worked together. Lots of people came and we had a great time. At the end we counted the money and I couldn't believe it. We had more than enough to create a really great garden! Everyone was so generous.

Sue:
There was a programme on TV last night about Alicante, a city in Spain. They talked to a lot of people about the holidays they spent there. Some of them said good things and some said bad things, but they all liked one particular hotel and showed lovely photos of it. It looked like a great place to go and it didn't seem too expensive! I took down the details – maybe next year?!

Sarah:
Have you seen the latest Dan Fisher film? It's out now and Charlie and I went to see it on Saturday. It's definitely as good as all his others. But it was so sad! I was crying at the end. It's about a man who falls in love with a woman who lives on the other side of the world. Apart from Dan Fisher, the other actors aren't very famous, but they are really good. I can recommend it. But if you watch it you'll definitely need tissues.

Developing speaking p45

1 ▶ 20

A: I am so bored. Why don't we do something, go somewhere – I don't know.

B: Good idea – I haven't done anything apart from watch TV all day.

A: Me neither. Shall we go shopping? There's a sale on at Frank's.

B: I'm not sure. I haven't really got enough money. I mean, I can't buy anything really.

A: Yes, but we can just look at things.

B: That's not much fun when you can't buy anything!

A: Hmmm … I know what you mean. How about taking your dog for a walk along the river? We can get some fresh air.

B: But what about the weather? It's going to rain later.

A: OK. You're probably right. We don't want to get wet. I know, let's call Maddy. She's usually got some suggestions.

B: Great! She might invite us over to play her new computer game!

A: Yes! Good thinking!

PRONUNCIATION p45

4 ▶ 21

/ei/	/ae/	/eə/
game	am	air
made	ankle	
play	at	
rain	haven't	
sale	Maddy	
taking	shall	

DESCRIBING PICTURES p45

6 ▶ 22

There are four girls in the photo and they're looking at something. They're all teenagers and three of them are sitting very close together on the sofa. One girl is holding something in her hand. I imagine it's a remote control for a television or maybe for a game? I think it's for a television and they're watching it together. They look very interested in the programme and I think something exciting is happening on the screen because they're watching very carefully! I think they're enjoying the programme and want to see what happens next.

Unit 6

Developing vocabulary and listening p51

2 and 3 23

A: In our science class yesterday we got some really interesting homework from Miss Barber. It's a project about what we can do in our area to help slow down climate change in the future. If we make some changes now, the weather in the future might not be so bad. I know that we've caused lots of problems to the planet with all our pollution, We can't go back in time and change things. All we can do is try to help a bit now.

B: I'm actually quite interested in that topic. Did you know my dad works for a company that looks at different ways of getting energy from the wind and the sea? He says the situation is getting worse and it's not going to get better. They've got the right technology, but they have to get permission from people to build wind farms and solar farms in different areas. My dad gets very annoyed when people refuse. I mean, if the wind or solar farms are near people's houses, they don't want them.

A: I know what he means – and I'm going to say that in my project! We have to think about the future, don't we? Perhaps your dad can get me some information and pictures. I tried to go online on my mobile to look last night, but if I go online where I live, I don't get a good signal. It was hopeless.

B: I'm sure he can. I'll ask him tonight and he'll email you some information when he gets to work tomorrow. He's always keen to help people understand more about environmental problems.

A: Thank you so much! But perhaps he can give you the information for me instead of sending it? My mobile will probably take forever to download it!

B: No problem.

Developing speaking p53

1 24

Katie: What are you up to tomorrow?
Tom: Nothing really. What about you?
Katie: Nothing planned. Do you fancy going to the Planet Earth exhibition in town?
Tom: Sure. What time shall we meet?
Katie: How about half past ten?
Tom: Fine. Why don't we meet at the bus stop next to my house?
Katie: OK, but where shall we meet if it rains?
Tom: Come straight to my house.
Katie: Good idea. I'll see if Amy wants to come.
Tom: Great! See you tomorrow.

PRONUNCIATION p53

3 25

1 What are you up to tomorrow?
2 What about you?
3 Are you up to anything tonight?
4 Where shall we meet?
5 What time shall we meet?
6 Do you like art exhibitions?
7 How about half past ten?
8 Why don't we meet at the bus stop?
9 Do you fancy going to an exhibition?

DESCRIBING PICTURES p53

5 26

There are two people in the picture. I think they're friends and they're cycling together. They're in the countryside and it looks very beautiful. In the background there's a lake or a river and they are cycling on a track going past it. There are some mountains in the background and the weather looks very good. The people are perhaps on a cycling holiday or perhaps they're cycling at the weekend for fun. I think they're enjoying the activity. It's good to see lovely countryside and it's good to be healthy, too.

Gateway to exams: Units 5–6

Gateway to exams p56

2 27

Interviewer:
There are lots of examples of famous people – singers or actors usually – who talk about the environment or natural disasters on TV or in magazines. We wanted to know what you think about that, so we went out onto the street and asked you. This is what you told us.

Speaker 1:
Well, some people think it's OK, but I hate seeing famous people talking about things like that. I think most of these famous people, when they do that, you know, they just want publicity for themselves. They just want to advertise their new film or album. They start talking about the environment and, two minutes later, they're telling you the title of their new record and talking about how brilliant it is!

Speaker 2:
I don't know. I think the good thing is that they help people to see that there are really serious problems in the world and we need to do something about it. They usually get people to help and give money, and that money can be really important. You know, famous people attract lots of publicity and they use the attention to tell people about some of the terrible things that are happening in the world right now. That's a good thing. Often people don't really care about these disasters if famous people don't talk about them.

Speaker 3:
I just think that these celebrities, these singers and actors, they're really rich. That's the biggest problem with famous people. They're too rich. They're millionaires. If they want to help, why don't they just give their

own money? Normal people like me aren't rich enough to give much money, but these celebrities could give enough money to stop some of these problems tomorrow, instead of buying mansions and sports cars and expensive clothes. They're millionaires. Why don't they just give money instead of telling us what to do?

Speaker 4:
Well, I think it's stupid. What does an actor know about the environment or about global warming? Actors don't know enough to be able to inform us, they aren't experts. I want famous singers and actors to talk about music and film, not about the ozone layer and global warming. I want to learn about world problems from the experts, people who really know what they're talking about.

Interviewer:
As you can see, not everybody agrees then about the question of celebrities, but one thing is …

Unit 7

Developing vocabulary and listening p61

2 and 3 28

A: Have you decided what subject you're going to study at university next year yet?

B: I have a couple of things I'm thinking about, but it's hard. I mean, you have to think about what you want to spend the rest of your life doing. If you make a mistake now, it could be a real problem later on.

A: Oh, I don't know that that's true. Yeah – for our parents it was important to make the right choice because then it was normal to spend your whole working life doing one job or profession. Today it's much easier to change career if you want to. In fact, I think people expect you to. My sister went for a job interview recently and they were quite surprised that she only had experience of one job!

B: I know what you mean. But I don't want to waste time doing a course that isn't going to lead to a good job. So, I think it's important to make the right decision now.

A: So what are you thinking about?

B: Well, you know my dad's a computer engineer? He enjoys his job and it's very well-paid. I think I might do that.

A: OK, if you were good at computer science then that would be a great choice – but you don't really like it much, do you?

B: But that's lessons at school – I'm sure it would be better at university. And there are lots of jobs for computer engineers.

A: That's true – but it isn't only about the money. You're really interested in the environment. Why don't you think about studying that?

B: But it's really hard to get a job with environmental sciences. My cousin did that and he's still out of work. He's had to take a part-time job at a fast food restaurant! I don't want to do that.

A: But … oh well, I still think you should study something you actually like. I'm thinking about doing drama. I know working as an actor is hard and it's usually badly-paid, but I love acting. If I were an actor, I'd enjoy every day.

B: I think that would be a good choice for you. You're very good, you know. And you say badly-paid, but if you got a big part in a film, you'd be really well-off! You might even get really well-known!

A: Perhaps you should think about that too then!

PRONUNCIATION p63

3 29

1 Can you tell me when the job starts?
2 Could I ask if you need any experience?
3 Can you tell me how I can apply?
4 Can you tell me what we have to do?
5 Could I ask what the basic wages are?
6 Can you tell me what your address is?

DESCRIBING PICTURES p63

5 ▶ 30

There are four people in the photo. Three of them are sitting at a table in a restaurant and they are ordering a meal. The waitress is writing down their order. I think it's lunchtime because they're wearing summer clothes that you wear in the day time. I think the waitress is a student in her summer holidays. Perhaps she wants to earn some extra money. I think the people at the table are feeling happy because maybe they've been shopping and they're having a break. They're probably hungry, too! The waitress doesn't look very busy so she's probably enjoying her job. It's not a very well-paid job, but if you're good, the customers leave you tips.

Unit 8

Developing vocabulary and listening p69

3 and **4** ▶ 31

Hi – I'm Zac and I'm 15. I'm here to tell you about an amazing friendship I have. Is it someone I met at school? No, it isn't. Or someone who lives near me? No, it isn't. In fact, my closest friend isn't human at all. She's a dog! You see, when I was seven I had a bad illness and I was in hospital for ten weeks. When I went home again, I couldn't go back to school for a few months. Loneliness and boredom are big problems when you're recovering from an illness so my parents had a good idea! They bought me a dog, a black Labrador called Betsy. She's absolutely wonderful and I really love having her around. She's always by my side and I walk her every day before and after school. We go to the park where she has some freedom to run around and explore. She has a great relationship with my friends, too. They love playing with her and they try to give her biscuits. That's not good as she has a weakness for biscuits. She also knows when I'm feeling sad and she puts her head on my knees.

Developing speaking p71

1 and **2** ▶ 32

A: Hi Nick! Did you have a good weekend?
B: Yes I did, thanks. Saturday was very busy, but it was good fun.
A: What did you do?
B: Well, it was my older brother's birthday – Tony, do you remember him?
A: Yes. He's at university in France, isn't he?
B: Yeah. Well, he came home on Friday and he got a big surprise! Mum and Dad had organised a big meal at a restaurant for him and friends at The Hotel on the Park.
A: How fantastic! My aunt used to work there. She says the food there is wonderful.
B: It certainly is! We all arrived at about 6.30 – Mum had booked the table for 7.30 – so we had a chat before dinner. Then we all sat round an enormous table in their main restaurant. There were twenty of us!
A: Did you know everybody?
B: Not everybody. But most of the people were family and Tony's friends from his old school. I knew them. But there were two new friends that had come over from France with him. And his new girlfriend! She's called Ella and she's really nice.
A: So, what did you eat?
B: I ordered fish in a delicious sauce. Then while we were all having coffee at the end of the meal, Dad stood up and spoke about how proud he was of Tony! I think Tony was really embarrassed!
A: What a great way to celebrate a birthday.
B: It was.

PRONUNCIATION p71

4 ▶ 33

1 How fantastic!
2 Did you know anyone?
3 What a surprise!
4 He's at university, isn't he?
5 That's brilliant!
6 I love it!

DESCRIBING PICTURES p71

6 ▶ 34

I can see some young people. They're teenagers and there are some boys and some girls. I think they know each other. They're wearing casual summer clothes – like T-shirts and shorts. They're on a beach because I can see the sand and I think there are some plants in the background. They're probably having a party. I imagine it's someone's birthday and he or she has organised a barbecue or a picnic. Some of the teenagers are sitting on a blanket and most of them are chatting and eating watermelon. They look relaxed and happy and I think they're really enjoying the afternoon.

Gateway to exams: Units 7–8

Gateway to exams p74

2 35

Ben: Hi Sophie, I haven't seen you for ages! How's life at university?

Sophie: I'm having an amazing time. The course is quite difficult, but it's very interesting and I'm getting on OK.
Ben: Do you have to get up really early to go to lectures?
Sophie: Gosh – no! It's not like school at all! There are some lectures that we have to go to, but we don't have to attend all of them. Usually my first lecture starts at 11.30 on Mondays and the rest of the week it's 10.30 – so that's not too bad. I must admit that I miss quite a few of the ones I don't have to go to – I know I should go to more, but sometimes I'm just too lazy.
Ben: Wow! It sounds like a good life! Are you staying with family while you're studying there? I know it's at least two hundred kilometres from here, isn't it?
Sophie: You're right. I can't travel every day – I'd have to get up far too early! No, I'm sharing a flat with two other students. It's brilliant. Being independent is fantastic. We get on very well and we've all got a wide circle of friends at university so there are parties all the time.
Ben: That's why getting up in the mornings is a problem!
Sophie: It's only my first term. At school I used to have to get up at 6.30 every morning! So, now I'm enjoying spending a bit more time in bed.
Ben: If I shared a flat with friends I think I'd do the same.
Sophie: It's also cool living with people that you really like. We all study the same subject so we help each other with work and projects, too. One of my flatmates is brilliant with computers and technology – so she's always fixing my laptop. I love cooking, too, and I've become a really good cook!
Ben: So, if I came up to visit you I would get a good meal?
Sophie: That would be so good Ben. Why don't you come up next month? You can sleep on the sofa. It's a nice big one and it's very soft!
Ben: Thanks! I must come up – and meet your flatmates. But you must start doing some work soon, too!

Unit 9

Developing vocabulary and listening p79

3, 4 and **5** ▶ 36

Speaker 1:

In my opinion, reading and writing these days is very different from when my parents were young. When they were at school they had to look up new words in a dictionary and it could take ages. Now I just go online, type in the word and I get the meaning immediately. You don't have to turn over a lot of pages and waste time. Also, instead of looking questions up in an encyclopaedia you can ask the questions online, too, and get answers very fast. Yesterday I asked a website who had written the first cell phone novel. I got the answer in seconds!

Speaker 2:

I asked my mum what the biggest difference was between the work I do at school and the work she used to do. She said it was writing. When my mum was at school she had to write everything by hand. If she made a mistake she had to cross it out. She said her essays were really messy because she used to make lots of mistakes! Today we just type our work on our laptops and print it out or send it to the teacher online. If we make a mistake we delete it! Easy! Also it's much easier to fill in forms online, too. And faster! I'm glad I'm at school now and not thirty years ago.

Speaker 3:

For me, the biggest change I've noticed with reading and writing is that so many people read books online now. Everywhere you go you can see people reading on their e-readers, tablets or laptops – even on their phones. It's convenient, I know and it's especially good for people when they're travelling, but I don't really like it. I prefer the way a real book feels – you know what I mean? I like turning over real pages and I like flicking through a new book before I buy it – you can't do that online, can you? And the smell of a new book – that's magic!

Developing speaking p81

1 37

Hi! I'm going to talk about a book I remember from when I was younger. We've all got favourite books from that time in our lives and mine is called *The Wind in the Willows*. I'd like to begin by saying that I first read this when I was quite young, but I've read it several times again since then. It's a beautiful book. First of all, I love the location. The story happens in a very peaceful part of the countryside and when you read it you can see sun, blue skies and almost hear the noise of a gentle river! It's about the lives of different animals. The descriptions are very good and what's more – it's very funny, too! It's also true that this book has a special message. It's not just about animals and what they do or don't do, it's about the modern world and technology and how it is changing the countryside. It makes us think about what we are losing. Last but not least, the book is about friendship and helping other people. It tells us that when life is difficult we need to help each other. To sum up, I think both children and adults can learn a lot from *The Wind in the Willows*. It was written a long time ago, but I think it's even more important for people today.

PRONUNCIATION p81

3 38

1 I'd like to begin by saying that
2 Last but not least
3 It's also true that
4 Another thing is that
5 To sum up

DESCRIBING PICTURES p81

5 ▶ 39

Well, there are a few people and they're in a bookshop. On the right and in the foreground, there is a young woman, I imagine she's a student. She's wearing casual clothes. On the left there's an older man. They're all looking at books from the shelves. I think it's a bookshop and not a library because the people are standing up. In a library they would sit down to look at the books. I imagine these people are flicking through some books before they decide if they want to buy them. The people are reading and they look quite serious. I think they are concentrating hard because they want to know if the book is a good one for them to buy.

Unit 10

Developing vocabulary and listening p87

3 and **4** ▶ 40

Situation 1

Belinda: Hi, Paul!

Paul: Belinda – hello. How are you doing?

Belinda: OK, thanks. I just wanted to ask you about the website to get information about the job you mentioned.

Paul: Oh – I sent that and some more information to you yesterday. Didn't you get my email?

Belinda: Yes, I did – thanks. But unfortunately I deleted it! I was sent a lot of advertising emails yesterday and I deleted them all. The problem is – yours was accidentally deleted, too. Could you possibly resend the information? Sorry to be a pain.

Paul: No problem – that's easy to do. I'll email them to you again now. This time – download the attachment immediately!

Belinda: I will. Thank you.

Situation 2

Daniel: So, Ella, are you coming at the weekend?

Ella: Sorry? What's happening at the weekend, Daniel?

Daniel: The trip to London. I sent you an email about it yesterday.

Ella: Oh – I didn't get an email from you. And I checked my emails several times yesterday. When did you send it?

Daniel: About 11.30. I wondered why you didn't ring me.

Ella: I'm so sorry – it never arrived. Did you use the right email address?

Daniel: Yeah – I sent it to EllaMarks@ webnet.com

Ella: No! There's no 's'. It's EllaMark – M-A-R-K, I had to choose that because there's someone else with EllaMarks as her email address.

Daniel: Oops! Must remember that. I didn't realise I'd made a mistake because it didn't bounce back.

Ella: Yeah. I imagine this other Ella Marks has got a lot of my emails in her inbox! I must change my email account.

Situation 3

Ben: Where's Penny?

Tammy: Oh – she was sent home from school today.

Ben: Really? Why was that? What did she do?

Tammy: Well, nothing terrible. She's often told off for using her mobile in class. Well, today the teacher got really fed up with her. She was seen checking her emails in the middle of the lesson again.

Ben: I often do that. But I'm careful to do it when the teacher isn't looking.

Tammy: That is *so* bad! You should concentrate on the lesson. You'll get caught one day.

Ben: I have already been caught. Last month my phone was taken away for a whole day.

Tammy: Oh, well, there you go!

Developing speaking p89

1 ▶ 41

OK, so yes, both of the pictures show people using computers, but they're using them in different places and for different reasons. In the first photo, the older people are looking at a computer together whereas, in the second photo the people have got their own computers. The older people look really happy and they're smiling. They're probably enjoying the activity. However, in the other photo the people are concentrating and they look very serious. I think they may be at a big meeting. Another big difference is what the people are wearing. The older people are wearing casual clothes. In contrast, the people at the meeting are all wearing smart clothes. One similarity between the photos is that the computers are clearly important for the people. But apart from that they don't have a lot in common. My grandparents were given a computer last year. They love it. My dad is a bit like the people in the second photo. He takes his computer to meetings all the time.

PRONUNCIATION p89

3 ▶ 42

1 Another important thing is the location.
2 This weather is normal for this month.
3 These are my brother's clothes.
4 Thank you for your kind thoughts.
5 My teeth were checked on the third of June.
6 I threw away the dirty cloth yesterday.

DESCRIBING PICTURES p89

5 ▶ 43

OK, well – there are five people in the picture, two boys and three girls. They look like students. I'm not sure if they're English, they might be foreign students in England or people in another country. It's autumn because there are leaves on the ground. They're outside and I imagine it's in the countryside or a big park or garden. There is a lot of grass and behind the people I can see a lot of trees. It might be a forest. They're sitting on the grass and they're looking at computers. I think they're talking about what they have found or what they can see. I think they're very relaxed and enjoying the situation because they're smiling.

Gateway to exams: Units 9–10

Gateway to exams p92

2 ▶ 44

Situation 1

Sam:	Hi! What are you doing here, Tony? You don't usually buy books in shops. You said you got everything online these days.
Tony:	I know! It's a bit of an emergency. I'd forgotten it was Sally's birthday today and I'm looking for a book for her. Any suggestions?
Sam:	Well, I know your sister loves crime stories, but I imagine she's read all the latest ones.
Tony:	That's what I thought. Do you think she might like a romance novel?
Sam:	She once told me that she hated romance novels – so maybe a science fiction one might be a better idea.
Tony:	I'm hopeless. I never know what she's reading. But that's a good idea.
Sam:	I read this one last month – it's really good. I think she'll love it.
Tony:	Thank you so much. You've saved my life!

Situation 2

Martha:	How's your project coming on, Ben? The teacher wants it in by tomorrow.
Ben:	Oh, it's going really slowly, I'm afraid. I've been working non-stop, but I'm having some problems.
Martha:	Is there anything I can do to help?
Ben:	That's really kind of you, but I think I'll be OK. One thing was – I wasn't given all the information at the beginning of the project so I've had to spend some time researching that.
Martha:	That is such a pain. Are you still having problems with your broadband? That doesn't help.
Ben:	Not really. It seems to be better these days. No, I'll spend a lot of time on it today and this evening and it should be ready for tomorrow.
Martha:	Good luck!

Situation 3

Kay:	What are you reading, Miranda? It looks interesting. And it's a very thick paperback!
Miranda:	It's a crime novel. Lucy told me it was the best she'd ever read so I've borrowed it from her.
Kay:	And is it very good? I love crime novels, too, but I haven't read that one.
Miranda:	It's excellent. I just love the idea. Most crime novels are about the police who have to solve a murder. But in this one the detective isn't from the police. It's a teenage boy who's on holiday. There's a series of robberies and he suspects the policeman who's in charge of the investigation.
Kay:	OK.
Miranda:	And his uncle who is on holiday with them has just disappeared. It's getting really exciting.
Kay:	Excellent. I'll ask Lucy if I can borrow it after you?
Miranda:	Sure, I know Lucy won't mind.

Situation 4

Mandy:	I see you've got a new smartphone, Tom. Are you happy with it?
Tom:	On the whole, yes, I am. Kathy's got one of these and she told me that they're excellent and easy to use. But there are some things on it that I really don't understand!
Mandy:	Well, there's always a lot to learn with a new phone, isn't there? Phones can do so many things these days.
Tom:	You're right. But I was really looking forward to getting it and now I think I prefer my old one. I keep clicking on the wrong icons and there are so many different menus.
Mandy:	Well – don't get angry with it and throw it away! You could take it back and change it if you really need to. But you'll work it out soon, I'm sure.

Notes

Macmillan Education
4 Crinan Street
London N1 9XW
A division of Macmillan Publishers Limited

Companies and representatives throughout the world

ISBN 978-0-230-47092-7

Text, design and illustration © Macmillan Publishers Limited 2016
Written by Anna Cole and Ursula Mallows

The authors have asserted their right to be identified as the authors of this
work in accordance with the Copyright, Designs and Patents Act 1988.

This edition published 2016
First edition entitled *Gateway B1 Teacher's Book* published in 2011

Designed by emc design ltd
Cover design by emc design ltd and Macmillan Publishers Ltd

Authors' acknowledgements
The authors would like to thank the Macmillan team.

The publishers would like to thank the staff and pupils at the following
schools in Mexico and Spain for helping us so enthusiastically with
our research for this second edition of Gateway: Concha Campos, IES
Burgo de Las Rozas, Las Rozas, Madrid; Félix Gaspar, IES Las Encinas;
Villanueva de la Cañada, Madrid; Cristina Moisen, IES Joaquín Turina,
Madrid; Colegio Montessori Cuautitlán; Colegio Conrad Gessner; Colegio
Erasmo de Rotterdam; Colegio Kanic, Centro Educativo Erich Fromm;
Universidad Franco Mexicana; Centro Pedagógico María Montessori de
Ecatepec; Instituto Cultural; Escuela Maestro Manuel Acosta; Liceo Sakbé
De México.

The publishers would also like to thank all those who reviewed or piloted
the first edition of Gateway: Benjamin Affolter, Evelyn Andorfer,
Anna Ciereszynska, Regina Culver, Anna Dabrowska, Justyna Deja,
Ondrej Dosedel, Lisa Durham, Dagmar Eder, Eva Ellederovan, H Fouad,
Sabrina Funes, Luiza Gervescu, Isabel González Bueno, Jutta Habringer,
Stela Halmageanu, Marta Hilgier, Andrea Hutterer, Nicole Ioakimidis,
Mag. Annemarie Kammerhofer, Irina Kondrasheva, Sonja Lengauer,
Gabriela Liptakova, Andrea Littlewood, María Cristina Maggi,
Silvia Miranda Barbara Nowak, Agnieska Orlinska, Anna Orlowska,
María Paula Palou, Marta Piotrowska, N Reda, Katharina Schatz,
Roswitha Schwarz, Barbara Scibor, Katarzyna Sochacka, Joanna Spoz,
Monica Srtygner, Marisol Suppan, Stephanie Sutter, Halina Tyliba,
Prilipko, Maria Vizgina, Vladyko, Pia Wimmer, Katarzyna Zadrozna-Attia
and Katarzyna Zaremba-Jaworska.

Full acknowledgements for illustrations and photographs in the facsimile
pages can be found in the Student's Book and the Workbook.

The authors and publishers would like to thank the following for
permission to reproduce their photographs:
Shutterstock/ively p11, Shutterstock/Artem Kovalenco pp11, 17, 18, 19;
Shutterstock/M.Stasy p12.

Printed and bound in Thailan

2020 2019 2018 2017 201
10 9 8 7 6 5 4 3 2